THE SECRET ENEMY:
AUSTRIA-HUNGARY AND THE GERMAN ALLIANCE, 1914-1918

GARY W. SHANAFELT

EAST EUROPEAN MONOGRAPHS, BOULDER
DISTRIBUTED BY COLUMBIA UNIVERSITY PRESS, NEW YORK

1985

EAST EUROPEAN MONOGRAPHS, NO. CLXXXVII

for
Thomas Lithuainius

CONTENTS

PREFACE: THE PROBLEM

> Well, then, what are our secret enemies, the Germans, doing, and the German Kaiser, the play-actor?

Franz Conrad von Hötzendorf, early 1915[1]

It is something of a historical truism that the Austro-Hungarian Monarchy should never have existed, or at least existed as long as it did until the 20th century. Like its octogenarian reigning monarch, it continually baffled its critics by refusing to collapse, and it took the cataclysm of the First World War finally to destroy it. The complexities and paradoxes of its existence accompanied it to its end. During the war, the Habsburg Monarchy was threatened by all the major countries around it; but as the conflict progressed, Serbia and Rumania were overrun, Russia collapsed in revolution, and the armies of Italy were thrown back into their own territories. From the embrace of only one state was the Monarchy unable to free itself—Imperial Germany. Ironically, Germany was not an "enemy," but Austria-Hungary's chief ally. Its alliance with Germany had formed the cornerstone of Austrian peacetime policy for over thirty years. It was the Monarchy's greatest source of external strength. But while Vienna was able to overcome the combined threat of its enemies on the battlefields, the bond with its ally—whose aid on those battlefields was essential to it—ultimately proved fatal.

The Dual Monarchy was by far the weaker partner in the alliance between the two countries. This fact alone would have caused discord in a wartime situation requiring mutual cooperation; coalitions have rarely been characterized by complete harmony of interests, and weaker members have usually had to make more concessions to their stronger partners than they would have liked. During World War I, however, Austria-Hungary faced a situation in which its stronger partner's war aims came to threaten its own existence, and where it itself became a war aim of its ally.

The outbreak of the conflict in 1914 locked the Monarchy into a position from which the connection with Germany prevented any easy escape. Vienna had extracted itself from previous lost wars with the cession of a few peripheral provinces—but not this one. On the contrary, Germany dragged it toward a common fate of either complete victory or complete disaster. The Austrian decision for war in 1914 was taken to "preserve" the Monarchy, but it soon became apparent that the conflict's continuance would destroy it. Austria-Hungary simply lacked the strength and cohesion to withstand a modern total war, though its leaders tried to ignore the fact as long as they could. The more it came to need peace to stave off total collapse, however, the weaker it became either to influence German diplomacy in that direction or to break with Germany and attempt a separate peace on its own. The Austrians were thus compelled to remain in the war as long as Germany remained in it. But German plans to dominate Central and Eastern Europe meant that even a German victory would have seriously injured the Monarchy's continued integrity as an independent entity.

The repercussions of the alliance were equally momentous in their domestic implications, for the German bond was integrally connected with the Austrian internal order. That order was already tottering in 1914, and the pressure of the war put it under intolerable strain. Fearing a complete collapse, the preponderant Austrian German and Magyar groups turned increasingly to Reich German support to fortify their position within the Monarchy. This, however, hastened the very dissolution it was intended to counteract; the resulting dependence on Berlin undermined the worth of preserving the Habsburg state for the other nationalities. The Monarchy ceased to be any sort of "European necessity" if it was reduced to the position of a German satellite. A regime that could avoid this condition and still hold the divided loyalties of the Empire's various ethnic groups became ever more unlikely the longer the war lasted. Ultimately, the only policy that could preserve the old domestic order was the "German Course" with Berlin, and the "German Course" finally made the end of the Monarchy inevitable.

The problem of Austrian wartime relations with Germany has often been examined in the literature on the war. The early controversies over war guilt and responsibility for the collapse in 1918 could hardly avoid it. *Unser Österreich-Ungarischer Bundesgenosse im Weltkriege,* the memoirs of August von Cramon, the German liaison officer with the Austrian High Command from 1915 to 1918, appeared as early as 1920. They received a rejoinder of sorts from the Austrian side in *Deutschland als Verbündeter* by

Karl Freiherr von Werkmann, the Emperor Karl's Press Secretary; and in the memoirs of Karl's Foreign Minister Ottokar Czernin. Former German Chancellor Theobald von Bethmann Hollweg considered the question of the alliance so important that he intended to have an entire chapter of his own memoirs deal with it, and only his premature death prevented that section from being written.

Most of these early accounts were products both of the shock of defeat and collapse in 1918 and of the postwar search for a new order that would somehow reverse them. A great deal of the German historiography on the subject tended to take Austria-Hungary (and the last Emperor, Karl) to task for having undermined the German war effort through incompetence and defeatism, if not downright disloyalty as in the case of the Sixtus negotiations. Richard Fester, *Die Politik Kaiser Karls und der Wendepunkt des Welt-krieges,* is a good example of this tendency. The other extreme, typified by Werkmann or Arthur Polzer-Hoditz, Karl's Cabinet Chief, in *The Emperor Karl,* were in essence legitimist defenses of the Habsburg dynasty. Czernin's wartime policies put him into a third category practically by himself, since he alienated the extreme nationalists in Germany by his supposed defeatism and the Habsburg apologists through his "betrayal" of the Emperor in April 1918. Recent biographers of the Emperor, such as Gordon Brook-Shepherd in *The Last Habsburg,* still attempt to portray the Austrian Foreign Minister in as negative a fashion as possible, while emphasizing Karl's virtue and foresight.

The situation after the Second World War made new perspectives possible, both because the files of the Ballhausplatz and the Wilhelmstraße for the war period were finally opened to research, and because the old questions of war guilt and responsibility no longer had the same immediacy that they had possessed in the interwar period. Fritz Fischer's monumental *Germany's Aims in the First World War* (originally published in German in 1961; in English translation in 1967) did more than reopen an old historical controversy on a new documentary basis; it also suggested a host of new approaches to the old problems and spurred interest in issues previously overlooked. Since then, there has been an outpouring of work on the problem of war aims and politics during World War I. Some of this material has been directly tied to the "Fischer controversy" over German imperialism before and during the war (notably the last two volumes of Gerhard Ritter's *The Sword and the Scepter*). A great deal, however, has dealt with broader aspects of the diplomacy of the time, such as Wolfgang Steglich's studies of the peace efforts of the Central Powers or Fritz Klein's work on the structure of the Austro-German connection before the war. Similarly, interest in the causes of the dissolution of the Monarchy has led to a host of recent studies, both on the dissolution itself (the books of Arthur J. May, Z. A. B. Zeman, and Leo Valiani) and on specific areas of Austrian wartime diplomacy (particularly Ingeborg Meckling's *Die Aussenpolitik des Grafen Czernin*). In all of these works, the complications of the Austro-German alliance occupy a conspicuous place.

The general dimensions of the problem have thus been long familiar to specialists in the field. All these recent scholars have used the main archive collections which form the basis for the present work. What this study seeks to offer is not so much new information on an old issue, but rather to put both old and new information into new perspective. Surprisingly, despite all the monographs and special studies that have appeared in the last years, there is still no work in either English or German which concentrates on the role of the German alliance per se in Austrian wartime policy and traces its implications all the way from Sarajevo to the end of hostilities.

This study is an attempt to fill some of that gap. The emphasis is political-diplomatic, but other areas are covered when they impinge on this central concern. And while much is said about German policy toward Austria, it should be repeated that the focus is on Austrian policy toward Germany: the center of attention is Vienna, not Berlin. How much freedom of initiative in foreign affairs did the Monarchy still have by 1914? How did its leaders make use of it? To what extent did their own actions contribute to the Monarchy's final demise? What do their policies say about more general problems of alliance cohesion and wartime politics? Many men and institutions were involved in foreign policy in the last years of the Habsburg Monarchy, but only a small number of them were at the heart of the Austrian decision-making process. It is on these individuals and their immediate institutional framework that this work is centered. By putting its emphasis here, it will attempt to show how the alliance, over the course of the war, progressively limited the Monarchy's options and contributed to driving it into a blind alley from which there ultimately was no escape.

All manuscripts adopt certain conventions of expression or organization which may not be entirely clear to their readers, and this one is no exception. For reasons of simplicity, "Austria" is used to refer to the non-Hungarian and non-Bosnian sections of the Monarchy, though technically it would be more correct to say "the kingdoms and countries represented in the Reichsrat." "Austria" is also used to refer to the Monarchy as a whole, as in "Austrian statesmen" rather than "Austro-Hungarian statesmen." Whether the term refers to the western half of the Monarchy alone or to all of it will, I hope, be clear from the context. "Vienna" is used in the same manner. In the notes,

I have tried to cite English versions of works rather than their German (or French) originals, unless the former were drastically altered in translation. This should make it easier for a reader with no foreign languages to investigate my sources, should he so wish. I have not emphasized foreign words in the text as is generally done since some of the principals I quote (particularly Hohenlohe) commonly used both foreign phrases and emphasized words in their correspondence; rather than trying to distinguish between my emphasis and theirs, the simplest thing seemed to be to avoid any emphasis at all unless it appeared in the original document. Any emphasized words and phrases in the quoted material thus come from the quoted writer himself. Unfortunately, I do not read all the languages of the Monarchy. I can only plead in extenuation that the official documents are in German, as well as a good number of private papers.

This study is a revised version of a doctoral dissertation completed in 1977. It was only thanks to the help of a number of people that it arrived at its present state, and I would like to acknowledge their aid. Gerald Feldman, William Slottman, and Paul Seabury supervised the initial research and writing. Alfred Clark and Rodney Ottinger suggested areas for subsequent revision, while Edward Segel's aid was invaluable in sharpening the manuscript's clarity of expression. A Fulbright Fellowship allowed me to spend the year 1975-1976 in Austria. Of course, that leaves the most important people in all this for the last: the archivists of the various document collections cited in the bibliography, particularly those of Haus-, Hof-, und Staatsarchiv in Vienna. Without their organizational work and constant readiness to fulfill the most obscure requests for information, none of this would have been possible.

I close with the no doubt familiar reminder that however much assistance I may have received, any errors that remain in the text are all of my own doing.

McMurry College

September 1984

Chapter 1

THE BRILLIANT SECOND
August 1913-June 1914

I

The Austro-Hungarian Monarchy before World War I was a state like no other in Europe. On a prewar map of the continent, it extended from Switzerland in the west to the Carpathian Mountains and Rumania in the east. Its size was second only to that of Russia, and within its borders it encompassed regions of every geographic description. It was ruled by one of the oldest European royal dynasties and was numbered among the select circle of states known as the European Great Powers.

What made it unique was not its size, but its constitutional and ethnic complexities. The political problems which its rulers faced are well known. Because of the Ausgleich, or Compromise, of 1867, the Habsburg Monarchy was in reality not one unified whole, but two, usually quarreling, separate states in one: the unified polity of Hungary or Transleithania, and the conglomeration of Crownlands grouped about it, usually referred to as Austria or Cisleithania, even though it had no official name until the war. The small Leitha River provided part of the border between them, hence its incorporation into the Monarchy's unofficial nomenclature. The two states shared a common monarch, foreign ministry, and army (though each had a separate military organization as well). A common minister of finance oversaw the revenue provided to maintain those common institutions. Separate governments in Vienna and Budapest handled all other affairs independently and provoked periodic crises with each other whenever the provisions of the Ausgleich regulating what proportion of the common revenue each had to pay came up for revision. A common tradition was often difficult, if not impossible, to distinguish. Even the monarch exhibited a sort of split personality, being Emperor in Austria but only King in Hungary, and

1

thus both "imperial" and "royal" at the same time. Austria-Hungary had the smallest military budget of all the Great Powers (including Italy) before the war because the two parliaments could never agree on military expenditures. Similarly, the province of Bosnia-Herzegovina, formally annexed in 1908, was still in a state of constitutional anomaly when the war broke out in 1914 since neither half of the Habsburg state would allow it to be incorporated in the other. Such was the often less than edifying reality of the grandiloquent sobriquet "imperial and royal" ("kaiserlich und königlich," "k. u. k." for short) officially attached to all the Monarchy's common institutions.

The Monarchy's convoluted political structure was the direct result of its ethnic complexity. Nine major languages were spoken in a realm that encompassed national groups in all stages of cultural and economic development from sophisticated Viennese bankers to illiterate peasants in the Bukovina. The original logic of the Ausgleich had been to simplify the nationality problem by dividing the hegemony of the Empire between the then most powerful nationalities—the Germans west of the Leitha and the Magyars east of it—at the expense of the other ethnic groups. In the long term, the Ausgleich only further complicated the issue. Hungary became even more strongly dominated by a small oligarchy of Magyar landowners applying a systematic policy of Magyarization on the non-Hungarian population and blocking any measures elsewhere in the Monarchy that seemed to threaten its entrenched position of power. The result in Cisleithania was less obvious, but only because the Germans failed to maintain the absolute dominance which the Magyars achieved in Hungary.

This is not to say that the Monarchy was simply the "prison of the peoples" of nineteenth century liberal mythology. The Poles, for example, enjoyed virtual autonomy in Galicia and exercised considerable authority in the government. Even the Czechs, if usually in opposition, were still an important part of the Austrian political system. The division of power between the various nationalities was complex and uneven. But however much the "Old Austria" accommodated itself to the demands of the other ethnic groups, until its final end in 1918 it remained ultimately German in character. The higher reaches of the bureaucracy were staffed by a disproportionate percentage of Austrian Germans, and the officer corps of the common army was almost exclusively German. Those non-Germans who entered these preserves of authority usually did so by assimilating themselves to the dominant national ethos, and thus did little to change their established character. As the other nationalities gained greater political awareness and economic power, they became more and more unwilling to accept this state of affairs, while their demands for change fortified those whose positions were imperiled to block any changes at all. Often, what was demanded would simply have replaced one abuse with another; the Czechs in Bohemia demanded the same right to dominate the Germans there that they complained was currently being exercised by the Germans against them.

The controversies that racked the Monarchy politically spilled over into its economic life. In theory, Austria-Hungary was an almost completely self-sufficient economic unit, the industrial areas of Bohemia and Upper and Lower Austria complemented by the great Hungarian granary of the Alföld. In reality, Hungary attempted systematically to encourage its own industry in order to make itself economically independent of the rest of the Empire and blocked all economic development projects that threatened its special interests. The two halves of the realm were constantly at odds over tariff and commercial policies. Economic unity may have been dictated by the Monarchy's geography, but it was resisted by its political system.

The Monarchy's economy could hardly afford such political burdens. Except for Italy and possibly Russia, Austria-Hungary had the weakest economic base of any of the Great Powers. Economic development varied immensely from area to area, and even in supposedly industrial regions hand and craft workers retained a much more important role than in more industrialized nations. Compared with England or Germany, the process of industrialization was just beginning. Railroad mileage for the entire Monarchy totaled 27,000 miles; Germany, with a smaller land area, had three times the amount of mileage.[1] The agricultural sector presented a similarly mixed picture. In good years, Austria-Hungary produced enough grain to satisfy its domestic needs, but poor harvests after 1909 often required large-scale importation. Because the yield per acre was much lower than in Western Europe, it was impossible to build up enough domestic reserves from good harvests to compensate for bad ones.[2] Sizeable imports of grain or other commodities, unless they were offset by exports elsewhere, threatened the stability of the Monarchy's traditionally weak financial structure. Austria-Hungary experienced a negative trade balance in the immediate prewar years even before it was subjected to the added strain of the war itself.

Historians continue to debate whether the Monarchy's internal weaknesses made its dissolution in 1918 inevitable, or whether different policies could have saved it. There is general unanimity that it could not have been saved within the constitutional system of the Ausgleich. By the twentieth century, that system was under assault by the non-privileged nationalities on the one hand and Magyar chauvinism on the other. Even the loyalties of the Austrian Germans, the traditional "people of state," could no longer be assumed without question. The demands of the Slav groups in Cisleithania spawned

among some Austrian Germans a Großdeutsch or Greater-German nationalism; they argued as early as 1882 in the so-called Linz Program that only
the closest association of Austria (minus Galicia and Hungary) with the
German Reich would allow them to keep the pretensions of the Slavs under
control. With the central Reichsrat or parliament in Austria often paralyzed
by the obstructionism of one national group or another, government
continued to be possible only through Article 14 of the constitution, which
provided for rule by imperial decree in the absence of parliament. The
parliamentary system still appeared to function in Hungary, but only because
an ethnically and socially manipulated franchise shut all but the privileged
Magyar elite out of the halls of government. The growth of mass political
parties demanding political and social democracy further complicated the
political process. Surveying the chaos of conflicting groups and demands,
Karl Lueger, the famous prewar mayor of Vienna, could well lament that true
Austrians could be counted on the fingers of one's hands.[3]

These domestic weaknesses necessarily impinged on the realm of foreign
affairs. In perhaps no other country of Europe was domestic and foreign
policy as closely intertwined as in the Dual Monarchy. Vienna's traditional
policy of supporting the international status quo was dictated by the fact that
almost any other course threatened to undermine the entrenched position of
some domestic group or to overburden the financial structure—a state of
affairs which became even more obvious after 1914, when Vienna attempted
to fashion a coherent set of war aims. But passivity alone provided no final
solution to its problems, as was painfully clear by its failure to combat the
growth of national irredentism. The "South Slav" problem involved not just
discontented Serbs in Hungary or Bosnia, but the attraction exerted on them
by the Serbian national state beyond the Monarchy's borders. The issue was
made explosive by the support which Serbia and later Rumania received
from Czarist Russia. Nor were the Balkans the only area where irredentism
seemed traceable to St. Petersburg. The early months of 1914 also witnessed
the so-called Bobrinski trials of alleged Russian-paid agitators among the
Ruthenes in East Galicia. The Czechs appeared if anything even more
susceptible to Russian blandishments, and seemed less immediately dangerous only because there was no alluring regime of co-nationals bordering on
the Czech areas of the Monarchy. Covert Austrian encouragement of anti-
Russian Polish defense organizations in Galicia did little to discourage the
Russians from attempting to profit from the Monarchy's nationality
problems.

Faced with these manifold weaknesses, the men who ran the Dual
Monarchy turned to foreign support to redress the balance. They were well

aware, even before the beginning of the war, that Austria-Hungary's superficial position as a European Great Power was dependent on the solidity of its alliance with Wilhelmine Germany. Its domestic problems made its ties with Berlin a matter of vital necessity. Those ties complemented and stabilized the precarious balance of domestic forces within Austria-Hungary and created a similar, interrelated balance on an international level between the two empires.

The German alliance, from its inception until the final collapse in 1918, was the cornerstone of all Austrian foreign policy. It originated in 1879 as part of Otto von Bismarck's system of alliances to safeguard the newly-created German Reich; Italy was added in 1882, forming the famous Triple Alliance of the history books. Bismarck was careful to maintain its character as a defensive, essentially conservative, alliance, and as such it assured Vienna (whatever Vienna might have wanted to do with it) of the support it felt it needed against the seemingly limitless power of Czarist Russia in the East.

But the alliance cannot be understood in terms of the exigencies of foreign policy alone. It was also firmly anchored in the domestic order of the Monarchy. Count Ottokar Czernin, Austrian Foreign Minister during probably the decisive phase of the war, later described it not as a normal alliance, but an alliance of blood between the Germans of Austria and those of the German Reich.[4] Its maintenance involved interests and loyalties deeper than those of pure raison d'état; deep enough, in fact, to raise the question of whether some Austrian statesmen during the war were not actually more loyal to the alliance than to the Monarchy itself. In effect, it allowed the Germans of Austria to think of themselves as both German and Austrian, and thus solved (or at least deferred) the question of ultimate loyalty for all those Germans who had been shut out of Bismarck's Kleindeutsch Reich at Königgrätz. It assured them that Austria would retain its German character. Similarly, the alliance buttressed the authority of the Magyars in Hungary. It was quite clear to both groups that the tie with Berlin was one of the chief supports of their domestic position. In the face of the demands of the other nationalities, they could hardly have maintained the status quo without it.

This had not exactly been Bismarck's original intention. As he wrote to one of his ambassadors, whether Carinthia and Carniola spoke German or Slavic was all the same to him; all he cared about was his ally's military worth.[5] The growing nationality conflicts within the Monarchy, however, seemed to threaten that worth directly, by weakening its army in particular and the cohesiveness of the state in general. Maintaining the position of the Austrian Germans and the Magyars against the other nationalities increasingly appeared the best way of guaranteeing Habsburg military dependability, while the demands of the Slavs, if satisfied, might either destroy Austria-Hungary's political cohesion entirely or, given their assumed pro-Russian proclivities, take it into the opposite alliance system. Thus it is not surprising how much Germany even before the war was drawn into the internal affairs of the Monarchy. During the Badeni language controversy at the turn of the century, Berlin intervened actively to encourage Austrian German and Magyar pressure against the domestic course of the Vienna government.[6] German Kaiser Wilhelm left little doubt about his concerns in a meeting with István Tisza, the Hungarian Minister-President, in early 1914: They were both threatened by a rising Slavic wave, he said, and the "best defense against this danger" would be "a German Austria and a Magyar Hungary." A few days later he emphasized to the Archduke Franz Ferdinand that the Czechs had to be set in their place.[7]

Such interventions were heartily welcomed by many Austrian Germans. Paul Samassa, an Austrian member of the radical nationalist Pan-German League (Alldeutscher Verband), wrote to League president Heinrich Claß on the eve of the war: "A strong popular movement in Germany in favor of the Austrian Germans would certainly make an impression among the leading circles here, just as it did at the time of Badeni."[8] Even a relatively moderate Austrian German statesman like Joseph Maria Baernreither, a member of the Herrenhaus, the upper chamber of the Austrian Reichsrat, and a former Austrian Minister of Trade, could not imagine the Monarchy existing without close ties to Germany and maintained numerous political contacts with the Reich. The Magyar oligarchy found the German tie no less essential. During the war, Tisza went so far as to describe Hungary as "the advanced vanguard of Germandom in Southeast Europe."[9] The alliance was thus as closely bound up with the question of domestic reform within Austria-Hungary as was any of its domestic institutions. It was no accident that the Czechs and the small group of Hungarians around Mihály Károly who were so opposed to the existing political and social order were also the loudest critics of the continued maintenance of the alliance with Germany. The defenders of the status quo within the Monarchy needed the Germans just as much as the Germans needed them; each supported the other. This was the essential inner dynamic of the alliance.

Until the outbreak of the war, the alliance both shored up the position of Austria-Hungary as a Great Power and reinforced the Ausgleich. It guaranteed that the Monarchy would be pro-German without being a mere German satellite. Consequently, it seemed to give those at the Ballhausplatz, where the Austrian Foreign Ministry was situated in Vienna, the diplomatic latitude for preserving Vienna's claim to be treated as a major European entity. In actual fact, by the twentieth century the balance between Vienna and Berlin within the alliance had become as precarious as the balance of domestic forces upheld by the Ausgleich. If the war upset it forever, the direction of its fall was becoming evident even before Sarajevo.

Most Germans knew little about the complexities of the Monarchy's domestic structure and cared less. Like Bismarck, all they wanted was dependable diplomatic support, however that was to be achieved. It was a common complaint in Vienna that Berlin showed no understanding of its problems. Yet, if misunderstood, Austria-Hungary was too valuable to be forgotten. Faced by the supposed encirclement of the Entente, Germany felt with increasing urgency the need to retain and buttress its last remaining ally in Europe; for if Vienna were lost to it, it would be completely isolated. Austria-Hungary was, moreover, a valuable economic object. German investments there were greater than those of France and Great Britain combined, and many German banking institutions were linked with those of the Monarchy.[10] It further provided the land bridge for German economic penetration of the Balkans and Asia Minor. Retaining the Austrian ally, however, was seen as no unmixed blessing in Berlin. Its weaknesses constantly appeared to demand assistance and support. If Austria-Hungary was the recipient of large sums of German money before the war, many of them were political loans which would have done more good for the German economy elsewhere.[11] The Germans would certainly have preferred to have been allied to a power of greater strength and cohesion—if any had been available. A month before Sarajevo, Heinrich von Tschirschky, the German Ambassador in Vienna, lamented their predicament:

> How often I consider the question, whether it is really worthwhile for us to bind ourselves so tightly to this state structure cracking in all its seams, and to keep on with the tiresome work of dragging it along with us. But I see no other political constellation which as a substitute could offer us anything more than the alliance with this Central European power. Since without this alliance, our policy would of necessity have to be directed towards a partition of the Monarchy.[12]

Tschirschky aptly voiced the dilemmas which the Monarchy presented to Berlin before the war: it managed to be both a necessity and a liability at the same time. Many of the German plans for relative or absolute control which developed during the conflict were in part attempts to put an end to such an anomalous and frustrating situation.

If the alliance as it then stood was a source of concern in Berlin, that was no less the case in Vienna. Austria-Hungary had always aspired to a position of equality in its relations with Germany, and there was a certain logic in having a close connection with the conservative, satiated Germany of Bismarck. But in the years before the war, the Monarchy found itself tied to a state whose dynamic growth far outstripped its own and progressively distorted the relative balance of power within the alliance. It has been estimated that the ratio of German to Austrian military strength was 4:3 when the alliance was first created. It had shifted to nearly 2:1 by 1914 and 3:1 by 1917, a mark of Germany's explosive industrial expansion and its more efficient political and military organization.[13] Moreover, Wilhelmine Germany aspired to be not simply a Great Power but also a World Power, one whose political and economic ambitions throughout the world had conjured up the Triple Entente against it. The Habsburg Monarchy had no immediate conflicts of interest with Britain or France—hardly any areas of overlapping concern at all—but its tie with Germany automatically ranged them against it in international crises and blocked the political or economic support it might otherwise have found from them. In 1912, Alexander von Spitzmüller, the director of the Austrian Kreditanstalt bank, complained of the Monarchy's misfortune at being allied to a power which could offer it little financial support—an obvious allusion to the fact that its alliance with Germany closed the much-needed French money market to it.[14]

Ironically, the same weaknesses which German statesmen deplored as limiting the Monarchy's effectiveness as an ally also assured them a position of authority which they certainly would not have enjoyed in a more equal relationship. As German power and ambition grew, Austria-Hungary found itself dragged increasingly by its powerful ally into a subordinate role within the alliance. The Habsburg Monarchy was Germany's "brilliant second," Kaiser Wilhelm loudly proclaimed after the first Morocco Crisis. His words were resented in Vienna and not quickly forgotten.

The increasing subordination of the Monarchy to Germany was registered in the economic as well as in the political sphere. Many Austrian businessmen had good reason to fear being pushed out of traditional markets by the aggressive and economically more advanced German counterparts. The Balkans were not only an area of acute political importance to Austria-Hungary; they were also its most important source of foreign trade, next to Germany itself. But if the Balkans had not been worth the bones of a Pomeranian grenadier to Bismarck, they were worth a good deal to his successors. While the Monarchy's political standing deteriorated in both Serbia and Rumania, the Germans' remained excellent, and they were more than willing to take economic advantage of the fact. Austrian businessmen there discovered to their increasing dismay that their chief ally often was also their chief competitor. During the so-called Pig War of 1906-09 between the Monarchy and Serbia, the Austrian attempt to boycott the Serbs economically merely gave the Germans the chance to step in and appropriate the former Austrian markets for themselves, not to mention thereby strengthening Serb economic independence. Throughout the Balkans, the German share of the market increased, while that of Austria-Hungary declined.[15] Joseph Baernreither reported after a trip to Rumania in early 1914 that the Germans were outpacing the Monarchy "all along the line." This he attributed not only to better German business practices but to German diplomacy itself: "The German Minister in Bucharest is concerned, first and foremost, in getting orders for Germany."[16]

Austria-Hungary's economic vulnerability was also evident outside the Balkans. Germany accounted for around 40% of Austrian foreign trade in the years before the war, while Austria's share of German foreign trade, never more than 20%, diminished steadily. Germany was far more important economically to Austria-Hungary than was Austria-Hungary to Germany, and Berlin when it chose could exert an economic weight on Vienna which could not easily be countered.[17] József Szterényi, a former Hungarian Minister of Trade, told the Vienna Industrial Club in March 1914 that the Monarchy's economic future was hopeless and that it was no longer possible for it to have an economic policy separate from that of Berlin.[18]

Thus, even before Sarajevo, the balance of power in the alliance was progressively shifting to the Monarchy's disadvantage. The responses in Vienna were a foretaste of what was to come. Count Alois Lexa von Aehrenthal, Austrian Foreign Minister from 1906 to 1912, tried to maintain at least the appearance of Austrian parity in the alliance, dissociating the Monarchy from Berlin as much as possible in the Second Morocco Crisis and in Germany's continuing naval rivalry with Britain. Both Aehrenthal and the Archduke Franz Ferdinand advocated an understanding with Russia and a resurrection of Bismarck's Dreikaiserbund. Such a course would have meant a lessening of Austrian dependence on Germany, but in the strained international environment of the time neither had any real idea how to carry it out. Other voices were raised for a rapprochement with the West. Establishment of close ties with Britain or France was an appealing prospect on paper, but of little worth in reality so long as the Monarchy's main foreign adversary remained Russia. If war broke out between the two East European empires, how would British or French aid help stem a Russian invasion of Galicia? In such a situation, the Germans, for all the problems they brought in their train, could still offer far more than either of their western neighbors.

Whatever their doubts, in practice the Monarchy's leaders continued to direct their steps in the well-worn traces of the alliance. They continued to believe, despite all their premonitions of weakness, that they could go on drawing the benefits they had traditionally derived from their ties with Germany without paying the rising cost. This was clearly becoming a dubious proposition even before the events of the war swept it away altogether.

II

The complicated institutional structure of the Monarchy guaranteed that only a small body of men actually made the foreign policy decisions aimed at coping with all these problems. Actually, to say that they "made" policy is probably too positive an expression. It was easy for someone at the center of power to come to a decision; but Austria-Hungary's institutions frequently made it impossible for that decision then to be carried out—or at least carried out effectively. Where diplomacy impinged on domestic politics, the Foreign Ministry often found it could do nothing without first securing the cooperation of the respective Austrian or Hungarian ministries, a time-consuming task at best. More typically, it tried to ignore them, with an impact on the coherence of general policy which is easily imagined. Baernreither, after his trip to Rumania, complained that the Monarchy's trade relations there were represented by no less than three separate groups—the Austro-Hungarian Consulate, a trade representative from the Austrian government, and a trade representative from the Hungarian government—all working at cross purposes with each other.[19] More well-known is the course of the July Crisis of 1914. The decision to attack Serbia was generally agreed on within a few days of the assassination, but it took a month before the ultimatum was presented to Belgrade. By then, the initial shock in foreign capitals of the Archduke's death had worn off, and any chance of a quick fait accompli was gone. Had the Monarchy been capable of more rapid implementation of its decisions, the outcome of the crisis might have been far different.

There were few official channels through which the direction of foreign policy could be influenced. The Reichsrat in Austria and the parliament in Hungary were concerned with domestic, not foreign, affairs. Although they selected the Delegations which met periodically to approve the policies of the Foreign Minister, the Delegations usually acted as little more than rubber stamps of the Foreign Ministry. Since the Austrian Reichsrat was prorogued early in 1914, they never even met for the first half of the war. That left the separate Austrian and Hungarian ministries, but only the Minister-President of each was entitled constitutionally to a voice in foreign policy. The other ministers were usually allowed no input beyond their immediate bureaucratic jurisdictions. Consequently, very little of the imposing governmental apparatus of the Dual Monarchy was actually involved in the making of foreign policy. Or rather, since its institutions were denied any positive role, their chief impact was the negative one of complicating the actions of those who were involved in the actual decision making.

The effectiveness of unofficial channels in influencing foreign policy— through personal influence or organized pressure—varied with the circumstances. Any number of groups were interested in foreign policy—the various national clubs, the big newspapers like the *Neue Freie Presse,* the Socialists, the business organizations. But again, these were usually more successful in blocking government measures than in effecting measures of their own. Magyar opposition was instrumental in causing Count Agenor Goluchowski's resignation as Foreign Minister in 1906. But such cases were more the exception than the rule. The Pan-German League, for example, would certainly have liked to have influenced Austrian policy; two of its members, Paul Samassa and Edmund Steinacker, were involved in Franz Ferdinand's Belvedere Circle, and Samassa enjoyed ties with German Ambassador Tschirschky.[20] Its actual influence, however, failed to match its expectations. Samassa and Steinacker were not among the Archduke's most intimate advisors, and Samassa's ties with Tschirschky were hardly more productive. Tschirschky was an intelligent man, but his sharp German nationalism and (often justified) impatience with Austrian ways of doing things did not make him a very popular one. He was heartily disliked by the Austrian Foreign Ministry, which in fact attempted several times to have him replaced. Nor did others fare much better. During the war, some of the leading figures of the Austrian German parties in the prorogued Reichsrat attempted to maneuver the Austrian Minister-President, Count Karl Stürgkh, out of office. They got nowhere. As long as Stürgkh enjoyed the Emperor's confidence, he was untouchable. Perhaps typical in all this were the reactions of the frustrated Austrian scholar and Reichsrat deputy Josef Redlich. Even though he knew personally many of the men at the center of power in the Monarchy, he could only fulminate ceaselessly against them in his diary.

Those directly involved in the conduct of foreign policy thus occupied a position of power perhaps possible only in a state like Austria-Hungary. In a real sense, they were accountable to no one but the Emperor and each other for what they decided; but what they decided was usually blocked or distorted by the institutional jumble around them. Their mentality has frequently been described: "desperate but not serious," fatalistic, stubbornly immobile. In many regards they formed a closed circle, living in an insulated world where success was still determined by aristocratic family pedigrees or royal favor, and becoming a privy councillor was more important than winning an election. Even if they were aware of the new social and economic forces around them, they had little idea how to deal with them. Society in Germany may have been dominated by the East Elbian Junkers, but there was room for rye to merge with iron; successful businessmen like Albert Ballin attained access to the inmost circles of authority. Their expertise was welcomed there. Few Albert Ballins numbered among the central policy-makers in Austria.

These constraints naturally affected the behavior of those in positions of authority. By 1914, Austria-Hungary was in a sense a complex balance of interlocking crises; and to the men who actually held the reins of power, the only solution often seemed to be to avoid any solution at all, somehow to smooth over each crisis as it came along and thus to postpone any drastic shock that might finally upset the whole fabric: to muddle through as always. They were in fact set not only against the growing demands of the Slavs, but also against the shrill cries of the various Großdeutsch-oriented Austrian German groups to repress the Slavs once and for all. In the final resort, their policy was not national; it was dynastic. Yet though they managed to uphold the complex polity of the Old Austria, at least superficially, into the first months of the war, there was an inner sense of futility that gripped nearly all of them. Even Franz Conrad von Hötzendorf, the bellicose Army Chief of Staff, predicted to his future wife on hearing of the Sarajevo assassination that Serbia and Rumania would become the nails of the Monarchy's coffin and that the impending struggle (which he himself advocated) was hopeless.[21]

The final arbiter of all policy in Austria-Hungary on the eve of the war was the old Emperor Franz Joseph. In 1914, he was nearing the end of the longest reign in modern European history. Franz Joseph was rigidly conservative, after the early disasters of his reign content to preserve rather than to innovate, even though a policy of "preservation" did little to solve the manifold difficulties confronting the realm. It was his prerogative to select the Foreign Minister, the two Minister-Presidents, and the chief officers of the army, who carried out the policies he desired. Because of personal inclination and age, however, his role was usually the passive one of approving ideas proposed by others, rather than that of actively initiating them himself. His well-known care in reading and approving dispatches was more characteristic of a dedicated bureaucrat than of an innovative states-man. To what extent he was influenced by his immediate entourage at Court—officials such as High Court Chamberlain Prince Alfred Montenuovo or the head of the Military Cabinet, Arthur Freiherr von Bolfras, or other members of the imperial family—is difficult to say. Most likely, they simply confirmed him in the routine to which over the years he had become accustomed. Many of the Court officials were nearly as old and set in their ways as was the Emperor himself.

The Imperial and Royal Minister of the Household and of Foreign Affairs held immediate responsibility for the conduct of foreign policy. From 1912, this was Count Leopold Berchtold. Berchtold has received a great deal of attention, most of it unfavorable. Much of this is unfair; he was neither lazy nor frivolous nor stupid. Yet though a successful ambassador to Russia, he accepted the office of Foreign Minister only at the insistence of Franz Joseph. He felt himself temperamentally unsuited to the task of conducting foreign policy and was much more at home elsewhere; the burden of office rested heavily on his shoulders. Just how heavily is indicated by his relief in escaping it. A day at his country estate at Buchlau in Moravia meant "having the good fortune to get away from the simmering cauldron at the Ballplatz, even if only temporarily, for a few suggestive hours in the service of art."[22] His own feelings of inadequacy made him heavily dependent on the advice and opinions of those around him, with the result that the policies he advocated were often the result of following the line of least resistance among his colleagues rather than having clear opinions of his own. This tendency gave an importance to the views of his otherwise obscure confidants—to Count Alexander Hoyos, his Cabinet Chief, and to Count János Forgách. Forgách as Minister to Belgrade had discredited himself by uncritically providing forged documents for the Agram (Zagreb) treason trials of 1909. He had subsequently been shipped off to Dresden but returned to the Ballplatz in the fall of 1913, where he remained a Section Chief until 1917. More importantly, it accentuated the influence of Count István Tisza, the Hungarian Minister-President.[23]

If any single man could be said to have been the moving force behind Austrian policy in the last year before the war, that man was Tisza. Tisza's unbending Calvinist personality impressed most of those who met him, especially since it contrasted so conspicuously with the passive resignation of so many other statesmen of the Monarchy. But if his fanatical sense of purpose inspired the respect of his friends, his dictatorial methods made him thoroughly hated by most of his opponents—the leaders of the other Magyar parties as well as the non-Magyar nationalities of Austria-Hungary. As head of the " '67" Party of Work in Hungary, where he presided over an impressive majority in the Hungarian parliament, his good standing was guaranteed with Franz Joseph, for he firmly blocked the demands of the

" '48" factions to loosen further the bonds of Hungary with the rest of the Monarchy. Rather, he upheld the 1867 Ausgleich as the chief bulwark of Magyar predominance over the other nationalities in Transleithania. He was less chauvinist than those inspired by the 1848 struggle for complete Hungarian independence only to the extent that he, unlike they, believed that a close association with Vienna was essential to preserve Magyar power in Central Europe. Tisza took special interest in the decisions of the Foreign Ministry, received access to all important dispatches, and made sure nothing was decided without his consent. "It was well known that foreign policy could not be made without Tisza," Karl Freiherr von Macchio, then First Section Chief at the Ballplatz, later wrote.[24]

The force of Tisza's judgments was exercised over the other ministers of the Monarchy as well as the head of the Foreign Ministry. If there was any general policy-making organ shared by both halves of the Monarchy, this was the Gemeinsamer Ministerrat or Council of Common Ministers. The council was an informal body whose decisions were not constitutionally binding. However, it allowed the government leaders in Vienna and Budapest to come together to consult over general issues of concern. It consisted of the Common Ministers for Foreign Affairs, War, and Finance (who also administered Bosnia-Herzegovina), the Austrian and Hungarian Minister-Presidents, and, when their presence seemed necessary, the army Chief of Staff and the heads of individual Austrian or Hungarian ministries. The Foreign Minister usually presided over its deliberations, and it met whenever consultation appeared called for. Leon Biliński, the Common Minister of Finance, later described to the Austrian journalist Heinrich Kanner the extent of Tisza's influence: "In the Common Ministers Councils Tisza's opinion was always decisive; we really had nothing to say about it, mostly we kept quiet."[25] The extent of Tisza's power makes it easy to see why many Austrians before the war could worry about a Hungarian stranglehold on the Monarchy.

The Hungarian position in the Habsburg policy-making elite was further represented by Baron István Burián. Burián was Minister a Latere, that is, the representative of the Hungarian government with the Court in Vienna. He had access to the principal leaders there as well as to the Emperor, giving him a sometimes influential, if shadowy, behind-the-scenes authority. He was such a close friend of Tisza that he was often considered little more than Tisza's yes-man. Even if his standpoint usually corresponded with that of the Hungarian Minister-President, Burián nonetheless had a stubborn, often doctrinaire mind of his own. He had earlier served as Common Finance Minister, and his ties with Tisza would lead him to the position of Foreign Minister in little over a year.

The same right of access to foreign policy decisions of which Tisza made so much use was also available to the Austrian Minister-President, Count Karl Stürgkh. Yet Stürgkh, an upstanding but unimaginative bureaucrat, did little with it. "He has never had a single independent aim, never followed a single plan of his own, never held high a single idea," Baernreither grumbled about him in his diary.[26] Stürgkh concerned himself almost exclusively with domestic policy, except when domestic affairs impinged on foreign policy considerations or foreign policy questions came up for discussion in the Common Ministers Council.

Tisza's most powerful opponent among the makers of Austro-Hungarian policy was one who held no official office in the foreign policy decision-making structure at all: the Heir Apparent. The Archduke Franz Ferdinand had reputedly sworn that his first act in ascending the throne would be to topple Tisza from power before Tisza could have time to incite a revolution against him. Franz Ferdinand's actual impact on policy is hard to calculate. Even though he was already drawing his advisors around him at the Belvedere in preparation for his ascent to the throne, his influence rested on anticipation of his future position, not on his existing one. He generally advocated a peaceful foreign policy that avoided confrontation with the Monarchy's neighbors, if for no other reason than to preserve the realm intact until he could become Emperor and initiate his schemes of reform.

Those who, on the contrary, believed that Austria-Hungary's problems were no longer amenable to peaceful solution found their most influential representative in Franz Conrad von Hötzendorf, the Chief of Staff of the army. Most memoirists after the war discreetly underplayed their role in the decisions that led to the conflict. Conrad, on the other hand, paraded his bellicosity before the public's eyes in his reminiscences and argued unabashedly that the Monarchy had been done in not by unleashing the war, but only by unleashing it too late. His constant urgings for a preventive war against Serbia or Italy—or both at once, depending on the circumstances—are well known. The Austrian military possessed nowhere near the influence of its counterpart in Imperial Germany; any other Austrian general who spent as much time meddling in the business of the Foreign Ministry would probably have been dismissed in short order. Aehrenthal managed to get Conrad removed from office, but he was reinstated in 1912 under the weaker Berchtold. His view of the situation, and his efforts to upgrade the army accordingly, struck a responsive chord in the Austrian establishment. By the close of the Balkan Wars, both Stürgkh and Alexander von Krobatin, the Common Minister of War, had been won over to his position. Franz

Ferdinand's admonition to Berchtold "not to let yourself be influenced by Conrad!"[27] gives some indication of his prewar influence.

The policies formulated in Vienna were influenced and implemented by the Monarchy's representatives abroad. Some of these had acquired considerable weight for their judgments, both at home and in their countries of accreditation. Mention need be made only of Count Albert Mensdorff in London or Margrave János Pallavicini in Constantinople. The Monarchy's interests in Berlin were represented by Count Lászlo Szögyény. Szögyény had held the position since 1892 but was slated for retirement by the time of the July Crisis because of his advanced age. His successor, who took office in August 1914, was Prince Gottfried zu Hohenlohe-Schillingsfürst, a member of the Austrian branch of the family that produced the German Chancellor Chlodwig Hohenlohe. Gottfried Hohenlohe, who had earlier served as Military Attaché in St. Petersburg, was convinced that only a close association with Germany would allow the Monarchy to solve its increasingly paralyzing nationality problems, which he blamed on the selfish demands of the Slavs and the Magyars. He had little sympathy for Habsburg bureaucrats like Stürgkh, whose slackness and immobility were a constant source of irritation to him. Hohenlohe's energy and judgment made him a key link in the alliance, and while he sometimes seemed to have more faith in Germany than in his native country, there is no doubt that his efforts contributed substantially to smoothing over the disputes that soon arose between the two allies—certainly more so than was the case with his German counterpart in Vienna.

These were probably the chief makers of official policy in Austria-Hungary on the eve of the war. And it was these men who, faced with a deteriorating situation nearly everywhere they turned in the last year before the conflict, finally decided on the ultimatum to Serbia in July 1914.

III

The Treaty of Bucharest of August 10, 1913, which ended the Balkan Wars, ratified a near-total disaster for Austrian foreign policy. Between 1912 and 1913, the small Christian states of the Balkans came together under Russian aegis to form a Balkan League which practically drove the Ottoman Empire out of Europe. Vienna dreaded that Austria-Hungary would now inherit its position as the sick man of Europe. Serbia was nearly doubled in territory, with a corresponding boost to its irredentist ambitions against the Monarchy. Rumania, secretly affiliated with the Triple Alliance since 1883, experienced a similar enhancement of its national ego, and began to realize that it, too, had an irredenta in Austria-Hungary, in the Rumanian-populated areas of Hungarian Transylvania. The single success that the Ballplatz had to show from the diplomatic infighting that accompanied the military campaigns was the erection of the new state of Albania, whose main purpose was to block Serbian access to the Adriatic. Unfortunately, the new polity threatened to collapse almost as soon as it had been created.

Austria-Hungary had never really found a satisfactory way of dealing with the Christian peoples of the Balkans. Vienna seems to have been unable to make up its mind whether they should be considered fellow Europeans or potential colonial subjects; Metternich's quip that Asia began on the Landstraße still held true for it. But for all the anxiety they caused, irredentist Serbia and Rumania could hardly have threatened the Monarchy much by themselves. Russian backing made the danger they posed so formidable and the Austrians so hard put to find a way to counter it. The specter of Russian expansion westward had haunted Vienna for over a century. In the years before the war, it acquired almost nightmare proportions. South Slav terrorism in Bosnia or Ruthene subversion in East Galicia were all seen as having their ultimate origins in Russia, and they could now be expected to take on even more dangerous proportions. As the Balkan Wars drew to their close, even such a relatively enlightened Austrian statesman as Baernreither could look at the Monarchy's predicament and conclude: "Thanks to its passivity during the war, and its absolutely unclear policy towards the Balkan states, it was now faced with a fait accompli whose consequences it had got [sic] to avert at any price."[28]

As far as those in Vienna were concerned, the alliance had done little to avert this catastrophe. The Germans had in fact often worked against them. Berlin had refused to intervene actively in the conflict and had discouraged the Austrians from taking any forceful actions on their own. Berchtold's Cabinet Chief Hoyos referred to German acceptance of the final treaty of peace, which the Ballplatz had hoped to modify, as "Austria's diplomatic Olmütz."[29] Berchtold fumed:

> If we can thank this alliance for the unpleasant fact that the French and English money market is closed to us and we are heading towards a financial catastrophe, they [the Germans] should at least help us out politically in the single foreign policy showplace where vital interests of the Monarchy are at stake.[30]

Vienna set itself after the close of the Balkan Wars to reverse the political situation created by the Treaty of Bucharest on its southern borders, or at least to keep affairs there from getting any worse. The war party around Conrad continued to press for a preventive war against the Serbs, but Berchtold was not yet ready for this and Tisza decidedly against it, as was the Archduke Franz Ferdinand. These hoped instead to contain the Serbian threat through diplomatic means. Their fear was a resurrected Balkan League centered on Serbia, supported by Russia, and directed against the Monarchy. To block it, they wanted a longterm diplomatic offensive to isolate the Serbs from the other states of the Balkans. Such an offensive could be successful only if it were conducted in the closest harmony with Berlin; without consistent German support, the Austrians felt powerless.

Restoring the harmony of the alliance (on Vienna's terms) thus seemed to be the main precondition for any Austrian foreign policy in the summer of 1913. Austrian policy-makers may have been divided over many issues, but they all viewed the German alliance as a vital necessity for the Monarchy. A month earlier, Franz Ferdinand had lectured Berchtold on the importance of maintaining smooth relations with Germany in general and the erratic Wilhelm in particular. "I can't always go off on boar hunts to calm him down," he had pointed out.[31] There was an essential contradiction here: to play the role of a European Great Power, Austria-Hungary found German backing essential; but if it was unable to pursue an independent policy without German support, then it no longer possessed the power base to be a Great Power in the first place. The very fact that the Austrian leadership felt the need for such support so strongly already indicated the beginning of the dependence that was to become so evident during the war. But in 1913, Vienna still thought of itself as an equal in the alliance and actually expected priority in Balkan questions. It believed that Germany could be made to serve Austrian interests rather than the other way around, despite all the evidence to the contrary.

The harmony that Vienna sought in the last year before the war was never really achieved. Baernreither, a well-informed observer, made a revealing notation in his diary in March 1914 after a visit with Wilhelm and Gottlieb von Jagow, the German State Secretary for Foreign Affairs:

> As usual, here in Berlin, self-confidence runs high; at the moment, indeed, excessively high. These men lay down the law, and are little inclined to pay attention to the opinions of others. There is insufficient knowledge of our Austrian conditions, with the result that the difficulties with which we have to contend are underestimated. Hence, the professorial tone that sounds in nearly all they say.[32]

If the Monarchy's leaders structured much of their foreign policy around the problem of somehow containing the Serb threat as they saw it, they were never able to convince the Germans of the seriousness of that threat until Sarajevo. The situation might not have been so intolerable had Berlin at least had a consistent policy of its own toward the Balkans, but it did not. The Germans wanted a solution to any problem that menaced the effectiveness of Austria-Hungary as a German ally, of course. But they really had no idea how to bring it about, and were likely to respond differently in every situation.

The October 1913 crisis between the Monarchy and Serbia has sometimes been interpreted as the point at which the earlier differences between Vienna and Berlin were finally bridged, and where Vienna secured for itself the support it had sought so long. In actual fact, whatever harmony was displayed during the crisis disappeared almost as soon as it was over. Alarmed by the continued failure of the Serbs to evacuate their troops from territory that had been designated part of the new Albanian state, the Austrians on October 18 sent an ultimatum to Belgrade demanding withdrawal of those forces within eight days. Berlin approved completely. Kaiser Wilhelm informed Conrad: "In a few days you must be in Belgrade. I was always an advocate of peace, but that has its limits. I've read a lot about war and know what it means, but finally the situation comes when a Great Power can't look on any longer, but must grasp the sword." [33]

The Serbs quickly gave in to the ultimatum (which, unlike that of July 1914, was not specifically designed to be incapable of acceptance), and Vienna seemed to have achieved a major diplomatic victory. But victory or not, Vienna and Berlin remained as far as ever from real harmony. Wilhelm's words to Berchtold a week later when he visited the Austrian capital have frequently been cited. The German Kaiser was effusive that war between East and West was inevitable and that the Serb problem had to be solved by force if no other means proved effective. Belgrade would be bombarded and occupied until Franz Joseph's will was carried out there, and Vienna would have complete German support for such an action.[34] These assurances may have had value for a future crisis, but they did little to exorcise Vienna's immediate fears of a resurrected Balkan League or to provide a practical plan for frustrating it. Their real effect was to avoid any discussion of practical reality at all. As Burián noted sarcastically in his diary on the occasion of Wilhelm's visit, "He only wants us not to ask too many questions or to have doubts." [35]

Burián's skepticism was borne out in the following months. By March of 1914, Wilhelm had changed course entirely and with Jagow was urging an Austro-Serb rapprochement and customs union.[36] "It's easy for the gentlemen in Berlin to give good advice," Berchtold could only exclaim in frustration. "They're far from the shooting!"[37]

Probably the most obvious example of the continuing disharmonies in the alliance was the Ballplatz's failure, in a year of effort, to change Berlin's orientation to Rumania and Bulgaria, which it considered necessary if Belgrade were to be diplomatically isolated from its neighbors. The Monarchy's relations with Rumania had already begun that steady deterioration that led to open hostilities three years later; Ottokar Czernin, the Austrian Minister in Bucharest, reported that Rumania's secret treaty with the Monarchy had become little more than a "worthless scrap of paper."[38] Vienna was increasingly skeptical that the Rumanians' loyalties could be regained in light of Bucharest's designs on Transylvania, but it felt unable to take any decisive action without German support. Berlin, however, refused to admit that a problem scarcely existed right up to the eve of the war, optimistically assuming that Rumania, as a non-Slav power, somehow had a natural community of interests with the Triple Alliance. The only step it was ready to take was to recommend domestic concessions to the Hungarian Rumanians, a policy it would continue even more forcefully after the outbreak of hostilities. In the last year of peace, Vienna tried repeatedly to convince the Germans of the worsening situation in Bucharest, but to no avail.

To compensate for the potential defection of Rumania, the Ballplatz hoped to establish closer relations with its Balkan rival, Bulgaria. Bulgaria harbored territorial claims on both Serbia and Rumania, but was one of the few states of the area with none against the Monarchy. But the anti-Bulgarian sentiment that had prevailed at the Wilhelmstraße during the Balkan Wars persisted beyond them despite all Vienna's efforts to alter it. Again, the Austrians felt powerless to act without German backing. The most Vienna was able to squeeze out of Berlin was support for the Bulgarian loan of 1914, something it believed absolutely essential to prop up the current Austrophile government in Sofia. Even this came only after considerable pleading on Berchtold's part. The fact that Vienna had to turn as a supplicant to Berlin for the loan was an indication of its financial as well as its political weaknesses. The Monarchy could clearly do little in Bulgaria without German approval. Forgách summed up his colleagues' frustrations soon after Kaiser Wilhelm again visited Vienna in March 1914. "A complete conformity of our and Germany's policies in the Balkans is still not attained, despite all our efforts," he noted ruefully.[39] More and more, Vienna feared that if something were not done soon, both Bulgaria and Rumania would be lost to the rival Entente camp.

These difficulties were accompanied by a similarly deteriorating situation on the Adriatic, the one area where Vienna thought it had salvaged something from the Treaty of Bucharest. An initial threat came from the possibility of a union of Montenegro with Serbia, which would give the hitherto landlocked Serbs an outlet on the Adriatic Sea—something Berchtold had labored tirelessly to prevent during the negotiations of the Balkan Wars. Vienna believed firmly that it was a vital interest of the Monarchy to block such a development; or, if the union actually took place, to annex the Montenegrin coast including the Lovčen, the mountain dominating the Austrian naval base at Cattaro (Kotor). But it received no German support for any of these ideas. Wilhelm minuted on a dispatch from Belgrade: "The union is absolutely not to be prevented; and if Vienna should try, it will be committing a great stupidity and conjuring up the danger of a war with the Slavs, which would leave us completely cold"[40]—hardly the same Wilhelm who in October advocated bombarding Belgrade. Simultaneously, the Austrian client state of Albania disintegrated into anarchy. Austrian requests for financial or military support for it were received with undisguised indifference in Berlin; the Germans had never considered Albania viable to begin with.

These complications raised the further danger of a major crisis with Italy. Though allied with Austria-Hungary, Italy, like so many other neighbors of the Monarchy, had an irredenta there: the Trentino, Trieste, and areas of the Dalmatian coast. Moreover, Rome had claims in the Balkans as great as Vienna's, and it would tolerate nothing that seemed to favor Austrian Balkan interests over its own. It staunchly opposed Vienna's plans in the case of a Serb-Montenegrin union and was the Monarchy's chief rival for influence in Albania. The two capitals watched each other with scarcely-veiled suspicion, which any major upset on the Adriatic was likely to fan into open hostility.

Vienna could expect no more German support in its growing difficulties with Italy than it found anywhere else, for what Berlin wanted to avoid above all was an open conflict between Italy and Austria that would destroy the Triple Alliance. This meant in practice to refuse any active backing to the Monarchy where it was in conflict with Italy, in order to conciliate the Italians. "It is a little like the situation of a husband who is sure of his wife and therefore spoils his mistress," Kajetan Mérey, the Austrian Ambassador to Rome, complained in July.[41] An Austrian attempt to carve out a sphere of influence for itself in Anatolian Turkey foundered on the opposition of both Rome and Berlin, each of which had established claims there already and felt no inclination to share any of them with its partner in the Triple Alliance.[42]

Austrian relations with Germany thus remained in a state of disarray and tension, whatever image of solidarity was presented to the public, right up to the eve of Sarajevo. The men who made Austrian policy saw the Monarchy's position rapidly deteriorating and felt themselves ignored or actively blocked by their German ally in their anxious efforts to cope with it. Only a week before Sarajevo, Conrad sketched the Monarchy's situation as he saw it: It was surrounded on two sides by aggressive enemies in Russia, Rumania, Serbia, and Montenegro; an unreliable ally, Italy, on the third; only on the fourth, from Germany, could any assistance be expected—and the Germans were equally threatened by France and Russia, not to mention the British.[43] Czernin in Bucharest, railing at his superiors' apparent paralysis and exasperated with German blindness to the whole situation, was no less vehement:

> Before us in broad daylight, openly and distinctly, clear as the sun, with shameless audacity, step by step, the encirclement of the Monarchy is being completed; under Franco-Russian patronage a new Balkan League is being forged together, whose aim, today still seemingly complicated, will soon become apparent with startling simplicity—against the Monarchy.[44]

Tisza was equally alarmed, as he made clear in a lengthy policy recommendation in March. The Entente was working single-mindedly to encircle Austria-Hungary and to cement its hegemony on the continent. To block its efforts required a longterm diplomatic campaign to set up a grouping of the Balkan states favorable to the Triple Alliance. "It is wholly impossible to achieve anything," he wrote, "unless the complete harmony of our policy with Germany's comes into effect in word and action all along the line."[45]

Vienna's repeatedly-expressed appeals for German assistance and understanding indicate how desperate and vulnerable the Monarchy's leaders felt by the spring of 1914, and how little real assistance they believed they were getting from Berlin. This is not to say that if they had gotten more German support for their views, things would have been any better. Often, Germany's was a voice for sanity and restraint. Without that voice, an Austrian intervention in the Balkan Wars might have led to the First World War breaking out several years earlier than it actually did. But for all its confident posturings, in the last resort Berlin was at as much of a loss how to deal with the situation as was Vienna.

The result was a willingness at the Ballplatz to entertain measures whose level of risk would never have allowed their consideration under more stable circumstances. The Austro-Hungarian decision for war in 1914 was not the culmination of a long period of close cooperation with Berlin, but rather of its precise opposite. After Sarajevo, the Germans finally seemed to offer to the harried Austrian leaders the support for which they had been pleading so long in vain. The frustrations of the past year made it an opportunity which no one in Vienna was about to pass up.

Chapter 2

VA BANQUE
July 1914

There is a certain irony that Austria-Hungary used the occasion of the Sarajevo assassination for its final showdown with the Serbs. Franz Ferdinand had been seen as an unsettling, if not dangerous, factor by many circles in the Monarchy, especially the Magyars, who undoubtedly breathed more easily once Gavrillo Princip's shots had done their work. Moreover, far from having been directed against the South Slavs, his reform plans were reputed actually to have favored them; and while this is open to question, there is no question that he would have liked some kind of understanding with Russia. The Archduke had not been a member of the war party in Vienna and probably never would have countenanced the use to which his assassination was put by his compatriots there.

The events in Sarajevo not only eliminated one of the chief influences for peace among the Austrian policy-making elite; they also sealed the adherence of Berchtold to the war party. Long before Sarajevo, Berchtold had concluded that only a drastic solution of the Serb problem was possible. That solution, he had noted in November 1913, "either will leave only faint traces of the present Serbian state or will shake Austria-Hungary to its foundations." [1] But his actual policy had been to prepare for that future moment through diplomatic means, not to provoke an immediate military decision. As he wrote a year later after leaving office, he had been convinced ever since the close of the Balkan Wars that a reckoning with Serbia would have to come; his only doubt had been of his own suitability as the person to carry it out. [2] The assassination overcame his last hesitations.

Even if Berchtold had not been already at least intellectually convinced of the need for action, he would have been hard put to resist the pressure of those around him. His confidants, Hoyos and Forgách, argued for a forceful course of action, as did Conrad; and Hohenlohe, soon to be Ambassador in

25

Berlin, admonished him: "Count, be hard!" and threatened to refuse his new post if energetic measures were not taken.[3] Franz Joseph as well proved to be convinced of the necessity of a military action against Serbia.[4] Only Tisza argued against a forceful action against the Serbs—a lonely but important exception.

Whatever Vienna thought the situation called for, however, it felt that it could do nothing without the support of Germany. For such an action against Serbia, the assent of Berlin was decisive. "Do you think we would have dared to go to war if we had not known Germany wanted it?" Leon Biliński, the Common Finance Minister at the time of the July Crisis, asked rhetorically two years later in an interview with the Austrian journalist Heinrich Kanner. "Without Germany, it would have been impossible for us to do it."[5] The decisiveness of German support is understandable only in the context of the disharmonies since the Treaty of Bucharest. The July Crisis was an attempt not only to come to terms with Serbia, but also with Germany, to recover the German support that had been so painfully lacking over the last year. The two were inseparably connected in the minds of the Austrian leaders. Berchtold later listed as the determining factors during the crisis not only the threat from Serbia and Russia which had to be countered, but also the possibility of losing Germany as an ally.[6] If the Austrian leadership (excepting Tisza) was unanimous at the beginning of July 1914 that the time for a showdown with the Serbs had arrived at last, it was the assurance of German support, combined with the fear—after the events of the last year—that it might never again be available, that turned its resolve into action. The promise of German backing was so important that it became the chief means of pressure on Tisza to alter his position against going to war. Throughout the crisis, while Vienna kept one eye on Belgrade, the other was turned towards Berlin; and practically until the final declarations of war there remained always a modicum of apprehension that it might at the last minute again find itself abandoned by its German ally.

Vienna made its proceeding against Serbia dependent on German approval. When Tschirschky, who at first had urged moderation, reversed his position, advocating a forceful action against the Serbs and promising complete support from Berlin, Berchtold initially could not hide his skepticism. He noted "that this had been repeatedly assured to me, but that in practice I had not always found the support of the Berlin Cabinet and therefore did not know to what extent I could count on it. . . ."[7] Franz Joseph was equally uncertain what to expect from Berlin, telling Conrad a few days later that he had asked the Archduke to get a definite promise of support from Wilhelm at their last meeting at Konopischt, but that Wilhelm had avoided committing himself. "I had the impression that His Majesty did not feel certain of Germany and therefore hesitated to make any decisions," Conrad later wrote.[8]

These doubts were overcome by Tschirschky's systematic pressure in Vienna, by Austrian Ambassador Szögyény's reports from Berlin of German promises of support, and by the assurances given to Hoyos who on the 4th was sent to Berlin specifically to request German backing. Not that the Germans may have not had their own doubts; Kurt Riezler, the close advisor of German Chancellor Theobald von Bethmann Hollweg, recorded Bethmann's quandary: "Our old dilemma with every Austrian Balkan action. If we encourage them, then they say we've pushed them into it; if we discourage them, then it means we've left them in the lurch."[9] But in July 1914, those in Berlin, despite their public displays of confidence, were becoming as worried about the diplomatic situation as the Austrians, and equally inclined to desperate expedients. They decided that the moment for an Austrian showdown with Serbia had come and promised their complete support even if that action led to a war with Russia. This "blank check" of support was blank only to the extent that the Germans overestimated their ally's ability to make quick use of it; it was clear to both of them what it was intended for. Whatever doubts Berlin may have had were given no expression in Vienna. The only German doubt the Austrians received concerned whether the alliance could be maintained if the Monarchy failed to take the agreed-upon forceful action against the Serbs. Forgách wrote Austrian Ambassador Mérey in Rome:

> We are *completely one* with Berlin. Kaiser and Chancellor etc. determined as never before, they send complete backing against Russia, even au risque of a not-at-all impossible world war, consider the moment favorable . . .[10]

When the Austro-Hungarian Common Ministers Council met on July 7, Berchtold was able to assure those present that the Monarchy had unconditional German support for a war against Serbia. All those except Tisza agreed that a mere diplomatic success would not be enough, even though further action brought with it the risk of hostilities with Russia. Of course, the Germans had just indicated their support against this eventuality—if they were not actually anticipating it. Similarly, the support the Monarchy had received from Germany might never come again if the present opportunity were missed; Stürgkh emphasized that to hesitate ran the danger of "no longer being so sure of this unconditional German support at a future point in time."[11]

Because of Tisza's position in the Monarchy, his opposition alone could block the intent of the other ministers, and therefore it had to be overcome. It took another week before this was accomplished. Though the grounds for his final conversion are still debated, the role of the German alliance seems to have played a major part in them. However much Tisza valued German assistance, he refused to surrender all initiative to Berlin to get it. When Berchtold emphasized at the July 7 meeting German readiness to back any proceeding against Serbia, Tisza protested vigorously: "It is not Germany's business to judge whether we should attack Serbia or not." [12]

To Tisza, unconditional German support was as important as it was to Stürgkh or Conrad or Berchtold. But in early July 1914 he was not convinced that a diplomatic solution of the Monarchy's problems in the Balkans was no longer possible. On the contrary, he was against war with Serbia precisely because the diplomatic situation at that time was so unfavorable. It had to be altered before the possibility of war could be considered. Once this were done, a final reckoning with Belgrade might be possible—but not before. [13] His resolve was actually strengthened by the type of support the Germans appeared to be offering after Sarajevo. Not only did they agree to an Austrian military action against Serbia, but they also agreed at last to support an Austrian diplomatic effort to win Bulgaria over to the Triple Alliance so long as their obligations to Rumania remained untouched. [14] A success here might have made an attack on Serbia unnecessary. Immediately after the Common Ministers Council, Tisza in a memorandum for Franz Joseph argued that the German assurances of support should be used to launch a new diplomatic offensive against the Serbs, not a military one. "The means to exercise a decisive influence in the Balkans and to bring about a constellation there more favorable to ourselves have just been put in our hands," he wrote. [15] The proposed ultimatum to Serbia should be severe, but not incapable of fulfillment.

What changed his mind? By July 1914 after the experiences of the last months, no other major Austrian leader believed in the efficacy of a longterm diplomatic campaign, let alone that Germany could be expected to support it consistently. But it soon became evident even to Tisza that Berlin was far more interested in a quick reckoning with the Serbs than with long range diplomatic plans anyway. On July 8, Berchtold informed Tisza that Tschirschky had just told him that Berlin was awaiting an action against Serbia and would not understand the Monarchy's missing the opportunity to carry it out. Moreover, the German Ambassador hinted that such a failure would be seen in Berlin as a sign of weakness "which could not remain without effect on our position in the Triple Alliance and on the future policy of Germany."[16] A few days later, Tschirschky again urged Berchtold to prompt action. Under this pressure, Tisza was forced to modify his position, and his friend Burián was instructed by Franz Joseph himself to get him to give up his last objections.[17] Burián's influence may finally have tipped the scales; so Forgách later claimed.[18] In any case, on July 14 Tisza informed Tschirschky that he had finally agreed to the action against Serbia. Having at last decided for war, Tisza remained one of its firmest supporters up to the final collapse of the Monarchy in October 1918.

The German alliance not only pressed on Tisza to give up his initial opposition to war; it also fortified the other Austrian leaders to resist his arguments. Tisza had previously been able to force his will on his weaker, more unsure colleagues. In the July Crisis, however, he signally failed to do so because the assurance of complete German support, and their fear of the consequences should they not take full advantage of it, gave them the determination not to be dissuaded from the planned showdown. Berchtold, who had been widely criticized for his vacillations in earlier crises, never wavered in this one so long as he was sure Germany was behind him. Crucial was the position of the Emperor Franz Joseph, whom Tisza attempted repeatedly to sway, but in vain. Franz Joseph's course proved to be determined as much by Berlin as by Belgrade, and this was decisive in his refusal to accept the views of the Hungarian Minister-President. Two days after the Common Ministers Council, Berchtold presented both his and Tisza's viewpoints to the Emperor. He recorded in his diary that Franz Joseph was "concerned that a weak attitude would discredit our position towards Germany."[19] Tisza himself in his talk with Tschirschky admitted that "the unconditional stand of *Germany on the side of the Monarchy* was decidedly of great influence for the firm position of the Emperor."[20] Tisza's position thus remained an isolated one; moreover, in maintaining it, he ran the risk of destroying his personal influence—and that of Hungary—not only on the common policies of the Monarchy, but in Berlin as well. This must have been an important consideration in his final conversion to the war party. His firm resolve to maintain Hungarian interests as he saw them in both Vienna and Berlin was something that could never be called into question.

It was nearly a month after the Sarajevo assassination before the proposed ultimatum could finally be delivered to the Serbs. The delay was due first to the time it took to become assured of German support, then to overcome Tisza's opposition, then to collect as much information as possible to implicate the Serbian government in the assassination. Once this was done, delivery was postponed until Poincaré, the French President, ended his scheduled visit to Russia. The Germans had expected a quick reckoning, a fait accompli before the shock of Sarajevo in the other capitals of Europe had worn off. The continued delays made them increasingly nervous, and they redoubled the pressure on Vienna to act. "We absolutely want to avoid the world war," Forgách wrote to Mérey on the 16th, "although Germany is completely ready to carry it out."[21] Berchtold almost defensively assured the German Ambassador that the only thing holding up the note was Poincaré's presence in Russia; there was no question of hesitation or indecision in Vienna.[22]

At the same time, Vienna became increasingly apprehensive itself that it was about to be undercut by Germany over Italy. Berchtold wanted to keep the entire action against Serbia secret until the ultimatum was actually delivered, fearing Italian leaks to Russia but fearing even more Italian demands for compensation under Article VII of the Triple Alliance Treaty. Article VII stipulated the right of either power to claim compensation if conditions in the Balkans were altered in favor of the other. While the Germans on the one hand urged Vienna to hurry up with the ultimatum, on the other they exerted increasing pressure to make concessions to Italy to assure its loyalty to the alliance. On the 15th, Jagow instructed Tschirschky even to suggest the Austrian Trentino as an object of compensation if the moment seemed opportune.[23]

Vienna thus found itself under a double compulsion from Berlin, fearing first to forfeit German support if the action against Serbia were not pushed to a swift conclusion, and second to be undercut by rising German pressure in favor of Italy the longer it took to complete that reckoning. On the 19th, the Common Ministers Council met to approve the ultimatum. Berchtold emphasized that they could not wait any longer to hand it to the Serbs because reports of the intended action were leaking out to Italy and because people in Berlin were getting nervous. The note was approved by all, Tisza demanding only that no annexations be made from Serbia since these would threaten the position of Hungary in the Ausgleich.[24]

The ultimatum was delivered to Belgrade on July 23. The Serbs surprised everyone by answering most of its points affirmatively; but Vienna broke off relations with Belgrade anyway and, to block the possibility of third powers attempting to mediate, declared war on July 28.

The events of the last days of July followed one another in confusing rapidity. The day before the declaration of war, Berchtold noted to his son Alois that the war ardor in Berlin was unmatched since the mobilization against France in 1870, adding that in Vienna it was so great that they were hesitant to let Franz Joseph even be seen there for fear he would inadvertently be torn apart in the popular enthusiasm.[25] Such was the popular wave which the crisis under German encouragement had called forth and which now strengthened Berchtold's resolve to press things to a final conclusion. Yet having encouraged Austrian bellicosity for the last three weeks, Berlin began to worry that Vienna was leaving it in the dark about its actual intentions in order to assure itself of German support under all circumstances.[26] The Germans had hoped that any war would remain localized or that England would stay neutral, and they suddenly realized that the crisis was beginning to develop faster than they had intended. As a result, they now attempted to rein Vienna in, and the Austrians feared that they were about to be abandoned again as so often in the past.

German support remained ultimately uncertain to the Ballplatz up to the last day of the month. As Russia threatened to mobilize, the British put forth various meditation proposals, which Berlin passed on without comment to Vienna or actually advised it to reject.[27] This Berchtold did. His chief concern was to know what Germany planned to do in the light of reports of Russian mobilization against the Monarchy; Conrad had to know whether to order a campaign only against Serbia or against Russia as well. But when Berlin realized that British neutrality in a continental war was a pipe dream, Chancellor Bethmann Hollweg completely reversed his stand on mediation and telegraphed urgently to Tschirschky for Vienna to accept it. Tschirschky read Bethmann's telegram to Berchtold on the 30th, reporting Berchtold "pale and silent." Hoyos and Forgách protested that merely occupying Belgrade or some other Serbian city and then waiting for mediation was out of the question.[28] At the same time that Bethmann pressed for acceptance of the English mediation proposal and Kaiser Wilhelm was engaged in trying to convince the Russian Czar of his peaceful intentions, Helmuth von Moltke the younger, the Chief of Staff of the German army, complained to Conrad of Austria's seeming disinclination to mobilize against Russia. Berchtold, now committed to a course of action the Germans had encouraged since the beginning of the month, could in his confusion well ask about Berlin: "Who rules—Moltke or Bethmann?"[29]

Clarity was established only on the 31st, when Moltke telegraphed that Germany had decided to mobilize. Conrad brought Moltke's telegram to Berchtold, who admitted he had been under the impression that Germany was giving way: "Now I have the most reassuring declaration from the most authoritative military authority."[30] Shortly afterward, Franz Joseph was asked to approve general Austrian mobilization. On the same day, Wilhelm urged him to concentrate his forces against Russia. Austria-Hungary was certain of German support at last, but only at the price of a world war which was now inevitable.

Moreover, the terms of that support had changed considerably in the course of the crisis. The events of July had begun with Germany assuring its backing for a campaign against Serbia; they ended with Germany demanding that the Monarchy direct its forces against Russia so that Germany could launch its own campaign against France. If there had earlier been any doubt about where the center of initiative in the alliance lay, the outbreak of the war brought clarity here too. The Germans declared war on Russia on August 1; Austria-Hungary did not follow suit until the 6th, and only after considerable prodding from Berlin. It continued to be at peace with France and Britain, both now engaged in hostilities with Germany, for another week. The initiative for the final declaration of war came from London and Paris, not Vienna. The Austrians had finally secured German backing—but not for a localized war against Belgrade, rather a world war against the Entente; and thus ultimately not for the Austrian interests but for German ones.

Vienna's decision to go to war in 1914 was a calculated risk, one that was accepted because the events of the past years had convinced nearly everyone in the policy-making elite there that the odds against them in the future could only get worse. Conrad told his friend Leo Chlumecky: "In 1908-09 it would have been a game with all the cards laid out to view, in 1912-13 still a game with chances, now it is playing va banque."[31] It was the assurance of complete German support after the conflicts of the last few years which made that risk acceptable—an assurance of support which might never be repeated. Yet if Vienna was playing va banque that a conflict with Serbia could be localized and won, it was also playing va banque that it could maintain German support and keep it from undermining its own interests. The Habsburg domestic structure, precarious in any case, threatened to collapse from one direction from the South Slav agitation. Yet Sarajevo, the latest manifestation of this pressure, opened the door to the Germans of the Monarchy, encouraged if not actively backed by Germany itself, to topple it from the other. Stürgkh, dimly perceiving this danger, immediately after the Sarajevo assassination urged the Statthalter of Bohemia to get the Czechs to demonstrate their loyalty to the Monarchy:

I also consider this especially important for further domestic developments, since a great part of the German press and also many politically authoritative German circles will naturally try to use this crime from the Slav side to represent as absolutely necessary a fundamentally anti-Slav regime, and one which in my view would be incompatible with the Austrian conception of state.[32].

If the Monarchy had a South Slav irredenta, in a sense it also had a German one, and in this context the German alliance in a wartime situation could exert a dynamic which posed just as great a threat to the multinational basis of the Monarchy as did the agitation from Belgrade.

The events of July 1914 hardly provided an auspicious example of interalliance crisis management. By the end of the month, however, most misgivings had been either forgotten or swept aside. Austrian policy in the wake of Sarajevo was aimed not only at ending the Serb threat once and for all, but in securing German backing to do it; and the support Austria appeared to have received in Berlin overcame all its hesitations. If anything, the possibility that Germany might end by undercutting the Monarchy's position only spurred it to further actions before the promised support could be withdrawn. As the armies began to march, Vienna seemed to have secured everything it had wanted. "We are in no unfavorable situation," János Forgách had remarked soon after the assassination. "The first military power of the world is our ally!"[33]

Disillusionment would come later.

Chapter 3

THE SHORT WAR
August 1914-January 1915

I

Austria-Hungary was not ready for a long war in 1914. In both halves of the Monarchy, there were laws providing for the exercise of emergency powers by the governments in the case of war, but little had been done in practice to anticipate the economic demands of a major conflict. There were no stockpiles of either military supplies or foodstuffs, no plans for maintaining adequate reserves of raw materials. Practically the only prewar planning for a conflict at all involved the initial army mobilization, and it would quickly prove itself anything but complete or systematic.

In this regard, the monarchy was typical of all the European powers in 1914. Even Germany decided on war with hardly more preparation than the famous Schlieffen Plan; once this failed, putting together a long range war effort had to be largely improvised. Austria-Hungary's weak political and economic structure, however, made it especially vulnerable to the strains of a modern total war. It had fewer resources with which to support a war effort than the other European Great Powers. Agriculture had already faced problems before the war, but under the initial dislocations of the conflict the 1914 grain harvest in Hungary actually fell from 60 million quintals to 40 million.[1] Moreover, the Monarchy's institutional conflicts made it more difficult to mobilize effectively what it had. The war had scarcely begun when the Hungarians closed the border with Austria to a free flow of commodities, refusing to release their grain to Cisleithania except at the price of political and economic concessions. Vienna and Budapest eventually spent almost as much time wrangling with each other over the allocation of foodstuffs and military contracts as they did fighting their enemies on the battlefields. Even if Austria-Hungary had been a smoothly-functioning economic unit, it was likely that a long war would accentuate its weaknesses and drive it into economic and financial dependence on its stronger German ally.

The prospect that Austria-Hungary would emerge unscathed from an extended struggle was thus highly questionable. Why, then, did its leaders act as they did in July 1914? For many of them, the decision to go to war was a measure of desperation. Nevertheless, the war to which they consented was far different from the conflict as it actually developed. In 1914, they expected a quick, short war, one that in a few months' time would solve all their foreign policy problems with a minimal expenditure of resources. It would be over before their political or economic weaknesses could become a factor in the scales. Berchtold spoke for all of them when he later admitted to the historian Luigi Albertini: "Nobody here thought of a long war." [2]

This belief was not confined just to the Monarchy's foreign policy elite. The news of war was greeted throughout Austria-Hungary by outpourings of enthusiasm and patriotism, just as in the other involved states of Europe. Momentarily, the political controversies that had afflicted the Monarchy so long seemed submerged in a common wave of ardor. Count Albert Apponyi, one of the " '48" Hungarian opposition leaders, greeted the declarations of war with the words "At last!" [3] and even the Social Democrats appeared to support it. As the army mobilized, there was no repetition of the disorders among Czech units that had characterized the precautionary mobilizations of the Balkan Wars—somewhat to Conrad's amazement. "As never before, thousands and hundreds of thousands felt what they should have felt in peacetime, that they belonged together," the writer Stefan Zweig recalled in his memoirs. [4] The sudden political truce was, however, less durable than that being enacted at the same time in the other European capitals. Although the established Magyar political groups were united in their support of the war, their hatred of Tisza made any sort of coalition government there impossible so long as he held office. In Austria, the Reichsrat remained prorogued. Stürgkh was afraid that to reconvene it might provide a forum for unpatriotic demonstrations by dissatisfied Slav deputies.

The outbreak of hostilities inevitably complicated the decision-making process in Austria-Hungary. The supreme army commander was the Emperor Franz Joseph, but Franz Joseph delegated his authority to the Archduke Friedrich, who left all real power in the hands of the Chief of Staff, Conrad von Hötzendorf. Because of his advancing age, the old Emperor's role became more passive than ever, generally approving his subordinates' actions without comment unless they proposed something especially outlandish. The Austrian staff officer Edmund Glaise von Horstenau recalled an audience with him towards the end of 1915: The Emperor complained that Conrad did not keep him properly informed, then momentarily dozed off in the middle of Glaise's report.[5] Franz Joseph occasionally presided at meetings of the Common Ministers Council and continued his habitual routine, reading and approving dispatches, almost to the day of his death. But he was clearly no longer able to muster the energy to make major decisions or directly supervise the war effort.

The result was that there was little if any coordination of policy between the civil and the military authorities within the Monarchy. It was obvious to all how desirable in a wartime situation such coordination was; but without a strong guiding hand, the institutional structure of Austria-Hungary as usual prevented it from happening. With the outbreak of hostilities, the Austrian High Command (Armee Oberkommando, or AOK as it was generally called) received a great addition of power as large areas of Cisleithania were declared to be war zones and put under military administration (Tisza, needless to say, was able to prevent similar military encroachments in Hungary). Military command was also extended over the major Austrian war industries. The military was further responsible from 1915 for administering conquered enemy territory. These various activities involved the High Command in political and economic, as much as purely military, decisions. Issues of allocation of resources between the Monarchy and Germany, or administrative guidelines for the occupied areas, might be decided by Vienna and Berlin; but it was the respective military commands in the field which actually implemented them.

Conrad had little inclination to share any more of this authority with the civilian leadership than he had to, and did all he could to keep matters under his immediate jurisdiction out of civilian purview. The Foreign Ministry assigned a special representative to the High Command to keep it informed of military developments, but his effectiveness was hamstrung by Conrad's efforts to make it as difficult as possible for him to gather information or to communicate it in unaltered form to the Ballplatz. The Foreign Minister, the two Minister-Presidents, even Franz Joseph himself, were told little more about military operations than was the general public.[6] Requests for more cooperation elicited sharp protests from the sensitive Conrad. "I did not have the least intention of wanting to exercise even an indirect influence on military operations," Berchtold protested after one such run-in, noting that he could hardly conduct foreign policy without knowing what the military situation was.[7] Conrad, on the other hand, complained constantly of being left in the dark on political matters. The situation persisted until 1916, when the massive military reverses of the summer finally forced the Austrian Chief of Staff to be more accommodating.

In the light of these conflicts of authority within the Monarchy, it is perhaps surprising that the channels of communication between Austria-Hungary and Germany functioned as well as they did after the outbreak of hostilities. On the political level, day-to-day relations continued to be conducted through the two countries' ambassadors, Szögyény and then Hohenlohe in Berlin, and Tschirschky in Vienna. These channels were supplemented by periodic meetings of the foreign ministers and other high officials.

Coordination of military policy before the war had been limited almost entirely to personal contacts between Conrad and his German counterpart, Helmuth von Moltke the younger. After the commencement of hostilities, each power attached a liaison officer to the high command of the other. Josef Stürgkh, the brother of the Austrian Minister-President, was the Monarchy's first representative at German headquarters. He was soon succeeded by Alois von Klepsch-Kloth. Their functions remained minimal, however, because most military liaison matters were handled by the German representative at the Austrian High Command, August von Cramon. Cramon held this position from January 1915 to the end of the war; he enjoyed the trust of both Conrad and his successor, Arthur Arz von Straussenburg. It was an often unenviable job. Conrad never got on well with Erich von Falkenhayn, who replaced Moltke as German Chief of Staff after the Battle of the Marne, and Cramon sometimes had all he could do just to keep the two of them on speaking terms with each other.[8]

Since nearly everyone in Austria-Hungary expected a speedy, decisive victory, it is not surprising that a discussion of war aims began there almost as soon as the mobilization order had been given. Like Bethmann Hollweg's so-called September Program, the war aims that emerged in Vienna in August and September 1914 clearly presupposed that the Central Powers would be able to dictate their terms to the enemy. Those terms would end the external threats confronting the Monarchy and secure its Great Power status for all time. Unfortunately, beyond these general desiderata, the complex domestic structure made it impossible for the leading figures to agree on specific goals that did not conflict with their own respective separate interests.

The initial cause of the war was Serbia. Serbia had been the occasion for the ultimatum, and a victorious war meant preventing Belgrade from ever again posing a threat to the Monarchy. But what would happen then? Tisza had demanded that the Monarchy make no annexations in Serbia, so there was no clear conception of what would be done to the country after a military victory except that pieces of it might be taken over by Bulgaria and Albania.

Yet it was not Serbia which attracted the chief interest as a war aim that summer, but Poland. The problem of Poland developed into one of the greatest single controversies between Austria-Hungary and Germany during the war. It became a central war aim of each, and only the final defeat of both of them in 1918 ended their bitter duel for predominance there. The germs of the controversy dated from the very opening of hostilities.

Poland had been partitioned between Prussia, Russia, and Austria over a century earlier. The largest part, including the former capital of Warsaw, Congress Poland, belonged to Russia; but the sizable province of Galicia was ruled by Vienna. Galicia occupied a unique place in the Monarchy. It enjoyed local autonomy, giving the aristocratic Polish authorities there nearly complete freedom to oppress the largely Ruthene (Ukrainian) population of East Galicia. In return, the Galician Polish landlords proved the most accommodating subjects, staunchly supporting the domestic status quo and the government in Vienna. If it was a truism that the Austrian Reichsrat could not be run without the Germans, it was equally true that it could not be run without the Poles. That loyalty was not entirely genuine, however; the Poles under Austrian rule simply enjoyed more freedom than their compatriots in Germany or Russia, but the final loyalty of most of them was to a future reunited Polish state. With the outbreak of the war and the possibility that that state might actually come into being, the loyalty of the Galician Poles, and their votes in the Reichsrat whenever it should be reconvened, were immediately called into question. Vienna saw itself facing a potential Polish irredenta whose consequences seemed to dwarf the South Slav agitation that had been the initial occasion for the war—unless that future Polish state could itself be made a part of the Monarchy. Then the attractive power of an independent Warsaw on Galicia would become harmless, for both would lay under Austrian rule. This was the so-called Austro-Polish solution to the question.

The future of Poland, even more than that of Serbia, was thus directly involved with the domestic order of the Monarchy. Even before the war, Poland had been a point of worry for the Austrian leadership; Vienna and St. Petersburg had both been drawn into shadowy intrigues among the conflicting currents of Polish and Ruthene nationalism. A return to that unstable status quo ante was hardly acceptable after the outbreak of hostilities. The only alternative appeared to be the annexation of all Congress Poland to the Monarchy. Initially, no one in Vienna seems to have considered that Germany, with its own Polish areas in Poznan and Silesia, might also be concerned about Polish irredentas and thus interested in the future fate of Russian Poland. This omission was all the more striking, considering the fact that the policy of Germanization pursued in the Polish areas of Prussia, watched closely by the Galician Poles, had been a latent source of tension within the alliance for years.

As early as August 7, Burián noted in his diary that the leading circles in Vienna favored annexing Congress Poland to the Monarchy once victory was achieved. The only question was how constitutionally to do it.[9] Hoyos was in favor of a federal solution, which he described to Josef Redlich the same week: Poland should be united to Galicia, which would receive its autonomy. East Galicia and Bohemia would also become autonomous. Such a solution would enable the Poles to be removed from the Reichsrat, assuring it a German majority.[10] The hope that acquiring Poland could at the same time provide a basis for solving the nationality conflicts of the Austrian half of the Monarchy by guaranteeing German control of the Reichsrat was often to be repeated. The idea became even more attractive when the Austrians encountered their first opposition from Germany, because they knew that Berlin, with its Slav phobias, was likely to be more susceptible to this argument for the Austro-Polish solution than to any other. A week later, Berchtold transmitted his own views through Szögyény to the Germans. He wished Congress Poland to be united with Galicia, the resulting entity to be constitutionally equal in status to Austria and Hungary. East Galicia would get autonomy, but there was no mention of Bohemia. This was more of a trialistic than a federal conception. Again, the Poles would no longer be represented in the parliament in Vienna. Such a solution would not further Slavicize Austria, he argued, but restore German national predominance there.[11]

A coherent Austrian policy towards Poland, like that towards Serbia, was complicated by the position of Hungary in the Monarchy. The acquisition of Poland as a third constituent member of the state—its transformation from a dualistic to a trialistic entity—would mean an end to the Ausgleich and to Budapest's special position as the co-equal and usually decisive partner of the realm. Tisza admitted to Burián that if an independent kingdom of Poland were set up in Warsaw, that polity would eventually cost the Monarchy Galicia. But if this was to be prevented by making Congress Poland part of the Monarchy, it would have to be done without upsetting the Ausgleich—no matter what sort of constitutional contortions that led to. Rather than becoming a separate area equal in status to Austria and Hungary, Poland/Galicia would have to be united entirely with Austria, so that the constitutional position of Budapest remained untouched. This conception was soon to become known as the sub-dualistic version of the Austro-Polish solution. Further, if Austria, which already possessed a greater population than Hungary, acquired Poland, Hungary would have to get compensation somewhere or be completely overawed. Tisza suggested that Bosnia-Herzegovina, and perhaps even Dalmatia, accrue to Hungary—even though he had just rejected any annexations from Serbia as likely to bring too many Slavs into Hungary to be assimilated. He himself conceded that such a compensation would be more than enough for the Magyar state to digest. The important thing for him—his central standpoint throughout the war—was that Hungary could not be allowed to sink to the position of a mere province in an enlarged Habsburg Empire. Shortly thereafter, he made these views clear to Berchtold and Stürgkh: Budapest would consent to an acquisition of Congress Poland only on the basis of an enlarged dualism. Far from simplifying the Monarchy's institutional problems, the acquisition of Poland thus threatened to complicate them still further. The difficulties which the whole issue raised were aptly summed up in a cynical Viennese witticism of early 1915: Whichever side lost the war should receive Galicia.[12]

To these problems was soon added the significant further complication that Austrian annexation of Poland was opposed not only by the Russian army but by the Germans. Berchtold's communication to Szögyény advocating his trialistic Austro-Polish solution was in response to rumors that Berlin was considering setting up Polish and Ukrainian buffer states after the war. Vienna had already made plans to divide Poland into Austrian and German administrative areas and expected to install an Austrian governor in Warsaw as soon as the city was captured.[13] Consequently, Berchtold was unpleasantly surprised to discover a few days later that the Germans intended to put their own governor there once it fell to their armies.[14] Not only that, but he began to be afraid that the Germans were thinking of a longterm occupation. Hohenlohe, who now replaced Szögyény in Berlin, was told that it was essential to assure the Poles that incoming German troops intended only to make possible their unification with their co-nationals in Galicia under Austrian rule. Arthur Zimmermann, the Undersecretary at the German Foreign Ministry, was "not exactly pleased" when Hohenlohe conveyed these sentiments to him. He indicated that Prussia had certain industrial interests in Congress Poland which would have to be reserved for future discussion.[15]

How did the Monarchy propose to respond to this unexpected German opposition over Poland? In the face of continued German interest in fostering a Ukrainian separatist movement in Russia, Stürgkh saw a clear German tactic to force the Monarchy's interests from Poland to the Ukraine and Volhynia.[16] Tisza, on the other hand, almost welcomed the German interest in Russian Poland. Since the whole complex posed such a threat to the Ausgleich were it not handled properly (or, for that matter, even if it was), the German opposition could be used as a convenient means of dampening potentially dangerous expectations among the Poles. True to his belief that the interests of Hungary were maintained by a close connection with Berlin, he in no case wanted the Monarchy's relations with Germany muddied because of Warsaw. "In my opinion, it would be a mistake to get into unpleasant arguments with the Germans over Poland," he warned Berchtold.[17] Hohenlohe in Berlin also desired to mute the initial friction between the two allies as much as possible. He assumed that the Austrian army would defeat the Russians while the Germans subdued France, after which Vienna would have no trouble with Berlin in realizing its claims.[18]

Like everyone else, Hohenlohe counted on a quick victory, with the Austrian army playing a substantial role in it. For Austrian war aims and, indeed, the Great Power status of the Monarchy itself, rested ultimately on the battlefield performance of the Habsburg army. The assurance of German support had pushed the Austrians over the brink into war a month earlier; but they had expected the impressive German military machine to guarantee the success of their own military effort—not to supplant it. By the end of the month, all these assumptions were turning out to be disastrously wrong.

II

Prewar Austrian mobilization plans had reckoned on both a war against Serbia alone and one against Serbia allied to Russia. Certain contingents were meant to mobilize on the Serb border, while others were to go to Galicia; and a third group of units was designated for either theater depending on whether Russian participation was expected or not. Military coordination between Austria-Hungary and Germany before the war had been minimal. Although the bulk of the German army would be turned against France, German Staff Chief Moltke had promised a German attack out of East Prussia against Russia; this would still leave the Austrian army the task of bearing the brunt of the pressure from the Russians, but it would only have to hold them off for six weeks. Then the campaign in France would be completed victoriously and the rest of the German army would be shunted to Poland to help finish off Russia as well.

In the event, everything miscarried. To begin with, Conrad, apparently hoping for a quick prestige victory against the Serbs while the Germans in East Prussia diverted the Russians, sent his third group of units to mobilization points on the Monarchy's southern borders. This was no part of the prewar understandings with Berlin. Then, on August 3, Conrad learned from Moltke that, again contrary to their earlier agreements, there would be no German attack from East Prussia. The entire weight of the massive Russian army would fall on Austria-Hungary alone. As this became apparent, Conrad frantically attempted to reroute the extra units sent south in the opposite direction, to the Monarchy's northern border with Russia. But because of the limitations of the Monarchy's transportation network, they could not be moved north immediately against the Russians; they had to travel first by rail to their Serb debarkation points and then be re-embarked to Galicia. And on top of all this, the Russians managed to mobilize faster than anyone had anticipated.[19]

Conrad nevertheless ordered an offensive out of Galicia. After a few tactical victories, the Austrian forces were overwhelmed by their more numerous Russian opponents. The Galician campaign was a disaster from which the Austro-Hungarian army never really recovered. The Austrians were driven out of East Galicia to the passes of the Carpathian Mountains; losses were estimated at 250,000 dead and wounded with another 100,000 taken prisoner. Losses from the officer corps were to prove irreplaceable.[20] By the end of September, rain and biting cold had set in, turning the primitive roads to quagmires; and in addition to the weather, for which the troops were unprepared, cholera broke out.

The summer campaign in Galicia was only the beginning chapter in a long history of disharmony and friction between the armed forces of the two states supposedly fighting side by side in Bündnistreue. It has often been noted just how little harmony there actually was between the two allied powers. Controversy arose from major issues of military strategy to supposed slights in allied press releases. Tschirschky made no secret of his feelings: "God preserve my poor fatherland from ever again making war with Austria as an ally," he lamented[21]—a sentiment which did nothing to enhance his already scanty popularity in Vienna. To the Germans, the Austrian military often seemed incompetent and superficial, constantly clamoring for help because of its inadequacies and then refusing to be properly grateful once it had gotten it. But the Austrian leadership, as it constantly reminded the Germans in response to such criticism, faced problems in running a multinational and multilingual army of which they had little comprehension. German military men could be woefully ignorant about the ethnic complexities of the Monarchy. Some were surprised to discover that there were other peoples besides Germans among the Austrians; others, that anyone in the Monarchy even spoke the German language.[22] Some differences could be attributed to temperament. Austrians claimed to get along much better with Bavarians or

Saxons than with Prussians. As even a Großdeutsch-oriented Austrian officer was later to point out, German military superiority would not have been so insulting had it not been made so deliberately apparent all the time.[23]

Still, the frequent German complaints were far from groundless. An Austrian staff officer, Theodor von Zeynek, later summed up in his memoirs the difference between the two allied military commands: "We unfortunately lived by improvisations, while on the German side the most solid organization was the basis of every undertaking."[24] Austrian assertions that they faced insuperable nationality problems with their men were true to a point, but they could also provide a convenient excuse for their own shortcomings in leadership. Supposedly unreliable Czech or Ruthene troops often performed without reproach when put under German, rather than Austrian, officers. Many Austrian officers also preferred serving under German command since they then received more artillery and recognition.[25] The lesson was obvious: Austro-Hungarian troops fought as well as any when properly led and supplied. But while the front line troops bled and suffered, following the initial battles the Austrian High Command settled into a comfortable existence in Teschen, a pleasant town in Austrian Silesia, where life was marked by candlelight dinners with Court table service, tennis, horseback riding, and visits to local coffee houses.[26] The situation was made worse when Conrad's new wife, a divorcée, moved into his quarters to share in the general Gemütlichkeit. A more military regimen was not initiated until two years later, when the new Emperor Karl had the whole command moved to Baden outside Vienna. It is not hard to see why many Germans had difficulty believing that their Austrian allies were really as serious as they ought to be about the war effort.

But the differences ran deeper than this. While it was quite true that greater coordination of operations would have led to a more successful overall conduct of the war, to the Austrians it was obvious that their pretensions to Great Power status and equality in the alliance could only be met if they could claim military successes on their own. Unfortunately, to try to do that, they usually overtaxed their limited resources and ended up by making their position worse than it was to start with. The Brusilov breakthrough in 1916 was due in part to the fact that the Austrian units which should have been there to stop it were occupied instead with an independent offensive in Italy. Moreover, German and Austrian wartime priorities differed. Vienna for obvious reasons was always more interested in the Eastern Front than about what was happening in France; coordination of operations often meant Austrian sacrifices for purely German military interests. Much of the lack of military harmony in the alliance, whatever its consequences, arose from very real Austrian fears that they would be dominated completely by their German ally.

The practical consequences of the Austrian campaign in Galicia were that the Monarchy bled itself white to save Berlin from the Russians. While the Germans advanced victoriously into Belgium and destroyed a whole Russian army at Tannenberg, the Austrians were being crushed by the main Russian forces in Poland. Where were the promised German reinforcements? If Moltke had overestimated the capacity of the Austrian army to protect the German rear in the East, the Austrians had made the same mistake in reverse; they had not expected the German offensive in the West to result in a stalemate. In six weeks, those reinforcements should have been free, but on September 9 the Battle of the Marne turned into a German retreat. The short war was over.

As the Austrian situation in Galicia became more desperate, any thought of expansive war aims for the Monarchy were put aside, and all thoughts turned to the promised German reinforcements—which still had not materialized. "The German victories are achieved at our cost," Conrad wrote at the end of August, complaining that Germany allowed the enormous burden of the Russian army to fall almost entirely on its weaker ally. A week later, he agreed with Bolfras, Franz Joseph's Military Cabinet Chief, that Berlin had left the Monarchy in the lurch.[27] The Germans, Conrad reflected, were apparently ready to see their ally sacrificed with equanimity, even though it was not Tannenberg but the Austrian army that had blocked the main Russian forces from marching on Berlin. By November, after three months of fighting in common with the German military, Conrad wrote in disgust that although he had to make a public show of harmony and agreement, within himself he had had all that he could take of them.[28]

Such sentiments were not confined just to the Chief of Staff in the field. Forgách reported the situation in Vienna: "We can't think about anything except the bloody battles in Galicia. The loss of Lemberg is extremely deplorable. I am quite concerned and am afraid of the humiliating necessity of the Germans having to 'save' us."[29] Forgách was probably no less bitter than Conrad, for if the Monarchy faced disaster in Galicia, it was those potential German "saviors" who were again seen as the cause of it. He wrote a week later: "I am *very* concerned. But the collapse of our Polish campaign is the fault of the Germans, whose *agreed* cooperation on the left wing failed to appear."[30] Berchtold, equally shaken, also complained of being abandoned by Germany to the Russians. But repeated calls to Berlin for assistance brought only a minimal response. At the same time, in the wake of the defeats, the Germans applied pressure for territorial concessions to the wavering neutrals, Italy and Rumania. In his frustration, Berchtold even instructed Hohenlohe to hint that Austria would conclude a separate peace if Germany continued to refuse the agreed-upon military help and instead proposed giving away Habsburg provinces.[31]

Before the war was over, such Austrian complaints would become a frequent source of irritation in Berlin. The Germans often assumed that any German interest must also be an Austrian one, and reacted to Austrian objections with the feeling that their allies were either short-sighted or unappreciative of their help. But they had good cause for resenting the Austrian leadership's tendency to blame its failures on everything except itself. In his complaints after the Galician debacle, Conrad conveniently forgot the role his own errors of judgment had played, especially with the bungled mobilization. And while more German troops would have helped the situation on the Eastern Front, so, too, would the Austrian units that were retained in the south under the independent command of Oskar Potiorek, the military governor of Bosnia. Conrad, unable to lead the crusade against Serbia in person, protested loudly when Potiorek was given the opportunity. The result was an Austrian offensive on both fronts, with insufficient forces to succeed on either. Whether more German units in the East would have made much difference under these circumstances is debatable. Hohenlohe, who was probably as disgusted with the Austrian military performance as the Germans, pointed out in a private letter to Berchtold that, if Conrad was in such dire need of German assistance, there was not much sense in his launching an attack on the Russians by himself.[32]

Of the major figures in Vienna, only Tisza's faith in the German ally remained unshaken. As the reports from Galicia came in, Tisza minimized the defeats and emphasized his belief that the might of the German Empire would save the situation. It was the strength of his belief in German might, after all, that had probably won his consent for war to begin with. At the beginning of September, he admonished Berchtold to show a strong front; a military spirit had to rule at the Ballplatz, and no hint of discouragement or defeatism could be allowed to leak out. This applied especially to the Germans, for otherwise the Monarchy's position as an equal in the alliance could be endangered. " . . . We must not for a moment look like the weak, fearful protégé," he declared, "since that would receive not only the complete protection, but also the complete burden, of the German protectorate." When he heard of Berchtold's hint of a separate peace if no aid from Berlin were forthcoming, he reprimanded him; this would cause a "very bad impression" there.[33]

How the weak protégé could avoid the consequences of that weakness was a problem which faced the Austrian leadership throughout the war. Josef

Stürgkh, at this time Austrian liaison officer with the German High Command, later noted in his memoirs that in his continual requests for aid he often felt like a beggar asking for alms.[34] In response to the repeated Austrian cries for help, German units by the end of September finally began to be shifted to the East, but hardly in sufficient numbers from the Austrian viewpoint to be very effective. Erich von Falkenhayn, Moltke's successor as German Chief of Staff, believed firmly that the war would be decided in the West, despite the failure of the Schlieffen Plan. The Austrian army remained locked in costly but indecisive combat, while Falkenhayn burned up his reserves in a futile effort to take Ypres. Nor was operational coordination any more improved. The Germans refused to allow their forces serving in conjunction with Austrian units to be put under direct Austrian command, so that when the idea of a common overall command in the East—under German leadership—began to be mooted at the end of October, Conrad, arguing that it would destroy the independence of the Austrian army, scotched the whole project by threatening to resign.

This, then, was the result of the summer campaign in Galicia. The Austrian army was thrown back and decimated by the Russians, and the Monarchy was forced to implore military aid from Germany to save the situation. Rather than a short, victorious campaign, Austria-Hungary found itself locked into a grueling war of attrition with the apparently inexhaustible forces of Czarist Russia while its German ally expended its chief energies elsewhere. The Galician campaign nearly broke the back of the Austrian army and assured its military dependence on Germany for the rest of the war. And with that, in one campaign, an independent Austrian foreign policy lost its main pillar of support.

Less dramatic, but no less dangerous in its longterm implications, was the impact of the war on the Austro-Hungarian economy. If the war were going to last longer than a few months, wartime agencies to control resources and production would have to be organized; and in late September, under German initiative, agreements to pattern Austrian economic mobilization on German were reached. This was a longterm measure; more immediate were the Monarchy's financial needs. "Money runs just like water in the war ministry," Stürgkh told Redlich in the same month. "We'll hopefully get a war indemnity; otherwise, there would be a general financial catastrophe."[35] Like most countries during the war, the Monarchy resorted to borrowing and outright expansion of the money supply to finance its war effort. In other states, the resulting inflation was kept under some restraint by the government controls imposed on the economy. The Monarchy's controls were less effective and many eventually broke down completely. Scarcely three months into the war, the exchange rate of a hundred Kronen had sunk from 84¾ Marks to 77-78—a 9% drop.[36] The depreciating currency not only threatened Austria-Hungary's economic viability; it also affected its ability to pay for imports of vital war commodities, largely from Germany. "The creation of foreign means of payment is one of the most important economic-financial tasks of the war," Tisza emphasized to Stürgkh at the end of October.[37] To support the exchange rate and keep inflation under control, the Monarchy had to have German financial support. For most of the conflict, Austria-Hungary received payments of 100,000 Marks a month in exchange credit from Germany. This still failed to keep the Krone from sinking to between 1/14 and 1/16 of its prewar value by the time of the armistice in 1918.[38] In the economic as well as in the military sphere, the disasters in Galicia forced the Monarchy to turn to the Germans for assistance, but the cost was a financial dependence on Berlin which threatened to grow to alarming proportions and further undercut the possibilities of an independent foreign policy.

That those possibilities had already been considerably undermined was revealed in the first efforts to win over the adjacent neutral states to the cause of the Central Powers. The July Crisis had reversed earlier German policy and finally convinced Berlin to try to pull both Bulgaria and Turkey into association with the Triple Alliance and active participation in the burgeoning conflict. Vienna suddenly found itself almost pushed further than it wanted to go by Berlin's efforts to accomplish this, but nevertheless supported the German initiatives. Turkey declared war at the end of the summer; Bulgaria, a year later. But in the case of the other neutrals, Rumania and Italy, both of whose territorial ambitions would be satisfied much more by fighting against the Monarchy than with it, Vienna found itself under pressure from its German ally to give away whole provinces to make those supposed allies honor their treaty obligations or at least remain neutral. The Austrians had gotten a foretaste of this treatment from Germany before Sarajevo, but nothing on this scale. Fear of violent dismemberment had decided Vienna to go to war; now, it was exhorted by its ally to dismember itself voluntarily. Its reaction was obvious. But the disasters of the fighting put the Monarchy in a poor position to resist. Franz Joseph's remark was to the point: "How on earth can we pursue even a tolerable foreign policy when we fight so badly?"[39]

At the outbreak of the war, both Rumania and Italy declared their neutrality. Because their loyalty to the Triple Alliance before the war had been questionable anyway, this action was not entirely unexpected—at least in Vienna. In the case of Rumania, it further increased the pressure on the

Austrian army; the last mobilization plans had hoped for Rumanian assistance against the Russians. As the Galician front began to buckle, the Germans urged far-reaching concessions from the Monarchy to get the Rumanians into the war, as well as promising them Bessarabia from Russia. Those concessions were both territorial, affecting Transylvania and the Bukovina; and political, dealing with domestic political and cultural concessions (if not complete autonomy) for the Hungarian Rumanians. Hohenlohe actually reported after a trip to German General Headquarters in late September that if the Rumanians marched into Transylvania, Kaiser Wilhelm thought the Monarchy should do nothing more than protest, treating it as if they were acting to "protect" the area from the Russians. It should certainly not declare war against Rumania.[40] While the Germans hoped that such concessions would buy a Rumanian entry into the war, the Austrians were convinced that Rumanian neutrality was the best that could be hoped for, and that any concessions would serve only to reveal the Monarchy's weakness and hence make more likely a Rumanian intervention against them.

In the Rumanian question, Tisza's position as Hungarian Minister-President was decisive, since concessions concerned the Hungarian far more than the Austrian half of the Monarchy. In his judgment, Rumania would eventually join whichever side it thought would win. Even the most far-reaching concessions would have no effect on its conduct. Of course, concessions which might in any way impinge on the unity of the Hungarian state he resisted absolutely. On this point, as on so much else, he was totally inflexible. Even in the unlikely event that Rumania would agree to attack the Russians, he was only prepared to cede to them the district of Suceava— which was a part of the Bukovina, not Hungary. At the same time, he worked for minor concessions to the ethnic Rumanians of Hungary, though far less than the Germans urged, and left no doubt that however much he might be willing to discuss such measures with Berlin, they remained a "purely internal affair of Hungary" in which foreign governments had no business interfering.[41]

Tisza made sure that the Ballplatz presented a firm front to Germany on the issue of the concessions, though other Austrian leaders were scarcely inclined to act differently. What would happen to a state of nationalities like Austria-Hungary if it seemed to accept the prerogative of all its irredentist neighbors to claim special jurisdiction over the areas of their co-nationals within its borders? On September 20, the Common Ministers Council met to discuss the issue, and all present were agreed that concessions were out of the question. "We must not let the German Kaiser press and entice us into

making concessions which would later prove to be worthless," Stürgkh
argued. He added that Wilhelm's idea of allowing Rumania peacefully to
occupy Transylvania was the most impossible he had ever heard; even the
demand to cede the Trentino to Italy paled by comparison.[42]

The controversy led to recriminations between the two allies over their
respective responsibility for the war before the conflict was scarcely half a
year old. German Chancellor Bethmann argued that the decision for war was
Vienna's; Berlin had simply "taken on the struggle at the request of the
Emperor Franz Joseph who called on our loyalty to the alliance." Vienna
should now show a similar spirit of self-sacrifice and make the necessary
concessions to the Rumanians.[43] Bethmann's notion that all the initiative in
July 1914 had come from the Austrian side received an emphatic denial from
Tisza:

> First of all, let it be emphasized that before undertaking our Serbian action we
> went to Germany for advice and carried through the démarche in Belgrade with
> the direct encouragement of the German government, and with its declaration that
> it considered the situation then favorable for the reckoning which was becoming
> ever more threatening.[44]

Tisza obviously felt the Monarchy under no moral obligation to Germany
for what had transpired after Sarajevo. What limited concessions he was
willing to make to the Rumanians were published shortly thereafter, and
towards the end of the month he went himself to Berlin and German General
Headquarters to thrash out the whole question. Afterwards, he reported that
he had at least momentarily chased the idea of further concessions from the
heads of the German leaders, including Wilhelm. But if the pressure from
Berlin seemed to abate, it was also obvious by the end of November that
Rumania was unlikely for the moment to join either side, so the issue was
no longer acute.

Such was not the case with Italy. Berchtold had done his best (or worst)
to ignore it during the July Crisis, but with the outbreak of war and the
declaration of Italian neutrality, German pressure rose for territorial compensation to the Italians to keep them in the alliance. It was obvious to the
Ballplatz that such compensation ultimately meant the Trentino, for it was
afraid Italy would be satisfied with nothing less. To all the fears of showing
weakness and creating subversive precedents that were involved with
Rumania, there was added over the Trentino a certain emotional bias against
dealing with anything Italian. Vienna may have forgiven Königgrätz, but it
never forgave Solferino; and when war with Rome finally did come a year

later, it proved to be the one enemy against whom all the peoples of the
Monarchy could equally unite.

Had the war ended quickly, there would have been no Italian problem.
At the beginning of August, a Common Ministers Council discussed the
question of compensation; the Germans were pressing for an intensification
of earlier exchanges on the subject between Rome and Vienna. It was agreed
to continue the conversations in a nonbinding manner until a military
decision was reached in France and Russia. The assumption, of course, was
that that decision would make it possible to refuse to give the Italians
anything. Berchtold maintained that promising Italy even the Trentino would
accomplish nothing; as soon as the Monarchy suffered a reverse, Italy would
attack it to get the city of Trieste. Tisza was equally adamant against
concessions, and blamed Germany for the fact that Italy was not honoring
its alliance obligations. Italy could not easily enter the war on the side of the
Central Powers and expose its long, vulnerable coastline to the British fleet;
but if the Germans had not violated Belgian neutrality, Britain might still be
neutral. Stürgkh agreed.[45]

With the failures of the campaigns in Galicia and in France, the bottom
was knocked out of the Austrian position. Vienna attempted to keep the
conversations with Rome nonbinding as long as possible, while the Germans
did all they could to make the Ballplatz more accommodating. The Austrians
feared that one concession to Italy would just whet its appetite for others;
they feared even more that German softness in Rome would undercut the
whole position and encourage the Italians constantly to raise their demands.
Tisza told Berchtold that he was "painfully" affected by repeated German
suggestions that the Monarchy should cede the Trentino, and hoped that they
would show more consideration in the future: "I think it would be good to
tell the Germans this in a friendly but very serious manner, and to exclude
this subject from all further conversations."[46] Yet on the same day, Vienna
had to accept the Italian interpretation of Article VII of the Triple Alliance
Treaty (on compensation), applying it to the entire Balkan peninsula, and
waived its earlier condition that in return Italy had to enter the war.

Starting in November, the German pressure on Vienna to appease the
Italians was constantly increased. In the middle of the month, Count Anton
Monts, a former German Ambassador to Italy, appeared in Vienna to sound
out Berchtold about ceding the Trentino. Monts seemed to believe that such
a concession would buy not only Italian neutrality but its actual belligerency
on the side of the Central Powers. Berchtold contended all it would do would
be to begin a process of blackmail just to retain its neutrality. At the same
time, it was announced that Prince Bernhard von Bülow, the former German

Chancellor, was being sent on a special German mission to Rome. Karl Freiherr von Macchio, since August the Austrian Ambassador there, reported that the whole Italian press expected Bülow to bring the Trentino with him. The Ballplatz urged Berlin vigorously to deny it. Instead, Berchtold was told by Tschirschky that Italy had requested German support for formal discussions with Austria over compensation, to which Germany had agreed since otherwise Italy might go over to the side of the Entente.[47]

By the end of the year, it was quite clear that the Central Powers would be lucky even to retain Italy's neutrality. Rome was ready to sell its position to the highest bidder, and at issue was simply whether it could gain more from Vienna by remaining neutral or from the Entente by declaring war. The Austrians were uniformly outraged at the situation. Italy was demanding compensations on the basis of an alliance treaty which, by remaining neutral, it simultaneously refused itself to honor. Worse, they found the Germans working openly against them; no sooner was Bülow in Rome than he fulfilled their worst expectations. Macchio reported that Bülow let it be known that the Monarchy had to make concessions and that German denials were not meant to be taken too seriously. "The natural result of this talk," Macchio added, "is that people here get the impression that Germany is on their side and is busy only against us . . ."[48] Berchtold hoped to satisfy Italian compensation demands in Albania instead of the Trentino, but the German activities in Rome undermined his whole position. Bitterness was not confined just to the diplomats. Berchtold noted in his diary after an audience with Franz Joseph: "Emperor again complains greatly about the Germans, with whom working together is very difficult. Bülow, Tschirschky are both very harmful, Jagow is an enemy of Austria and the Chancellor very weak, the Kaiser unpredictable."[49]

With the Monarchy's armies locked in combat with Russia in Galicia and the Carpathians, and with the imminent possibility of a Russian breakthrough into Hungary, an Italian declaration of war would be a disaster—even more so because it was feared that Italy's entry into the war would be followed immediately by that of Rumania. Under these circumstances, both Berchtold and Forgách were inclined to be conciliatory. "Berchtold and I were by no means completely unapproachable to the greedy Italian demands," Forgách later wrote.[50] Macchio in Rome also urged greater flexibility.

Tisza, however, refused to concede anything. Rome was bluffing over the Trentino in order to get more concessions elsewhere: only if Germany led the Italians to believe that they could really get it would a conflict with them become inevitable. Or so he told Berchtold.[51] By January, Tisza was as concerned with showing a strong front to Berchtold as he was to the

Germans, for he was determined that the Monarchy not yield the Trentino to Italy and believed that only a united show of strength by Austria and Germany would make it give up its demand for territory there. He was undoubtedly afraid such a precedent in the Austrian half of the Monarchy might lead to a repetition in Hungarian Transylvania. No matter how pliant Berchtold might be, Tisza feared his weakness would lead him to compromise the Monarchy's position with the Germans. Worried about a coming trip Berchtold planned to make to Berlin, Tisza confided to Burián: "We can get him to send a specific declaration there. But if he goes there, he will be exposed to their concentrated attack alone. Even if he does not knuckle under, he will in no case leave the impression of a resolutely determined man. His behavior will definitely only encourage the Germans to continue assailing us." [52] Tisza's apprehension that Berchtold was too weak to stand up to the Germans was a major reason for his removal as Foreign Minister a week later.

Thus by the end of the year, Austria's military defeats had also endangered its diplomatic position. Germany had proven to have few inhibitions about giving away Habsburg territories to its avaricious neighbors, which the Monarchy, already sliding into military and economic dependence on it, was hard put to resist. This was not at all what had been expected in July and August 1914; this was no brief, victorious war but a life-and-death struggle which already threatened permanent damage to the Empire. The expectations of the summer, the presuppositions under which the Monarchy's leaders had originally gone to war, had all proven themselves false. How could Austria-Hungary maintain its position as a Great Power and an equal in the alliance under these new circumstances? Tisza's response, as he made abundantly clear, was a show of strength through sheer will power. But was this the only answer?

III

This was not the first time that the Habsburg Monarchy found itself locked into a war which threatened it with disaster. In earlier wars, the sale of a few provinces had brought a cheap end to hostilities. Austria had repeatedly ceded territories to Napoleon and fifty years later resorted to the same expedient with his nephew. The situation by the end of 1914 was hardly promising; all the summer's hopes had been shattered. The result was gloom and uncertainty in Vienna. Macchio, called home from Rome for direct consultation with Berchtold at the end of December, found the mood depressed and pessimistic, with Berchtold himself having no idea what to do.[53] It was not surprising, then, that some in Vienna should begin to consider the prospects of ending the war before the situation got even worse. If this could not be achieved through a status quo ante peace with the Entente, historical precedent might again be followed, with the Monarchy ending a bad war by giving up some of its own territory in order to preserve the rest.

Almost as soon as Vienna contemplated the chances of peace, however, it had to consider its relations with Germany. And the Germans evinced no interest in any quick peace settlement that stopped short of total victory. In mid-November, on the occasion of a mediation offer by American President Woodrow Wilson via his confidant, Colonel House, the Ballplatz approached Berlin on the question of war aims. Berchtold believed such a discussion necessary in order to avoid "the dangers which could be involved in stubbornly insisting on aims which are in the last resort too extensive." It took Bethmann two weeks to reply; and when he did, he made no mention of any war aims discussions.[54] In December, there was talk in Berlin of the possibilities of concluding a separate peace with Russia in order to defeat Britain and France. Nothing came of it, but the rumors deepened fear in Vienna that the Germans were turning the war from its supposed original purpose—to end Russian expansionism in the East—into a struggle for supremacy with England.[55] Such a conflict might drag on indefinitely, and it was one from which the Monarchy had little to gain.

By the end of the year, Vienna's war aims had shrunk considerably from what they had been in August, and even Conrad admitted that the Monarchy would be lucky to get out of the conflict with nothing more than a "black eye."[56] Germany, however, seemed intent on driving the war to an unambiguously victorious conclusion. As it became obvious that this would be far more costly than anyone had imagined, the Monarchy's leadership had ample cause to reflect on its future course of policy. At the end of August, Tisza had pondered what would happen when the expected victory was achieved: he would urge the Germans to be satisfied with relatively moderate terms, although he considered it understood that "completely different terms" would have to be demanded if the Central Powers were compelled to fight to the finish.[57] Now, after the summer defeats, he devoted himself entirely to achieving that final victory, cost what it would. If he had doubts that the war could be won or that the Monarchy could maintain its independence within the alliance, he kept them to himself. His associate, Burián, was even more inflexible. Berchtold, however, was obviously wavering. Though he had insisted that the war could not be ended until at least Serbia was properly beaten, by the end of December the second Austrian attempt to do that had failed as ignominiously as the first. His November exchange with Bethmann had indicated an interest in discussing peace terms, and with the Serbian defeats and the growing problem of Italy, his desire to get out of the conflict could only have increased. His weakness and fatalism, however, held him immobile against the combined front of Tisza and the Germans. If he had received enough support from the other direction, he might have mustered the determination to try to alter their position.

By the beginning of the new year, that support was beginning to materialize. To two other members of the Austrian policy-making elite, the dangers to the Monarchy of continuing the conflict at the side of Germany far outweighed the possible rewards; they had decided that to allow Berlin to hold them longer in the war could easily lead to fatal consequences.

The first was Margrave János Pallavicini, the Austrian Ambassador in Constantinople. Pallavicini was an influential figure whose judgment carried considerable weight. Not only had his years of experience with the Porte won him an enviable position of authority there, but he had served as de facto Foreign Minister during Aehrenthal's last illness and later would be asked in vain by the Emperor Karl to resume the office. Pallavicini was already worried that Germany would push the Monarchy completely out of any meaningful role in the Ottoman Empire if the war continued, and by the end of November he saw no reason why a compromise peace was not theoretically possible. There was no more danger of a Balkan League arrayed against Austria-Hungary, and Germany had established its predominance in the Near East. He also realized that as long as the Germans intended to annex Belgium, England and France would continue to fight bitterly. "I now ask myself," he wrote, "should we bleed ourselves white in Poland and Galicia because Germany wants to annex Belgium?" He hoped that both Belgium and Serbia (he assumed then that it would soon be conquered) could be used as bargaining counters for an essentially status quo ante settlement. Somewhat toned down and without the above-quoted sentence, his letter was printed for circulation among the members of the Austrian foreign service. A few weeks later, in January, he discussed the possibility of using the concessions Austria-Hungary would have to make to Italy to get it to mediate a peace settlement for it. Germany had pushed Italian concessions in order to make possible a continuation of the Central Powers' war effort; Pallavicini turned Berlin's argument on its head by arguing instead that they should be used to get out of it.[58]

Pallavicini was in essential agreement with another figure considerably closer to the center of power—János Forgách. Forgách had now become First Section Chief in the Foreign Ministry, and he was one of Berchtold's closest advisors. By January 1915, Forgách had decided that the war had to be ended. His exultant war optimism of July had since plummetted to despondency; and at the beginning of the new year, he prepared for his chief a long memorandum on the subject. The war situation was bleak: Russia had not been defeated, and Italy and Rumania threatened to intervene at any time. The chances of an improvement were "very slim." To achieve peace, he was ready to sacrifice the Trentino to Italy to get its mediation and even East Galicia to Russia in exchange for some compensation in Western Poland. But an end to the war could be gotten only with the Germans; hence it was urgently necessary to convince them that a settlement had to be reached. Many of the disasters of the past year were Germany's fault. The Germans had mishandled both Italy and Rumania, they had failed to send enough troops to achieve victory on the Eastern Front, and they had botched their invasion of France through Belgium. After that performance, Berlin should be as satisfied to get out of the war as Vienna. In exchange for occupied Belgium, it ought to be able to buy a status quo ante peace. Forgách admitted that both the German and the Austrian publics would have a difficult time adjusting to such an end to the war. But he emphasized that a quick settlement could still preserve the Great Power position of the Monarchy, while a continuation of the conflict would have catastrophic consequences and entail wholesale economic devastation.[59]

Thus Tisza's position of blind adherence to the alliance and the war effort was not the only one circulating in Vienna by the beginning of the new year. If Forgách and Pallavicini painted the immediate military prospects blacker than they actually were, their perception of the long range dangers facing the Monarchy was grimly realistic. What would have happened if Vienna had decided in early 1915 to end the war at the cost of a few provinces—before it was totally exhausted by a long war of attrition and before Italy or Rumania had become belligerents—and done all it could to get German agreement for a quick peace settlement? The immediate possibilities of such a course were hardly promising; neither Germany nor the Entente was ready for peace in 1915. But the longterm effects are less calculable, for the Monarchy would certainly have been able to exercise on its ally a more effective weight for peace had it begun systematically to do so in 1915 instead of waiting until two years later. More flexibility might also have prolonged Italian neutrality. As it was, Tisza prevented any such policy from being adopted. If Austria had in a sense pulled Hungary into the war in July 1914, it was now Hungary in the person of Tisza that determined to keep it there. Forgách's memorandum was never delivered. By the time it was ready, Leopold Berchtold was no longer Austrian Foreign Minister.

Chapter 4

**THE HARD LINE
January 1915-December 1916**

I

"In his usual manner like a good child," as Tisza put it, Berchtold agreed to leave the Foreign Ministry.[1] Berchtold seemed no longer willing to maintain the uncompromising stand against the Italians (and hence the Germans) which Tisza deemed necessary, nor did he have the determination which the Hungarian Minister-President believed called for to continue the war. Therefore Tisza came to Vienna and convinced Franz Joseph to dismiss him. Berchtold raised no opposition. Franz Joseph wanted Tisza himself to be Berchtold's successor; this Tisza refused, suggesting his friend Burián instead. On January 13, 1915, Baron István Burián formally became Austro-Hungarian Foreign Minister, a post which he held for the following two years.

The new regime firmly blocked any chance that there might have been an early Austrian attempt to end the war. It in fact blocked almost any chance for change at all. While Berchtold had tended to be equivocal and open to outside influences, Burián was scarcely open to anything, save the influence of his friend and mentor Tisza. With the assured backing of Franz Joseph, Tisza and Burián were now in a position to monopolize almost all foreign policy decisions. Forgách later wrote that under Burián he soon lost all influence.[2] A lower official in the ministry, noting the same inflexibility of opinion, reported optimistically: "A firm hand is at the rudder."[3] Yet the performance of that firm hand disappointed most of the hopes placed in it. Burián had worked closely with the Foreign Ministry since the outbreak of the war and was thus no stranger to the problems it faced. He had been seriously considered by Franz Joseph as Aehrenthal's successor in 1912. But his vaunted strength often turned out to be mere stubbornness and blind obstinancy. He was a knowledgeable and demanding minister, but he was also doctrinaire and pedantic, unable to fit his flights of rhetoric to practical realities. Those in contact with him often compared him to a long-winded professor whose main talent seemed to be giving interminable monologues, an impression reinforced by his pince nez and manicured beard. His stubbornness and inflexibility endeared him to few of his associates, least of all the Germans. German Undersecretary Zimmerman complained to the journalist Kanner after a year of contact with him:

> Nothing can be done with the man. It is always the same. When you want to discuss something with him, he gives an endless learned lecture, at whose conclusion you're completely exhausted; and if you try to make a reply, then he sits down and repeats the same lecture all over again. And then everything is over; you can't go on. How are you supposed to come to a conclusion with the man? It is impossible.[4]

Of course, such obstinacy was precisely the "determination" Tisza had been urging ever since the collapse of the Galician campaign, though in Burián he undoubtedly received more than he had bargained for. If Austria-Hungary's Great Power position could be preserved by a show of strength, the requisite men were now in control; for Stürgkh was scarcely any more amenable to outside influences than Burián, and Tisza's position with Franz Joseph made him the undisputed arbiter over them both. This triumvirate—Stürgkh, Burián ("Burián-sturian" to the critics, "stur" meaning "obdurate" or "pig-headed" in German), and Tisza— now monopolized the Monarchy's power with an exclusiveness and rigidity that was to last until the fall of 1916.

It was perhaps no accident that the architects of the policy of strength were both Magyars. While relations between the Monarchy and Germany were conducted officially from the Ballhausplatz in Vienna, unofficial channels of influence between Berlin and Budapest persisted from the time before the war, often directed from Budapest against the Austrian half of the Empire. In the fall of 1914, pro-German sentiment among the Magyars was so strong that it almost seemed to Redlich that the country wanted to become a part of Germany itself.[5] As successive defeats discredited the largely Austrian army leadership, there was heavy support in Hungary for its replacement by German commanders. Count Gyula Andrássy the younger, one of the main Hungarian opposition leaders, approached Tschirschky in the middle of the Brusilov offensive in 1916 to plead for German military leadership, since with the Austrians he contended that everything was going to ruin.[6]

Berlin was often ambivalent in its assessment of the value of Hungary as an ally. Kaiser Wilhelm, however much he admired the strength and energy of Tisza, nevertheless criticized him for applying all his gifts towards strictly Hungarian interests. But as August von Cramon, the perceptive German liaison officer with the Austrian High Command, later noted, Germany in general looked on the Hungarians as the strongest supporters of the alliance within the Monarchy.[7] Tisza's own reputation in Berlin was such that at one point Burián actually had to remind the Germans after a visit there by the Hungarian Minister-President that Tisza had no authority to discuss anything but internal Hungarian matters.[8]

The Magyar elite always conceived its ties with Germany as those between strict equals. Backed by a long historical tradition and convinced of their right to dominate the neighboring ethnic groups, its members had no intention of accepting second place to Berlin, and before 1914 they had in no way done so. The reality that Germany was far more powerful in economic strength or sheer numbers of people had no effect on them. Both Tisza and Burián accepted this close, but equal, identification of the two states. At a Common Ministers Council at the end of 1915, Burián described the history of Hungary as that of a nation "which had joined itself to the greatness of the German Reich and yet had known completely how to preserve its independence."[9] The supposed special relationship between Budapest and Berlin certainly underlay much of the confidence of Tisza and Burián that they could maintain the German alliance as one between equals and prevent it from coming to dominate them. Tisza was under no illusion about German ambitions. As the first Mitteleuropa plans for Austro-German economic union began to be discussed, he observed shrewdly: "No one values our ally more than I, but they have the cute habit of grabbing at your entire hand as soon as you extend your little finger to them."[10] Such "healthy German egoism" (as Burián put it) could be contained, however, by a strong, forthright defense of the Monarchy's own interests. "We will find understanding with our ally in every regard," the new Foreign Minister wrote with his typical stolid complacency after a year in office, "but not without some struggle."[11]

In reality, the show of strength, the hard line, was to have just the opposite result to what Tisza hoped for at the beginning of 1915. Paradoxically, the dismissal of Berchtold for being too soft with the Germans and the initiation of a tough policy of asserting the Monarchy's equality with them had in the long run the very outcome which it was intended to avoid, for it grossly overestimated Austria-Hungary's powers of resistance to the enormous pressures of the war. Berchtold had always been conscious of the Monarchy's weakness, hence his constant efforts to guarantee German support and his fears of losing it. This standpoint undoubtedly implied a certain degree of Austrian dependence on Germany, which he was ready to accept. The wartime plans for Mitteleuropa found his quick approval as a means of assuring firm German ties with Vienna for all time. For Tisza, however, as the Hungarian Minister-President asserted to Berchtold in a conversation in 1916, Austria-Hungary was more important to Germany than the other way around.[12] He and Burián had no hesitation about being more obstinate towards Berlin than Berchtold ever would have dared. Such rigid obduracy in the long run only worsened the position of the Monarchy, because it overtaxed its dwindling resources and thus made it ever more vulnerable to the very German domination it was supposed to prevent.

II

The question of what to do about Italy had brought Burián into the Foreign Ministry. His solution was to do nothing at all. Burián contended that Italy was not prepared to go to war, or at least would not be prepared for the next few months, and that any concessions until then would be meaningless. Until it was ready to commence hostilities, Italy's policy could only be one of bluff, to extract as much from the Monarchy as possible—the Trentino would be just the beginning, not the end. There could be no assurance that ceding it would permanently assure Rome's benevolent neutrality in any case. Of course, once Italy was ready for war, Burián could argue that all concessions were useless since Austria-Hungary would be attacked no matter how forthcoming it acted. In either case the conclusion was the same: simply to play for time. Though talks should be pursued with Rome about compensation, they should be drawn out and complicated as much as possible. These were the same arguments and tactics of the previous year, though with a stubbornness absent under Berchtold. If Burián conceded that when the "psychological moment" came some concessions might have to be made, he also spoke blandly of "shooting the Italians" if they attempted to take the Trentino by force.[13] His hope, like Tisza's, was that if concessions could be put off long enough, the war situation would improve and allow them to be put off altogether. An Austrian winter offensive was planned in the Carpathians. "We will not break the thread, but rather attempt to draw out the negotiations without committing ourselves so that the favorable military situation which has to be created can have its effect," Tisza wrote.[14] In this they had the full support of Franz Joseph, who was firmly set against parting with any of his patrimony. But to stake everything on such a problematic turn in the fortunes of the war was the same va banque policy that had led the Monarchy into the war in the first place.

The initial prerequisite for such a course was to stop once and for all the continued German efforts to appease Italy, which undermined the whole Austrian position. Burián traveled to German Headquarters at the end of January to present his view of the matter. No territorial concessions at all were possible; the situation would improve of itself through a show of calmness and strength. Above all, Bülow's machinations in Rome had to be put under control. But where was that strength to be found? Falkenhayn argued in vain that Germany had nothing to spare to defend the Monarchy against an attack from Italy and Rumania. Hohenlohe wrote afterwards that Burián practically talked his German colleagues to death, who finally stopped arguing with him out of sheer exhaustion. No agreement was reached.[15] A month later, Burián conferred with Bethmann and the other German leaders at Teschen, with similar results.

To Berlin, Berián's intransigence was infuriating. The Germans believed that the Italian military preparations were far more advanced than Burián or Tisza were willing to admit, and recognized much more clearly the seriousness of the concurrent Italian negotiations with the Entente. Even the Austrians had to agree that a simultaneous Italian-Rumanian attack would find the Monarchy defenseless; the forces of the Central Powers were tied down on the other fronts, with no reserves to spare. Austria's collapse would probably decide the war. "As even Baron Burián admits, an Italian attack on Austria will lead to a catastrophe which will ruin not only Austria-Hungary but us as well," Bethmann wrote urgently to Tschirschky. That Vienna was willing to run such a risk in order to save one small province was simply incomprehensible. "All considerations for our ally and for its entirely understandable objection against a concession to the blackmailer have to take second place to our concern for Germany's existence," Bethmann made clear.[16]

So, the pressure on Vienna was tightened. The Wilhelmstraße repeatedly demanded that the Austrians give way. Falkenhayn wrote to Conrad in the same sense, and the Austrian Chief of Staff, despite his Italian phobias, agreed that everything must be done to keep Italy out of the war. Additional influence was brought to bear by means of Austrian domestic channels. Berlin had utilized such channels before in order to squeeze cooperation from Vienna when normal diplomatic argument failed, and the wartime situation gave them an added importance for political leverage. Tschirschky made sure that Stürgkh and Burián were put under pressure by members of the Austrian

German national parties to give in on the Trentino, and did what he could to get the Christian Socials and the Polish Club to follow their example. Statesmen from former Foreign Minister Agenor Goluchowski and the earlier Austrian Minister-President Wladimir von Beck to such influential Reichsrat members as Baernreither—and even the Socialists Viktor Adler and Karl Seitz—all made appearances at the Ballplatz to argue for concessions. Burián complained that the German actions threatened to give the impression that the Austrian government had abdicated all ability to make independent decisions about its own vital interests.[17] It was indeed another example of the influence Berlin possessed to manipulate Austrian domestic politics, given the complex national and alliance loyalties of the various parties and leaders in the Dual Monarchy. Those overlapping loyalties guaranteed it a strong voice in whatever happened there no matter how much it professed its theoretical non-interference in strictly internal Austrian affairs.

A good deal of the increasing bitterness towards Germany over Italy in Austrian government circles was not just due to the repeated use of such pressure tactics, but to the fact that Berlin seemed to be pushing the Monarchy to make all the concessions in a crisis in which both powers had equally as much at stake. If Italy was blackmailing Austria for chunks of territory, certain leaders in the Monarchy were not above suggesting that Vienna should use the same tactic against Berlin. At the end of February, Conrad, who repeatedly admitted that the Monarchy was finished if war with Italy could not be avoided, proposed to Burián that the time had come to demand of the Germans how much they were willing to pay for Austrian concessions to Rome. If they did not like the idea, they should be told: "Either you agree, or you fall into the water with us."[18] Berlin was more than ready to agree. The Germans promised the coal area of Sosnowiec in Russian Poland to the Monarchy in return for a cession of the Trentino, and in their desperation even went so far as to consider giving up a section of Prussian Silesia if it became necessary.[19]

Burián's response to the German campaign was simply to entrench himself further. He wrote of the Germans: "The men are not to be brought away from the fallacy that, because a danger exists, one should use a means against it whose ineffectiveness—even injuriousness—is clearly obvious. Political judgment in Berlin today is insufficient and we must certainly not let our course be dictated from there."[20] The exasperation towards Germany at the Ballplatz was well expressed by Forgách, who described Bülow's activities in Rome as simply "*unbelievable.*" Yet much of what Bülow was urging there Forgách had himself suggested in his January memorandum. By the end of February, Forgách was complaining to Macchio that Burián had broken the original thread with Rome and added that, thanks to the Foreign Minister's conduct, he was afraid the Monarchy would be faced with war with both Italy and Rumania in another two months.[21] Nor was Forgách the only Austrian official frightened by Burián's refusal to show any inclination to appease the Italians. Before Berchtold's dismissal, Hohenlohe had argued that however much he disliked the Italian demands, sacrifices would have to be made if the Monarchy was not strong enough to resist them. And Macchio in Rome cautioned Burián a month later that the Italian demands were not necessarily a bluff. All such warnings were to no avail.[22]

Whatever can be said against the German pressure for concessions on ethical grounds, Berlin's standpoint at least had the virtue of flexibility. The promise of Austrian territory might not have had much effect on those currently in power in Rome. But used as part of a resourceful diplomatic campaign, as later events would show, it might have significantly strengthened the neutralist forces in Italian political life and seriously complicated Foreign Minister Sonnino's ability to deal with the Entente. Italy might still have intervened against the Monarchy, but it would have been an even more prolonged and painful process than it was. All these possibilities were blocked by Burián's uncompromising attitude.

The Austrian position was finally undermined by the Russians rather than the Germans. Tisza and Burián had expected Austro-German victories on the Eastern Front that would call the Italian "bluff." None were forthcoming. A German attack out of East Prussia achieved a tactical success, then bogged down. Conrad's Carpathian offensive scarcely managed even that. It began on January 23, with the goal of pushing the Russians out of the Carpathians and relieving the great Austrian fortress of Przemyśl in Galicia where 120,000 Austro-Hungarian troops had been under siege since November. It achieved little except more frightful losses. A second offensive fared no better in the difficult, often snow-bound terrain. Przemyśl surrendered on March 22. By April, the Russians were attacking in their turn, and, as the Austrian lines were pressed back toward the Hungarian plain, it began to look as if the Habsburg forces might collapse entirely.

Even before the fall of Przemyśl, Vienna had been forced by the military failures to agree in principle to a cession of the Trentino. The decision was confirmed at a meeting of the Common Ministers Council on March 8, 1915. Bitterness at the meeting was almost greater towards Germany than towards Italy. Burián complained about German pressure, while Tisza remarked that it was only due to German intrigues in Rome that the Italian appetite had grown as large as it had. Conrad perhaps outdid them all. "If Italy could not be satisfied with this heavy sacrifice and made new demands," he argued, "in his opinion it would be better to go to ruin and drag Germany along with them, than to give in to more of such blackmail." Stürgkh and Franz Joseph both agreed that Berlin should not be told the Monarchy's maximum concessions lest it give them away too quickly; Burián assured them that no such thing would happen.[23]

Vienna still drove a hard bargain with Berlin. In return for giving up the Trentino, Burián expected to get Sosnowiec (with future claims to the rest of Russian Poland still open), a guarantee against further Italian demands, a sizable loan, and a free hand in the Balkans. But the pace of the exchanges between Vienna and Rome continued to be as slow as ever; the Trentino was no longer sufficient for those Italian appetites, which now hungered for a border on the Isonzo River and the city of Trieste. Moreover, the Italians demanded an immediate occupation of the areas to be ceded to them, not wishing to wait until the end of the war—a demand perhaps justified by all the reservations at the Ballplatz against any cession at all.

The Germans thus found themselves putting even more pressure on Vienna to make concessions to the Italians before Italy went entirely over to the opposite camp. Rome had to be offered enough to make it more worthwhile to stay neutral than to make war for the additional Habsburg territories the Entente dangled before it. The German Reichstag deputy Matthias Erzberger scurried unofficially back and forth between Rome, Vienna, and Berlin trying to find an agreement, and Zimmermann made a special trip to Vienna to press for further concessions. But there were limits to how much even Berlin could do—at least, at this stage of the war. At his January meeting with the German leadership, Burián had argued that an Italian attack would not necessarily doom the Monarchy, which had always found a way out of such crises. Bethmann's secretary Riezler drew the deduction: "He means therefore peace with Russia."[24] That fear was not limited to Riezler, and for the first time in the war Berlin began to worry about an Austrian separate peace if it put too much pressure on Vienna.

Tschirschky had written in November that no influential person in the Monarchy seriously considered the possibility of a separate peace, despite all the friction between the two allies over the failures of the first military campaigns.[25] But by the end of February, Jagow confided to Bülow in Rome that an Austrian separate peace with the Russians was in no way impossible, especially since a circle of the Bohemian nobility seemed ready to buy it at the cost of East Galicia (which Russia already occupied anyway) so that all Austria's strength would be available against the Italians. If too much pressure drove the Monarchy to leave the war, Germany would be left to face the

Entente alone. "We have no means of compulsion against Austria," Jagow concluded regretfully.[26]

Jagow's fears were not entirely imaginary. In April, Conrad repeatedly urged peace with Russia in order to contain Italy. He proposed to give the Russians East Galicia in return for peace and a free hand in the western Balkans. Russia would be allowed to satisfy its aspirations in the eastern Balkans, though he admitted this might cause some difficulties with Austria's supposed ally in Constantinople. But Conrad was careful to note that such a step had to be taken in full agreement with Berlin; he was proposing a separate peace at the expense of the Turks, perhaps, but not the Germans.[27] As became obvious in 1917-1918, when the question of a separate peace without Germany reached acute proportions, any such peace involved domestic repercussions which most Austrian leaders—and certainly Conrad—could never accept. Whether other voices in favor of building "golden bridges" to Russia went so far as to consider a separate peace without Germany, as Jagow feared, seems unlikely, and for the same reasons. János Pallavicini in Constantinople still argued for a quick end to the war, seeing an Austro-Russian understanding as the most promising way of achieving it; he remained concerned that German designs on Belgium would prolong the conflict. But he also realized how difficult a separate peace without Germany was made by the Monarchy's complex national loyalties. As he told his German colleague in Constantinople, such a peace "would without fail lead to the dissolution of the Austro-Hungarian Monarchy—since the Germans of Austria and also the Hungarians would more likely support Germany than their [own] government."[28]

The worsening situation also spawned interest in a general peace with all the Entente powers, similar to that contemplated by Forgách and Pallavicini before Berchtold's dismissal. By the middle of April, over a month after its reluctant agreement eventually to cede the Trentino, Vienna suddenly realized with a shock that Burián's "psychological moment" might finally be at hand. The military situation had continued to deteriorate, and it appeared that the Russians might soon break through the Carpathian passes into the flatlands of Hungary. In sharp contrast to his earlier standpoint, Tisza anxiously wrote Conrad that the Monarchy would now have to make heavy sacrifices to keep Italy neutral; and if it failed, Rumania would follow Italy into the conflict and there would be nothing left for Germany and Austria except to conclude peace with everybody as quickly as possible. He repeated the same arguments to Burián, only in even stronger terms: Italian entry into the war would end any prospect of victory, and instead they would be forced to beg the Entente for peace terms. Therefore, they would have to make more concessions to

Italy than they had previously been willing to do, though of course the weakness of the Monarchy's position had to be hidden from Berlin or else their standing there would be undermined completely. Nonetheless, there had to be more detailed talks with the Germans about possible peace terms if an Italian attack could not be avoided.[29]

The sudden need for peace was contemplated by others besides Tisza. Although the immediate occasion was the impending calamity of Italian intervention while all the Monarchy's forces were occupied on the Eastern Front, it was Germany, not Italy, that was seen as the initial obstacle to be overcome. Count Miklós Szécsen, the former Austrian Ambassador to France, wrote several memoranda on possible peace conditions in April and May. A peace program had to be settled in advance with Germany, for Szécsen feared that otherwise Berlin might draw up a program on its own as a fait accompli—at the Monarchy's expense. "Germany's attitude in the Trentino question should serve as a warning for us about that," he observed. The heart of the problem was not the Trentino, but Belgium. If Germany gave up Belgium, England's war aims would be met and then England could perhaps induce France and Russia to stop fighting as well. He noted prophetically that a continuation of the war could lead to the complete destruction of the Dual Monarchy. Germany, however, being an ethnically unitary state, might be defeated, but it could not be destroyed.[30] Stürgkh was thinking along similar lines; he remarked to Leo Chlumecky that Vienna had to make it clear to the Germans that the Monarchy could not go on fighting just so that they could annex Belgium.[31] At the end of April, Burián asked Bethmann in Berlin if concessions on Belgium would make it possible to conclude peace with England, which would then free the necessary military forces to deal with the Italian threat. Bethmann answered negatively and referred to the need for German "guarantees" there.[32] What had been indicated by the thinking of Forgách and Pallavicini at the beginning of the year was again illustrated: When Austrian statesmen considered the prospects of peace—no matter how strong and unshakable their faith in the German alliance—they found that the first obstacle to its attainment was their bond with Germany.

Whether a peace offensive had been at all possible in January, now, in April, thanks to Vienna's own obstinacy, it was too late. Burián might have changed his mind at last about the Italian "bluff," but the change seemed to be strictly academic. Forgách complained that he still did not do anything about it unless pushed by Tisza. Conrad and Falkenhayn, involved with plans for the spring offensive that led to the Gorlice breakthrough against the Russians, agreed that the attack's political precondition was continued Italian neutrality; troops could not be spared to deal with an Italian belligerency as well, while a clear victory in the East, if it came in time, might yet keep Italy neutral. Conrad pressed Burián to do everything possible to keep the Italians out of the war at least until the offensive was underway. As late as the beginning of May, though, Burián was reported still to be optimistic about further drawing out the negotiations without making any significant concessions.[33]

Finally, on May 9, Bülow and Macchio on their own initiative drew up a list of Austrian concessions and presented it to the Italian government. Austria would cede the Trentino to the German language border, Gradisca, and the west bank of the Isonzo. Trieste would become a free port with an Italian university, and Italy would be granted a free hand in Albania. But Sonnino had already concluded the Treaty of London with the Entente on April 26, which not only promised Italy everything conceded by Bülow-Macchio, but South Tyrol to the Brenner, the cities of Gorizia and Trieste, and part of Dalmatia with its offshore islands in the Adriatic. These territories included not just Italians, but sizable numbers of Austrian Germans and South Slavs. The treaty put Rome at odds with the expansive aims of the Serbs for the rest of the war. Bülow and Macchio hoped to provide the final impetus to the Italian neutralists under former Prime Minister Giolitti to return to power, but nevertheless Burián and Tisza were upset with their unauthorized move. Conrad even suggested pressuring Germany for more territory.[34] Italy seemed poised on the brink of revolution as neutralists and interventionists battled each other in the streets, but on May 23, Rome finally declared war on the Dual Monarchy.

The full consequences of the Italian declaration of war only became obvious later when Vienna began in earnest to try to pull out of the war and discovered a chief stumbling block in all the concessions promised Italy by the Treaty of London. Fortunately, the Austrians did not face an immediate crisis, but only because the Italians had still not assembled enough forces to mount a successful attack. Moreover, German troops had finally begun arriving on the Eastern Front in large numbers. On May 2, the great Austro-German offensive from Gorlice-Tarnów began, and though the steady advance failed to prevent the Italian declaration of war, it did deter Rumania from following suit as everybody had expected. By the time the Italians finally mounted their offensive, the Eastern Front was out of immediate danger and an Austrian army had been scraped together along the Italian border to oppose it.

Italy's entry into the war in no way ended the friction that had built up between Austria-Hungary and Germany since the beginning of the year. As

Burián accepted the inevitability of Italian intervention against Austria-Hungary, he pressed for a positive military agreement with Berlin to deal with it. When the break with Italy came, however, Berlin refused to declare war against the Italians. The ill feeling which that refusal caused in Vienna, especially considering the urgency with which the Wilhelmstraße had argued for Austrian declarations of war against France and Britain in 1914, needs no further comment. It was not until 1916 that the situation was changed by an Italian declaration of war on Germany.

The German pressure that had earlier been exerted on behalf of Italy was now transferred to Rumania. It was feared in Berlin in the months immediately following the Italian entry into the war that Rumania would imitate its example, cancelling out all the victories of the Gorlice offensive. But even Rumania'a continued neutrality was not sufficient. At the end of April, the British Gallipoli campaign opened. The Turks rapidly exhausted their supplies of munitions, and Berlin was faced with the prospect of Constantinople's falling to the Entente and Turkey's being knocked out of the war. With no possibility of supply shipments through Serbia, the only means of sending essential war material to the Turks was via neutral Rumania, but the Rumanians refused to allow transit of any appreciable quantities. Once again, Berlin demanded that its ally make territorial sacrifices to save the common cause—from the Bukovina if not Transylvania—and enact domestic reforms for the Hungarian Rumanians.

Burián and Tisza agreed that there could be no sacrifices of Hungarian territory. The Germans again dangled the prospect of annexing Sosnowiec before their eyes. Tisza agreed to cede several districts of the Bukovina to Rumania as well as to making minimal concessions to Hungary's Rumanian population. But Burián refused; when Bethmann and Jagow came to Vienna at the end of May, he told them that the Bukovina concessions were far too much just for the right of munitions transport. He would offer them only for Rumania's active participation in the war on the side of the Central Powers, and even then the offer would have a thirty-day time limit. Berlin railed and worried again about the chance of an Austrian separate peace with Russia if Vienna were pressed too hard. Meanwhile, Burián reiterated all his old arguments for presenting a strong front, not encouraging blackmail, and in general remaining calm.[35] The stalemate eventually was resolved by the failure of the Gallipoli campaign and the realization that Bucharest was still not ready or willing to enter the war openly on either side.

The first fruits of Tisza's and Burián's policy of strength were increased friction within the alliance and the active belligerency of Italy. By gaining a new enemy on its southwestern border, the Monarchy now needed German military aid even more than at the beginning of the year, for it could defend the Isonzo only by transferring units there from Galicia and Serbia. Instead of strengthening the Monarchy's position towards Berlin, Burián and Tisza had weakened it. No doubt, as the initial reports from the Gorlice offensive came in, the Austrian leaders assumed that their earlier difficulties with Berlin would fade away and that they would finally begin to reap the rewards so optimistically anticipated in the summer of 1914. It was a false hope.

III

The Gorlice offensive continued for most of the summer, as the Russian army was pushed out of one stronghold after another. Przemyśl was recovered and the threat of a Russian invasion of Hungary through the Carpathians vanished. At the same time, the Austro-German armies overran much of Russian Poland; Warsaw fell to the Germans on August 5. Finally, in the fall, as the front against the Russians stabilized, a successful campaign was finally mounted against the Serbs.

Credit for the successes can be attributed in part to Conrad, who convinced Falkenhayn that a major effort should be mounted against the Russians, though the multiplying signs of Austrian military collapse undoubtedly lent cogency to Conrad's arguments. But what really made the campaigns possible was the German army. Without German troops, the Austrians could scarcely even maintain a defensive in the East—much less mount an attack there. Tisza in January had told the publicist Viktor Naumann that no German troops should be sent to Serbia; "Austria-Hungary's influence in the Balkans is destroyed forever if we call on the Germans for help."[36] But in the successful Serbian campaign in October, both German and Bulgarian divisions participated alongside those of the Monarchy. The best the Austrians could manage on their own was to subdue Montenegro—not a particularly impressive accomplishment.

The campaigns of early 1915 also revealed the first signs of national disintegration within the Habsburg army. The mobilization in August the year before had proceeded smoothly, but under the grueling pressure of the conflict and the blunders of the Austrian military leadership, some members of regiments of the more dissatisfied nationalities—Czechs, Ruthenes, Rumanians—either failed to fight effectively or deserted to the enemy. At the same time, Austrian weak points were reinforced with German units, a practice first begun as a stop-gap measure during the Carpathian campaign of the winter. It continued over the next two years, until divisions of the two armies were inextricably mixed together. The fact that the Austrian army could not even hold an independent section of the Russian Front without German reinforcement humiliated no one more than the hypersensitive Conrad. "I cannot at all express how distasteful is the infiltration with German troops," he wrote, "but the heart has to follow the head."[37] The weakness of the Austrian army, which repeatedly required new infusions of German forces, naturally entailed increased German pretensions to ultimate control; and these overflowed from the military into the political sphere. Burián in late October 1915 complained to Conrad that the unreliability of Czech and Ruthene units was undermining his bargaining position with Berlin; with their "greatly-intensified self-esteem" as a result of the victories, the Germans were already hard enough to deal with.[38] The prospect of further German influence actually increased the alienation of the dissatisfied nationalities in the long term, making their military loyalty still more questionable. Thus the victories of the summer and fall of 1915 brought with them on a military level an intensification of the difficulties posed to Austria-Hungary by the German alliance. In any case, they were tactical rather than strategic successes and failed to bring about a successful conclusion to the war. On a strictly political level, however, the controversies those victories unleashed were perhaps even greater. What Vienna wanted to do with the successes was not at all what Berlin had in mind—as the Ballplatz soon found out.

A year earlier, Vienna had contemplated the annexation of Russian Poland, a design which had been shelved with the defeats of the fall. The success of the Gorlice offensive put Poland back on the agenda. Since most of Poland had been captured by German arms, the Monarchy was forced to content itself with a small administrative area around Lublin while Berlin set up its jurisdiction in Warsaw to administer the rest. This was just a temporary measure. What was to be the ultimate fate of the territory? For a while, there seemed a possibility that it might be returned to Russia to buy its way out of the war, but as the likelihood of this faded, the claims of both Vienna and Berlin hardened. "During the war, Polish affairs sometimes severely tested the harmonious relations between Austria-Hungary and Germany," Burián later wrote in his memoirs[39]—an understatement even for him.

As in 1914, the leaders in Vienna, fearing the loss of Galicia, convinced themselves that Congress Poland had to be joined to the Monarchy; and Tisza and Burián, fearing the loss of the Ausgleich, agreed that only the subdualistic solution was possible. The question of just how that feat was to be accomplished without making the Monarchy totally ungovernable remained as difficult to answer as ever. In a meeting of the Common Ministers Council on October 6, Tisza reiterated his support of the sub-dualistic solution; the Ausgleich could not be touched, and any other solution would allow the anti-German Poles too great an influence on foreign policy. Of course, if Poland joined the Austrian half of the Monarchy, Dalmatia and Bosnia would have to revert to Hungary. Yet no one was really enthusiastic about annexing Poland at all, given all the problems it brought with it. Stürgkh was afraid it would destroy the character of Austria, and Tisza himself wanted no commitments that might prevent an eventual status quo peace with Russia.[40]

The Germans, on the other hand, in actual possession of most of Congress Poland except for the area around Lublin, feared for the Austrian domestic order no matter how Poland entered the Monarchy. Berlin had always been concerned about the strength (or weakness) of the roots of the alliance in Austro-Hungarian domestic politics, or, more specifically, the ability of the Austrian Germans and the Magyars as its chief proponents to maintain their predominant position in the Empire. Tschirschky from the beginning of the war had been outspoken about the dominant role the Austrian Germans were supposed to play in the Austrian half of the realm, hence much of his unpopularity at the Ballplatz. It was difficult for Berlin to see how that role would be strengthened if those Austrian Germans, already on the defensive against the political demands of their Slavic fellow citizens, now had to contend with an additional 12 million Slavs in the form of Congress Poland. Baernreither noted after a visit to Berlin:

> I found everywhere the strongest determination against agreeing to any form of constructing Poland or attaching it to the Monarchy which would injure the Germans in Austria or tend to lessen their influence. People have finally recognized that the preponderance of the Germans in Austria is an indispensable condition for the assured continuation of our alliance.[41]

There could be for Berlin no question of any Austro-Polish solution which did not simultaneously ensure the continuance of the Austrian Germans as the dominant national group in Cisleithania. This became clear shortly after the fall of Warsaw, when Burián met with Bethmann to advocate the Austro-Polish solution and found himself having to argue that the incorporation of Congress Poland into Cisleithania would not undermine the political position of the Austrian Germans. Ominously, the Germans indicated that they would expect border rectifications and economic concessions in Congress Poland no matter how it was constitutionally attached to the Dual Monarchy.[42]

Three months later, Burián again met with the German leaders in Berlin, on November 10 and 11. Bethmann announced that the constitutional proposals which Stürgkh had sketched out since their last meeting for connecting Poland sub-dualistically to Austria "did not seem to guarantee satisfactorily the safeguarding of the Germans in Austria which was so important." Burián complained about Bethmann's apparently sudden interest in the Austrian Germans; they were Austrians first and Germans only second. To Berlin's assertions that the Slavs formed a common danger to Germandom, he argued (unlike Tisza in the Common Ministers Council) that the Poles had always been in favor of the German alliance.[43] His listeners remained skeptical. They now made counter-demands which went beyond Poland to the constitutional order of the Monarchy itself. In effect, they were willing to yield control of Congress Poland to Vienna only for control of the whole Monarchy in return. Such a demand had already been implicit in the repeated calls for guarantees for the position of the Austrian Germans, but at the October meeting Bethmann formally made his acceptance of the Austro-Polish solution conditional on Austrian compliance with his plans for Mitteleuropa, which had as its goal the permanent binding of Austria-Hungary to the German Reich.

IV

The question of Mitteleuropa was, in its various guises, the central issue of the alliance. It involved not only the whole question of Austria-Hungary's future relations with Germany, but constitutional development within the Monarchy itself. Mitteleuropa or "Central Europe" was the term given to the idea that Germany and Austria-Hungary should form the core of some sort of future association of the various nations of Central Europe and that the relations that had hitherto existed between the two empires would be deepened and made more durable. The advocates of Mitteleuropa usually discussed it on three levels: political (a strengthening of the Austro-German alliance), economic (increasing the economic ties between the two states), and military (a military convention to supplement the alliance treaty). Ideas on the specific mechanism and extent of the connection varied widely, for the disparity between the two states and the multinational character of the Monarchy meant that any sort of "closer connection" between them could easily lead to overt German domination. Some Mitteleuropa advocates hoped to avoid this—but others openly welcomed and promoted it.

Consideration of the idea in Austria-Hungary pre-dated the war, but the outbreak of hostilities led to an extensive popular discussion. In the fall of 1914, Austro-Hungarian and German politicians began exchanging visits to consider the matter. The following months saw a gradual crescendo of such contacts, of articles on Mitteleuropa in the press, and of joint meetings between German and Austro-Hungarian pressure groups aimed at popularizing the concept and influencing the actions of their respective governments. The agitation reached its peak at the end of 1915 with the publication in Germany of Friedrich Naumann's famous book entitled, appropriately, *Mitteleuropa.*

The Mitteleuropa idea was generally discussed in economic terms. The wartime situation strengthened the belief that Austro-German economic cooperation was necessary to withstand the economic power of the Entente. The Entente powers had organized a common economic as well as military effort against the Central Powers, the results of which were most apparent in the blockade that sealed off Austria-Hungary and Germany from the resources of the rest of the world. Many feared that this Entente economic cooperation would persist into the postwar period, even after military hostilities had ceased. Under those circumstances, Austria-Hungary seemed to have no choice but to strengthen its economic ties with the German Reich. Where else could it turn to assure its continued economic development?

There was little agreement, however, on how this should be achieved, and the Monarchy's economic leaders were actually some of Mitteleuropa's least enthusiastic supporters. Austro-Hungarian businessmen feared that too close an association with the Reich—especially a removal of all customs barriers—would allow Germany's more developed industries to put them out of business. "The Austrian, and even more the weaker Hungarian, industrialists are striving hand and foot against a customs union," the German Consul in Budapest reported in August 1915.[44] Former Hungarian Trade Minister József Szterényi, an active proponent of the Mitteleuropa idea, was emphatic in drawing the line before a customs union with Germany: "The idea of a union, with or without an inner customs line, is incapable of being carried out and would simply destroy the national independence of the Monarchy in commercial relations, without even mentioning the economic side of the question."[45] The best economic argument that Baernreither, a warm advocate of Mitteleuropa, could present to the Lower Austrian Chamber of Commerce at the end of 1914 was that the increased German competition that would follow a lowering of tariffs would force Austrian industry to modernize.[46] His listeners, many of whom might be the first casualties of such a process, no doubt received his words with mixed emotions.

Why, then, did Mitteleuropa arouse such a popular agitation within the Monarchy in the first years of the war? The answer is that its ultimate implications were political and national far more than they were economic.

Mitteleuropa's most fervid supporters were not businessmen, but Austrian German politicians and intellectuals. Of the organizations or towns which passed resolutions for closer economic ties with Germany, virtually all were Austrian German in origin.[47] Baron Heinrich von Tucher, the Bavarian Envoy in Vienna, reported that those groups with an economic stake in Mitteleuropa were openly alarmed by the idea's chief advocates. They were afraid that the latter were ready to sacrifice Austro-Hungarian economic interests to their political goal of achieving as close a tie with Berlin as possible.[48]

Since the domestic order in Austria-Hungary and the alliance were so closely bound together, any deepening of the ties between the Monarchy and Germany could not fail to have an effect on its chief domestic institutions. Those who wanted to extend Austro-German ties the farthest tended to be the members of the splintered Austrian German nationalist parties of the Monarchy. They hoped that the war would tie the Monarchy to Germany so firmly that their position in Austria would be safeguarded against the Slavs for all time. Gustav Groß, the head of the Austrian German Nationalverband, the umbrella organization of the German parties in the Reichsrat, wrote his colleagues in late August 1914 in this sense; and one of them, Josef Dobernig, agreed that the government would try to reward the Slavs for their wartime loyalty *"unless we keep it from doing so"*—a fitting comment on the position of Vienna between the popular demands of both the Slavs and the Germans within the Monarchy.[49] Such sentiments soon led to the plans expressed in the so-called Easter Demands of the Austrian German nationalists, to split Galicia and Dalmatia from Cisleithania in order to give it a permanent German majority, and to make German the official state language of Austria just as Magyar was that of Hungary, all within the framework of a "constitutional" bond with the German Reich. The old Linz Program of 1882 was thus revived in the course of the war.

These ideas called into question the continuation of the Monarchy's independence itself; they exposed the ambiguous loyalties of the Austrian Germans to both Vienna and Berlin, one of the residues of Bismarck's incomplete solution of German unification in 1866. In October 1914, Rudolf Pogatscher, a secondary official at the Ballplatz, had noted uneasily: "Despite the suspension of domestic political life, at least in its outward appearances, a Großdeutsch-national movement sometimes shows itself very noticeably." The Monarchy, he continued, would have to be careful not to fall into dependence on Germany and thereby become unfaithful to its historic mission.[50] His thoughts were well taken. Interest in Mitteleuropa was notably absent among the non-German population of the Monarchy, which clearly realized its political implications. The Slav nationalities could hardly accept a program that made the Monarchy a permanent appendage of the German Empire and froze their domestic status to one of permanent inferiority. Yet this was precisely the reason why so many Austrian Germans supported it. The German Consul in Prague reported the Czechs to be decidedly reserved about the whole issue.[51] Nor were the Magyars any more enraptured, except for some agrarians hoping to penetrate the German agricultural tariff wall. Their chauvinistically-nurtured infant industries were probably more susceptible to German competition than those of Austria. Moreover, a Mitteleuropa agreement would require putting the Ausgleich with Austria on a more longterm basis, something the Hungarians had opposed for years. The Hungarian opposition leader Albert Apponyi could support a longterm agreement with Berlin only while firmly rejecting any such thing with Vienna.[52]

As the Mitteleuropa agitation among the Austrian Germans grew, the Austro-Hungarian administration had to define its official position on the issue. Many of its members were quite favorable to it. Hohenlohe had complained in October 1914 of Stürgkh's ties with the Czech leader Kramář; "We have to stop ruling Slavically for a while!" he had asserted.[53] Mitteleuropa seemed to offer the assurance that Austria would not be ruled "Slavically" for a long time. Hohenlohe explained his position to Berchtold at the end of 1914: "I also believe that all of this will have to happen as soon as possible after the war, so that the *economic* common interest helps us over the *national* antagonisms, since the anti-German demands in the Monarchy after the war will be *very* great."[54] Hohenlohe hoped that closer ties with Germany would give the Monarchy the strength to create an efficient central government that would no longer be hamstrung by the selfish complaints and obstructionism of the non-German nationalities. He was not alone in his views. Berchtold's Cabinet Chief Hoyos talked about trimming the pretensions of the Austrian Slavs so much that Redlich wrote in his diary that his utterances sounded scarcely any different than those of German Ambassador Tschirschky.[55] Whether Berchtold himself went so far is unlikely, but he also welcomed the closer ties with Germany that Mitteleuropa would bring. So did Conrad.[56]

Such beliefs were not, however, shared by the central policy-makers in Vienna once Berchtold left office. Stürgkh was stubbornly set to preserve the status quo in Cisleithania from both German as well as Slav demands for change, if only because he was too rigid to accept any major deviation from the existing order. He had little sympathy for the various schemes of Mitteleuropa brought into circulation by the war, and did what he could to hinder their spread. Baernreither grumbled: "They do not have the least interest for it with the government, which is all the more remarkable since even some section chiefs working in their company are heart and soul for the thing."[57] At the same time, Tisza in Budapest set his immense energy against the whole idea. In April 1915, he reiterated his conviction that the Monarchy had to exert its position of equality in the alliance, adding, "I have also never made it a secret that I consider the propaganda emanating from certain Austrian circles for an economic union with Germany to be short-sighted, unpatriotic, and harmful."[58] Burián's position was hardly any different.

The Austrian leadership was able with little difficulty to ignore the noisy Austrian German groups agitating for Mitteleuropa, just as it tried to ignore so much else in the Monarchy. But Germany itself was another matter. The Ballplatz was already uneasy about the increasing activities of the annexationist groups in Germany and their influence with the government there. In the fall of 1915, when Berlin linked further discussion of the Polish problem to the issue of Mitteleuropa, official Austrian policy finally had to come to grips with the question.

As early as 1914, in his so-called September Program, German Chancellor Bethmann had proposed a customs union of all Central Europe (and adjacent areas) under firm German control. Whether it was still going to include the adjacent areas after the Battle of the Marne remained an open question, but there was no question that it was going to include the Monarchy. The German leadership had been haunted for years about the impending dissolution of its last certain ally in Europe, and the difficulties of its prewar relationship with Austria-Hungary were accentuated by the events of the war. If the Germans ignored it, they ran the risk of its collapsing entirely. If they aided it, they had no guarantee that their aid would not simply be squandered through misuse or outright incompetence. They felt constantly put upon to rectify disasters which, under their own leadership, they were sure never would have happened. And no matter what course they took, the Austrians seemed ungrateful. The implementation of Mitteleuropa appeared to offer a solution to all these worries and a permanent safeguard for Germany's political and economic stake in the Monarchy. Differences remained in German official circles over what priority to assign to Central European interests; while some groups believed that the Entente blockade proved that Germany should concentrate all its attention on the continent, others hoped that it could still realize political and economic ambitions overseas as well. But the general consensus was that, somehow, Austria-Hungary had to be brought under tighter German control.

In the fall of 1915, with the victories of Gorlice behind them and the question of Poland requiring solution, the Germans began to consider concrete steps to this end. Falkenhayn demanded an indissoluble bond between the two states under German hegemony: "Austria-Hungary must give up as much of its sovereignty as this requires. Since it will not do that willingly, it will have to be compelled, at the latest at the conclusion of peace." Bethmann protested that Vienna could hardly be given such a reward if they won the war; the controls would have to be more subtle. Therefore Berlin demanded as a minimum the maintenance and strengthening of the Austrian Germans in Cisleithania; hence the joining of the question of Poland and Mitteleuropa at this time. Tschirschky wrote that the erection of Mitteleuropa would not only reverse 1866 and permanently chain Austria to Germany, but solve the Polish problem by giving Congress Poland to the Monarchy while leaving it open to economic exploitation by Germany.[59]

Berlin's Mitteleuropa proposals were formally presented to Burián at the Berlin meeting of November 10 and 11, 1915, where guarantees for the Austrian German position in Cisleithania were demanded as the precondition for Berlin's assent to the Austro-Polish solution. Bethmann proposed restructuring the alliance treaty and extending its duration, concluding a military convention to make possible a more unified organization of the two armies, and gradually erecting a customs union between Germany and the Monarchy. Such a deepened alliance was more than enough to guarantee the Germans of Austria a position of domestic hegemony, for the Monarchy itself would have been subordinated to the hegemony of Berlin.

Burián replied that in principle he was in favor of deepening the alliance, but that "in details the affair would have to be carefully considered." The independence of the Habsburg army had to be preserved, and he refused to go beyond consenting to the principle of preferential tariffs as a basis for future economic negotiations. He also pointed out that trade talks would have to be coordinated with the current negotiations to renew the Ausgleich, which were dragging along interminably between Vienna and Budapest. His response to Mitteleuropa, if theoretically positive, was thus hardly enthusiastic. His main goal was probably to assent only to as much as was necessary to get Poland. As he himself afterwards admitted, the Germans displayed "very far-reaching claims" to him.[60]

Three days later, Jagow produced a memorandum for Vienna which further detailed the German Mitteleuropa proposals. The original basis of the alliance, Austrian German hegemony in Austria and Magyar in Hungary, no longer existed; therefore Jagow demanded that Austria as the "Germanic Eastern March" take measures to secure German preponderance over the

Slavs there for all time.[61] Berlin could hardly have been more blunt in expressing its belief that the multinational Monarchy (or at least its Austrian half) was little more than an extension of the German Reich, or in applying pressure to change its internal constitutional structure. Nor did the memorandum express views exclusive to Jagow. It had been prompted by Tschirschky and said nothing that Kaiser Wilhelm himself had not often affirmed. The intention to Germanize Austria received further expression in a memorandum Cramon sent to Falkenhayn at this time. Cramon was no extremist, and, as German liaison officer with the Austrian High Command, had a great deal of sympathy for the Monarchy. Yet he wanted a military convention between the two states that would instill "German spirit and German character, German discipline and order, German sense of duty and German precision" in the Austrian officer corps; he also desired suitable measures against the restive non-German nationalities. Sweeping changes would probably not come from Franz Joseph, so he set his hopes on the heir to the throne, Archduke Karl, proposing to attach a liaison officer to him to exercise "a definite, if also circumspect, control." His experiences with the Austrian military had apparently convinced him that Vienna could never overcome its traditional Schlamperei on its own.[62]

It did not take long for the Ballplatz to respond to Jagow's memorandum, and it emphatically rejected his contention that Austria was merely a "Germanic Eastern March." Burián reminded him that the German Austrians were only one of the many nationalities of the Monarchy. He also rejected Jagow's specter of a "progressive Slavicization of Austria." The increasing importance of the non-German nationalities was a positive development; and in any case it would "never be injurious to the foreign interests of our alliance."[63] Whatever Vienna's anxieties about dealing with the rising expectations of its Slav subjects, there could be no doubt that those in control there intended to solve their nationality problems without outside interference from Berlin. They knew full well that the cost would be their own independence. Yet Vienna had in fact opened the door to such interference after Sarajevo, and the dynamic of the war only made it more likely.

Burián had agreed in principle to begin discussions on Mitteleuropa, but he took no initiative. He contended that the talks could not begin until the concurrent Austro-Hungarian Ausgleich negotiations had reached a conclusion, since the economic provisions to be negotiated with Germany could not be determined until those between the two halves of the Monarchy had first been regulated. This was true enough, but the Austrian leaders had no particular interest in embarking into so complex and potentially dangerous an enterprise as Mitteleuropa any sooner than they had to. The dilemma they faced was enunciated by Alois Klepsch-Kloth, Cramon's Austrian counterpart with the Germans. Since Germany was more powerful than Austria-Hungary and egoistically viewed everything from a purely Prussian standpoint, "common" interests in any union between them would actually mean little more than "Prussian" ones. But in practically the same breath, he asserted that the alliance had already become a sine qua non for the Monarchy.[64] How, in other words, could Austria-Hungary maintain a "necessary" alliance with an ally whose latest demands threatened its own independence?

The answer, if it could be called that, was to ignore the whole problem as long as possible. Hohenlohe argued in vain that Berlin was becoming irritated at Vienna's seeming lack of interest in the Mitteleuropa negotiations; further delays might actually lead the Germans to turn to an economic orientation with Russia.[65] The Germans finally proposed beginning preliminary talks without awaiting the result of the Ausgleich negotiations. Reluctantly, Vienna agreed. Stürgkh noted that continued delay would not only exacerbate Berlin, but could also "obstruct and injure the beginning and further progress of the more important forthcoming discussion of political war aims, which it is in our interest to encourage as much as possible." [66] Once again, the Monarchy had to retreat before Germany's demands. But the first talks, over unifying the tariff schedules between the two states, began only at the end of April 1916. While Berlin ultimately wanted a full customs union, Vienna was unwilling to consent to anything more than preferential tariffs, and the negotiations dragged out inconclusively for the rest of the year.

Vienna's procrastination in bowing to Germany's Mitteleuropa desires cost it the Austro-Polish solution. Poland occupied a major place in the "forthcoming discussion of political war aims" which Stürgkh desired; if the Ballplatz continued to let the fate of Congress Poland hang indefinitely, it was afraid it would lose the support of the Poles there as well as in Galicia. At the beginning of April 1916, worried that groups in Poland might be acquiring the unwelcome expectation of complete independence, Vienna called for a clarification of the whole question. Austria would receive Poland, while Germany would get all the other conquered areas of Russia; the position of the Germans in Austria would be assured by shutting the Poles out of the Reichsrat.[67]

Unfortunately, the Germans had continued to consider the question since the previous fall, and they liked the Austro-Polish solution even less by 1916 than they had before. As Jagow wrote to Tschirschky in mid-February, continued exchanges of ideas on Mitteleuropa indicated little Austrian willingness to offer the kinds of guarantees for German national predomi-

nance in Cisleithania that Berlin considered necessary if Poland was going
to be attached to the Monarchy. Furthermore, the Monarchy already
expected to acquire Serbia and Montenegro in one form or another; if it got
Congress Poland as well, Germany in comparison would be left with only
Lithuania and a slice of Courland as Eastern war gains.[68] Tschirschky agreed
that the Austro-Polish solution could make the Monarchy too powerful for
German interests. He noted: "It has to be maintained under all circumstances
that Austria-Hungary, if not in dependence, nevertheless must remain in such
a relation to us as is determined by our incumbent protection of the entire
German Volk." [69]

Burián came to Berlin to meet with the German leaders on April 14 and
15. He thought the final details of the Austro-Polish solution would be settled.
To his astonishment, he was told that the solution itself was no longer
acceptable. "Just because of its geographical position, Poland in exclusive
possession by the Monarchy would of necessity constitute a constant standing
danger to four Prussian provinces," Jagow declared.[70] Burián argued stubbornly that the Austro-Polish solution posed no danger to Prussia; but Jagow
and Bethmann were adamant that Congress Poland would have to be made
autonomous—with ultimate control, of course, firmly in the hands of Berlin.
This became known as the German-Polish solution. Germany could hardly
assimilate that many Poles itself, but if it did not want them to go to Austria,
autonomy under veiled German domination was the only other alternative.

"It was debated back and forth for hours, without being able to reach any
agreement," Jagow reported afterwards.[71] Nor was any consensus reached
over the next few weeks. Burián refused to budge an inch, contending that
the German-Polish solution would create such an irredenta in Galicia that
the province would be made ungovernable, and that ultimately all the Poles
would be thrown into the arms of Russia. Berlin made counter-proposals to
soften Burián's opposition, but in vain. The first victories in the war thus
loosed new controversies with Berlin, and now actually confronted the
Ballplatz with the prospect that, rather than winning Poland, it might
eventually find itself losing Galicia. And the "greatly intensified self-esteem"
of the Germans combined with the Mitteleuropa issue indicated that the
bonds of the alliance itself could be exploited by Berlin to force the Monarchy
into a position of permanent dependence on its stronger ally.

V

It was probably becoming apparent in Germany by 1916 that the war
situation by itself was steadily pushing Austria-Hungary into dependence on

it, whether it agreed to formal German demands for Mitteleuropa or not. It was certainly apparent enough in Austria. Already in the winter of 1914, shortages in the weak Austrian economy began to make themselves felt, and by the spring of 1915 Tschirschky could report that much of the available bread in Vienna was of poor quality and that flour was scarcely available at all.[72] The government attempted to remedy the situation, but its efforts were fruitless; and the 1915 harvest proved to be smaller than that of 1914, which had already been below normal levels. Efforts to equalize the burden also accomplished little; the rich suffered visibly less than the poor, to the scandal of many German observers who saw in the discrepancy only another proof of Austrian incompetence and blundering.

A rational allocation of available resources was complicated by the internal conflicts between the two halves of the Monarchy. The economist Gustav Stolper later wrote that Hungary's food policies contributed more to the defeat of the Central Powers than the Entente blockade.[73] While the poor in Cisleithania were threatened with hunger, agricultural Hungary seemed almost to enjoy a surplus of foodstuffs, which it refused to share with the other half of the Monarchy except in return for political concessions. Stürgkh repeatedly begged Tisza for more grain supplies, while Tisza stubbornly insisted that Hungary had no surpluses to relinquish. Sealed off from the rest of the world by the Entente blockade, the Monarchy could turn only to Germany to cover the food deficit it was unable to provide for itself— but such imports failed to fill the ever-widening gap between available stocks and the needs of the population. As the transportation network strained against the limits of its capacities, even possession of food supplies was no assurance that they could be distributed where they were needed. Stürgkh wrote dismally in November 1915:

> The English war of starvation, as a result of three bad harvests following one after the other, has brought us into the most difficult situation. We have done everything that was possible. . . . We have to recognize, however, that after a certain amount of time, which can be predicted with all too much certainty, we are going to be at the end.[74]

By the beginning of 1916, Austrian reserves were long gone, and many areas were provided with food only on an ad hoc basis. That the situation was not even worse was due only to increased numbers of emergency shipments from Germany. In January, Stürgkh, pleading again with Tisza for more Hungarian grain, indicated how much the Austrian half of the Monarchy had

become dependent on Berlin for its sheer existence. "I just mention that last
year in June we were only able to prevent a catastrophe in Vienna because
we received from Germany—I repeat: from Germany!—2000 wagons of
flour." Tisza in reply advised Stürgkh to get the Germans to agree to a bigger
quota of the Rumanian grain export for Cisleithania, and not to hesitate too
long in trying.[75]

Nor was the Monarchy any better off financially. However successful its
initial domestic war loans, its indebtedness to Germany increased with each
month of the war at a rate which frightened many of its leaders. At a meeting
of the Common Ministers Council in June 1915, the financial state of
Austria-Hungary was discussed in detail, and the participants complained
loudly of Berlin's financial policies towards them. They freely admitted that
the Monarchy was financially dependent on Germany; in fact, one complaint
was that it was not receiving enough financial assistance. Ernst von Koerber,
the Common Finance Minister at that time, pointed out that England
subsidized its allies much more generously than Germany did its. Berlin's
financial assistance seemed deliberately calculated to further its political
ambitions; János Teleszky, the Hungarian Finance Minister, referred to efforts
to force the Monarchy under German economic domination, and Tisza
agreed that "Germany's tactic is to drive us financially and economically into
a blind ally." But what could be done? If Germany was a financial necessity
already, it would be even more so once the war was over and the work of
reconstruction began. Vienna could hardly expect financial assistance from
England or France, its former enemies. Koerber cautioned: "It therefore
would not be advisable also to close the German capital market to ourselves
through unfriendly economic relations." Tisza had to agree, despite his
objections to Mitteleuropa.[76] Yet it was obvious to all that the financial and
economic problems would only increase the longer war lasted. Half a year
later, at another Common Ministers Council, Tisza argued that the Monarchy
would have to include an indemnity among its war aims simply because of
the war's crushing economic dislocations. "He could not at all imagine how
our continued economic development after the war could be assured if we
did not succeed in getting this minimum," he confessed.[77]

After the first year of war, and then with increasing urgency, those running
the Monarchy began to realize that if the war lasted indefinitely, Austria-
Hungary would collapse from within no matter how many victories were
won on the battlefields. Even as the victorious reports from Gorlice came in,
their time was spent trying to solve economic problems that simply could not
be solved so long as the war continued. As Stürgkh had put it, the point at
which their domestic supplies of raw material and manpower would be

exhausted loomed ever nearer; and then the collapse would come—unless the conflict could be brought to a speedy conclusion beforehand.

The question of peace had not been forgotten since the Italian declaration of war. Throughout the summer of 1915, the possibilities of splitting the Entente by getting the Russians to conclude a separate peace had been kept in view. Conrad had repeatedly urged this; and Bethmann had found Tisza filled with "strong inclinations for peace" in June. Yet the Russians even after Gorlice showed no interest in a separate peace, and in September Forgách worte glumly to Berchtold: "There are unfortunately no peace possibilities at all, since our opponents are still one in hoping for victory and Germany's humiliation and our dismemberment." [78]

If victory could not be achieved nor the Entente broken, the only other possibility of ending the war was through a general compromise peace. The first prerequisite for this was for Vienna and Berlin to work out a comprehensive war aims program. Hohenlohe in Berlin repeatedly urged that this be done as a basis for a general peace proposal to the Entente. But though Burián and Bethmann touched on war aims parenthetically in their meetings over Poland and Mitteleuropa, it was only to agree that any such step would seem a sign of weakness. Burián telegraphed Hohenlohe in November 1915: "I share the view of the Reich Chancellor that such an offer right now would be harshly rejected and would only kindle the war fervor of our enemies. . . . The cause of peace at the moment is best served through an energetic continuation of the military operations." This was once again Burián's doctrinaire policy of preserving a strong front with no concessions in any direction. But thinking of peace reminded him of Belgium; and he pointed out that if an inclination for peace were going to be produced in England, Germany should make assurances that Belgium's sovereignty would be restored. "It would be commendable to keep bringing up this subject with the Reich Chancellor," he noted. Hohenlohe did so and quickly encountered a host of German reservations.[79]

Burián in the meantime continued to maintain that the initiative for peace should be left to the Entente, no doubt assuming the victories in Russia and the Balkans would have their effect, while the domestic situation in the Monarchy continued to crumble. At the end of 1915, a practical opportunity for Vienna to express its peace inclinations actually materialized—but instead Burián opted for a hard line of no compromise, which did no good and was in fact carried out over the objections of Berlin.

As the diplomatic and military preparations for the fall campaign against Serbia were completed, Berlin pressed Vienna for an agreement on Balkan war aims. The Serbs could then be presented with easy terms if they sued for peace, a contingency which would have a good propaganda effect on the rest of the world by demonstrating the Central Powers' moderation. Ironically, the Ballplatz was to spend the final two years of the war repeatedly begging the Germans to do the same thing over Belgium and the Baltic, but the Balkans were an Austrian war aim, and here Vienna would not hear of it. Burián told Tschirschky that if the Serbs made a peace offer before the opening of the campaign, it should not be allowed to interfere with the sequence of operations. The Monarchy's earlier defeats there had to be suitably avenged —at whatever cost. Tisza even complained about German agents in the Balkans trying to conclude peace with the Serbs behind their backs.[80]

The campaign opened at the beginning of October, and by the end of the month the capitulation of the Serb forces seemed imminent. Burián demanded nothing less than their unconditional surrender, to Jagow's repeated protests. "German troops are fighting in Serbia, therefore our interest [is] a deciding one," he telegraphed to Tschirschky.[81] But whatever chance there might have been of a formal peace with the Serbs was missed. King Peter and his army managed to escape across the mountains of Albania to the safety of an Entente fleet. A few months later, the whole process was repeated when the Montenegrins actually did ask for terms. The Germans wanted them made easy; they thought that a moderate peace would have a strong moral effect on Italy and Russia. Burián, however, wanted to dismember the entire kingdom, with the Monarchy getting the Lovčen and Albania inheriting portions of the remainder. He asserted that any sign of conciliation would only increase the aggressiveness of their enemies. "But if we continued along the way dictated by our interests with unshakeable calm," he added, "that would certainly have the most favorable effect and contribute most to the shortening of the war."[82] Montenegrin King Nikita fled to Italy, leaving the already-designated Austrian negotiators nobody to negotiate with. Of course, even Burián's conditions were too mild for Conrad, who had launched the Montenegrin offensive without telling the Germans and wanted to annex both Serbia and Montenegro outright.[83] In typical fashion he was soon complaining that his successes in the Balkans were being wasted by the Foreign Ministry. He even fretted that Bulgaria was taking over what ought to be Austrian preserves in Southern Serbia and Albania, and Falkenhayn had to intervene after an armed clash between Austrian and Bulgarian troops there in order to delimit their respective occupation areas.

Burián's obstinacy evoked a worried response from Tisza. During a visit of Kaiser Wilhelm to Vienna at the end of November, Tisza was concerned to find the Kaiser buoyantly underestimating the strength of the Entente, not to mention the extent of the difficulties Germany and Austria-Hungary faced themselves. A month later, he wrote Burián anxiously that although earlier he had fought faint-hearted pessimism, now he had to warn against too much optimism. "We must spare our strength and achieve peace before much longer," he said, "or else such an exhaustion of our human resources and economic strength will set in, that, even if it did not lead to our collapse in this war, it would still permanently cripple us afterwards and endanger our future." It was no longer possible to compel the enemy states to accept peace; the Entente had to be persuaded that it could win nothing by continuing the war, and this could be attained only through moderate war aims. But what was moderate? "Moderate" to Tisza still meant the virtual disappearance of Serbia as an independent entity.[84]

Hohenlohe's reaction was even stronger. He was already anxious that Burián's inflexibility over Poland and Mitteleuropa was exacerbating Berlin to no end; he complained that Burián's "talks" at the Wilhelmstraße were merely long-winded lectures which just left the Germans feeling more and more frustrated and angered. "I've warned more than once," he had written Berchtold in October, "that people here will proceed to regulate the future *without* us if we—that is, Ballplatz and Wilhelmstraße—do not *really* come closer together." At the beginning of the new year of 1916, he expressed his growing worry that the longer the war lasted, the more difficult it would be to achieve an eventual peace. The Entente, Hohenlohe posited, had perhaps had enough of the war and only fought on because it did not know their peace conditions. He continued:

> The eternal anxiety of showing weakness—on which Burián and Bethmann always insist and with which they reject my opposing suggestions—gives me much more the impression . . . that they plainly do not *know* what they want. Neither of the two is *the* statesman qui saurait *imposer* his will on all the party and nationality demands. Bethmann trembles before the conservatives, Burián before the god-like man from "Trans" [Transleithania, i.e., Tisza].

The result, he concluded, was that the war continued because the Central Powers could not formulate any war aims and fanatics like Poincaré and Nicolson remained in power in the Entente—which was critical "because we also will not be able to hold out ad infinitum."[85]

Yet nothing was done. Burián waited for an initiative from London or Paris or St. Petersburg, and he waited in vain. Far from actively and consistently working to coordinate a peace program with Berlin, he concentrated his energies on countering Germany's own claims to Poland and Mitteleuropa.

He may have thought that the longer he could put off considering peace conditions, the better he could defend the Monarchy's claim to be an equal co-belligerent in the alliance. Reality finally shattered all his pretenses in June 1916.

VI

Of all the perils threatening the Dual Monarchy, few people expected a renewed threat from the East after successes of the Gorlice offensive a year before. "A complete collapse of the Russian Empire is no longer far away," Hohenlohe wrote to Burián on June 4.[86] Ironically, the opening bombardment of the fateful Brusilov offensive began against the Austrian lines the same day. The Austrians were taken completely by surprise; they had had advance warning of the attack but had considered it nothing to worry about. In the disaster which followed, the Austrian army as an independent fighting force on the Eastern Front was broken once and for all. By the end of August, 614,000 Austrian troops had been lost.[87] Conrad, confident that the Russians were no longer capable of mounting an offensive, had sent many of his better units to Tyrol for his pet project of an offensive against Italy. Falkenhayn had protested, but in vain. Once again, the Monarchy, grasping for too much, lost all. The Asiago campaign in Italy, scarcely begun, was abruptly cancelled. It was too late. Most of the reinforcements that finally stopped the Brusilov armies were German, not Austrian, and with that the German voice in the alliance became decisive. The Austrian leadership could hardly resist all Berlin's political and economic demands at the same time that it called frantically for help to keep its own territories from being overrun. In the last months of 1916, the hard line that Vienna had tried so stubbornly to maintain was breached at one point after another.

The successes of the Brusilov breakthrough at Lutsk affected the leaders of the Monarchy as perhaps no single event of the war since the defeats in Galicia in the fall of 1914. Conrad, realizing full well that the Monarchy's whole position with Germany had been demolished, wrote Burián two weeks later to urge the necessity of coming to a speedy agreement with Berlin over war aims and the division of future acquisitions. Asserting that the Monarchy's aims were in the Balkans, he advised Burián to yield to German wishes over Poland. Burián replied calmly that there was nothing to worry about, but even he was not able to hide his pessimism. The general mood at the Ballplatz was summed up by Alexander Freiherr von Musulin, the official who drafted the text of the Sarajevo ultimatum in 1914. Even if the Russian

offensive was stopped, with Russia's immense manpower reserves, he saw no
guarantee that Russian offensives would not be repeated spring after spring,
ad infinitum.[88]

Perhaps most negative of all was the reaction of Hohenlohe in Berlin. In
a remarkable letter to Berchtold on June 27, he voiced his conclusion that
the Monarchy could no longer survive the war. Disgusted by repeated
instances of incompetence and failure among Austria's leaders, he wrote
dismally:

> The deplorable thing about it is only that we are no longer going to get out of
> this quagmire, since corruption and complete intellectual confusion—even among
> otherwise entirely upstanding people—have taken on such dimensions that, as I
> see it, there is hardly any way out of these conditions any more. Here lies the *great*
> tragedy of the Monarchy today: that it will no longer have the strength to
> overcome the difficult operation posed by the war. . . . Its *inner* organism is no
> longer capable of overcoming this great crisis; this conviction *unfortunately*
> becomes ever stronger with me. I also see the people running things as only the
> tools of the irresistible fate of the Monarchy; Burián-Tisza-Stürgkh and all the rest
> of them—each in his own way chosen by higher powers to be gravediggers of the
> Old Austria and to shovel the grave for the new Austria-Hungary.[89]

This essential pessimism formed the key to the Austrian Ambassador's
position for the rest of the war, and it was an evolution not limited to him
alone. If the Monarchy as he knew it was no longer capable of saving itself,
then the only possibility of regeneration lay in Berlin. "I was never in doubt
that the longer this great struggle lasted, the more dependent the Monarchy—
quite naturally—would become on Germany," he wrote to Burián several
months later. Even to stand on its own feet again after the war, it would have
to have German aid, and he pleaded for Vienna to avoid any unnecessary
friction with Berlin since to "tread on the Prussian curassier boots" while
Austria-Hungary was so dependent on its assistance was simply foolhardy.[90]

Militarily, the first result of the Brusilov breakthrough was the establishment of that Unified High Command on the Eastern Front which Conrad had
managed to frustrate back in 1914. Conrad was no more in favor of it now;
he argued that it would complicate military operations and in fact threatened
the continued independence of the Monarchy itself. His protests were
unavailing. Since the beginning of the war, the civil authorities had resented
Conrad's incursions into politics and his unwillingness to discuss military
matters with them. The failures of the summer of 1916 so discredited the
Austrian military leadership that most people in Vienna saw their independ-

ence more threatened without a Unified High Command than with one. Bethmann noted after a trip there in August: "The authority of the Army High Command is completely buried, with the Emperor as well as the field army and the population."[91] In 1914, Conrad had been supported in his position by Franz Joseph; now, no one supported him. When the Germans renewed their demands for a united command structure, Burián and Franz Joseph agreed. On July 27, General Paul von Hindenburg, the victor of Tannenberg and the German commander on the Eastern Front, formally assumed overall command over the northern sections of the front. This was a temporary measure to stem the Russian advance. A Unified High Command was officially set up over the entire front on September 6, with the German Kaiser in the supreme position. It was a measure of Conrad's distrust of the Germans—as well as egoism for his own position—that he was able to incorporate a secret clause into the agreement: If the Austrian High Command could not agree to some measure which affected the integrity of the Monarchy, Kaiser Wilhelm would not act without first getting Franz Joseph's approval. But except for this loophole, the direction of the Eastern Front now passed officially into German hands.

The second military military consequence of the Brusilov offensive carried far greater longterm consequences for Austria-Hungary. In late August, encouraged by the Russian offensive, Rumania finally declared war on the Monarchy. After the start of the Brusilov advance, Burián, nervously remembering Germany's reaction to Italian belligerency a year earlier, had repeatedly prodded Berlin to learn its reaction to a Rumanian attack on Transylvania. This time, the German response was all that could have been desired. A German declaration of war followed immediately and a lightning campaign—led by German generals and made possible only by German troops—quickly cleared Transylvania of hostile forces and proceeded to occupy all of western Rumania, including Bucharest. But if Vienna had feared a Rumanian attack, Falkenhayn, the German General Staff Chief, had not; he was already under attack from various quarters in Germany, and this oversight cost him his job. The day after the Rumanian declaration of war, he was replaced by Hindenburg. Erich von Ludendorff, Hindenburg's Chief of Staff, now became Quartermaster General of the German army. The new position of Hindenburg and Ludendorff in the German Army High Command (Oberste Heeresleitung, or OHL) was anchored not only in the immense prestige that the two of them enjoyed in Germany as a result of their Eastern victories, but in the entrenched position of power held by the army and conservative interest groups there.

The pressure of the annexationist groups in the Reich was now consolidated in a ruthlessly annexationist German High Command against which even Bethmann's famous "policy of the diagonal" could have little impact. A month after the formal initiation of the Unified High Command on the Eastern Front, Conrad sent a long letter of warning to Vienna. Despite all his personal conflicts with Falkenhayn, he maintained that Falkenhayn's measures had not involved the full sovereignty of the Monarchy. But Ludendorff, who he correctly saw as the dominant force in the new command structure, intended nothing less than the complete military and political subjugation of Austria-Hungary to Germany. "He is attributed with the statement, 'Germany's victory prize in this war must be Austria,'" Conrad noted. The Germans would now quicken the tempo of their dealings with Vienna with "Bismarckian ruthlessness." What was to be done? Conrad urged a clarification of the Monarchy's relations in a binding state treaty with Germany as soon as possible.[92] His position thus became similar to Hohenlohe's: to come to terms with Berlin before it was too late. But it was already too late for Conrad himself to influence policy further in this direction. Continuous defeats had sunk his influence far below what it had been at the outbreak of the war.

The effect on the Monarchy of the change in the German High Command would soon become apparent. The pressure began, however, even before Hindenburg-Ludendorff came into power, as the initial breakthrough at Lutsk destroyed the Austrian bargaining position in the alliance and the Wilhelmstraße moved to take advantage of the fact. Burián later admitted to Baernreither that the Austrian collapse at Lutsk was the final blow to the Austro-Polish solution.[93] At the time, he attempted to remain as unyielding to Berlin as ever, but it was an untenable position and the Germans knew it. "It has to become clear to our allies that it will not do to go to the strong brother to get help in time of need, and then to empty his pockets after the danger is over," Jagow wrote to Tschirschky.[94]

By late July, both Tisza and Stürgkh had reconciled themselves to giving up the Austro-Polish solution. The weakness of the Monarchy in the alliance made that decision inevitable for them; the Austro-Polish solution could not be carried out against German opposition and therefore had to be sacrificed. Tisza wanted the Monarchy to abandon not only the Austro-Polish solution, but all claim to equality with Germany in Poland whatever the solution. He calculated that Vienna's claims would otherwise merely cause more friction in the alliance, and to no result since the Monarchy, being weaker than its ally, would still have to yield in the end. Furthermore, he knew that the Poles would be enraged to be turned over to German control, but assumed that if the Monarchy dissociated itself from Poland completely it would escape the odium for such a thing. The harmony of the alliance took precedence over all Austrian claims to Russian Poland, especially if the complications could be transferred onto German shoulders. Of course, Tisza had never been particularly enthusiastic about the Austro-Polish solution in any case because of the dangers it posed to the Ausgleich. Stürgkh's position was similar; it was simply a question of power, and maintaining the alliance was more important than fruitless protests against the German position. Both of them agreed that the economic weakness of the Monarchy made continued resistance inadvisable, and both hoped for further German support of the Monarchy's faltering financial structure in return for acceding on this issue.[95]

Tisza and Stürgkh finally brought Burián to accept the inevitable, and on July 27 he formally gave up the Austro-Polish solution. But the hard line persisted; Burián made Austria consent subject to various safeguards for Austrian interests in Congress Poland, and, whatever Tisza had advised, demanded complete parity for Austrian and German influence there. Berlin simply refused. The problem was further complicated by the question of a Polish army, which came to the fore with the Brusilov offensive. To the German military, acutely conscious of its strained manpower resources, the possibility of recruiting a Polish army to share some of the weight of battling Russia was an enticing prospect. But a Polish army could not be created unless the Polish soldiers were given some positive goal that they would fight for. Berlin therefore wanted not only the end of the Austro-Polish solution, but the proclamation of Poland as an independent state (at least in name) as the basis for recruiting an army.

As these plans became concrete, it became obvious in Vienna that the Monarchy would have scarcely any voice in the future of Poland as the Germans intended it. Burián's bitterness can be imagined. He stubbornly refused one German demand after another, while both sides became more and more angry and suspicious. When Bethmann came to Vienna on August 11 and 12, it was decided that Poland would become a constitutional monarchy tied to the Central Powers; but that was practically all that could be decided. Burián conceded German control of the projected Polish army, but he protested emphatically that Bethmann's intentions to include Poland in the German customs union would injure Austrian economic interests. A month later, Hindenburg proposed uniting the two occupation areas of Congress Poland under the Warsaw government as the basis for recruiting a unified army. To this, Burián reacted sharply that there could be no question of the Monarchy evacuating its sphere in Lublin to the Germans. The Austrian-organized Polish Legion caused endless friction. By October, Tschirschky was asserting to Burián that Germany had to have political control in Poland to realize its military predominance there, while Burián reiterated stubbornly that such a demand violated the August agreement and was simply "unacceptable."[96]

The Pleß meeting between Burián and Bethmann on October 18 finally resolved enough differences that it could be decided to proclaim the independence of Poland as soon as possible. The Polish army was put in German hands, but the two military occupation areas of Congress Poland remained separate. Burián's subsequent resumé of the meeting gives a good idea of how he and his German colleagues by this point were conducting business with each other:

> Indeed, in the course of the conference, which, with a pause at noon, lasted for nearly the whole day, the complete register of German debating skills came into use: now the emotional appeal to allied friendship and trust; then the pathetic reference to the seriousness of the whole situation; then, with the true ring of conviction, the emphasis of military categorical imperatives; and finally, dialectical attacks and attempts at distortion.[97]

The conference seemed to preserve Austrian political equality with Germany in Poland, but the transitory nature of the solution did not take long to become apparent. Scarcely a week later, Leopold Freiherr von Andrian, the Ballplatz representative with the German administration in Warsaw, voiced his suspicions that the Germans had only postponed their intention to drive the Monarchy out of Poland entirely and continued their work of undermining Austria-Hungary's prestige there.[98] The independence of Poland was officially proclaimed on November 5. At the same time, Vienna, its anxieties unallayed that the step would eventually cost it Galicia, proclaimed its intention of granting that province a special position within the Monarchy. Berlin reacted sharply to the Galician declaration, seeing it as another Austrian attempt to strengthen its position in Congress Poland. A week later, the Germans unilaterally called into being a Polish State Council, provoking even sharper protests from Vienna. All the conferences and exchanges over Poland had accomplished little, except to show how hopeless was the conflict between Austrian and German aims and how little faith either of them had in the ultimate intentions of the other.

The protracted negotiations and recriminations over Poland indicated clearly the gradual crumbling of Burián and Tisza's policy of the hard line towards Germany. Burián may have been an expert at doctrinaire stubbornness and opposition, but such a position was in the long run untenable under the crushing military and economic burden of the war. The result was that he usually found himself having to abandon his position anyway, but only after embittering everyone he worked with and getting nothing in return. After nearly two years of such conduct, he was isolated in the Foreign Ministry and government from nearly all his colleagues except Tisza. Forgách thought he should be removed from office, not only because he had lost contact with reality, but because his personality was unnecessarily complicating the alliance. Hohenlohe was so exasperated with him that he actually suggested to Bethmann that the German Chancellor should declare that he could no longer work with him—rather astonishing advice for an ambassador to give a foreign head of government. Hohenlohe's behavior pointed out the limits to which any Austrian leader could go in taking a strong stand against Germany without losing the loyalty of his own subordinates; Burián had reached the limit. Even Franz Joseph appeared to be tired of him.[99]

The Germans felt the same. Tschirschky at the end of September had described conditions within the Monarchy as simply catastrophic, with Stürgkh incompetent and Tisza interested only in Hungary. Burián was oblivious to the whole situation. Improvement would come only if their regime was replaced by one with the initiative to deal actively with what was happening. Bethmann agreed and recommended that Kaiser Wilhelm discuss the situation with the heir to the throne, Archduke Karl. Wilhelm made no secret of Berlin's disgust with Burián when he met Karl in Pleß a week later: "With Burián, nothing can be done." Burián, no less bitter towards the Germans, was meanwhile doing all he could to get Tschirschky replaced by a new German Ambassador in Vienna.[100]

It was in this atmosphere that Burián finally suggested to Bethmann that the Central Powers present a formal peace proposal to the Entente. By the end of the summer, the Brusilov offensive had been beaten back, Rumania was being overrun, and the Entente had failed to break the German lines in France. After these accomplishments, it could at last be argued that a peace proposal would not look like an admission of weakness. Burián made the suggestion at the same October 18 meeting at Pleß that supposedly settled the future of Poland. It was long overdue. Hoyos had noted in August that although even Burián saw the need for peace, his personality was such that he would take no initiative unless pushed into it by Tisza.[101] And so nothing had been done throughout the summer months, nothing until the fate of Poland was theoretically decided in October.

Burián's and Tisza's alliance policy towards Germany, already undermined, received its final blow with the Central Powers' peace note. Burián proposed that the Central Powers officially publish their peace conditions, so that even if they were not accepted by the Entente, their moderation would have a good propaganda effect on the enemy and neutral states. But Bethmann refused to agree to a publication of concrete terms, not only because he feared that the action would rob him of any negotiating flexibility, but perhaps even more because a publication of German aims would have had an anything but favorable propaganda value in the rest of the world. It would undoubtedly have complicated his domestic position between the rival German political parties. So all he was willing or able to do was to issue a joint statement that the Central Powers were willing to end the war, without describing under what conditions.

When Vienna finally proposed a formal peace note by the Central Powers, it consequently found its wishes for a straightforward peace proposal blocked in Berlin, despite its urgent need to get out of the war while the situation still remained at all favorable. It was eventually forced to agree to a peace note without conditions. Burián persisted in trying to formulate a common war aims program between the two capitals, even if it would not be published. But here, as he discovered in Berlin in the middle of November, the Germans insisted on plans for control of Belgium and northern France which he could only describe as impossible to fulfill.[102] A quick end to the war seemd to be blocked by German annexationist aims and noncooperation. Unfortunately, Burián's own proposed aims hardly looked any less annexationist: He suggested border rectifications against Russia and Rumania, restoration of Serbia minus Macedonia and its Albanian-populated areas (not leaving particularly much to restore), Montenegro's annexation by the Monarchy, and the prohibition of any economic warfare against the Central Powers after the conclusion of peace. Germany would give up most of its gains in the West, to be compensated by Lithuania and Courland in the East; and the new entity of Poland would remain on the map.[103] These hardly looked like the aims of a power which had to get out of the conflict before it collapsed from internal prostration, and Berlin replied heatedly against Burián's own extensive war aims. How, after all, could Vienna argue for the necessity of ending the war while at the same time presenting a catalog of demands like that?

Nothing in Burián's points received a colder response than his demand that Germany guarantee the territorial integrity of the Monarchy at the peace conference. In July, when Burián finally gave up the Austro-Polish solution, he had not only demanded parity of interests with Germany in the new Polish buffer state, but German acceptance of the principle that "to get back territory of the Central Powers still occupied by the enemy at the end of the war, *all* captured enemy areas in our possession remain liable as securities which can be used as objects of exchange, depending on how necessary this is made by the war situation."[104] In practical terms, this meant that since East Galicia was still occupied by the Russians, while virtually none of Germany was in enemy control (outside of a small strip of Alsace-Lorraine), Burián wanted German-occupied areas (Belgium, northern France, Lithuania) as well as those under Austrian control (Serbia, Montenegro) subject to exchange to restore the Monarchy to its 1914 borders at the conclusion of peace. The Ballplatz had occasionally considered the chances of exchanging Congress Poland to get East Galicia back, but after it gave up the Austro-Polish solution, it no longer had Poland to exchange. The old demand of the summer was now renewed. Burián proposed an official agreement that the occupied areas would not be evacuated until all the Central Powers' territory had been given back.[105] Vienna was obviously afraid that at the peace conference Berlin might not be above buying peace at its ally's expense, just as Berlin had tried earlier with Habsburg territory to keep Italy and Rumania out of the war. But the Germans saw no reason to pledge themselves to give up their own conquests to restore East Galicia to the Monarchy, or to continue fighting just so that Austria-Hungary came out of the war intact. If there was going to be talk of territorial integrity, Berlin wanted all its colonies included as well—an obviously impossible demand.[106]

The Central Powers' peace note was issued on December 12, 1916, couched in the general platitudes Bethmann had insisted on earlier, even though Vienna and Berlin were nowhere near agreement on war aims. It was rejected by the Entente two and a half weeks later. The war aims Burián had proposed would have made Entente acceptance unlikely in any case; but German refusal to state any conditions at all made rejection certain and also robbed the note of any propaganda effect.

The inadequacy of Burián's methods of diplomacy was now fully apparent. Burián had persisted in an essentially negative policy, allowing the Germans the initiative in most things and simply opposing them when German initiative seemed to threaten the Monarchy's own interests—which was more and more often. For all his intransigent opposition to specific German demands, he had never called the alliance itself into question. Even to take enough initiative to propose the peace note to Bethmann had followed only after months of prodding by practically everybody else with a voice in making Austrian foreign policy. Austria-Hungary did not have much to show for his efforts. It was as far away from a solution to its problems as ever; and the longer the war lasted, the worse its position would logically become—if it did not simply fall to pieces first.

Yet there were other channels of action which Burián with his lack of imagination had never considered. For two irreplaceable years, Austrian leaders had persisted in holding unrealistically extensive peace conditions while they set all their hopes on Berlin's finding a way to end the war for them. Perhaps, however, there were possibilities that Vienna could itself find a way to end the war—or at least revitalize its position within the alliance— if only it mustered the energy to seize the initiative. In November, Macchio, back from Rome, told the German publicist Viktor Naumann:

> You naturally have the better trumps in your hand now since you are militarily and organizationally superior to us. But you should not forget that we will have the better diplomatic position in the end, since the neutrals are more favorable to us and on the other side they hate you far more than they do us.[107]

His words were not just idle talk, for Bethmann was well aware that the Monarchy had no real conflict of interest with England or France even after two years of war. He feared that if Germany pressed it too hard, it could join them against Berlin at the peace conference.[108] If those in Vienna had periodically thought about this aspect of their position over the last two years, especially in early 1915 before the Italian declaration of war, they had never done much to exploit it. As the situation within the Monarchy deteriorated and Vienna found its role in the alliance hamstrung by one German demand after another, could these potential ties to the West not be utilized in some way or another before it was too late?

This was a question which the old order in the Dual Monarchy would not be able to answer. At the end of October, Stürgkh was assassinated by the Socialist Friedrich Adler. A month later, Franz Joseph breathed his last. The death of the Emperor had been anticipated and feared for years; and now, in the third winter of the war, it finally came to pass. Archduke Karl, his grand-nephew, inherited a throne burdened with crushing problems the solutions to which had been postponed for decades, and a war that could no longer be won. One of his first acts was to dismiss Burián from office. A new beginning would have to be made, and it was going to be made by new men.

Chapter 5

THE NEW MEN
December 1916-March 1917

I

At the end of September, Tschirschky sent a long report on conditions in Austria-Hungary to Berlin. It was one of his last acts as German Ambassador in Vienna, for he died in office a few weeks later. "The longer the war lasts, the more acute becomes the anxious question of how much longer the Austro-Hungarian Monarchy will be able to endure the struggle, economically as well as militarily," he wrote. Militarily, complaints against the officer corps were universal, and morale negative and resigned; the Monarchy was nearing the complete exhaustion of its manpower reserves. Economically, the situation was no better. Tschirschky described economic conditions as "simply wretched," complaining that there was no economic organization whatsoever. Inchoate Austrian attempts to mobilize the economy for war had foundered under the weight of Schlamperei and corrupt favoritism. The population in the suburbs of Vienna was starving. An economic catastrophe could soon be expected, as well as the bankruptcy of the entire state because of its tottering financial structure. Tschirschky further noted that the Austrian and Hungarian halves of the Monarchy, instead of working together to combat the common danger, were now after two years of war farther apart than ever. His conclusion, needless to say, was that Berlin would have to intercede and repair the damage, since otherwise Austria-Hungary could suddenly collapse and pull down its German ally with it. Bethmann forwarded Tschirschky's report to Kaiser Wilhelm, noting, "I am afraid Herr von Tschirschky does not paint too blackly." [1]

Tschirschky's dispatch showed clearly the paradoxical, if not tragic, results of the Burián-Tisza alliance policy. The alliance had allowed the status quo of Burián, Stürgkh, and Tisza to be maintained; but that system was simply not up to the monumental task of providing for the demands of the war. Whether some other regime would have been any better, given the Monarchy's basic weaknesses, is open to question; but by the close of 1916, the failures of the existing one were obvious. Yet those failures opened the door to the very German influence that Burián and Tisza had wanted to prevent. If Austria-Hungary could not maintain an efficient war economy on its own, its shortcomings virtually invited its powerful German ally to bring order out of the chaos—on its own terms. The Germans were hardly likely to provide economic aid without some sort of assurance that it was put to what they considered good use and not simply squandered; and "good use" involved political as much as economic considerations.

The Germans were soon surprised to discover that conditions within the Monarchy were even worse than Tschirschky had reported, for Burián had attempted to underplay the Monarchy's economic difficulties as long as possible in order to bolster his diplomatic bargaining position. Now, time was running out. Industrial production had actually increased in 1915 and 1916, but from the end of 1916 it began to fall drastically until it reached a condition of complete collapse in 1918. The scarcity of coal was first apparent in the winter of 1916-1917; in January and February 1917, despite critical grain shortages, there was no coal to be spared to run the mills in Budapest.[2] Transport difficulties increased; the amount of rolling stock in service steadily declined. Iron and steel production faltered. As conditions in one industry worsened, they affected those in related or dependent industries, and shortages and declining production began to derange the entire economy despite everything the centralized wartime economic organizations attempted to counter the process.

Nowhere was the situation worse than in the area of foodstuffs. From the beginning of the war, agricultural production began a precipitous decline uninterrupted by any improvement. Each successive year saw a greater grain deficit than the year before. Reliable figures were never achieved, but it has been estimated that even in 1914 the Monarchy was 9.8 million quintals short of meeting its own grain needs—a figure which increased to 37.1 million for 1916.[3] The decline was due to a number of causes—shortages of labor as peasant field workers were called into the army, lack of sufficient fertilizer, inefficient government regulation, hoarding. Because of the Entente blockade, the only external sources of supply were Rumania and Germany. Characteristically, Burián tried to ignore the whole problem as long as possible. In July 1915, he optimistically informed a meeting of the Common Ministers Council that the Monarchy was no longer dependent on imports of Rumanian grain.[4] He was soon proven wrong. The speedy occupation of western Rumania following the Rumanian declaration of war in 1916 kept its grain reserves open to the Monarchy; but Germany assumed control of the occupation administration, so that no allocation of grain from occupied Rumania could be made without German agreement. In any case, even such imports could not bridge the constantly widening gap between supply and demand in the Monarchy.

The food problem, which by the end of 1916 had begun to assume catastrophic dimensions, was a major cause of the Monarchy's growing dependence on Germany. At the beginning of September, in the wake of the Rumanian declaration of war, a Common Ministers Council was held to discuss the situation, which Burián admitted was becoming ever more serious. Stürgkh was pessimistic, describing conditions in Cisleithania in dismal terms and asserting that it was impossible to lower the per capita ration of flour there. Alexander von Krobatin, the War Minister, pointed to signs of malnutrition diseases in the army. Yet no real conclusion was reached, beyond Burián's hope that the Germans, in relatively better condition, would spare some of their grain supplies in return for Austrian oil. But he noted that Berlin would undoubtedly attach conditions to any grain it shipped to the Monarchy.[5]

Nothing concrete was done. A month later, Simon Joannovics, the department head in charge of economic affairs in the Foreign Ministry, wrote worriedly to Burián that getting more supplies of grain had become "an unpostponable necessity."[6] Burián agreed that Germany would have to be told the proportions of the crisis. On October 16, at another Common Ministers Council, he announced that the Germans had in the meantime told him that they could send no help because of a bad potato harvest, which Tisza greeted almost with relief, not wanting to become any more dependent on Berlin than was already the case. Stürgkh was far less relieved at the news. Negotiations with the German government were "imperative," he asserted. A long verbal tussle over supply inequalities between Austria and Hungary followed. The two halves of the Monarchy could still not agree between themselves on the dimensions of the crisis.[7]

But that there was a crisis could scarcely be denied, and another meeting of the Common Ministers Council in January finally agreed to renew Austrian pleas for more German assistance. Not only did general food supply negotiations begun in November have to be completed, but the Monarchy had to get a larger allocation of grain from occupied Rumania. A near-term grain deficit of 12 million quintals was expected.[8] When Hohenlohe told Karl Helfferich, the German Finance Minister, how great the deficit was, Helfferich was "most painfully surprised" that it had reached such a size and was visibly shaken in view of the problems in meeting Germany's own needs.[9] Food supply shortages had reached a point in the Monarchy where German aid had literally become a matter of life and death. In March 1917, when Bethmann was due to visit Vienna for political consultations, even Tisza was ready to tell the Ballplatz: "His stay in Vienna must be intensively used by all of us to get the absolutely necessary German assistance in the food supply question."[10]

The rivalry between the two halves of the Monarchy continued to hamper any effective solution of the crisis. It was only on February 27, 1917, that an Empire-wide organization to coordinate food supply, headed by General Ottokar Landwehr von Pragenau, was set up—a measure long overdue. Budapest, intent on preserving its special status within the realm, had consistently opposed the formation of any new agency common to both Austria and Hungary; the policy of the Magyar oligarchy was to loosen the bonds tying it to Cisleithania, not to create new ones. Landwehr's organization was placed directly under Emperor Karl so that no constitutional precedents unwanted by Budapest would be created. It had authority only to persuade, not to command, and each half of the Empire continued to have its own separate food administration as well. Magyar chauvinism merely drove the Monarchy further into dependence on Berlin, for if the Hungarians refused to send more of their grain to the Austrian half of the state, Germany was the only other place to turn. Despite his protests, Landwehr was unable to compel Hungary to make greater sacrifices.[11] The Hungarians' behavior afforded Berlin ample reason not to concede the Monarchy anything, as the Austro-Hungarian delegates reported ruefully after a March 1917 meeting with Hindenburg and Ludendorff in Berlin. "The Germans would continually point out that German officers coming from Hungary declared unanimously that the food supply question in Hungary was incomparably better than in Germany or Austria," they noted. Their attempts to counter the German assertions "remained completely ineffective."[12]

Nor was the political situation within Austria-Hungary much more reassuring after two years of war. The popular enthusiasm of the weeks following Sarajevo had long since melted into dull apathy or opposition. In those areas of Cisleithania where military administration had replaced civil, a forceful policy against proven or suspected enemy sympathizers, mainly Slav, had been initiated, culminating in the famous treason trial of the Czech leader Karel Kramář. The Reichsrat remained prorogued. In Hungary, where parliamentary life—such as it was—continued, Mihály Károlyi and his small band of followers broke openly with the pro-war parliamentary majority in 1916, forming a separate faction to work for a speedy end to the conflict as well as an extension of the Hungarian franchise and a further loosening of the constitutional ties with Vienna. They were supported by the Hungarian Social Democrats. By the beginning of 1917, it was becoming apparent in both halves of the Monarchy that the national and social demands of large groups of the population, momentarily dampened by the outbreak of hostilities, had in no way been satisfied.

In 1914, many had recognized the Monarchy's structural problems and speculated on its future viability. But even its most vehement critics had usually not advocated its dissolution as a positive goal to strive for. Now, however, those nationalities who found their demands within the framework of the Monarchy denied were presented the alternative of satisfying them by destroying that framework entirely—by linking up with the Entente in a program to shatter Austria-Hungary into its constituent national parts in order to win the war. At the end of 1914, Tomáš Masaryk left Vienna for Rome and in the following year became head of a Czech National Committee in London. Masaryk was only the most successful of several nationality leaders working in exile in the Entente states. Their success would mean the end of Austria-Hungary as a unified political entity.

The exile leaders did not face an easy battle in working for recognition and support among the Entente powers. Their aims conflicted not only with each other but also with many of those of the Entente itself. Neither London nor Paris, where they sought their greatest aid, had much desire to destroy the Monarchy as the exiles advocated. The primary aim of the British and the French was to defeat Germany, and what happened to Austria-Hungary was for them strictly secondary. They would treat the Monarchy in whatever manner seemed most likely to advance victory over the Germans. This in practice meant either of two policies, depending on the course of the war. One was to relegate Vienna to the position of war booty with which to acquire new allies (and hold onto old ones); already they had promised large areas of Tyrol and Dalmatia to Italy, Bosnia-Herzegovina to Serbia, and Transylvania and the Banat to the Rumanians, while leaving Russia a free hand to deal with Poland and Galicia. The result of such amputations would hardly have left a viable Habsburg state in Central Europe.

The second course involved a special arrangement or separate peace with the Monarchy, a desire which became especially strong in 1917 after the abdication of the Czar. If Germany could not be defeated by direct assault, perhaps victory could be achieved by isolating it from its chief ally. Such a policy meant not the dismemberment of Austria-Hungary, but its preservation essentially intact; the Monarchy would replace collapsing Russia as a brake on German power in Central Europe. This line of reasoning received its strongest support from the British, particularly British Prime Minister David Lloyd George. The French seem to have been more reluctant, or at least more sensitive about antagonizing Italy by tampering with the terms of the Treaty of London. Neither Britain nor France, of course, had any territorial claims on the Monarchy themselves, though they had signed treaties underwriting those of its more immediate neighbors. If a deal that would end the war could be made with Vienna, could they be expected to continue fighting just so Rome could annex the Brenner, or Rumania Transylvania?

The possibility of such an arrangement with the Entente depended on the Monarchy's ability to preserve its integrity from all the powers around it. Yet the longer the war lasted, the more it appeared to become merely a satellite of Berlin, making its present or future use as a counterweight to Germany in the European diplomatic system impossible. German de facto domination of Central Europe through a totally subservient Austria-Hungary was something no Entente government could accept—as the exile groups never ceased to remind them. Growing Austrian dependence on Germany pushed the Entente towards acceptance of the radical exile program of dissolution as the only alternative. The January 10, 1917, answer of the Entente to American President Wilson's 1916 mediation offer was a clear indication of the fate in store for the Monarchy if it remained firmly tied to Germany while losing the war; the Entente note called for "the liberation of Italians, of Slavs, of Rumanians, and of Czechoslovaks from foreign domination."[13]

Since the outbreak of hostilities, Austria-Hungary's leaders had held to a policy of domestic and foreign immobility, freezing the internal order as much as possible and blindly assuming that close adherence to the German alliance would eventually lead to victory. Instead, it had led to military defeat, economic chaos, and rising political unrest. The losses on the Russian front had been tremendous; and if the lines there seemed to have been stabilized with German help by 1917, in the southwest against Italy one Isonzo battle after another was straining the army to its limits. Despite all the problems and contradictions besetting it, the Monarchy still somehow held together— much to the amazement of many foreign observers. But the policy that had hitherto been followed had clearly reached a point of bankruptcy. A reappraisal of the status quo, and even more of the German alliance that held it together and also held Austria in the war, was obviously necessary.

II

The passing of Franz Joseph marked a major watershed in the history of the Dual Monarchy. Kaiser Karl, his successor, was not yet thirty when he ascended the Habsburg throne, unknown and untried to those around him. Whatever the old Emperor's failings, few had questioned his essential decency of character; that, and his very longevity, had inspired a loyalty among the polyglot peoples of the Monarchy that Karl could only hope to replace with youthful idealism. "Sense of duty and goodwill were certainly his characteristic qualities," Landwehr later reminisced of the new Emperor.[14] Yet those were practically the only qualities he possessed with which to face the problems confronting the realm—those and an almost intuitive belief that things could no longer continue as they were. Before Sarajevo, there was little to distinguish his life except an almost idyllically happy marriage to Zita of Parma; his political experience was nil. He was intelligent, sensitive, pleasant, deeply religious, and naive: capable of compulsive measures but without the willpower to sustain consistent policies against determined opposition. This was his great weakness. Anatole France later called him a saint,[15] but an other-worldly saint was the last thing Austria-Hungary needed during the First World War. Nevertheless, where Franz Joseph had little more than passively approved his advisers' policies in the last years of his reign, Karl intended to take an active part in decision-making, and, despite his inexperience, to alter both the domestic and the foreign policy basis of the Monarchy. Moreover, he intended to begin without waiting for the end of the war, despite the danger that he might just undermine the old order through precipitate measures without replacing it with anything else. It soon became apparent that he had scarcely any idea how to effect the transformation he desired. Yet his intuition of the changes necessary if the Monarchy were to survive the war was often of greater perception and foresight than the opinions of all his supposedly more experienced advisers.

Nowhere was Karl's conviction firmer than in his belief that it was his duty to end the war as quickly as possible. He was a devout Catholic, and the strength of his desire for peace was grounded in religious as much as practical considerations. His pacifism was expressed to almost everyone who talked with him; it was the subject of his first proclamation as Emperor and quickly became a cause of concern for the Germans. Count Botho von Wedel, who replaced Tschirschky as German Ambassador in Vienna after the latter's death, had much more understanding and tolerance for the Monarchy's problems than Tschirschky had ever been able to muster; but even Wedel was alarmed at Karl's longing for peace and made clear his belief that for

Austria-Hungary's own good it should be toned down.[16] Many of the Monarchy's statesmen were inclined to agree with him. Karl's idealistic pacifism might be muted momentarily by his advisers, but it remained the burning passion of his reign—the more so the longer those advisers themselves failed to produce any end to the hostilities.

Karl's ascent to the throne also marked a watershed in the alliance with Germany. Cramon later wrote: "Austria-Hungary ceased to be loyal to the alliance in the fullest sense of the word."[17] Much of Cramon's judgment reflected the post-Versailles German search for scapegoats to explain their loss of the war, but it was not entirely without foundation. Karl shared neither the domestic nor the foreign policy assumptions that had guided his predecessor. The Ausgleich, the domestic anchor of the connection with Berlin, was anathema to him, and his inarticulate but nevertheless real desire to transform the Monarchy into some form of federal state would have destroyed once and for all the alliance's traditional basis among the Austrian Germans and the Magyars. Nor was his love of Germany any greater; Germany had become a "pure military dictatorship," he informed Burián at the beginning of December.[18] In a long summary of his views five months later, he made his position even clearer. Reflecting his own Habsburg dynastic loyalty, he wrote that the work of the Hohenzollerns was to reduce the Monarchy's relation with Germany to that of the status of Bavaria, by encouraging Italy's pretensions against it and by exploiting the war to make it militarily and economically dependent on Berlin. "A smashing German victory would be our ruin," he noted grimly. This was assuming that Germany won the war—but what if it lost? In that case, "Going to ruin with Germany just out of pure noblesse cannot be reconciled with Germany's previous behavior." On the other hand, the Western powers of England and France were not really Austria's enemies, and he actually hoped once the war was ended for an alliance with France to lessen the Monarchy's one-sided reliance on Berlin.[19] As the Germans repeatedly blocked his efforts to stop the fighting by their demands for economic concessions and annexations of territory, his impatience with them grew.

Karl's desire for change—and its limitations—began to be manifest practically as soon as he became Emperor. Ernst von Koerber, who had been named Austrian Minister-President after Stürgkh's assassination, was replaced by Count Heinrich Clam-Martinic, a member of the Bohemian nobility. Karl gave Clam the task of preparing the reopening of the Reichsrat and the building of a ministry of all the Austrian nationalities. Tisza, deprived of the certain support he had enjoyed under Franz Joseph, was clearly on the defensive in Hungary. A new age seemed to be dawning. Yet the changes were often more apparent than real. Karl might appoint and dismiss ministers at will, but the basic order continued untouched. Clam was certainly more flexible than Stürgkh, for example, but no more inclined towards radical constitutional experiments or dramatic shifts in the Monarchy's relations with Germany.

Karl also asserted his initiative militarily, with similar mixed results. He announced that he would assume personal command over the Austrian armed forces. The Archduke Friedrich was eventually retired. He moved the location of the Army High Command from Teschen to Baden outside Vienna, where it was further away from Germany and more easily supervised from his own seat of residence. The Unified High Command agreement with Germany was renegotiated. Moreover, the military administration extended over much of Austria in 1914 was now dismantled, piece by piece. Karl's military initiatives culminated in Conrad's dismissal as Chief of Staff on February 27, after rising friction over both political and military matters. Conrad had resisted the Emperor's incursions into what he considered his own sphere of authority, and Karl resented Conrad's persistent attempts to wield political as well as military influence. Perhaps even more decisive than the conflict of authority between them was the question of the alliance. While Karl was deeply suspicious of the Germans, Conrad in the wake of Austria's defeats was inclining more and more to an accommodation with them, giving up as no longer tenable his earlier assertiveness towards Berlin. In the middle of December, he had again urged Burián to give way to German wishes in Poland before continued attempts at opposition cost them Germany's alliance support: "Every such attempt would only lead to the complete isolation of the Monarchy and the loss of that firm tie with the German Reich which has proved itself so much in this war and is alone capable of giving us a militarily acceptable solution for the future." [20] This was a far cry from the Conrad of the first years of the conflict.

Conrad's replacement was Arthur Arz von Straussenburg. Arz had none of Conrad's egocentric assertiveness and was certainly less forceful in expressing his opinions. He spent a good deal of time accompanying Karl on his numerous tours throughout the Monarchy, in part, according to the staff officer Glaise von Horstenau, to make sure that his opinions were heard at all.[21] In his absence from army headquarters, considerable military responsibility devolved on Alfred von Waldstätten, his Chief of Operations. This division of authority further weakened Arz's ability to speak with the same weight that Conrad had enjoyed. But if Karl hoped he could induce his new army chief to actively support his own political ideas, he was mistaken. Arz was a firm supporter of the alliance and the domestic status quo, justifying that position on the grounds of maintaining the efficiency of the army. He later noted in his memoirs:

> But since any alteration of the constitutional structure of the Monarchy would necessarily result in an alteration in the armed forces, I had to resist all such attempts just as much as a loosening or dissolution of the bond that tied us in strong unity to Germany.[22]

Despite Karl's attempts at reform, the military remained attached to the old order.

By far, the most momentous of all Karl's changes occurred in the Foreign Ministry. His replacement for Burián was Count Ottokar Czernin von und zu Chudenitz, who remained Austrian Foreign Minister until April 1918. Czernin remains as controversial a figure today as Karl himself. Much that he did, as well as his relations with Karl, have never been entirely explained. He was a complex, often contradictory, figure.

Czernin, like Clam, was member of the Bohemian aristocracy, no Austrian German nationalist but nevertheless strongly German in his personal identity. After a brief stint in the diplomatic service, he quit to become active first in the Bohemian Landtag, and later the Austrian Herrenhaus. Before the war, he was a close member of Franz Ferdinand's Belvedere Circle, and it was Franz Ferdinand who secured his appointment as Austrian Minister to Rumania in late 1913. He outdid even the Archduke in his violent conservatism—perhaps deliberately. In 1908, he published a book denouncing the recently-enacted extension of universal suffrage for the Chamber of Deputies of the Reichsrat, arguing that only the will of the Emperor could bring order out of the chaos of Austrian domestic life.[23] His absolutism was a result of the same profound pessimism that characterized so many other Austrians of the time. In his case, however, that pessimism provided a spur to often passionate action in defense of the old order. "Better to fall fighting honestly than to give up the struggle like a coward," he assured Alexander Hoyos in late 1913.[24]

Czernin's strivings in the Herrenhaus were directed towards creating an alliance of the Czech and German Bohemian feudal aristocracy that would bridge over the national conflict there; his ultimate goal, like the Archduke's, was the abrogation of the Ausgleich and the creation of a centralized Greater Austria under firmly conservative influences. Socialists, liberals, Freemasons, Jews, and Magyars were all relegated to the position of scum or worse in his correspondence with his mentor. "I do not interest myself *at all* for Count Tisza, just as little as for the whole Magyar company," he wrote in 1913.

"This Magyar clique is a plague boil on the body of the Monarchy, and that no *Austrian* patriot can doubt." [25] Such sentiments notwithstanding, he became good friends with Tisza after his appointment to Bucharest.

Czernin may have been deeply conservative, if not reactionary, but he was also extremely ambitious. Principle and expediency were inextricably mixed in his personality. That mixture was perhaps the key to his political career. He often talked of brutality and unscrupulousness and drastic constitutional changes; after the war, his attraction to such qualities led him to praise Italian dictator Mussolini as "the only really great statesman of the world." [26] Nevertheless, he always kept an eye on reality and was ever ready to find new means to his ends if his old ones no longer seemed to fit the situation. "The man is pure seventeenth century," Josef Redlich wrote in his diary after an interview with him in early 1917. [27] Yet he had a perception of the needs of the twentieth—if not always a willingness to fulfill them—lacking in almost all other high-ranking Austrian policy-makers. Against their stubborn passivity or lack of imagination, he was willing to try one expedient after another, to maneuver and to innovate. Most of those who met him commented on his forceful energy and apparent receptiveness to new ideas.

Czernin had few close friends. He could be charming and incisive, but also coldly brusque to people who taxed his patience. His health was poor, and he was often sick from pure nervous tension, acutely conscious of the pressure on him and quick to express his irritations. Glaise, who was attached to the Austrian delegation at Brest-Litovsk in the last part of the war, noted that he often treated officials who were not members of the high aristocracy, even those close to him like his press secretary Friedrich Wiesner, like "door mats." Glaise compared his character to that of an Arabian stallion, with the same smooth lines and high-strung temperament. [28] Both his ambition and his impulsive forcefulness set Czernin apart from the other officials in the Foreign Ministry, and he once described himself as an "outsider" there. [29] During his tenure at Bucharest, he was held at the Ballplatz as something of an enfant terrible, a dilettante whose often kaleidoscopic policy suggestions, if perceptive, were not to be taken too seriously. The feeling was reciprocated. "I ceaselessly receive 'instructions' which come from the Forgách-Hoyos kitchen, and have now had enough of them," he complained to Franz Ferdinand in February 1914. [30]

The contrasts in Czernin's personality between the brilliance and the shadow perplexed his contemporaries as much as later observers. Why, then, did Karl choose such a complicated, restless man as his Foreign Minister? The answer can probably be found more in Czernin's activity in Bucharest than in any supposition that he was Franz Ferdinand's intended future candidate for the post. His impatient proposals for policy initiatives were undoubtedly impulsive or contradictory and hardly endeared him to his superiors at the Ballplatz—especially when he railed against their seeming refusal to do anything at all. But his perception of the course of Rumanian politics was brilliantly accurate. Moreover, Czernin was a firm believer in a compromise peace. Even in September 1915, in the euphoria of the Gorlice victories, he had written: "I do not believe in a victory of the Empires in the sense that we will be able to dictate to a beaten Europe the conditions that we want." What he hoped for was an honorable peace that, simply by preserving the Monarchy intact, would lead to its political and moral rebirth. "Whether we get a sizable extension of territory as well seems to me practically inconsequential."[31] A year later, during the Russian Brusilov offensive, he was even more vehement—peace had become an absolute necessity at almost any cost; for the Entente, with the resources of the world available to it, could continue the struggle for years:

> For the war to continue for years, however, means with mathematical certainty the complete collapse of the Central Powers and their allies. In my humble opinion, our victory is therefore impossible and only one question can be raised: whether we can succeed in ending the war *with significant sacrifices in a phase militarily favorable to us.*

It was obvious to him that, strangled by the British blockade, Austria-Hungary and Germany were nearing the end of their strength. At the first opportunity, the Entente should be offered peace on the basis of no annexations (including Serbia), no reparations, restitution of Belgium, and an international disarmament conference—an almost Wilsonian program. Simply by surviving the war and thus demonstrating its viability, the Monarchy would have won a great deal.[32] Such sentiments were precisely those of Karl himself, and in Czernin he undoubtedly hoped to find a minister who would be able to realize them.

Czernin officially entered office on December 22, 1916, and once there wasted little time in making his presence felt. Averse by nature to sharing authority, he quickly moved to secure his freedom to conduct policy as he saw fit within the limits inevitable to any Foreign Minister of the Dual Monarchy. The first to be affected was Tisza. However much Czernin valued the Hungarian Minister-President's support, he had no intention of subordinating himself to Hungarian dictation, and soon demonstrated that Tisza's decisive influence under Berchtold and Burián was now a thing of the past. Nor was Tisza the only one affected, for Czernin moved to establish his independence from imperial interference as well. He hoped to advise the inexperienced Emperor on the policies to be followed rather than the other way around, and Karl seemed to accede to his wishes. To maintain close relations with the Court, Czernin appointed Count August Demblin, a young diplomat, to be a special liaison officer between the Foreign Ministry and the Emperor.

The Ballplatz was almost immediately altered under Czernin's new management. Forgách, who had complained of Czernin's insubordination in 1914,[33] was put on indefinite vacation, and many aging Austrian foreign representatives were retired. Hoyos was sent to Norway; Musulin, to Switzerland. Significantly, Hohenlohe remained in Berlin. Czernin also made an effort to explain the logic of his policies to his representatives abroad, unlike Burián, who had tended to send out turgid instructions while keeping their ultimate goals to himself. With an appreciation of the possibilities of the press that his predecessors had never grasped, Czernin set about to enlist it actively into his policies, rather than merely censoring it. His periodic interviews in the semi-official *Fremdenblatt* were intended to mobilize Austrian public opinion directly behind him—a popular appeal no previous Austrian Foreign Minister had ever considered. He also met with the representatives of the various parties in the Reichsrat to garner their support, or at least to mute their hostility. He even established ties with Károlyi, who, in the beginning of 1917, saw Czernin as a possible ally in his radical peace campaign.

At first, Czernin's energy and will for peace tended to obscure the essential differences between him and the new Emperor—differences which were ultimately irreconcilable and would destroy them both. Czernin had attacked the Ausgleich and Magyar oligarchy before the war, but one of his first acts as Foreign Minister was to declare officially to the other officials at the Ballplatz his complete support of the dualistic system.[34] This reversal of position was not just lip service but the result of the pressure of war—the same thing that determined the political evolution of Conrad and Hohenlohe. Czernin saw the Ausgleich as the only available source of internal stability against the increasing signs of dissolution within the Monarchy; and until peace came, stability was more important to him than attempting a constitutional transformation that even in peacetime could easily prove fatal. He was intent on a firmly pro-German domestic course in Cisleithania. "A majority must be created, and this is there in the German bloc," he told Redlich in a discussion of the reopening of the Reichsrat.[35] He emphasized his belief that the best way to create internal stability and solve the Czech-German national conflict in Bohemia was through an Oktroi or imperial

decree—in favor of the Germans. In any case, Czernin's autocratic, centralized Greater Austria had little in common with Karl's vague notions of
democratic federalism, except a mutual antipathy to the 1867 settlement.
Czernin, for all the apparent readiness to experiment with new ideas and
policies that he would demonstrate as Foreign Minister, was essentially far
less liberal or democratic than Karl, despite the latter's seemingly archaic
dynastic and religious loyalties.

The differences were to prove even greater on the subject of Germany.
Before the war, Czernin had underscored to Franz Ferdinand the importance
of the "Holy Alliance" with Berlin as a bulwark against both the Magyars
and the threat of revolution, and his loyalty to the German connection
underwent no change after the outbreak of hostilities. In October 1916,
Baernreither recorded a conversation between Czernin, Clam, Egon Fürstenberg, and himself. Czernin reiterated his conviction that time was working
against the Central Powers; the longer it took for them to conclude peace,
the worse the situation of the Monarchy would become. Neutral mediation
might possibly bring together a peace conference, and then popular opinion
would make it impossible for any power to leave it. But what if the Germans
refused to agree to a moderate peace program? Czernin had no intention of
concluding a separate peace without them. "Every step of the proposed
program must be made in the closest contact with Germany," he emphasized.[36] When Czernin became Foreign Minister two months later, Hilmar von
dem Bussche, his former German counterpart in Bucharest and now German
Undersecretary, voiced his assurance that his loyalty to the alliance "could
not be doubted."[37] Czernin's ideas on both domestic and foreign policy were
thus poles apart from Karl's; and the difference was bridged only by their
mutual belief in the need for peace.

The gap between the two men was made explosive by Karl's willingness
to take policy initiatives without the full knowledge of his official ministers.
None of the men he appointed to high office at the beginning of his reign
really shared his own inchoate ideas for drastic domestic and foreign policy
changes. To get what he wanted, Karl resorted to sometimes ill-conceived
actions on his own, and this led to considerable confusion and bitterness—
especially with Czernin, who wanted all the strings of policy between his own
fingers. The extent of the Emperor's private initiatives will probably never
be known. The most famous were the Sixtus peace feelers, about which
Czernin's own involvement remains a subject of controversy; and Karl's
summer Amnesty Degree, which was sprung on almost everyone by surprise.
As a loyal son of the Catholic Church and ruler of the only Catholic Great
Power in Europe (France and Italy having separated church and state), Karl

could also count on the good offices of the Pope, as became apparent with the Papal peace note of August 1917. Whatever secret contacts he may have had with the Vatican authorities have never been determined.

There were rumors that Karl's political interventions were the result of the influence of his strong-willed wife, the Empress Zita, and of her mother the Duchess of Parma. Prince Sixtus was Zita's brother, and Zita was alleged to be the center of a Parma camarilla at Court. A representative of the Pan-German League reported in late 1917 from Vienna that Zita wrote constant letters to Rome. How much fire there was beneath all the smoke of that and similar allegations is still disputed. Those who spread them were, after all, often willing to believe anything that cast discredit on the Emperor. The evidence is nearly all hearsay and consequently unverifiable. Zita no doubt strengthened the Emperor's resolve in various matters, but beyond this her influence is difficult to measure. The Austrian staff officer Zeynek later wrote that except for stopping the bombing of Venice and objecting at a luncheon gathering to a German admiral's opinions on submarine warfare, he had heard nothing about any mixing of the Empress in the Monarchy's military affairs.[38]

More clearly documented in its impact on events was an unofficial circle of advisers which soon came into being beyond the realm of Karl's official policy-makers. This was the so-called Meinl Group, introduced to the Emperor by Count Arthur Polzer-Hoditz, a boyhood friend whom Karl made his Cabinet Chief. Through Polzer, Karl met Julius Meinl, a successful coffee merchant; and through him Heinrich Lammasch, an authority on international law and another member of Franz Ferdinand's Belvedere Circle (where he had often been at odds with Czernin), and the German pacifist professor Friedrich Wilhelm Foerster. All these figures agreed with Karl's fears of Germany and the Ausgleich, and they were ready to urge him to take the more radical actions that his official ministers refused to consider. As the differences between Karl and Czernin widened in the course of 1917, Czernin, fearing his position was being undermined by their influence, did everything he could to destroy their authority with the Emperor.

These future sources of conflict were scarcely evident when Czernin first assumed office. Evident only was the fact that under the new leadership the Monarchy began to show an initiative that it had not displayed for years. The first few months of the new year were concerned more with grappling with problems left over from Burián's tenure of office than starting completely afresh; yet the break with the inflexible passivity of the past was apparent almost immediately.

III

If Burián had in a sense been appointed Foreign Minister to keep Austria-Hungary in the war, Czernin's primary task was to get it out. Czernin made no secret of the views he had already expressed while Minister in Bucharest. "A complete conquest of the enemy would belong in the realm of the impossible," he told his listeners at the January 12, 1917 meeting of the Common Ministers Council. "Therefore a compromise peace must be reckoned with." [39]

War aims and peace policy could not, however, be considered without also considering the Monarchy's relations with Germany. Unlike his predecessor, Czernin realized that if Austria-Hungary was going to remain allied to its stronger German partner, it could effectively defend its interests in Berlin only if it adopted a policy of flexibility and maneuver, using a resourceful diplomacy to buttress a bargaining position that it was too weak to maintain simply through strength alone. Further, he was willing to appeal to neutral and even enemy powers independently of Berlin in order to further his policies, so long as the alliance itself remained intact. He described to the journalist Kanner in April the result of Burián's methods of conducting diplomacy with the Germans: "People often made a lot of noise and raised difficulties, and then in the end still gave way. I proceed from the opposite principle, which seems like the right one to me." [40] It was more a change in tactics than in actual aims, but it had an immediate impact. The new Austrian Foreign Minister met with the German leaders for the first time at the beginning of January 1917 in Berlin. The meeting itself was largely inconclusive, but on a personal level Czernin did much to reestablish the authority of the Ballplatz as an institution able to bargain smoothly and credibly there. Hohenlohe, writing afterwards to Macchio, was favorably impressed:

> The discussions here—which is certainly no wonder—have taken place *much more* pleasantly and easily than under our esteemed departed chief; however pretty and logical his flow of speech was, *no one* has cried a tear from missing him. I can assure you that I have been granted a great relief not to have to make the good Burián palatable here any more—an art which even a better "cook" than I à la longue would hardly be up to! The Germans have felt this also, and so Czernin has made an excellent start and also exploited it very well. [41]

Czernin was going to need all the personal influence in Berlin that he could muster, however, for Germany's actions as the new year began hardly seemed calculated to alleviate its ally's burdens.

The Entente answer to the Central Powers' December peace note was to reject it sharply on December 30. Burián would probably have viewed the affair as closed, but Czernin refused to surrender the initiative. As he telegraphed to Hohenlohe on New Year's Day, 1917, he had expected a refusal, but hoped to keep alive the question of peace by issuing a further statement. "My impelling motive with this consideration is that I do not want to allow the thread spun out by Baron Burián to be broken, and in this way to nourish further the worldwide peace movement." He hoped that such a step might allow the question of peace in both camps to assume a more definite shape, adding: "It means a great deal to me for the Imperial German Government not to close its eyes to this line of reasoning and not to break all the bridges through an eventual sharp, hasty answer."[42] The Germans, however, decided on a bombastic proclamation from Kaiser Wilhelm to his troops. Czernin had Karl send a personal protest to Wilhelm that he would only hurt the possibilities of peace, but the proclamation was issued nonetheless a few days later.

Of far more momentous consequences for the future of the Monarchy, however, was the question of unrestricted submarine warfare. The issue had been slumbering since the beginning of the war. Increasingly throttled by the pressure of the British blockade and unable to break it through its surface navy, Germany turned more and more to the possibility of countering it through the use of its submarine fleet. The submarine promised to have a decisive effect only if its use were unrestricted, that is, used without distinction against both enemy and neutral shipping in international waters, but that procedure threatened the almost certain entry of the greatest remaining neutral into the war against the Central Powers—the United States. It was a classic case of political versus military considerations. German Chancellor Bethmann Hollweg realized the likely consequences of the entry of the United States into the conflict, but as the power of the German military grew, the pressure on him to accede to unrestricted submarine warfare increased proportionally.

The question was viewed with rising anxiety in Vienna, which hoped if at all possible to avoid American intervention in the war. The Austrians wanted to come to terms with the enemies they already had, not to take on new ones. In 1915, Germany briefly experimented with unrestricted submarine warfare, which led to a crisis in German-American relations when the *Lusitania* was torpedoed. Burián, alarmed, urged the need for compromise. That crisis passed, but the voices in Germany arguing for unrestricted use of the submarine were in no way silenced. A year later, Hohenlohe reported with concern that Bethmann was under growing attack for not giving in to them.[43] Vienna held the political ability of the German civilian leaders in little esteem; even Hohenlohe was not particularly impressed with them, calling them at one point "fearful, nervous, insecure people."[44] Nevertheless, the Austrians realized full well that the military alternative could be even worse, and followed the rise in power of the German military and related annexationist groups with mounting apprehension. The accession of Hindenburg and Ludendorff to the German High Command in the fall of 1916 made the pressure on the civilian authorities greater than ever. One of the first results was that Jagow was removed as Foreign Secretary, with Arthur Zimmermann promoted to his place. At the insistence of the military, the question of unrestricted submarine warfare now became acute. Burián, trying to buttress Bethmann's resolve, addressed a personal letter to him in October, emphasizing the danger of American intervention in the war. "Whether the disadvantages of such a danger in political, moral, and military respects will be balanced by the advantages of submarine warfare which will certainly take place, is questionable, and cannot be judged simply from military standpoints," he warned.[45]

At the beginning of 1917, Bethmann's position crumbled. Czernin, who had now replaced Burián, argued that Austria-Hungary would be affected by the consequences of the measure as much as Germany, since American entry into the war would follow immediately. He sent Ludwig von Flotow, a former Attaché with the Austrian mission in Berlin, as his special envoy to the German capital to try to delay a decision.[46] It was to no avail. On January 9, the Germans resolved to open unrestricted submarine warfare beginning on the first of the following month. Vienna was not even consulted in the decision. Two weeks later, Zimmermann and Admiral Henning von Holzendorff, the Chief of the German Naval Staff, travelled to Vienna to secure Austrian assent to the decision that had already been taken. The Germans argued that the measure would not bring the United States into the war and that American involvement would have little impact even if it did; Admiral Holzendorff guaranteed that England would be forced into submission in four months.[47]

Faced with this fait accompli, the Monarchy reluctantly agreed to associate itself with the German action. To refuse would have created a breach in the alliance that none of its leaders was willing to accept. As Czernin later put it to the publicist Viktor Naumann, had he not gone along with the decision "all of Germany would stone me and say: The Austrian has ruined our certain victory."[48] Czernin and Tisza made no secret of their doubts, and it evidently took all of the Austrian Foreign Minister's powers of persuasion to get Karl's consent. The following day, a Common Ministers Council accepted unrestricted submarine warfare only because it might help relieve the Entente pressure on the Western Front—not because of any belief that it would starve Britain into submission and achieve a quick victory. Clam urged that if, in the meantime, the chance of an easy peace presented itself, "this opportunity—perhaps from the hope of further uncertain successes—not be missed, but that the offered hand be seized with determination." Conrad, predictably, was enthusiastic about the submarine measure, but his days were already numbered.[49]

The German decision enormously complicated the possibility of bringing peace closer through the most immediate offered hand, that of American President Wilson. Wilson had made a mediation offer shortly after the publication of the Central Powers' December 1916 peace note, which he repeated in the middle of January. Czernin wanted a positive answer. Yet Berlin seemed to be doing all it could not just to antagonize America, but to drive it into active hostilities against them. The Germans answered Wilson's second mediation offer, a request to be informed confidentially of the aims of all the belligerents, by telling him only what their aims would have been if the Entente had accepted the December peace note—aims which, because of its rejection, they were no longer bound to observe. Vienna was not informed of the German reply until after it was sent. Again, Burián probably would have protested such behavior in Berlin but done nothing more. Czernin, however, took the initiative. Rather than leave the rest of the world with the impression that the Monarchy blindly accepted the German position, he issued his own reply to Wilson's offer. In it, he accepted the formula that Wilson had expounded in his famous speech two weeks earlier on January 22: a peace without victors or vanquished, annexations or indemnities. Zimmermann was infuriated. He complained that Czernin was encouraging Wilson to differentiate between Vienna and Berlin (which he was) and added revealingly in a telegram to Wedel: "We can carry through even our moderate demands only as victors."[50]

Actually, Czernin had no more wish to accept Wilson as a mediator than did the Germans themselves, for he feared the American President to be too partial to the Entente. He preferred no mediation at all, but rather direct exchanges of views between the hostile powers.[51] If there had to be mediation, though, his first choice was the King of Spain, a possibility he busily sounded out in the opening months of 1917, though without result. Yet he realized that Wilson's peace efforts could very well be of advantage in bringing the war to an end even if he rejected Wilson himself as a mediator; he consequently wanted to adopt a public position favorable to them in principle. He explained to the Austrian Ambassador in Madrid that he hoped

in so doing to drive a wedge between Wilson and the Entente.[52] As Czernin
had defined his war aims in both his 1916 peace memorandum and in the
January Common Ministers Council, his goal was a compromise peace on
the basis of the status quo ante for Austria-Hungary. If the United States
could be induced to bring pressure on the Entente to moderate the goal
proclaimed on January 10 of liberating the peoples of the Monarchy from
"foreign" domination, that would certainly be a long step in that direction.
Czernin's readiness to meet Wilson halfway resulted in a series of exchanges
with the American government in February and March, which culminated
in the offer of a separate peace for Austria-Hungary—something Czernin was
emphatic that he would never accept. Any peace he concluded would have
to involve Germany.[53]

Whether further exchanges would have borne fruit remained unanswered,
because the Germans managed to intensify the conflict by finally provoking
an American declaration of war. Czernin's policy in any case had been to
postpone the breach with America as long as possible, and, by emphasizing
to the Entente the defensive nature of unrestricted submarine warfare, to
sound as conciliatory as he could. He and Tisza repeatedly protested against
bombastic German declarations that the measure would starve England into
submission as only likely to make the English fight harder. But Berlin,
confident of victory, seemed uninterested in showing a conciliatory spirit. It
outdid even its previous efforts with the famous Zimmermann Telegram,
promising Mexico the Southwestern United States in return for a wartime
alliance against Washington. Whatever Czernin's hopes to stave off American
intervention, the telegram's publication after being intercepted by the British
made it inevitable. Czernin protested to Hohenlohe that the incident was only
the latest of a whole series of German blunders, which certainly did not
incline him to accept without question Berlin's leadership in the alliance.[54]
Hohenlohe's own reaction, expressed privately to Berchtold, was that if Berlin
often committed blunders, at least it acted; and a certain number of blunders
were thus to be expected. Vienna, he complained, no doubt thinking of
Czernin's predecessor, avoided the risk of blunders by not doing anything at
all.[55]

On April 6, the United States declared war on Germany. It did not,
however, declare war on the Monarchy; and although Vienna broke off
diplomatic relations, no declaration from the Austrian side followed either—
to the chagrin of Berlin. Of course, the Germans had acted similarly towards
Italy in 1915 after it declared war on Austria-Hungary, so they were in a
poor position to complain. Czernin thus managed to keep open the possibility

of future peace initiatives from America as much as was possible with a power now at war with his chief ally.

At the same time, the old controversies between Vienna and Berlin over the future of Poland continued to cause friction within the alliance. The independence of Congress Poland had been proclaimed in order to enable raising a Polish army against Russia. While it had finally been agreed to put the army under German control, the German military under Ludendorff went further to insist on an oath of loyalty to Kaiser Wilhelm, which Vienna decided it simply could not accept without destroying its prestige with the Poles as well as its control over the Austrian Polish Legion. Czernin at the beginning of the new year complained to German Ambassador Wedel that Germany was demanding complete control over Poland for itself without leaving any compensation for the Monarchy.[56] A few days later, at the January 6 meeting in Berlin, Poland was the subject of much of the discussion, and the main points of the controversy were left "open"— meaning no agreement could be reached.[57] The only agreement was on the Kuk-Beseler loyalty oath, a compromise formula for the proposed Polish army worked out by the respective heads of the Austrian and German military administrations in occupied Poland. It remained a dead letter because Bethmann's efforts to get Ludendorff to accept it failed miserably. The loyalty oath question was solved only because virtually no Poles volunteered for the army anyway; it made no difference what sort of oath there was because there were no Polish troops to swear it.

In the face of German opposition, the Austrian leadership remained as divided as ever on the Polish question. Czernin and the Foreign Ministry hoped somehow to resurrect the Austro-Polish solution, a tour de force they still considered possible after the January 6 meeting. Tisza, dubious, thought that harmony with Berlin was more important than Poland, and that the Monarchy should surrender its Polish interests to Berlin in return for economic compensations. Hohenlohe in Berlin, viewing all the Poles as incurably Russophile, thought a few border areas should be annexed but the bulk simply dumped back into the lap of the Czar. Furthermore, even if there were an Austro-Polish solution, how should it be implemented? In February, Czernin considered the idea of a personal union between Congress Poland and the Monarchy, which would have meant that Poland would have an autonomous constitution but would be connected to the Monarchy by virtue of the Austrian Emperor also being King of Poland. The person of a common monarch, in other words, would be the only tie between them. Whether this was any constitutional improvement over the old sub-dualistic solution remained to be seen. Czernin and Tisza both agreed that Austria-Hungary, despite German pressure, had to retain its occupation area around Lublin as a possible object of exchange against Russian-occupied East Galicia. But that, and the fact that German ambitions there threatened their own interests, was practically all the Austrian leaders could agree to.[58]

The immediate result of Czernin's first forays as Austrian Foreign Minister was thus to confirm what had already been implicit since the opening of the war: The outcome of the conflict and the Monarchy's goals in it could not be separated from the German alliance. The initial concern of any Austrian peace policy had to be Germany. All Czernin's initial attempts to establish contact with the Entente had been complicated if not simply blocked by the Germans. Moreover, the increasing ability of the German military under Hindenburg and Ludendorff to dictate to the Wilhelmstraße indicated that the situation in the future would get no better. As this became more and more apparent, the possibility that the Monarchy could achieve its goals only by breaking out of the constricting hold of the alliance began to assume altogether new dimensions. Czernin, by trying to spin out the chances of peace contacts with the Entente and the United States, and by publicly calling for a peace without victory to appropriate Wilson's slogan as his own, broke with the alliance barriers that had restricted Burián. He had done nothing to threaten the alliance itself, but rather had attempted to widen the Monarchy's field of movement within it. In the following months, beginning from this starting point, Austria-Hungary would launch a coordinated peace offensive against its German ally, straining the bonds of the alliance to their limits.

Chapter 6

PEACE AT HAND?
March-September 1917

I

The year 1917 transformed the dimensions of the war. The entry of America into the conflict was only a part of that transformation. In early March, worker strikes broke out in Petrograd, as St. Petersburg had been renamed; they soon expanded into a general strike there and in other cities of Russia. On March 15, scarcely a week later, Nicholas II abdicated. The Czarist regime in Russia had ceased to exist, and a new democratic Provisional Government was set up. At the same time, a revolutionary Soviet appeared in Petrograd. It called for ending the war without annexations or indemnities and under the principle of national self-determination.

The events in Russia shook all of Europe. Most immediately, they removed the military pressure on the Central Powers on the Eastern Front. After three years of bloodletting, the battlefield stalemate appeared finally to be broken, and peace for the leaders of the Central Powers seemed nearer than at any time since the end of 1914. Perhaps even a favorable peace would be possible if the opportunity could be decisively exploited.

The longterm prospects for them were less rosy. The collapse of the regime in Russia was an example of the fate of any country which stayed in the war beyond the endurance level of its social and economic fabric. The Central Powers were not in much better shape, and the success of the revolution in Russia threatened to radicalize their own discontented lower classes so long as the fighting continued. Nor did unrestricted submarine warfare, after a few critical months, succeed in forcing the western Entente powers to sue for peace. American entry into the war compensated the Entente for the gradual withdrawal of Russia; and while it would take some time for the United States to mobilize enough troops and materiel to make its weight really felt on the Entente side, each month would bring that moment nearer. If opportunity beckoned the Central Powers in 1917, it was clearly an opportunity with a time limit attached to it.

The new conditions had an immediate and drastic impact on the alliance. In the previous three years, the Monarchy's statesmen had found achieving their goals increasingly thwarted by their more powerful ally. Over Italy, Rumania, the future of Poland, Mitteleuropa, unrestricted submarine warfare, and a host of other issues, Austria-Hungary and Germany had differed rather than agreed. These conflicts had always been outweighed, however, by the mutual threat posed to both states by Czarist Russia. Russia was the great common enemy holding the alliance together. Whatever the Austrians may otherwise have thought about the Germans, they had had no doubt that they could not exist without German aid against Russia. All this changed as Russia dissolved in revolution. The earlier conflicts between Vienna and Berlin remained as intractable as ever, but a major compensating area of agreement between them now disappeared. By 1917, there were few reasons why Austria-Hungary should be allied to Germany, and compelling reasons why it should not.

The collapse of Russia, in fact, made acute a larger issue that underlay many of the other areas of conflict in the alliance, the question of how to end the war. Vienna, conscious of its rapidly deteriorating domestic situation, believed that the overthrow of the Czar offered perhaps the last chance for the Central Powers to terminate the hostilities short of complete surrender. The Germans, however, were more sanguine about their prospects. Austrian desires for a quick peace promptly ran up against German desires for a victorious one. Burián in December 1916 had hoped that one result of his peace note would be the propaganda effect of blaming the Entente for prolonging the war. The events in Russia had precisely the reverse effect. Now, suddenly, it looked as if Austria-Hungary could have a compromise peace for the asking on the Eastern Front, and only its alliance with Germany kept it in the conflict. From the time of the Revolution on, German Ambassador Wedel reported a rising longing for peace within the Monarchy, with or without Germany, coupled with a fear of German domination which he described in July as "practically pathological." [1]

Russia's disengagement from the war had the further consequence of presenting the Monarchy with a momentary freedom of action that it had not enjoyed since Sarajevo. It no longer needed German aid against the Russians, and it gained a sudden importance in London and Paris. It seems clear that the western Entente powers never seriously considered a compromise peace with Germany. But to weaken Germany, there were strong circles in both capitals willing to consider one with Austria-Hungary. Wedel wrote anxiously to Bethmann in mid-April: "I have often heard it said in Germany, Austria was completely dependent on us; whether it wanted to or not, it had to follow and obey us. That was once correct. But whoever believes that it is still so today misunderstands the situation." [2] The question of an Austrian separate peace with the Entente, earlier feared or threatened, became in 1917 a central concern for everyone connected with the alliance. Some worked to block it; others, to hasten it. 1917 was filled with secret peace feelers and rumors of such feelers between Austria-Hungary and Britain and France. The famous Sixtus contacts dated from Karl's accession and extended into March; the Armand-Revertera conversations began in August. Other more shadowy soundings were scattered throughout the period. What they all had in common was the message that Austria-Hungary could expect easy terms from the Entente powers if it left the war, whatever might be in store for the Germans. The message was not lost on Karl, nor on the pacifist figures around him.

Such, then, was the position of the Habsburg Monarchy during the first part of 1917. The apparent domestic political truce of the earlier years had fallen apart, and the events in Russia added the danger of social revolution to a system already burdened with multiplying political disabilities. Though the first harvests temporarily eased the food crisis, the accelerating economic breakdown pointed towards a coming winter which could be little short of disastrous. In the short term, however, the result of the events in Russia was to open possibilities not apparent since the original outbreak of hostilities. Austria-Hungary's future existence depended on its ability to get out of the war as best it could during that momentary respite.

II

Czernin still remains something of an enigma as Austro-Hungarian Foreign Minister. His impulsiveness and expediency made many contemporaries doubt whether he had any clear long range policies at all, especially since much of his work was camouflaged deliberately to hide its real intent. Often the camouflage was added afterwards to rationalize and obscure his own momentary shifts from one position to another depending on his current view of the war situation. Czernin's long range goal always remained the same: to get the Monarchy out of the war without breaking the alliance with Germany. But his day-to-day tactics changed constantly, in a continuous kaleidoscope of appearances and deceptions whose ultimate impact often turned out to be different than what he himself had originally intended.

Czernin's basic foreign policy assumption in 1917 was that time was working against the Central Powers, a view already forcefully expressed in his 1916 memorandum from Bucharest. Hence his willingness to seize any opportunity that seemed likely to lead to an end to the war, and his public advocacy of a peace of compromise without victors or vanquished. Yet despite the rising pressure for a separate peace, he refused to take the ultimate step of breaking the alliance with Germany. He feared such an action would undermine the whole Austrian domestic order. "We could have a separate peace with England in eight days," he told Baernreither on June 24. "It would be a momentary salvation, but in its aftermath the certain ruin of the dynasty."[3] Rather, he hoped to put the Monarchy into the position of mediating a settlement between the Germans and the Entente Powers. It had been obvious since 1914 that the enemy of England and France was Germany; so it followed that Vienna had a much better chance of reaching an accommodation with them than did Berlin. Czernin's goal was a general peace, not a separate one. The Monarchy, by mediating between the chief opposing forces, would preserve its own status by garnering the laurels of the middleman. Nor were the Emperor Karl's ideas, no doubt reinforced through Czernin's own influence, much different; in an audience with Musulin before the latter was sent to his new Swiss post, Karl dwelt on the same theme, specifically adding that Musulin's job as Minister there was to make Austrian readiness to mediate apparent to all.[4]

To mediate, Austria-Hungary had to assert its credibility as a power to be negotiated with, not merely a dependent satellite of Berlin. Hence Czernin's efforts to prove to the Entente that the Monarchy, while allied to Germany, was not subject to it, and that it retained the power to influence its stronger ally in the cause of peace. This, obviously, was easier said than done. At the same time that Czernin demonstrated his independence of Germany to the rest of the world, he had to reassure the Germans, and his own domestic supporters, that his loyalty to the alliance itself was unquestioned. As Baernreither later recorded his words in a conversation with him, "He held unconditionally with Germany. . . . But in complete agreement with Germany and for its benefit, he had to present the Monarchy as independent, since it ultimately had to be able to be the mediator of peace."[5] While applying pressure on his own far stronger ally, he had to make sure that the Entente did not mistake his will for a general peace as willingness to conclude a separate one. Moreover, to maintain his domestic position, Czernin had no qualms about playing off the various Austrian political groups against each other or even against the Emperor himself.

The idea that the Monarchy could somehow mediate the conclusion of the war was based on two assumptions. It assumed first that the Entente was ready to accept a general compromise peace with Germany, and second that expansionist German war aims could be reduced to the point that a compromise peace with the enemy coalition became possible. It assumed, in short, that both sides by 1917 were ready to conclude that the war had reached a stalemate and that absolute victory for either was impossible. But was this viewpoint realistic? After several months in Switzerland, whose neutral territory provided the chief meeting ground for covert contacts between the two coalitions, Musulin reported:

> My impression here is that we are stuck in a circulus vitiosus. If things are going well with the Entente or they expect successes in the near future, they cannot be had for any ideas of peace; if it goes well with us, then on the German side it is the slogan "For God's sake don't go too fast, don't ruin everything, wait; it has to get still better."

Musulin's sources indicated that the Germans were actually working to strengthen the impression in the West that the Monarchy was only a "docile second" to Berlin with no will of its own. Czernin, undeterred, replied the following day that he would continue on his chosen course. "In this regard, we have the double task of leaving the Entente in no doubt that we cannot be separated from our ally, but on the other hand of exerting pressure on Germany to achieve moderate demands." It was the job of the neutral press— especially that of Switzerland—to counter the impression that Austria-Hungary was a mere dependent of the Wilhelmstraße.[6]

Burián and Tisza had tried to assert the Monarchy's independence within the alliance for two years, and the result had been a dismal failure. Czernin had no illusions about the real power of Vienna in relation to Berlin, but hoped to moderate the balance in his favor through diplomatic manipulation of the various power groups in Germany. Czernin made a clear distinction between moderate and extreme groups in the Reich. Ludendorff was an "engine of destruction" who probably wanted no end to the war at all, Czernin declared emphatically in an April interview with the journalist Kanner. "The final decision must rest in the hand of the statesman; a certain counterweight to the military has to be created."[7] Czernin's policy of reducing German war aims assumed that creating that moderate counter-weight was possible. He established contacts with Matthias Erzberger and the other leaders of the German parliamentary opposition and later claimed that the famous Reichstag Peace Resolution was the result of his own efforts.[8]

Perhaps more devious were his machinations with important groups within the Monarchy itself. To what extent his aim was to maintain his own position in office, or to preserve internal stability, or to exert indirect pressure on Berlin, or all three at once, can still not be said with complete certainty. Both Czernin and Karl established contact with Károlyi to get him to tone down his anti-alliance activities, and Károlyi's colleague Tivadar Batthyány even became Minister a Latere. While Czernin assured the other Hungarian leaders of his trust in Germany, Károlyi was assured the exact opposite. Both the Emperor and his Foreign Minister informed him that they actually approved of a certain amount of calculated anti-German utterances on his part as a means of expressing things they could not afford to say publicly themselves.[9] No doubt, Czernin could then point to Károlyi's speeches in his efforts to wring from Berlin more understanding for his position. The connection lasted until the end of the summer, when it became clear to Károlyi that Czernin would never risk an open break with the alliance.

Czernin followed a similarly complicated course with the influential Poles. He repeatedly met with representatives of the Polish Club in the Reichsrat to assure them of his interest in the future of Congress Poland, and instructed Musulin to make sure that the Polish groups in Switzerland never forgot that Austria had traditionally shown far more willingness to meet Polish wishes than had Germany.[10] At the same time, in mid-1917, he had abandoned the Austro-Polish solution and was engaged in negotiations to turn Congress Poland over to German control once and for all—talks which he repeatedly (and understandably) stipulated had to remain absolutely secret until the close of the war.

Perhaps nowhere was Czernin's policy more complex than towards the Austrian Socialists, who were an increasingly important political force after the events in Petrograd. In public speeches and interviews in the *Fremdenblatt,* he called for a peace of understanding, repudiation of annexationist war aims, and international disarmament—adopting for himself the slogans of his opponents on the left. Heinrich von Tucher, the Bavarian Envoy in Vienna, complained of his "demagogic" appeal to the masses after the appearance of an interview on March 31. "This behavior of the government is dictated from fear of hunger revolts and revolution," he wrote, "and it can be clearly recognized that since the outbreak of the Russian Revolution, the government is seeking contact with the masses more than ever and shows increased consideration for the wishes of the Socialist Party."[11] What Tucher failed to add was that, however real the danger of revolution, that very danger became another weapon in Czernin's arsenal against Berlin's wishes to achieve total victory.

Again, Czernin's expedient tactics often left his colleagues breathless trying to follow the course of his policy. He and Clam-Martinic had both come to office with the intention of satisfying Austrian German demands in Bohemia through an Oktroi; such a step had been Czernin's most forcefully expressed domestic intention. But then on April 16, at a meeting of the Austrian government ministry, he insisted that the whole program of an Oktroi be abandoned. His main reason was to strengthen his bargaining position towards revolutionary Russia by improving his domestic position with the Austrian Socialists, who were certain to oppose legislation by imperial fiat. That, however, was not the only motivation; as he told the assembled ministers, the Monarchy could expect no peace offers from the Entente (the Sixtus feelers were still in progress at that point), unless everything was done to avoid the appearance of Austrian subservience to Germany. "The war is coming to an end," he argued. "How should peace be achieved? An Oktroi would be seen as a Diktat from Berlin." [12]

Czernin's treatment of the Austrian Socialists was in fact as deceptive as his dealings with most other Austrian political groups. He adopted their slogans and, over Tisza's objections, granted them passports to the socialist conference in Stockholm that spring; in return, the leaders of the party showed a surprising loyalty to him, especially during the massive strikes that swept Austria in January 1918. But Czernin's real intentions, as usual, were far different from the appearances he cultivated so assiduously. As he wrote to Tisza laying out his position on the Stockholm conference, he had to grant the passports to the conference to prove to the Socialists that the Foreign Ministry was doing all it could to end the war and that no stupidity at the Ballplatz was responsible for its prolongation. [13] He assumed that the conference would fail, but wanted to preserve the semblance of doing everything possible for peace in order to dampen radical tempers in the Monarchy. He had no intention of allowing a socialist conference somehow to conclude peace over his head, and in fact took positive steps behind the scenes to make sure that it failed. He explained to Pallavicini in Constantinople that, while doing everything possible to facilitate the convocation of the conference, he was also working to assure that the programs advanced by the individual delegations would be such as to make any general agreement impossible. [14] To this end, he instructed his representative in Stockholm to encourage the Bulgarian Socialists not to demand "rather *too little* for Bulgaria." [15] Nor were his public avowals of a peace without annexations undeviatingly held. To Bulgarian worries that Vienna intended to abandon its obligations to them, he commented ingenuously that his pronouncements were intended merely to soothe the temper of the Slav population in the Monarchy.[16]

Czernin not only intended to reverse the style of his obstinate but basically forthright predecessors; he was prepared as well with an entirely new plan of action. Burián and Tisza had attempted to counter their increasingly dominant ally with a façade of strength. Czernin, on the other hand, aimed to defend the Monarchy's integrity by proclaiming its weakness. It was the ultimate contradiction in a policy riddled with contradictions; he was going to reassert Vienna's position towards Berlin by telling Berlin how powerless he was. Actually, it was an elaborate game of diplomatic blackmail: If Germany refused to show more consideration for its ally's needs and desires, that ally would simply collapse in dissolution or accept a separate peace and stop fighting—leaving the Germans to face the Entente alone. Instead of concealing the difficulties he faced as Foreign Minister, Czernin went out of his way to emphasize them. In the succeeding months, the chaotic conditions in the Monarchy, and the many ways the Germans (unwittingly or otherwise) aggravated them, were used repeatedly to justify Czernin's pleas for diplomatic concessions from Berlin.

Unfortunately for Czernin, while the smaller paradoxes of his policy would be smoothed over or covered up, this final contradiction involved problems that even he could not manage to overcome. To proclaim that Austria-Hungary was on the verge of destruction meant a willingness to get out of the war at any cost. But Czernin could never wholly discount the chance of the war somehow reaching an abrupt, favorable conclusion, despite his consistent pessimism about its longterm outcome. If gains beyond mere survival for the Monarchy could somehow be achieved, he certainly was going to do his best to get them. To stress the Monarchy's desperate need for peace and then to anticipate future advantages at the peace conference only undermined his credibility in Berlin, however, and lent support to the suspicion there that he had not just lost his nerve but was deliberately crying "wolf." Moreover, in attempting to carry out his policy, he was repeatedly confronted with the dubious loyalties of his own subordinates and colleagues, no matter how much he attempted to explain all the apparent paradoxes to them. In cases where Czernin himself may not have known what his immediate goals were, it was hardly likely that fellow policy-makers in a realm with such confused domestic loyalties could be expected to give him complete cooperation. And often they did not.

Nevertheless, in the spring of 1917, the time appeared temporarily favorable for an active policy such as Czernin contemplated. The revolution in Russia not only gave the Monarchy greater diplomatic bargaining room; it also seemed to present the possibility of an early peace in the East. The chance of peace in the West also appeared with the attempts of Prince Sixtus of Parma, Karl's brother-in-law, secretly to discuss French and British peace conditions with Vienna. Czernin would shape his policy accordingly as the likelihood of peace seemed greater in either East or West, but his general aim remained the same throughout the summer of 1917: to mediate between Germany and the Entente in order to bring Austria-Hungary out of the war intact.

His general plan of campaign was sketched in a long memorandum he composed for Karl and presented to the March 22 Common Ministers Council for approval.[17] The first aim of any foreign policy was to preserve the integrity of the Monarchy. While East Galicia and the Bukovina could probably be gotten back from the Russians, those areas occupied by Italy were unlikely to be retrieved; so, compensation had to be found elsewhere. Moreover, the Monarchy could not afford the loss of prestige that would be involved if Germany, let alone Bulgaria, came out of the war winning territory while it did not. He wrote:

> No one in either Austria or Hungary would understand such a policy, and with good reason. Above all, it would not be understood by the non-German population of Cisleithania, because the superhuman achievements, historically unparalleled exertions, and heroic sacrifice—all of this only ad majorem gloriam Germaniae—would evoke a mood which would attack the life nerve of the Monarchy and the roots of the dynasty.

Czernin argued that the domestic order could not be maintained after the conclusion of peace unless the Monarchy gained something more tangible from the war than simply the aggrandizement of its allies. With this argument, he was no doubt playing on the anti-German susceptibilities of his monarch, but he was also expressing a fear that Berlin might abandon Vienna at the peace table unless safeguards were extracted from it in advance. The same suspicion had motivated Burián's efforts at the end of 1916 to get a guarantee of the Monarchy's integrity from Berlin. In any case, the key was Poland. Reasoning that there would be no Polish irredenta as long as Austria remained militarily strong—thus exorcising the old specter of the German-Polish solution—and that Vienna could never expect to fulfill its wishes in Congress Poland anyway as long as Germany was against them, he proposed to turn the whole area over to German hegemony. In return, the Monarchy would claim the Balkans and, even more important, occupied Rumania (which Czernin described as a "Milliardenobjekt," an object worth billions) as its own sphere of influence. All the dilemmas involved in the question of Congress Poland were solved at a stroke: Poland would be exchanged for Rumania. Moreover, Czernin's memorandum was not only a war aims proposal, but a strategy for peace. The Sixtus feelers seemed to indicate that German concessions to France, especially in Alsace-Lorraine, would buy peace in the West, and Czernin intended to use Congress Poland as the inducement to get Berlin to make the necessary adjustments there. In effect, Poland was not going to be exchanged just for Rumania, but for an end to the war itself. He concluded: "When Germany gives up France and Belgium and something else in addition, then peace is at hand." He said that he had already discussed this with Bethmann and had gotten his agreement.

The Common Ministers Council on the 22nd approved Czernin's program. Czernin proposed as a general policy goal that Germany guarantee the Monarchy's integrity and, if acquisitions were to be made, that the gains of Vienna and Berlin be reasonably equivalent. For Vienna, he had in mind the Lovčen, a shrunken Serbia in an Austrian customs area, and annexation of Wallachia in Rumania; Congress Poland was officially dropped. Despite the inevitable dispute between the two Minister-Presidents over how Wallachia would be constitutionally incorporated into the Empire, and Tisza's warnings against being too pessimistic and following a "desperado policy" of peace at any price, Czernin now had a positive program to present to Berlin.[18]

III

The course of the fateful Sixtus peace attempt has been often described. The soundings were begun through Karl's marital connections with the Bourbon-Parma family, and it was only after the initial contacts had been made that Czernin was informed. There were meetings in neutral Switzerland with intermediaries. In March 1917, Prince Sixtus and his brother Xavier travelled incognito to Vienna to confer in person with both the Emperor and his Foreign Minister, a trip repeated two months later in May. The terms Sixtus brought were German renunciation of Belgium and Alsace-Lorraine, the restoration of Serbia plus Albania, and the cession of Constantinople to the Russians. To such peace terms both Karl and Czernin were interested in responding positively; but when Sixtus returned to the West, he discovered Italian opposition blocking the whole venture, and his second trip to Vienna was intended to wring concessions for Italy out of the reluctant Austrians. Italian (or, more specifically, Sonnino's) obstinacy nevertheless proved to be the immovable obstacle which finally doomed the venture from the West.

Whether Italian moderation would have made any difference in the long run is, however, doubtful. For Sixtus' whole effort was intended as a separate peace attempt, to lure the Monarchy out of the war so that Germany could then be finished off alone. It was never construed in any other light by Entente statesmen, and it got as far as it did only because of the differences between Karl and Czernin. Czernin, though approving of the contacts as opening a possibility of peace (and perhaps even of splitting the Entente), was always cool towards them, distrustful of the true intentions of Britain and France, and undoubtedly preferring all such feelers to be pursued under his direct control through the Foreign Ministry. He would exploit them to bring his own goal of a general peace nearer but did not intend to become involved in a separate peace. In a note to Sixtus in February, he stated emphatically that the alliance with Germany was indissoluble and that a separate peace was out of the question. If Karl had not added his own qualifications to the note, the feelers would have ended then and there, and Sixtus would never have come to Vienna at all.[19]

Was Karl aiming at a separate peace in the spring of 1917? Sixtus told the French and British that he was, but he had to say so in order to keep them interested in his negotiations. Karl's son Otto of Habsburg later wrote that the Emperor was offering a negotiated peace and "would have accepted a separate peace if Germany had refused to negotiate."[20] The truth is probably that Karl, like Czernin, hoped to use the talks as a bridge to a general peace, but that he failed to make that distinction clear to Sixtus. It was probably not even clear to himself, given his views of the alliance. In any case, he not only promised to put pressure on Berlin to get it to make concessions (which Czernin did as well), but actually made the promise in writing to his declared enemies in the so-called first Sixtus letter. He praised the valor of France in resisting invasion and concluded in a sentence that would return to haunt the Monarchy:

> I will support the just claims of France concerning Alsace-Lorraine with all the means at my disposal and exert all my personal influence with my allies to this end.[21]

Even if Czernin knew that Karl had written the letter, which is still a matter of dispute, Karl's warmest apologists indicate that Czernin never actually read the final text. It was a mark of the Emperor's naive impulsiveness and the already perceptible differences between him and Czernin that such a note could be dispatched without the full knowledge of the Foreign Minister. Czernin himself may have told Sixtus and other informal emissaries like Berta

Szeps-Zuckerkandl the same things that Karl said in his letter; but he never wrote his words down on paper, so they could be disavowed without difficulty if it became necessary.[22] Not only did Karl commit himself in writing, but, as the Empress Zita later had to admit, he failed to keep for himself a clearly-marked duplicate of the final letter to Sixtus among the copies of the various drafts—an omission that shows that Czernin's distrust of the Emperor's methods of personal diplomacy was not completely unfounded.[23] The Sixtus talks were not the only time that the Emperor, in his desire for quick solutions to all his problems, would make sudden policy initiatives without fully consulting with his own chief minister.

Whatever the talks meant for Karl, for Czernin they meant the possibility of peace in the West, if the attempt for a separate peace could be expanded into a general settlement. Though Sixtus tried to interpret his sentiments otherwise in Paris, it was clear that if Vienna might be willing to put pressure on Germany, it was not about to break with it openly.[24] And that was the end of the Sixtus project.

It was only the beginning, however, of Austria's peace offensive in Berlin. On March 16, less than a week before Sixtus' first trip to Vienna, Czernin met there with Bethmann and the other leaders of the Wilhelmstraße. His duty, he told them, was to give them an objective picture of conditions in the Monarchy. "Unfortunately, he was not in the position of being able to present a rosy picture," he declared, "since the Monarchy stood at the end of its strength." The food supply had become critical; all sorts of shortages were spreading, and hunger typhus was reported in the Erzgebirge of Bohemia. Peace had to be made, and a peace feeler from France seemed to offer the opportunity. Czernin referred to a contact in Switzerland that Count Albert Mensdorff, the former Austrian Ambassador to London, was being sent to pursue; Sixtus was not mentioned. In fact, when Wedel heard from Cramon at the end of May that Sixtus and his brother were in Austria, Czernin denied it "on his word" (which was technically correct; they had just left a few days earlier).[25] In any case, Czernin wanted to know Germany's Western war aims. Bethmann answered that Germany could not give up Alsace-Lorraine for an agreement with France; he conceded that part of it might be relinquished, but only in exchange for the more valuable iron ore area of Longwy-Briey. If Czernin thought from this meeting that he had secured Bethmann's consent to the plan he preceded to set out in his March war aims memorandum, of buying peace with Alsace-Lorraine, he was either grievously mistaken or deliberately misleading his colleagues. He then turned his attention to the East, and, asserting that the Monarchy could not afford to come empty-handed out of the war, put in his claim for Rumania. The

Germans objected that this was too much to expect, and the discussion ended with Czernin proposing that the gains (or losses) of the two powers at the conclusion of the conflict should be in rough proportion to each other. Bethmann reluctantly agreed.[26]

Czernin's policy of emphasizing the Monarchy's desperate need for peace, while simultaneously trying to insure that that peace would treat it as generously as possible, was clearly expressed at the meeting. Unfortunately, the inconsistency of the two aims was equally clear, for the question of Rumania undercut much of the effect of his declarations on the urgency of peace. His efforts were continued a week later on March 26 at another conference in Berlin, where he officially offered to renounce Congress Poland in return for German concessions in Alsace-Lorraine and Austrian predominance in Wallachia. He further pressed Bethmann for a clear declaration over Germany's intentions in occupied Belgium and France. Bethmann's answer was that "guarantees" were needed in both areas, and he complained that a peace in which Austria survived intact but Germany lost its colonies, all its conquests, and Alsace was one which no one in Berlin could accept. Bethmann was now using the same argument for a parity of war aims as Czernin. The Austrian Foreign Minister was able to maneuver him into finally signing the common agreement on war aims that he thought he needed to safeguard the Monarchy's position in the alliance and at the peace table. If there were to be gains, Germany's would fall in the East and Austria's in Rumania; but if not, then a minimal program would consist of an evacuation of all occupied areas and a return to the status quo ante.[27]

The door to peace now seemed to be open, for Czernin appeared to have safeguarded the Monarchy with its ally no matter what happened. If favorable conditions could be secured, Berlin had finally agreed to Austrian parity in acquisitions; but if not, then Germany had assented to the principle of the status quo ante, so that German thirst for annexations no longer stood in the way of a compromise settlement of the war. Or so it looked. Actually, peace was as far away as ever, because the agreement never received the approval of the German military (Bethmann, in fact, communicated it neither to them nor to his own successor in office). The German Chancellor refused to let himself be pinned down specifically even on Belgium, let alone Alsace, where Czernin's proposals simply infuriated him. Wilhelm von Stumm, Undersecretary at the Wilhelmstraße, called them "grotesque."[28] So even if the Sixtus feelers had held more promise, German obstinacy still blocked the road to a general settlement.

Vienna further complicated the prospects of peace by its own stubbornness towards Italy. Czernin admitted in the March 22 Common Ministers Council that Italy could not be pushed out of the small tract of the Monarchy that it had managed to occupy after months of bloody fighting; but Italy was still Vienna's favorite enemy, and psychologically the most difficult to make concessions to. Czernin wanted peace with Rome only on the basis of the status quo ante; it was almost impossible for him to consider a settlement involving sacrifices. At his March 26 meeting with Bethmann, he insisted that the Monarchy give up nothing to the Italians, provoking the Reich Chancellor's caustic retort after his proposals for Alsace-Lorraine: "Count Czernin has just declared that he cannot cede a quadrameter of Austrian soil to Italy, but we should give the French a piece of the Reichsland."[29] A few days later, urging to Wedel a cession of Alsace, Czernin declared his readiness to give up either the Trentino or Galicia for peace, but simultaneously rejected out of hand a shadowy peace offer at the price of the former from Italy.[30] Then, in May, in the wake of the second Sixtus visit, Bethmann was called to Vienna to be told that Austria had been offered a "legitimate" separate peace from Italy in exchange for the Trentino and several Adriatic islands.[31] But except for Karl, Austrian readiness for any sort of concessions to Rome quickly died with the failure of the Sixtus feelers. It was buried for good in the fall at Caporetto.

Whatever Bethmann said to Czernin in March, such Austrian stubbornness was not wholly unwelcome in Berlin. As Zimmermann noted in May, the war against Italy was "an effective counterweight against the continuing desire for peace in Austria-Hungary," and therefore he had been reluctant to investigate any possible Italian peace feelers very closely.[32]

The failure of Vienna to achieve German concessions for a quick peace in the West was confirmed at the Homburg meeting of April 3, where both Czernin, Karl, and Arz conferred with their German counterparts. "I'll tell you something," Czernin informed German Admiral Georg von Müller, the head of the Kaiser's Naval Cabinet. "Unless the war ends within three months the people will end it without their governments."[33] Because the conflict could not be carried on beyond 1917, every possibility of peace had to be seized and far-reaching annexations renounced. Instead of talking of parity of gains from the war, Czernin now emphasized the reverse side of the agreement he had wrung from Bethmann and urged parity of sacrifices if peace could be achieved in no other way. The Austrians offered not only Congress Poland if Germany would give up Belgium and Alsace-Lorraine, but Austrian Galicia as well. There was no more talk of the "Milliardenobjekt" Rumania—only of the danger of internal revolution if a moderate peace could not quickly be achieved.[34] It was perhaps the most pessimistic stance Czernin had yet taken with the Germans since coming to office. But his words might have had more effect on their recipients if Karl and Arz had supported them better. Asked by Kaiser Wilhelm if Czernin's depiction of Austrian conditions was really that bad, Karl was reported by Cramon to have answered: "Count Czernin always exaggerates!"[35] Perhaps this was a misunderstanding from Karl's often-reported tendency to seem to agree with whomever he was talking. But Cramon also reported that Arz, who had been instructed to paint the situation as black as possible, simply refused to do so. And Arz later confirmed this himself in his memoirs.[36]

Homburg did not signal an end to Czernin's efforts to bring peace nearer, but it did indicate a shift in emphasis from West to East. A month after the outbreak of the Russian Revolution, its effects began to be perceptible, both in its threatened radical effect on the increasingly dissatisfied masses of the Central Powers and in the possibility that the new Russian government might be more ready to discuss peace proposals than its predecessor. Spurred by the first, Czernin hoped to take advantage of the second. It was in April that he reversed his stand on an Oktroi to cover his ground with the Austrian Socialists, and it was also then that he sent his well-known memorandum on the condition of the Monarchy to the Germans.

As the new Russian Provisional Government and the Petrograd Soviet began to issue statements that seemed to indicate that the Russians were ready to leave the war, Czernin pressed the Wilhelmstraße for a common policy. He wanted a positive response to the Russian declarations, to bring peace nearer if it were possible, and for the propaganda effect on his war-weary home population if it were not. By his reckoning, there was nothing to lose and everything to gain through publicly espousing the principle of a status quo ante peace with the Russians. On April 10, he telegraphed Hohenlohe that Vienna and Berlin should quickly agree to a public statement that they were willing to negotiate with Russia on the basis of no annexations or indemnities: "Germany must naturally renounce annexations in the East just like ourselves." Unfortunately, Berlin was not ready to give up its own Eastern aims whatever Vienna intended, and Hohenlohe answered the next day that the Wilhelmstraße considered the situation too uncertain and confused to take any positive steps.[37]

A few days later, Czernin's April 12 message was sent by special courier to German Headquarters. As at Homburg, Czernin declared that the Monarchy's strength was nearing its end and that another winter campaign was out of the question. To the privations of the war was added a new threat: the danger of internal revolution. He described the "dull despair" of the population in the Monarchy, which, because of its Slav nationalities, was particularly susceptible to the events in Russia. He added that despite its national homogeneity, conditions were scarcely any better in Germany, and noted darkly that five monarchs had already been overthrown in Europe since the war began. The impending Entente offensive would probably be repulsed, but then the Central Powers would have to make a new peace proposal involving unspecified "great and heavy sacrifices" before the enemy found out how bad their situation really was. Karl sent an accompanying letter: "We are fighting against a new enemy which is more dangerous than the Entente: against internal revolution, which finds its strongest ally in the general famine."[38]

The message was intended to shake German confidence in a decisive victory and to induce them to moderate their expansionist war aims. But the official leaders in Germany refused to be moved. "The Minister has completely lost his nerve," Zimmermann exclaimed after reading it.[39] The reaction in Berlin was to ignore Czernin's fears and to assure him that ultimate victory was certain as long as the Central Powers held out. This reaction was perhaps encouraged by Czernin's rash attempt to pin down a German offer to put a Habsburg archduke on the Polish throne at the same time that his message was calling for sacrifices to achieve peace. He simply could not do both without undercutting his whole position.

For the next two months, Czernin did everything he could to make the Germans agree to moderate terms that would entice the Russians toward a separate peace with them. His hope was that peace in the East would force England and France to consider peace on the other fronts as well. In the *Fremdenblatt* of April 15, Vienna welcomed the similarity in war aims between Russia and the Monarchy and expressed the view that an understanding would not be hard to achieve. The statement was directed towards Berlin as much as Petrograd, for the official German response to the declarations emanating from Russia was not nearly so conciliatory. Shortly thereafter, when the German Socialist leader Philipp Scheidemann demanded in the Reichstag that the German government officially declare itself in favor of a peace without annexations or indemnities, Czernin wanted to know how the Wilhelmstraße intended to respond and threatened to publicly adopt the position himself if they made no satisfactory statement—which he promptly did.[40]

These direct contacts having gotten nowhere, Czernin attempted to apply indirect pressure on the authorities in Berlin. He invited Count Georg von Hertling, the moderate Bavarian Minister-President, to Vienna, where he induced him to declare that Berlin should publicly renounce all annexations beyond strategic border rectifications.[41] He hoped this would pressure German Chancellor Bethmann to issue such a statement. He even approached

Ludendorff about a clear declaration of war aims. Both attempts backfired. Hohenlohe cabled excitedly from Berlin that if Vienna gave the impression through such actions that it had lost faith in the moderate Bethmann, the military would be quick to take advantage of the fact to replace him with a creature of its own.[42] Czernin issued hasty disclaimers of his recent actions and subsequently did all he could to buttress the Chancellor's position against the more extreme groups in Germany. Vienna obviously possessed little leverage with which to counter the growing power of the annexationists there.

Czernin's efforts for peace did not encounter opposition just in Berlin. Hostilities could not be ended quickly enough for Karl, but other Austrian leaders were already afraid (like the Germans) that Czernin was moving too fast. Tisza advised Czernin after reading his April 12 message not to repeat what he had said there: "A pessimistic tendency evinced now by the leader of our foreign affairs would ruin everything."[43] Tisza believed through reports from the Entente countries that the war was coming to an end anyway; there was no reason to sacrifice Austrian interests by trying to rush the process. Hohenlohe, as might have been expected, shared the same view, whatever he thought of the German military. A month earlier, at the March 26 conference with the Germans, he had openly objected when Czernin entertained restoring Serbia with an outlet to the Adriatic, and now he privately poured out his views to Berchtold:

> Between the two of us, people have become terribly nervous at the Ballplatz in Vienna, which does not do any good at all and only worsens our position towards Germany. I have told Czernin a hundred times, Germany *cannot* continue the war beyond the fall and peace *has* to come; but he continues to belabor the Germans that *we* can in no case hold out longer than the next months. They *also can't here*—so why prostitute ourselves completely superfluously now as the scapegoat for all times to come—all out of nervousness![44]

Arz, the Austrian General Staff Chief, believed that the progressive dissolution of the Czarist army put the Central Powers in a favorable position with no need to push for armistice talks with the Russians. Clam even went so far as to inform Wedel that Czernin's views were overdone, confessing that he had advised him to be more circumspect in the future.[45]

Czernin's interest in declaring for a moderate peace with Russia was as much tactical as substantial, of course; he had nothing against annexations per se if they could be gotten. He specifically excluded "border rectifications" from the general formula of no annexations. But Berlin refused to concede even the tactical flexibility that he was demanding of it to get Russia out of the war. While Czernin desired a "soft" peace (as Zimmermann put it), the Germans were aiming to make any peace as hard as possible. "We have no reason to avoid a discussion over war aims," Zimmermann wrote to Wedel, "but we want to avoid being led into Count Czernin's momentarily advocated program of a peace *without annexations.*"[46] Ludendorff was so confident of final victory with the collapse of the Czarist regime that he reckoned Germany could win the war even if the Monarchy was unable to continue fighting. His consideration for Berlin's chief ally was vividly demonstrated in his plans for Eastern Europe: Berlin had to get Lithuania and Courland or the monarchical authority in Germany would be impaired; but if Russia were paid for these cessions by Habsburg East Galicia, Austria would be none the worse for the loss.[47] On April 23, in a meeting with Bethmann, Ludendorff and Hindenburg affirmed their war aims program despite the Chancellor's weak protests: German control of Belgium, Luxembourg, Liège, and Longwy-Briey in the West; Courland, Lithuania, Poland, and various economic interests in Rumania and the Balkans in the East.[48] It was not simply a maximum program; as far as the military was concerned, it was the only program. The mercurial Kaiser Wilhelm, increasingly submissive to their dictates, was equally ebullient. In May, informed after the second Sixtus visit that Vienna had received a separate peace offer from the Entente, he retorted:

> The offer must be *rejected.* Entente will then be compelled to treat not with weaker Austria, but with powerful *Germany*, which Entente desires to *avoid;* they will come!—since the offer is a sign of weakness and feeling that they can no longer win the war.[49]

Czernin's campaign to moderate German war aims to get a quick peace (separate or otherwise) with Russia in the spring of 1917 received its final blow at the Kreuznach war aims conference of May 17 and 18 between Germany and Austria-Hungary. His hopes for minimal aims were swept aside; the emphasis was on the maximum program of Hindenburg and Ludendorff, and the best Czernin could achieve was acceptance of parity of war aims—which meant the Balkans and Rumania for the Monarchy. But even here, the Germans proclaimed their economic interests in the areas supposedly relegated to Vienna, wanted a larger Serbia instead of a small one as proposed by Czernin, and advanced the old Mitteleuropa plan to make sure their economic interests received adequate safeguard.[50] Austrian aims may have remained proportional to German on paper, but it was on the basis of a program that could be achieved only through total victory. Czernin's minimum program of mutual sacrifices was forgotten by everybody—including Czernin.

After the conference, Czernin expressed his general satisfaction about it to both Karl and German Ambassador Wedel.[51] Yet it did not take long for his better judgment to return. He worried that Germany was arrogating the kernel of Rumania to itself and leaving Austria with only the empty shell, as well as elbowing the Monarchy's interests out of Bulgaria entirely. At Kreuznach, he had made his final approval of the program dependent on its acceptance by the respective Austrian and Hungarian governments, and when he informed Bethmann a month later that this had been achieved, he noted explicitly that if Germany did not get Lithuania and Courland, the Monarchy would be ready to reduce its rights in Rumania to whatever Germany claimed in Poland.[52] In Berlin, his proposal was virtually ignored.

Thus, by June, Czernin's initial, often erratic attempts to find a way out of the war for the Monarchy had been blindly rebuffed by Germany—or at least the German High Command of Hindenburg and Ludendorff. Even German observers such as Wedel realized that Vienna was being put into an impossible position by Berlin's extreme expectations of victory. As he noted worriedly, Austria-Hungary was being faced with the choice of either accepting a favorable separate peace from the Entente, or continuing the war under such conditions that even if it won, all the spoils would go to Germany.[53] He saw with increasing anxiety the growing antagonism and fear against Berlin, especially among Court circles. "People are not only against seeing the struggle through to a definite conclusion because they are afraid of defeat and revolution," he reported, "but also because they consider a complete German victory a danger for Austria-Hungary."[54] It was no wonder that Vienna strove for a compromise peace: to save itself from the pretensions of its own ally as much as those of the Entente. But its efforts to achieve a speedy end to the fighting had so far failed.

IV

Like the other states of Europe, Austria-Hungary underwent major political changes in 1917. Karl had hoped after his accession to reverse the growing current of popular discontent, but his efforts had little success. In Hungary, he wanted to break the power of the Magyar elite by widening the franchise. It would be the first step in appeasing the discontent of the politically powerless masses, Magyar and non-Magyar alike. Tisza, stubborn as ever, refused to countenance such a move, which would have marked the end of Hungary as he knew it, and on May 22 Karl forced him out of office. His successor, Count Móric Esterházy, was unable to accomplish anything, and was replaced in August by Sándor Wekerle. Wekerle, a veteran in Hungarian politics and a former Minister-President, was known for his ability to compromise with powerful vested interests and to avoid pressing problems; he managed to maintain a motley minority government until the last days of the war. The franchise question, like all questions, was discussed, watered down, shelved, and then revived again; but nothing substantial was done until it was too late. Karl may finally have broken Tisza's hold on Hungary, but it was a hollow victory. He merely created a vacuum which no one else could fill. For all his blind adherence to the old order, Tisza had been an energetic leader; his removal meant not that Hungary now received progressive new leadership, but that for the remainder of the war it had practically no leadership at all.

The situation in Austria, where the nationality and social conflicts were not hidden by the façade of an artificially homogeneous parliament, appeared even worse. The Austrian Reichsrat finally met for the first time since 1914 at the end of May, and the expectations Karl placed in a reopening of parliamentary life were quickly dashed. The Czechs demanded the transformation of the Monarchy into a federal state, with the Czech and Slovak nationalities united together within it. The South Slavs wanted the establishment of a Yugoslav polity in the southern portions of the realm. The demands of both groups directly threatened not only the Ausgleich but the territorial integrity of Hungary. The Austrian German Nationalverband, which only a few months earlier had been hoping to end Czech pretensions once and for all through an Oktroi, was adamantly opposed to these demands, while the Poles, so long the mainstay of all Austrian governments, demanded their independence and went into opposition. Clam was unable to deal with the situation and resigned as Austrian Minister-President less than a month after the reopening of the Reichsrat. Ernst von Seidler, a pleasant but otherwise undistinguished bureaucrat, formed a caretaker ministry until a new government could be organized. Karl began interviewing prospective candidates to head it, but found something wrong with all of them. Seidler's very mediocrity was reassuring, and so the Seidler "caretaker" ministry remained in power until the summer of 1918. In Austria as in Hungary, the hopes for a political renewal after the death of Franz Joseph were stillborn.

The increasing political fragmentation was paralleled and reinforced by the food problem. In both halves of the Monarchy, the government was unable not only to procure enough food supplies, but even to distribute equitably what shrinking stores there were. Wedel wrote gravely from Vienna in June that while many "pale, emaciated, even half-starved figures" were in evidence, "Those who have enough money do not have to suffer any privations; they can live practically as well as in peacetime." [55] Food distribution was supposed to be centrally controlled, but the complications of the dualist system prevented it from being so, except on paper. In Hungary, the Esterházy government actually relaxed the regulations for state control of the summer harvest, allowing it to disappear from the market in a matter of weeks. [56] As the 1916-1917 winter ended and the first yields came in, the food situation eased somewhat, but the prospects for a fourth winter of war were dim indeed. In early August, the various Austrian Crownland Statthalter were asked by the Ministry of the Interior in Vienna whether their provinces could hold out another year. The answer was yes—but only if the food situation got no worse. Shortages of foodstuffs, shoes, clothing, and coal were cited, as well as political unrest arising from them, especially among the Czechs in Bohemia. Conditions were worse in the German areas of Bohemia, the later Sudetenland, than in the Czech ones, because the former were more industrialized and had less agriculture; this naturally did nothing to improve relations between the two ethnic groups. The industrial population of Linz in Upper Austria was "already near the limit of its endurance and tolerance," while the Statthalter in Galicia warned that the food supply situation could be allowed to get no worse or "the limit of endurance would be reached." [57]

Unable to supply the basic needs of its population from domestic sources, the Monarchy was thrown more and more onto hope of succor from the occupied areas. *"Because of the extreme shortage of supplies, it is only through imports from Rumania* that the Monarchy is in the position of halfway coming through until the new harvest," Arz reported in July. [58] The supply thread from Rumania was a tenuous one at best, though, and one that led through Berlin. It was Ottokar Landwehr's thankless task as head of the Food Supply Committee to have to beg the German High Command repeatedly for larger allocations of Rumanian grain. In April, he was in Berlin to work out a division of the Rumanian supply to last until the end of May, and then a new agreement had to be negotiated. In August, further negotiations set up quotas to be followed until November. Such shortterm agreements were only stopgap measures, and every negotiation put the Monarchy further into German debt since it felt it had to have more than a fifty percent share of the available Rumanian grain—and had to make up the difference elsewhere. [59]

With the prospect of a further fall in domestic agricultural production, even Rumania seemed unlikely to be more than a temporary palliative. Redlich complained in his diary that the needs of provisioning the army had left the markets of Vienna empty, and that the summer weather was threatening to destroy the harvest yields for the following year.[60] If the Monarchy's military dependence on Germany had been relieved by the events in Russia, its desperate need for food supplies promised to more than make up the difference. "It is becoming ever more clear to me that the food problem is becoming the most burning question of the whole war," Czernin told Hohenlohe in April, pleading for more help from Berlin.[61]

The spreading domestic chaos, coupled with the failure to achieve peace in either East or West because of apparent German stubbornness, brought into the open the latent differences between Karl and Czernin. Czernin's reaction to the internal crisis was to advocate a firm course of repressing the elements of dissonance. On June 28, he had Seidler read a declaration to the Reichsrat bluntly rejecting national self-determination as a basis of peace; peace would be made by the Emperor alone. Czernin obviously feared the corrosive impact of such a doctrine on a multinational state like Austria-Hungary, but his violent rejection of it seemed to be a slap in the face to the Slav deputies of the parliament. Polzer's plans for a parliamentary committee to reorganize the Monarchy on the basis of national autonomy further antagonized him, and he argued that the Poles and Czechs on it made it completely unworkable. Some of the Czechs were committing high treason; and even those who were not wanted only an internal reform that would allow them to oppress the Bohemian Germans. The Poles had no other interest than to join Galicia to Poland. Any constitutional scheme that did not begin with the Austrian Germans was utopian, and even reform on the basis of the Germans would be "frightfully difficult." [62]

But the Emperor Karl's reaction to the turmoil was to conciliate, not repress. On July 2, prodded by Polzer, he issued his famous Amnesty Decree. The decree granted a blanket amnesty to all those who had been sentenced by the hasty military tribunals set up during the first two years of war to control internal security—mainly Slavs, and including the Czech leader Karmář who in 1916 had been found guilty of high treason. Karl had emphasized to Matthias Erzberger when the latter came to Vienna in April that Austria could not be Germanized because the majority of the population was Slav,[63] and he naively hoped the amnesty would be the first step towards appeasing the non-German nationalities of the Empire. But the amnesty was not enough for the Czechs, while it outraged all the upholders of the status quo. Perhaps no one was more upset than Czernin. His first intimation that it was even being contemplated was during a dinner with Hindenburg and Ludendorff when he abruptly learned that it was already public knowledge.

Berchtold, who had become Karl's Court Marshal, recorded a meeting with him a few days later:

> Czernin quite enervated by the procedures of Almighty Sovereign, who received and listened to all possible and impossible people and then suddenly came to a conclusion and acted without asking the responsible adviser. In this way His Majesty did not tell him anything about the Amnesty and he was put before a fait accompli. . . . His Majesty was like a child, listened apparently contritely in such cases; but did exactly the same thing the next time when he felt like it. It could not go on like this. "You'll see, in a month I won't be here any more!" [64]

Grasping for support against the domestic unrest, Czernin turned to the very German alliance that was frustrating all his efforts to achieve peace. Four days after the issuance of the Amnesty, he notified Berlin that he would like Bethmann to praise the strength of the alliance in a coming speech. He commented revealingly: "It would be of great importance in view of the Czech tendencies here." A week earlier, he had declared to Redlich: "He would never participate in a policy of separating Austria from the alliance with Germany; there were enough people in Vienna who would be ready to do that, he would never do it!" [65]

As Czernin realized, the deepening domestic crisis signaled not merely an assault on the status quo, but also on the alliance; all the acrimony that was expressed in the Reichsrat against the internal order was directed by implication at Germany as well. German Ambassador Wedel realized as much, urging greater flexibility from the Wilhelmstraße to head off an open break. He noted that, until then, the alliance had been treated "more or less as a bond between two German states;" and that with the inevitable emergence of the non-German nationalities, it would have to be revised to accommodate them as well if it were to survive. [66] Such advice, however perceptive, contradicted most of Germany's wartime approach to the Monarchy and in Berlin was simply ignored.

But to no one was the connection more obvious than to Karl, who saw it as the main block at once to his longed-for domestic reconciliation and to peace. If Czernin's inclination in the face of the domestic crisis was to strengthen the tie with Berlin, Karl's was just the opposite. Redlich described in early July an audience at Baden outside Vienna in which the Emperor was not only emphatic in his longing to end the war as quickly as possible, but bitter over his relations with Germany. [67] Nor was this all. Distrusting his Foreign Minister's efforts to achieve peace, Karl did what he could to establish peace contacts with the Entente on his own. One semi-official emissary sent by the Emperor to neutral Switzerland later wrote that Karl deliberately kept his mission secret from Czernin.[68]

Anti-German sentiment was not limited to Karl. It was nationwide. By the end of July, Wedel was reporting in alarm that in the Austrian half of the Monarchy it had reached such a pitch that if there had been a plebiscite, the majority of the population would have voted for joining the war on the side of the Entente and marching against its own erstwhile ally. Even the Austrian Germans could no longer be reckoned on, except those living in Bohemia. Conditions in Hungary were better, if only because Czech pretensions to Slovakia had driven the Magyar elite into a pro-Berlin position after earlier wavering; but even here the Transylvanian Saxons were the sole group that was really trustworthy. The Berlin-Budapest connection, supposedly one of the firmest pillars of the alliance, was actually much less firm than it looked. "For the Magyars, the alliance is no bond of the heart, but is based solely on egoistic calculation," Wedel warned. "If they no longer get their money's worth, they are capable of any change of position." [69] His fears were echoed by Bavarian Envoy Tucher, who, after reporting Czernin's growing estrangement with the Court, noted: "But what is still more painful is the fact that even in the non-Slavic population, which until now allowed no doubt of its alliance loyalty to arise, a sentiment unfavorable to Germany and especially to Prussia is beginning to be diffused." [70] The German officer Hans von Seeckt, who had considerable knowledge of conditions in the Monarchy as a result of having served with Karl on the Eastern Front before the latter became Emperor, surveyed the entire situation there in late July. He concluded that developments were in progress in Austria-Hungary "which in the last analysis have in part as their goal the loosening or dissolution of the alliance with Germany, and in part must have that as their result." [71]

Karl's inclinations aginst Germany were encouraged and directed by the Meinl Group acting through Polzer. Meinl and Lammasch had viewed Austria's role as peace mediator much as Czernin had done in the first months of 1917, but the Foreign Minister's failure to drive that policy to a successful conclusion had pulled them apart by the summer. Unlike Czernin, they put strong faith in British and French willingness to accept a moderate peace settlement. The precondition was a domestic reform which would appease the nationalities and thus end all the irredentist demands on the Monarchy by satisfying them from within. If the war continued, it was because of the unquenchable militarism of Prussia-Germany. Even in January 1918, Meinl believed that mere autonomy for Alsace-Lorraine within Germany would satisfy the Entente and, with a declaration of German willingness to restore Belgium and accept a future League of Nations, lead to the beginning of peace talks—hardly a realistic assessment of the war aims of Lloyd George or Clemenceau. The Meinl Group also argued that the Monarchy could exert far more pressure on Germany than Czernin dared, not only to end submarine warfare but even to carry through a reform of the Prussian franchise as preconditions for peace negotiations.[72] The position could not have been made clearer than in a conversation Redlich recorded at the end of August with Lammasch:

> Lammasch considers the military authorities in Berlin the most serious obstacle to peace. He urgently wishes Austria to exert itself in the question of peace and seems to me in his emphatic disapproval of the Prussian-German leadership to want to go to the ultimate consequences.[73]

Such consequences meant only one thing: end the alliance if Germany refused to accept Austria's peace conditions and then get out of the war without it.

The increasing influence of Polzer and Meinl with the Emperor led to an open crisis with Czernin, who by July had made it clear that he would tolerate neither a radical domestic departure nor a real attack on the basic integrity of the alliance. Wedel reported on July 20 that Czernin's position was being steadily undermined with the Emperor, who was seeing the pacifists Lammasch, Redlich, and Foerster almost daily; and that Lammasch had proposed an ultimatum to the Foreign Minister: If Berlin refused to agree to give up Alsace-Lorraine in 48 hours, Austria should make a separate peace.[74] He considered Foerster, a German citizen, so dangerous that he recommended not letting him leave Germany again if he returned home to Munich.[75] Czernin insisted to Karl that a break in the alliance would lead to German invasion of Bohemia and Galicia and a revolt in the German-populated areas of the Monarchy. The Emperor's response was a mark of the religious preoccupation that colored so much of his thinking: If he could bring peace to the world, the Austrian Christian Socials and the Social Democrats would all join him in pilgrimage to Mariazell, the famous pilgrimage spot in Styria. As far as Lammasch was concerned, Czernin had come under the complete control of Berlin.[76] The crisis had certainly strengthened Czernin's position there, for whatever the Germans thought of his peace policies, he was definitely more acceptable than anyone who might replace him—especially since the replacement being recommended by "the professors" was reputed to be the Anglophile Count Albert Mensdorff. "We have to support Czernin, or else we are cutting our own flesh," Wedel wrote to Zimmermann.[77]

At the end of July, Czernin launched an attack on Polzer and threatened to resign. Confronted directly, Karl reaffirmed his faith in Czernin. Polzer's position at Court, and hence that of the entire Meinl Group, was weakened accordingly; but from now on the lines of opposition were clearly drawn between Czernin and the "peace party."[78] It required a constant and increasing effort on Czernin's part to justify his policies to an Emperor wanting more and more to get out of the war at any price but afraid to accept the consequences of a final break with the man he had appointed to make foreign policy. Czernin had blocked the circles in the Monarchy that were ranged against the alliance—but only temporarily.

V

The domestic crisis in Austria was paralleled by one in Berlin. Bethmann's worsening relations with the German military finally came to a head over his efforts to promise some sort of democratic reform of the Prussian franchise. He was forced out of office on July 13. Czernin had done his best to support Bethmann as the assault on his position mounted; and Hohenlohe had gone to Wilhelm on his own authority to try to talk him out of any change of Chancellors. "Bethmann's departure is a blow for us," Hohenlohe wrote afterward, expressing Czernin's sentiments as much as his own.[79] Czernin told Wedel that a new Chancellor from the right could give the impression in the Monarchy that the war was going to be prolonged and thus lead to more domestic unrest; but the new Chancellor, Georg Michaelis, was firmly in the hands of the military. At the same time, Czernin urged government promotion of the impending Peace Resolution in the Reichstag. Such a proof of German moderation, by calling for peace on the basis of the status quo ante, would prevent the formation of a Slav-Socialist coalition in the coming meeting of the Austrian Delegation. "The word 'status quo' would work like a magic charm here and lead to a change of front even among the Czechs," he informed Wedel.[80] The Peace Resolution was passed, but Michaelis' acceptance of it "as he understood it" immediately negated its practical impact.

Whatever Czernin's domestic difficulties, he still tried to pursue his old policy towards Germany. Again, he played up those domestic problems to win concessions in Berlin. At the end of July, in a meeting with Kaiser Wilhelm, he pleaded for a greater show of German moderation to make his own battle with Austrian opponents of the alliance easier.[81] Czernin still hoped to achieve a modification of German war aims which would then make it possible to reach an understanding with the Entente, either as a whole or separately—but without calling the alliance into question and so without disturbing the domestic equilibrium (such as it was) within the Monarchy.

By August 1917, the road to peace again appeared to be in the West. The Kerensky offensive, launched by the Russian Provisional Government, was quickly beaten back; in the ensuing counteroffensive, the Monarchy finally reoccupied those areas of East Galicia and the Bukovina so long in Russian possession. But the offensive, despite its failure, indicated that the new Russian government still intended to remain in the war. On the other hand, the Armand-Revertera talks revived Austrian hopes that France was willing to discuss peace terms. The conversations developed from unofficial contacts between the French army officer Abel Armand and Count Nikolaus Revertera, a retired Austrian diplomat, and led to two secret meetings between them on Swiss soil at the beginning and end of August. Revertera, in an audience with Karl before the first discussion, found the Emperor so impatient that he saw fit to warn him against "hasty steps" in developing the contact.[82] The French conditions, as Armand presented them on August 22, included German restoration of Alsace-Lorraine as well as Belgium, while the Monarchy would be expected to evacuate Serbia and Rumania and cede the Trentino to Italy. It was clearly a separate peace offer, whatever Vienna might earlier have hoped. Armand offered an association of Bavaria and Prussian Silesia with Austria to make the conditions more enticing.[83] Karl remained optimistic even after he heard the conditions. No doubt, he assumed that German acceptance of the French terms in the West could expand the offer from a separate peace into a general one; but Hohenlohe, called in from Berlin, emphasized that even over Belgium nothing but intransigence could be expected from the Germans. Armand never received an answer to his proposals.

Nevertheless, Czernin used the talks to renew his pressure on Berlin for moderation. On August 1, he had his first meeting with the new Chancellor Michaelis; he underlined his pessimism for the future and repeated the earlier offer of Poland in exchange for Alsace-Lorraine. He made it clear that "Poland" meant not just Congress Poland but Austrian Galicia as well—all this if Berlin would cede the Reichsland to the French to get peace with them. Galicia had been mentioned in April as a possible inducement for German concessions in the West, but the proposal had apparently not been taken all that seriously. Now, it was formally presented to the German government. Michaelis admitted that the offer had much to be said for it, but the Germans were skeptical and refused to entertain giving up more than part of Alsace-Lorraine in any case.[84] Two weeks later, Czernin traveled to Berlin to repeat his views, seeing Crown Prince Rupprecht of Bavaria along the way. He was trying to enlist Rupprecht, as well as all the other potential German allies he could contact, in his struggle against Ludendorff. Czernin complained to Rupprecht that the High Command had adopted the war aims of the Pan-Germans. Unfortunately, he spoiled an otherwise favorable impression by refusing to consider any Austrian territorial cessions to Italy.[85]

The Berlin conference took place on August 14. Czernin's exchange offer of Poland and Galicia for some sort of moderation in the West was now rejected out of hand. The military had restated its war aims to the Wilhelmstraße a few days earlier and even extended them towards the Russian Ukraine. When Czernin talked of a status quo ante peace in the West, his listeners agreed in principle and then contradicted on specifics. Even Hohenlohe was outraged at such undisguised aggressiveness and protested that Austria could not carry on the war forever. Czernin, nervous as always, was apparently reduced to tears as he argued that the Monarchy was on the verge of collapse and could fight no longer. The Germans, staking everything on their submarine campaign, were making a desperate gamble. "Suppose: Entente makes status quo ante peace offer," he argued. "You say fight on. We say end. Then reason for alliance drops." It was the ultimate threat, the threat Polzer and the Meinl Group were urging, but it was the final step that Czernin would never take. Yet without it he was powerless; his bluff had been called.[86]

The Pope's peace mediation offer was little more than a postscript to the meeting. It was issued in mid-August after earlier soundings in both Vienna and Berlin and proposed a peace essentially on the basis of the status quo ante. Czernin, reading the Germans' proposed answer, wanted them to express their willingness to make concessions on Belgium, if for no other reason than to put the odium for wrecking the offer on the Entente. But Berlin prevaricated, intending to wait for the Entente response and rejecting Czernin's suggestions. "Count Czernin's pressing is . . . a very deplorable renewed attempt to compel us to enter premature peace negotiations," wrote Richard von Kühlmann, who had succeeded Zimmermann as head of the German Foreign Ministry.[87] Eventually only a generalized, if positive, reply was issued, and the Pope's peace offer went the way of all previous attempts to end the war.

Czernin's efforts to achieve Austrian mediation of the struggle within the alliance had thus reached a dead end by the close of the summer. That policy had assumed the willingness of both Germany and the Entente to accept a compromise peace, an assumption that now appeared completely chimerical. Musulin registered the failure in Switzerland. In July, he had written that the Monarchy's efforts to reestablish its independent image in the rest of the world had been so successful that they had to be braked in the interest of the solidarity of the alliance. But by October, he noted sadly that the dream of Austrian mediation between France and Germany had been buried forever by German reluctance to make concessions in Alsace-Lorraine and French refusal to settle for anything less. The Monarchy was simply too weak to bridge the difference.[88]

The final blow was dealt by Kühlmann, who took charge at the Wilhelmstraße in early August. Kühlmann intended to wrest control of German foreign policy from Ludendorff and impose a moderate settlement in the West, and Czernin quickly established close contacts with him. But the new German Foreign Minister had no intention of allowing Vienna to direct the alliance—which he believed to have been the case ever since his Austrian counterpart had been in office—or to arrogate to itself the role of peace mediator. As he wrote to Michaelis at the end of August, letting Austria play the middleman endangered Germany's vital interests by turning them over to Vienna's disposal to be bargained away with the Entente as it saw fit. Entering peace negotiations in tow of Austria, he added a few days later, would make an already bad diplomatic situation impossible.[89] What freedom of initiative Czernin had been able to exercise over Berlin had been in part the result of Bethmann Hollweg's weak grasp on foreign policy, and now this was a thing of the past.

The end of the summer marked a real parting of the ways for Austrian alliance policy. The alternatives were indicated in a brief echo from the Armand-Revertera talks. Czernin had informed Berlin at the beginning of September that he was ready to go in person to Switzerland to confer with French Premier Paul Painlevé if a meeting there could be arranged, but Kühlmann quickly sabotaged the plan.[90] That ended the chance of peace with France for everyone but Karl. In early October, not wanting the French contact to be lost entirely, the Emperor summoned Revertera to an audience with him. Czernin, alarmed, pulled Revertera aside and told him bluntly that he did not want Karl's peace inclinations encouraged. The Foreign Minister complained that circles around Karl were pressing for a quick peace on the grounds that Austria was now fighting only for German interests, but that such a measure would be a va banque gamble that risked a German invasion of Bohemia. It might change the course of history, but it might also destroy the Monarchy. "I am not up to this responsibility," Czernin insisted. "I see all the disadvantages of such a policy too much."[91]

Faced with a possible way out of the war, Karl was ready to strike forward intuitively with little thought of the alliance; while Czernin, seeing only a yawning abyss, nervously pulled him back. Austria-Hungary could either

seek a quick peace or preserve its tie with Germany; Vienna's efforts since
the beginning of the year had proved that it could not do both. This may
not have been clear to Karl, who did not want to admit that "quick" peace
had become synonymous with "separate" peace. The Emperor hesitated to
break openly with Germany even though this was the logical consequence
of his ideas, and Czernin complained that as a result Vienna ran the risk of
destroying its credit in Berlin while gaining nothing with the Entente.[92] For
Czernin, the alternatives were obvious, and he espoused the alliance.
However justifiable, it was a decision that would have fateful consequences.

Chapter 7

THE GERMAN COURSE
September 1917-April 1918

I

The beginnings of the so-called "German Course" in Austria-Hungary cannot be pinpointed with any great precision. In a sense, such an orientation was implicit in Czernin's actions from the moment he entered office at the end of 1916, for the basis of his foreign policy never ceased to be the alliance with Germany. In a sense, it was also implicit from the first exchange of views after the Sarajevo assassination; Austria-Hungary even before the outbreak of hostilities was settled on a domestic and foreign policy "German Course." Yet, for most of the war, and especially in the first part of 1917, the Monarchy had attempted to assert its independence toward Berlin within the context of that alliance as far as it possibly could: It had attempted to preserve at least the appearance of its own power while simultaneously drawing on its ties with Germany. Under Czernin, it had done this more deliberately than ever, to improve its foreign image as a possible mediator of the war.

But in the last half of 1917, a perceptible change set in. The change was in part a result of the military situation. Superficially, this improved considerably in the course of the year. The Entente attack in the West broke itself at Passchendaele and the Aisne; the Nivelle offensive nearly destroyed the fighting spirit of the French army. In Italy, the Austrian forces, fighting doggedly, had repelled Italian assaults in one Isonzo battle after another, but they had been forced to give up Gorizia in August. The situation was reversed in October with the Caporetto offensive. A combined German and Austrian attack freed the areas of the Monarchy occupied by Italian troops and hurled the Italians with great losses all the way back to the Piave River. Shortly thereafter, the Bolshevik Revolution ended the Russian military threat to the Monarchy for good, and the famous peace negotiations at Brest-Litovsk

149

began. By late 1917, Austria-Hungary was completely free of foreign forces, and Austrian units occupied Serbia, Montenegro, northern Albania, and southern Poland; only in northern Italy was an Austrian army still confronted by a major enemy, though one which did not attempt a renewed offensive until the closing days of the war. Vienna in 1914 had had no doubt that it was going to war to preserve itself from foreign dismemberment. By 1917, all of its attackers had either been invaded in their turn or knocked out of the war entirely. If the Monarchy had needed Germany only to preserve its territorial integrity, the alliance had now fulfilled its reason for existence. Militarily, Austria-Hungary had achieved all of its initial war aims.

In reality, the military results of 1917 were more ambiguous. Even the victory at Caporetto was less than it seemed. Karl originally had wanted to conduct the attack solely with Austro-Hungarian troops, the Germans merely providing artillery support. Ludendorff, however, insisted on German infantry participation and tactical command of the operation. It could be argued that the limited success of the campaign actually worsened the Monarchy's position. A complete victory might have knocked Italy out of the war, which would have invalidated the Treaty of London and removed a major hindrance to an Austrian understanding with Britain and France—with or without Germany. As it was, Caporetto fortified the Italians' resolve to continue fighting. It also forced the British and French to increase their support of the Italian war effort. And since Vienna's armies now stood on Italian soil, the breakthrough made it psychologically more difficult than ever to consider buying an Italian peace with anything less than the status quo ante. Perhaps the only longterm gainers were the Germans, who saw the pressure on their ally's southwestern flank relieved without seeing it relieved so much that the Austrians might decide that they could stop fighting in the war altogether.

While the successes of 1917 failed to end the war, they did increase the German military's expectations of eventual total victory. As the Germans forged peace treaties in the East with Russia and Rumania, they began preparations for the final offensive that would break through to Paris and impose a similar peace in the West. But the Entente could never accept their terms unless utterly defeated; so it was unlikely that further German victories would bring peace any nearer. Even if Berlin did manage somehow to end the war victoriously, few of the fruits of victory were going to be given to Vienna. The situation Wedel had feared in May thus became reality: The Monarchy stood to lose more by staying in the war even if it could be won, than by breaking the alliance and contracting out while it still could.

Czernin's efforts to find a moderate middle course of a general peace in the first part of 1917 had proved only that such a third alternative did not exist.

Yet instead of attempting to escape the alliance, Vienna—or, more precisely, Czernin—set itself to do the exact opposite. Though Czernin continued to stress such Wilsonian goals as international disarmament, an international court, and a League of Nations, most notably in an October 2 speech in Budapest, he was not going to allow anything to imperil the integrity of the alliance. He had already in September instructed the Austrian missions in the neutral lands to make this clear, a definite shift from his earlier instructions to emphasize the Monarchy's independence from Germany.[1] On December 6, in a public address to the Hungarian Delegation, he displayed his loyalty to Germany before all the world and attacked the growing suspicion in Austria-Hungary that the war continued only to satisfy annexationist German war aims. The Monarchy was fighting for Alsace-Lorraine just as much as Germany was fighting for it; and if the war was prolonged, it was because of the Entente's thirst for annexations, not the reverse. "I see no difference between Strasbourg and Trieste," he concluded in a ringing declaration.[2] From the time of that speech, observers began to speak of the "German Course" in Austria. Prophetically, the United States finally declared war on the Monarchy the following day.

Vienna's options, momentarily promising in early 1917, were now running out. Czernin had hoped to strengthen the moderate forces in Germany against Ludendorff and the military, but the latter remained as decisive as ever. The founding of the Fatherland Party (Vaterlandspartei) in early September augured still greater military intractability for the future. "Had Germany been victorious," Czernin admitted after the war, "her militarism would have increased enormously."[3] The moment of decision was also arriving for the Entente. Throughout the first part of 1917, Entente statesmen, watching Russia crumble, had vacillated between somehow setting up the Monarchy as a substitute Eastern buffer against Germany in the postwar order, and the opposite policy advocated by the emigrés, to dissolve Austria-Hungary into its constituent national parts. Brest-Litovsk made the issue acute: Russia was clearly out of the war. There would be no compromise peace with Berlin, about that everyone in the West was clear; the Entente intended to continue the war until Germany was decisively defeated. If Austria-Hungary could not now be induced to leave the war to offset the loss of Russia, it would have to be destroyed in order to cripple the German war effort from the rear. Brest-Litovsk made its continuation in the German orbit not merely dangerous, but potentially suicidal. Yet, faced with maintaining the alliance in these circumstances, Czernin not only rejected any separation from the Germans, but actually worked to strengthen the Monarchy's ties with them. "A separate peace was a sheer impossibility," he asserted after the war.[4] Why did he take such a rigid stand against breaking the alliance?

Concluding a separate peace has never been an easy step for a state to consider, but two factors made the Monarchy's predicament especially difficult. First, Austria-Hungary faced major territorial claims on the part of many of its antagonists, which would have left little of it to speak of had they been carried out to the letter. By 1917, it was apparent in Vienna (which by then knew the general terms of the Treaty of London and its counterparts, and knew them specifically after they were published by the Bolsheviks), that those claims would not be carried out to the letter in the case of a separate peace. But to what extent would they be changed? When Entente contacts promised a moderation of them, could their words be taken at face value, given the Entente's earlier promises to its own allies? Ironically, it was German strength that gave the Monarchy the opportunity of a separate peace. In 1917 and early 1918, many in the West feared Germany would win the war: hence their interest in an arrangement with Vienna. If the Austrians abandoned that source of strength and German defeat followed, they felt that they had no surety that the Entente would not then revert to its earlier aims and partition it at will. A major hindrance to an Austrian separate peace was the doubts and complications entailed by all those former Entente claims on the Habsburg patrimony.

Astute diplomacy by a determined government with strong popular backing probably could have overcome these hurdles, meeting British conditions and thus enabling London to overrule the doubts of Paris or Rome to achieve a separate peace that preserved the Monarchy. Unfortunately, such a government was simply lacking in Austria-Hungary. This was the second factor which made the Monarchy's situation so difficult: its character as a multinational state. When Italy left the Second World War in 1943, for example, a separate peace meant a change of the regime; but the state itself survived. In the Monarchy's case, a collapse of the regime could well have led to the dissolution of the entire polity into its constituent national parts. A separate peace would be an admission by its rulers that they had involved it in an unwinable war. It might also entail an open conflict with its erstwhile ally Germany: Austrian and German troops were inextricably mixed on the Eastern Front, and the Germans might invade the Monarchy to secure their supply routes to Rumania and Turkey. At the very least, it would mean an end to German transfusions of grain and financial assistance, upon which Austria-Hungary was so dependent, and thus provoke an immediate economic crisis. Did the Habsburg Crown still possess enough prestige and authority to maintain under those circumstances the coherence of a state as internally divided as the Dual Monarchy?

Clearly, Czernin thought not. Austria-Hungary appeared to him and to many of his colleagues as no longer strong enough on its own to survive the consequences of the war. The domestic and foreign balance of forces that had been the essence of the "Old Austria" had been crumbling ever since Sarajevo. But by the end of 1917, it was clear beyond any doubt that the nationalities had ceased to accept the status quo. The old order by itself no longer had the power to resist them; this could be done only by appealing to the alliance with Germany. The alternative was to appease the nationalities through a drastic transformation of the Monarchy into some sort of federal state—over German opposition. A separate peace, by ending the German connection, would make the collapse of the old domestic order inevitable; once the tie with Berlin was gone, there would be nothing left to stop it. The pro-Austrians in the Entente camp in fact considered a federal transformation of the Monarchy the sine qua non of any arrangement with Vienna. It would be their guarantee that the Monarchy's break with Germany would be permanent. Charles Hardinge of Penshurst, the Permanent Undersecretary of the British Foreign Office, noted in early 1918: "We also would like a strong and independent Austria as a barrier to Germany, but this is only feasible as a federated empire in which the Slav states enjoy complete autonomy."[5] By 1917, the Ausgleich could be maintained only by complete dependence on Germany; breaking with Germany necessarily meant the end of the Ausgleich and a constitutional reconstruction of the Habsburg state. Karl saw the choice and opted for reconstruction, even if he hesitated before the final step of an open break with Germany. Both he and the Meinl Group, however utopian they otherwise were, reasoned correctly that the longer a domestic transformation was delayed, the greater would be the eventual risk in carrying it out.

But to other leading Austrian figures, the risk was already too great. To them, there was no guarantee that "reconstruction" would not simply mean "dissolution," especially given the Emperor's own lack of practical experience and willpower. What was to keep all the conflicting nationality demands from unleashing a civil war? The traditional instruments of authority—the bureaucracy and the army—were tottering after three years of bloody conflict; the economy was a shambles; political and social radicalism would soon find expression in massive strikes. Constitutional experiments could easily release forces which those in authority, however well-intentioned, would be powerless to control, and which would lead to the collapse of the entire realm. Conclusion of a separate peace thus involved repercussions for

Austria-Hungary which few other states contemplating such a step have ever had to consider.

These were certainly grave risks. But the risks of remaining in the war were equally great, as Czernin himself had often pointed out. What ultimately determined that the Monarchy would follow the latter course, cost what it would? A final risk was involved in striving for a separate peace and domestic reconstruction, one which Austrian leaders rarely mentioned openly either during the war or afterwards, and which many perhaps never even wholly admitted to themselves. Bismarck, writing about the alliance in his recollections, had observed that loyalty to a treaty could never be expected to take precedence over loyalty to the state itself. If the existence of the state were jeopardized by an alliance, no amount of "alliance loyalty" justified continued adherence to that treaty accord.[6] This, however, was a distinction which many in Austria-Hungary could no longer make. By the end of 1917, the two loyalties—to the state and to the alliance—had become virtually synonymous for them. A separate peace would mean a domestic transformation of some sort; but any such transformation would put all the Monarchy's nationalities on an equal footing—and thus deliver up both Austrian German and Magyar to a Slav majority. For the Germans and Magyars, this could never be accepted even if it was possible to implement it. Faced with the choice, they would prefer to see the Monarchy collapse than to "save" it at such a cost. Domestic reform had to be opposed not only because it might fail, but, in the final resort, because it might succeed. To block it, Austria-Hungary had to retain the German alliance even at the price of staying in the war to the bitter end.

Czernin had already made his position towards the alliance clear in July in his efforts to negate Karl's attempts at domestic reform, and he never changed thereafter. At the beginning of October, he told Prince Lajos Windischgraetz, who became head of the Hungarian food supply administration in 1918, that any radical solution of the South Slav problem had to be put off until the conclusion of peace. In December, he repeated the same message to Clam-Martinic: Satisfying one nationality would only antagonize the others, so however necessary reform might be, constitutional changes had to be avoided as long as the war lasted. He also noted to a friend that even if a tolerable peace could be found without Germany, the federal transformation which it would entail was impossible in the face of the Austrian Germans and the Magyars.[7]

Others were prepared to go equally far—or farther. Statesmen who earlier in the war had followed the Tisza-Burián line of asserting the Monarchy's independence within the alliance became staunch supporters of the tie with

Berlin at any cost when Karl's impulsive efforts at reform threatened to overturn the domestic order. Cramon, in a draft report at the end of July, noted how highly German efficiency was held even by groups critical of the alliance and added:

> This is above all the case with the circles who follow the domestic policy of the young Emperor with great misgiving and ultimately hope for their salvation from us. They frequently go so far as to actually demand our interference in the domestic relations of the Monarchy, because the Emperor's policies involve the fate of all Germandom.[8]

Cramon may particularly have had Conrad von Hötzendorf in mind as he wrote those lines. Conrad had been unremitting in his efforts to counter real and fancied German attempts to dominate the alliance for the first two years of the war. But he never called the alliance itself into question; he always viewed Germany and the Monarchy as bound tightly together. After the defeats of the Brusilov offensive made German aid essential to stave off total disaster, Conrad became much more amenable to infusions of German aid and control. Karl's attempted reforms and his own dismissal completed his shift from being a Habsburg patriot to an advocate of Großdeutsch nationalism. As a commander on the Italian front after his replacement by Arz, he explained to Cramon why he had been fired by Karl: "I had to be set aside first of all because of my position towards Germany, since I would never in my life have agreed to a conspiracy against Germany but resisted it with all my strength."[9] As the Old Austria died, Conrad was unable to transfer his loyalty to any possible federated successor, but found it instead in his German nationality. After the war, he wrote that the non-German nationalities had "betrayed" the Monarchy but consoled himself that the new Austrian republic was a German land that would serve as a bulwark of Germandom against southeastern Europe and someday become part of a single German Reich.[10]

Czernin and Conrad thus both ended in the position at which Hohenlohe had arrived earlier in the war: Whatever fate the alliance held for the Monarchy, it was infinitely preferable to the fate of existing without it. The evolution of their viewpoints was shared by many other Austrian bureaucrats and party leaders. Nor was that of the Hungarian oligarchy much different. It defended the Ausgleich tooth and nail as long as it seemed to preserve Magyar domination of Transleithania; but when this finally ceased to be the case, it was ready to secede from the rest of the state rather than accept any constitutional changes that impinged on its privileged position.

The essence of Czernin's German Course was to cement the Monarchy ever more firmly to Berlin as the pressure for both peace and domestic change grew. It was a bitter outcome for someone who had come to office intending to assert Vienna's initiative and to find a quick way out of the war. Superficially, Czernin continued to follow the same course he had pursued since the beginning of 1917: to seek peace with any belligerent willing to treat, aiming ultimately for a general compromise settlement. But the preconditions for such a policy had clearly disappeared. In reality, he was willing to accept peace only through German leadership, for the domestic crisis in Austria-Hungary made it impossible for him to conceive of the Monarchy existing without Germany—though it was becoming unlikely that it could exist with it. If risking the consequences of a separate peace was to play va banque, as he told Revertera, to refuse the risk was equally to go va banque. So Austrian policy in the fourth winter of the war became little more than a desperate stumble from one shortterm expedient to another with the hope that disaster could be staved off until salvation somehow miraculously appeared on the horizon. Revertera wrote in despair to Berchtold: "We are bleeding ourselves white for grotesque ideas and nevertheless cannot separate ourselves from Germany without approaching a catastrophe."[11]

II

In the fall of 1917, the old questions of Mitteleuropa and Poland both reappeared as subjects of discussion between Vienna and Berlin. The goal of their interchanges was to put the issues to rest once and for all in a comprehensive agreement. More than this, the discussions represented a last attempt on Czernin's part to counter the power of the German High Command. In German Foreign Minister Kühlmann, Czernin hoped finally to have found the counterweight to Ludendorff and the military in Germany for which he had been searching since March, someone who realized the need for a moderate program and was ready to fight the High Command to get it. Their community of interests was complemented by a personal affinity, so that the eventual result was probably the strongest personal tie cementing the alliance at any time during the war. In practical terms, it became an alliance of Vienna with the civilian authorities in Berlin against the German military. By the fall of 1917, however, the annexationist forces centering on Ludendorff and Hindenburg were so entrenched that even the combined efforts of Vienna and the Wilhelmstraße together could not seriously shake them. The negotiations ended in a hopeless impasse of contradictory demands and accusations, while Czernin's attempts to save something from the general wreckage further strained his ties with the Emperor Karl.

Mitteleuropa had actually been discussed in Vienna throughout much of the preceding year. Even when Czernin had been most active in promoting the appearance of Austrian independence of Berlin, in contrast to his predecessors he had looked with favor on "extending" the alliance with Germany. Ironically, the government took up the question after the popular agitation, which had reached its peak a year earlier, had begun to taper off. By 1917, Vienna was simply no longer strong enough to persist in its earlier disinterest. A renewal of the negotiations with Germany was agreed to at a Common Ministers Council on May 6, where it was hoped that an arrangement compatible with the Monarchy's independence could be found—or at least an arrangement that would appear to be compatible in the eyes of the rest of the world. Even Tisza, still worried about the Monarchy becoming economically bound to Germany, was forced to agree. He admitted that a close association had become a vital interest for both empires.[12]

Vienna moved to renew the negotiations because the economic chaos caused by the war seemed to leave no other alternative. The Austrian leadership may have felt threatened by Mitteleuropa in 1915 and 1916, but by 1917 it could no longer afford to reject the fringe benefits it might bring in its wake. Baernreither confessed to Redlich in June that they had to agree to German Mitteleuropa plans because they already owed Berlin four billion Marks;[13] and Alexander von Spitzmüller, then Austrian Finance Minister, underlined the need for more German currency support at the May 6 meeting. The specter of a financial debacle haunted Vienna by 1917. At a September meeting of the Common Ministers Council, it was agreed that the state of the Monarchy's balance of payments and gold reserves was catastrophic. Once peace was attained, enormous foreign debts would fall due. Assuming the currency system still functioned at all, more credit would have to be raised somewhere to refinance them or the monetary system would collapse completely. It was obvious that the single possible source was Germany; the only question was how to secure the best terms. Burián, who had returned to his old office of Common Finance Minister after his replacement by Czernin, perhaps summed it up best in a July discussion of Mitteleuropa. For the Monarchy to reap the greatest benefits, talks for it should be pushed as far as possible before the war ended. "One would find Germany much more willing to negotiate during the war," he argued, "because it would have to want to consolidate its relations with Austria-Hungary as completely as possible before peace, and because Germany would need the Monarchy much more during the war than after it."[14] This was hardly the Burián of a year earlier. But Austria's economic and financial dependence on Berlin was such by 1917 that most leaders felt they had to assure a continuation of German aid into peacetime even at the cost of Mitteleuropa. The one exception was Karl, who, in response to the May decision to reopen the negotiations, declared bluntly: "I do not agree at all."[15] He saw the whole plan simply as an attempt by Germany to subvert the independence of the Monarchy no matter how many qualifications there were, but Czernin momentarily managed to prod him away from his misgivings.

The renewed negotiations got underway in July and reached a stalemate in August. The Germans, whatever their earlier professions, proclaimed their intent to create an economic area equal to that of the British Empire or America in which the Monarchy would have lost all economic independence. At that point, the talks broke down, for this was a greater price for the future than Vienna or Budapest was willing to pay no matter how desolate their immediate prospects.[16]

Such was the state of the Mitteleuropa scheme by the end of the summer, when the problem of Poland again surfaced. The Austro-Polish solution had supposedly been buried for good in March, but by September Vienna had concluded that any other solution made the Poles in the Monarchy totally ungovernable, whatever Czernin's earlier expectations; and the dissatisfaction in the Reichsrat from the other nationalities made the goodwill of the Poles more important than ever. Czernin now informed Viktor Naumann that the only way of solving the question of Poland lay in the Austro-Polish solution after all, regardless of how Congress Poland were constitutionally joined to the Monarchy. In a talk with Wedel he interjected a further consideration: The German-Polish solution created so many difficulties that it would make a continuation of the alliance itself impossible. Wedel agreed.[17] Just how important Poland had become for Czernin, despite all his earlier plans, was indicated in a talk with Cramon during the Caporetto offensive. To get it, he was willing not only to make concessions in Rumania, but even to accept a "vassal relationship" of the Monarchy with Germany. When Cramon objected that Karl could never be had for such a course, Czernin reportedly answered: "Let me worry about this—I'll bring the Emperor around."[18]

The Germans—at least the civilians—were ready for a change of policy. Wilhelm had just returned from a visit to occupied Rumania and was enraptured with its prospects for economic development under German control. He was more than willing to give up Congress Poland for the Milliardenobjekt to the south. Wedel had been arguing for a return to the Austro-Polish solution since August as the only way of dampening the anti-

German trend among the Austrian population, by giving it some tangible reward for all its sacrifices. But most important of all, Kühlmann wanted to settle the Monarchy's relationship with Germany by linking Poland to the Mitteleuropa question. He hoped not only to block the rising pressure in Austria to terminate the alliance, but to assure a continuation of the tie into peacetime. If he could get the Monarchy's adherence to the Mitteleuropa plan by acceding to its wishes for Poland, both goals would be accomplished at once: Since Poland would be included in any German-run Mitteleuropa organization, it would not really be lost anyway. It was the same reasoning that had motivated the Wilhelmstraße to present its first Mitteleuropa plans to Vienna two years earlier, only with Jagow's heavy racial overtones now smoothed over. The end would be the same: German domination of the Monarchy. "Our policy hopes for a *penetration* of Austria-Hungary," Kühlmann noted.[19]

Thus, as in the fall of 1915, Poland and Mitteleuropa became different parts of the same complex, and Vienna was confronted with a new situation from Berlin—or rather, an old one now revived. The moment seemed to have arrived for a settlement of all the various issues outstanding between them, and so for a long-overdue "clarification" of the alliance itself. Czernin was more than ready. Here, finally, was a moderate German statesman with whom he could work. Mitteleuropa interested Czernin not so much as an economic issue per se, but as a bargaining counter with which to buttress his diplomatic position in Berlin. He wanted a return to the Austro-Polish solution by the fall of 1917, and, no less important, continued to stress the need for a moderate peace program. Mitteleuropa might involve some loss of the Monarchy's independence to Berlin, but Czernin considered that a small price to pay if in return it could be used to get the German military to relinquish its most grandiose war aims and accept a moderate, flexible peace program.

The path the two Foreign Ministers hoped to follow was sketched out in a non-binding personal agreement of October 22, in which they formulated the common war aims program they hoped to carry through with their respective governments.[20] Austria would conclude a new offensive and defensive alliance with Germany for a period of 20 years, enter into a longterm military agreement to standardize weapons and military organization, and begin talks to create closer political and economic relations between the two empires by removing as many tariff barriers between them as possible. Reversing the earlier agreement of the spring, Poland was returned to the Austrian sphere of influence (the Austro-Polish solution, this time in the form of a personal union), and Rumania allocated to the German;

Lithuania and Courland were to become autonomous but closely connected with Germany as well. Finally, Berlin obligated itself to find a formula for Belgium that would not hinder the attainment of peace. The agreement indicated how much sovereignty Czernin was willing to surrender in order to achieve his aims; the Austro-Polish solution was intended to calm the Poles and secure a majority in the Reichsrat, and he hoped moderation over Belgium would bring the Entente closer to peace negotiations.

This unfortunately soon proved to be a vain expectation. Hindenburg and Ludendorff were dead set against the Austro-Polish solution despite all Kühlmann's arguments; they maintained that a strong Austria would reduce Germany to vassalage and actually talked of the possibility of a future war with the Monarchy. Hindenburg communicated their views to the Wilhelmstraße:

> The High Command is against an Austro-Polish solution. It sees in the increase in power of Austria-Hungary the strengthening of the anti-German elements in Austria-Hungary, and in the envelopment of Germany by Austrian Poland from the south and east a serious danger for Germany.

To counter this threat, a list of no less than 23 conditions was demanded if Poland should nonetheless revert to Austria, ranging from complete German control of the Polish economy to a cession of Austrian Silesia to connect Germany directly with Hungary. Even then, large parcels of western Congress Poland would be annexed to Prussia. Kühlmann's Mitteleuropa plans left them equally cold.[21]

On November 5 and 6, Czernin met with the German civilian and military leaders formally to reverse the earlier Kreuznach agreement of May and return to the Austro-Polish solution. Or so they thought. Czernin and Kühlmann were both ready to exchange spheres in Poland and Rumania and to begin working to set up the Mitteleuropa plan. Czernin even talked of the old idea of reestablishing Austrian German predominance in Cisleithania by shutting the Poles out of the Reichsrat through the Austro-Polish solution. But all this was reckoning without the High Command. Ludendorff openly rejected the plans of his own government in front of the Austrians, and the meeting quickly devolved into an argument of Czernin and Kühlmann against him. The Quartermaster General insisted on extensive German annexations in Congress Poland even if there was to be an Austro-Polish solution, not to mention German control of the railroads and industry in what was left. Agreement was finally reached in principle on the basis of the October 22 pact; but in practice, the military's "guarantees" for the Austro-

Polish solution had not been budged an inch, and on that basis any agreement for Vienna was impossible. Czernin objected that they amounted to a new partition of Poland.[22]

For the next month, Czernin did what he could to defend his position. But while he tried to present a strong front to the Germans, his own authority with the Emperor was continually shaking, for Karl doubted if Poland was worth Mitteleuropa to begin with. Far from getting out of the war, the Monarchy seemed only to be getting further entangled in it. The renewal of Mitteleuropa in the fall revived all his already-expressed fears of German domination; even more than to the economic clauses, he objected to the proposed 20-year military convention, and Czernin found himself having constantly to argue against his misgivings about the whole undertaking. "If the common armament *at least* is not included in the treaty, getting the advantages which Your Majesty wants from the Germans is completely out of the quesion," he wrote on October 15. "In that case, a positive refusal is absolutely certain and I have no other idea what to do."[23] The negotiations dragged on; new talks between the economic specialists began, but the question of Poland remained in deadlock. Hohenlohe warned that the Mitteleuropa discussions were going so slowly that Berlin might be tempted to break them off entirely, while Karl decided he could accept the Austro-Polish solution only if Berlin renounced not merely Ludendorff's annexations, but all annexations no matter how small.[24] Even Czernin had no expectation of carrying through such a thing. The intended clarification of the alliance and its war aims left Vienna's relations with Berlin more contradictory and unclear than ever, and it was in this state that Austria-Hungary entered the first peace negotiations of the war—the conference of Brest-Litovsk.

III

The Russian Provisional Government had scarcely survived the reverses of the summer. At the beginning of November, it was overthrown by Vladimir Lenin's Bolsheviks. One of its first acts was to proclaim its willingness to conclude peace immediately on the basis of no annexations or indemnities.

Vienna's earlier hopes for a quick peace seemed on the verge of realization at last, for the new regime was clearly in no position to continue hostilities even if it had wanted to. Whatever qualms other policy-makers in Vienna might have had, Czernin was more than ready to negotiate with the revolutionary regime on the basis it proposed. Speed was all the more important for him because there was no telling how long the Bolsheviks might remain in power, hence advantage had to be taken of their willingness for peace while the opportunity still remained. As in April, though, Czernin's first hurdle was Berlin. The Petrograd coup was scarcely complete before he began badgering the Wilhelmstraße for an agreement on the basis of which if any Russian proposals would be accepted, so they could act as quickly as possible if the Russians made an offer. But the basic dichotomy in Czernin's policy emerged once again; he realized how necessary peace was to forestall domestic events in the Monarchy, but he also hoped to be able to reap some sort of material advantage from it. As he pointed out to Hohenlohe, speedy acceptance of peace on the basis of no annexations would be a formula that the rest of the Entente could not accept, opening the possibility of splitting Russia from the West and concluding a separate peace with it. The Bolshevik regime had proclaimed the principle of national self-determination for its non-Russian peoples, and Czernin was quick to see how this could be exploited in favor of the Central Powers if only peace talks could be started: "Since we then will not be having to negotiate with Russia, but with its 'liberated nations', it will not be difficult anymore to reach an agreement with the Russian areas that we occupy today, guaranteeing their connection to us." He proposed that they declare their readiness to treat with the new Russian government, recognize it, agree to peace without annexations, and accept a three-month armistice.[25]

But even with such prospects dangled before them, the Germans refused to act with the speed Vienna demanded. Czernin wrote Hertling, the new Chancellor, directly, but to no effect. Count Georg von Hertling had been a moderate as Minister-President of Bavaria, but his elevation to Berlin in October 1917 as Michaelis' successor was a disappointment for the Austrians. Partly because of his advanced age, his coming to office marked no change in the civilian-military power relationships in Germany. Yet even Kühlmann complained that Czernin, in his haste for peace, was discussing the Bolshevik proposals behind his back with the Turks and the Bulgarians in order to put pressure on him.[26]

The Germans were as determined to reach an understanding with Russia as Czernin, merely more confident in the strength of their position and the weakness of their adversaries. They were not about to throw away any possible advantages just to achieve peace a little sooner, even though they recognized the possibilities of closing down the entire Eastern Front and concentrating all their weight in France for a decisive offensive. It was not until December 3, after the Entente had failed to respond to the Russian proposals as Czernin had predicted, that armistice negotiations were formally opened; and then they threatened to founder on the inflexibility of the German military. General Max von Hoffmann, the German Chief of Staff on the Eastern Front, wanted Russian evacuation of Estonia to be one of the armistice conditions, provoking Austrian protests that such a demand was exorbitant and would endanger the negotiations. On December 7, Czernin held a meeting at the Ballplatz with the leading ministers of the Monarchy to discuss what to do if the talks broke down. It was clear that however much he might like to secure gains from a peace with Russia, the internal condition of the Empire demanded peace with no gains whatsoever if the alternative would be a prolongation of the war:

> Count Czernin now expressed the view that the work of peace must under no circumstances collapse on the territorial aspirations of the Germans. He was firmly resolved to carry out even a peace on the basis of the status quo ante, if better conditions were not attainable. In view of the nervous mood of the hinterland, Count Czernin felt it would be extraordinarily dangerous if the peace negotiators, through the fault of Germany, came back empty-handed.

His listeners agreed, as he went on to point out that they could not even demand anything from Rumania or Serbia—not if they expected to pare down Germany's ambitions. The Lovčen from Montenegro was all that they could hope for. If the Germans still proved obdurate, then Czernin suggested launching an "adroit and discreet" press campaign in order to appeal to the German people over the heads of the military. Even the ultimate course of a separate peace with Russia without Berlin, though fraught with difficulty, was mentioned; but here Wekerle, the Hungarian Minister-President, demurred against coming to any open break with the Germans.[27] If Berlin weighed the prospect of peace in the East with confidence, Czernin in Vienna grasped at it almost in desperation. Luckily, a compromise formula was found for the armistice, which was initialed on December 15. The way was now open for formal peace negotiations.

That accomplishment, a triumph of sorts for Czernin's diplomacy, was one he had little chance to enjoy. As the armistice terms were finally settled, he was preoccupied with defending his domestic position. Karl was frightened at the prospect of treating with the Bolsheviks, fearing they could use the opportunity to revolutionize the Monarchy. He worried about the reaction of the Austrian Social Democrats if the talks failed. Czernin answered that Vienna had no choice; the impending exhaustion of the Central Powers meant that no risk was too great to accept.[28] At the end of November, Polzer had been forced to resign, prompting Wedel to speak of a major defeat for the "Chocolate Party," as he referred to the Meinl Group because of Meinl's business in coffee and chocolate. But the friction between Czernin and Karl only increased. With the fourth winter of war that Vienna had so dreaded, the food situation became critical. Staving off domestic food riots became an almost daily concern of the Austrian Foreign Ministry. "I point out to Your Excellency again," Czernin wrote to Wekerle on the 12th of December, trying to get more supplies out of Hungary, "that, if help with grain supplies does not come as quickly as possible, we will stand before a *catastrophe* here. Vienna is provisioned for only a few days more." [29] Czernin's health, never good, broke down in the middle of the month; and when he defended his policies to Karl, he did so from his bed. He had intended to attend the peace negotiations personally but was forced to delegate Kajetan Mérey, who had been Austrian Ambassador to Italy before the war, to represent him until he felt well enough to travel.

The negotiations opened officially in Brest-Litovsk, the headquarters of the German army on the Eastern Front, on December 22. By then, Czernin had made his arrival, after missing the first preliminary meetings; one of his cares before coming had been simply to assure himself a properly-heated room in the ruined, snow-bound town. Hoffmann characterized him: "A clever, distinguished man, whose nerves were unfortunately entirely shattered." Kühlmann was on hand for the Germans, and he and Czernin even managed to go hunting between negotiating sessions—to the disgust, needless to say, of the German military. Kühlmann divided power with Hoffmann. The Turks and the Bulgarians both sent delegations as well, but generally kept in the background. The main battles were waged by the Germans against the Russian delegates.[30]

What did Czernin expect at Brest? Not knowing when he could arrive, he sent a list of guidelines to Mérey in his absence. They included making certain that peace was assured militarily, getting supplies of food and raw material from Russia, attempting to keep Poland out of Russian control, non-interference in Austrian internal affairs, and preventing the German military from endangering peace through inflexible demands. He concluded emphatically:

> It is known to Your Excellency that peace with Russia under all circumstances *must* come into effect, and that *all eventualities are possible except that of a collapse of the negotiations because of the Central Powers.* Even a separate peace between us and Russia would be preferable to the eventuality of a collapse through German wishes.[31]

But what would happen after peace? In a contemporaneous letter to a friend, Czernin hoped that peace in the East would enable a German offensive in the West that would force the Entente to come to terms. Yet he realized that if the Germans took Paris, their ambitions would become more extravagant than ever; they would demand a "good" peace. Such a peace, he conceded pessimistically, was impossible even under those circumstances. So, as soon as the Entente was ready to treat, he proposed to appeal publicly to the peoples of the Central Powers over the heads of the military to end the war. "The odium of having 'spoiled the peace' I will take upon myself," he wrote.[32] In January, he had specifically refused that odium when the Germans began unrestricted submarine warfare. Did he really think such an action would have any more effect now? The German moderates would be weaker than ever if the High Command succeeded in adding a victory in the West to its Eastern triumphs. Czernin's words exposed the desperation of his position even as he sat down to begin negotiations. What he wanted was a German victory that would be followed by moderate terms to the Entente; and given the mentality of the High Command, this was a total contradiction in terms.

The course of the negotiations soon made that painfully apparent. The Russians presented their peace conditions to the plenary session, and thus to the world, for on their insistence the negotiations were public. They demanded a status quo ante peace excluding any annexations or indemnities, and plebiscites for national groups without political independence. Kühlmann and Czernin then presented a qualifying gloss, hoping to disguise possible annexations under the cover of national self-determination. The argument was too devious for Hoffmann. He bluntly told the Russians a few days later that "no forcible annexations" did not exclude Poland and the Baltic area from being separated from Russia if their representatives agreed. Shaken, his listeners called for a recess and went back to Russia. Equally shaken, Czernin told Hoffmann he would conclude a separate peace with the Bolsheviks if German thirst for annexations sabotaged the conference.

The military was enraged, but without reason, for it was a threat Czernin could scarcely carry out without destroying his whole policy. Hohenlohe actually reassured Bussche in Berlin that he should know the Austrian Foreign Minister well enough by now not to put too much weight on his declaration: "Certainly that was not meant so seriously."[33] Czernin's words were repudiated by his own ambassador.

But while being undercut from Hohenlohe on one side, Czernin had to defend his position with Karl on the other. August Demblin, his representative with the Court, wrote worriedly that Karl kept coming back to the idea of offering peace on the basis of no annexations to all their opponents, despite his repeated efforts to convince him that such a course was impossible without prior German agreement. Karl insisted that a general peace had to be found and the Germans brought to reason. "Germany must declare: no Belgium, no annexations, in a word: status quo." Furthermore, the Emperor noted that American troops would soon be pouring into Europe; the U-boats had not stopped any of them yet, and the Central Powers no longer had the manpower to equalize them if they kept coming. Nor was Karl any more amenable on Poland and Mitteleuropa. He was afraid the economic negotiations would just compromise the Monarchy with the Entente without getting any tangible results from Berlin, he balked at entering any further into a military convention than he had to, and he declared himself emphatically against the Austro-Polish solution—the chief benefit that according to Czernin was supposed to accrue from Mitteleuropa to begin with.[34] Czernin retorted that a general peace was impossible at the moment and that Vienna could not afford to appear to "beg" for peace in any case; in so doing, it would only demonstrate its differences with Berlin, to the advantage of the Bolsheviks. The only course was to strive for peace at Brest and to hope that other powers would accede to it later.[35]

Czernin was as firmly committed to the alliance as ever, whatever his threats to conclude a separate peace with Russia, and whatever his doubts that the German military could be moderated. While he pressed for peace at Brest against the Germans, he had to take the opposite position with Karl, dangling all sorts of inducements to him to stay in the war. By the end of 1917, the main inducement was Poland. He notified Karl on Christmas Eve that if peace were achieved at Brest, Germany would make the "enormous win" of Courland and Lithuania, and continued:

> It is completely impossible for Your Majesty in this case to come out without anything, and to play the role of having fought for three years just so Germany can make conquests. *Your Majesty must therefore get Poland in order to maintain parity.*

It was his old argument of equality of war gains, first advanced in March 1917. But since they were in no position to stop Germany from getting the Baltic, while the Germans could block the Austro-Polish solution at will, they had to press forward with the Mitteleuropa negotiations for bargaining room.[36] By 1918, even "parity" was impossible except with German consent. Still more revealing was what the exchange said of Czernin's deteriorating relations with the Emperor. He had not only to find worthwhile goals to convince Karl of the need to continue fighting; but once he found them, he had to force further concessions from his unwilling ruler in order to get German permission to acquire them. It was another example of Karl's chronic inability to give force to his own inner convictions that, despite all his objections, he nevertheless yielded to Czernin in the end.

The Brest-Litovsk negotiations formally resumed on January 9, 1918. The Russian delegation was now headed by Leon Trotsky, whose aim was to use the proceedings as propaganda to appeal over the heads of his opponents to their domestic populations, drawing out the deliberations in the hope that revolution would accomplish against the Central Powers what the dissolving Russian army was no longer capable of. He brought with him a separate delegation from the Ukrainian Rada or council to demonstrate the supposed reality of national self-determination in the new Russia. Czernin repeated to the Germans his threat of a separate peace, but the hollowness of his position was obvious. He confided to Karl that the Russians had little interest in dealing with Austria-Hungary alone, while the Ukrainians would probably demand East Galicia and the Bukovina, the Ruthene- or Ukrainian-populated areas of the Monarchy, as the price of any agreement with them. "The situation is without doubt serious, and no one can say what the next days will bring."[37] He soon found out; they brought a complete collapse of his negotiating position.

The ferment of the nationalities within the Empire, as the war stretched on interminably and Vienna lost more and more initiative to Berlin, continued unabated. The Czechs issued their Epiphany Declaration at the beginning of the new year, attacking the dualist system and proclaiming their right to determine their future without any constraint from the Monarchy. While welcoming national self-determination for Russia, Czernin at Brest-Litovsk was trying to deny it for Austria-Hungary, and the Czechs demanded to be allowed to send their own delegation to the peace talks. Czech dissatisfaction was perhaps to be expected; but simultaneously Wekerle raised the old Magyar demand that Hungary be granted its own army. Before the war, the same demand had caused a crisis which had nearly paralyzed the whole country; in 1918, the Magyars had no qualms about exploiting the weakened condition of the Monarchy for their own ends, even though they were one of its chief beneficiaries. The whole question was momentarily shelved under protest from the Austrians that it would provide a dangerous precedent for the other nationalities, but it was a clear indication that the Empire was not threatened simply by the centrifugal desires of the "subject" groups alone.[38]

The crash came, however, as a result of the catastrophic food situation in Cisleithania. It had been long expected; it was perhaps surprising only that it did not come sooner. At the end of December, Czernin, exasperated with the failure of both Vienna and Budapest to take adequate measures for controlling the food supply, begged Karl to intervene personally to place more energetic men in control. He suggested putting Tisza—anathema to Karl—in charge of food allocation in Hungary. But the Emperor's inclination was to avoid any sort of forceful action that might involve unpopular or coercive measures. Three weeks later, spurred by a report of the desolate economic situation in Bohemia, Czernin demanded that the system be tightened up and Landwehr sent to Berlin with a direct appeal from Karl to Wilhelm for help. "The situation which has come about because of the frivolity and incompetence of the ministers is frightful and I am afraid that it is too late to stop the complete collapse which is to be expected in the next weeks."[39] He was right; but it threatened to come within hours, not weeks.

The January 1918 strikes in Austria, though they lasted little over a week, demonstrated clearly the radical mood of the practically starving masses in the urban areas. A lowering of the flour ration on January 14 provoked spontaneous strikes in Wiener Neustadt and Vienna, and within a matter of days work came to a complete standstill in Lower Austria, while the movement spread to Budapest and other centers of the Monarchy. The Austrian Socialist leaders were taken aback by the strike and then pulled along in the current, attempting to moderate it. In some factories, Russian-style soviets or workers' councils were set up, while mass demonstrations protested the tactics of the German military at Brest-Litovsk. Equally ominous was the fact that most of those involved were not dissatisfied Czechs or Serbs or Ruthenes, but members of the "dominant" and therefore supposedly loyal nationalities of the Monarchy. Wedel wrote to Hertling that Vienna might earlier have used the threat of revolution as a bargaining ploy against them, but now it had lost control and the possibility was only too real. He noted that the strikes were directed as much against German demands for annexations as for more food supplies.[40] As in many revolutionary situations, economic protest quickly spawned political demands. The government promised the Social Democratic leadership to do all it could to satisfy both; and Viktor Adler, the Socialist leader, praised Czernin's efforts for peace and said he would try to calm the workers. He emphasized, however, that only a positive success at Brest could save the situation.[41] Ultimately, it was the threat of military force, coupled with the fear of German intervention, that broke the strike; and from then on, ever greater contingents of Habsburg troops, themselves of increasingly doubtful loyalty, had to be removed from the front to insure the loyalty of the domestic population.

The reverberations of the strike on Czernin's position at Brest-Litovsk were immediate. Seidler, the Austrian Minister-President, telegraphed frantically to Czernin that immediate food shipments had to be gotten from Berlin. Czernin's words to Hohenlohe betrayed the Austrian Foreign Minister's desperation (or panic) at the disastrous course events had taken:

> In case Germany does not want to, or cannot, help us, nothing else remains for us but to submit ourselves unconditionally to England. There are positive signs that with the loss of some territories we would reach peace with the entire Entente through English mediation.[42]

How serious the Germans considered that possibility, at least from Czernin, is indicated by their reaction to the crisis. They were in no mood to relinquish any more of their scanty stocks of grain than they had to, and Landwehr had "ceaseless trouble" getting even the smallest scraps when he hurried off to the German capital.[43] Hindenburg noted that, though he would send what he could, depleting his food reserves would damage the efficiency of the German army and forfeit an otherwise certain victory in the war. "Compared with this, a collapse of Austria-Hungary would not play a decisive role," he declared with equanimity. "We would have to reconcile ourselves to it."[44]

While Czernin was forced to beg the Germans for more food supplies to save the situation in Vienna, Karl frantically urged him to conclude peace with the Russians as quickly as possible. The Emperor telegraphed at the height of the strike:

> I must emphatically impress upon you again that the whole fate of the Monarchy and the dynasty depends on the quickest possible conclusion of peace at Brest-Litovsk. We cannot upset the situation here for Courland and Livonia and Polish dreams. If peace is not made at Brest, it will be revolution here, no matter how much there is to eat.[45]

But how could Czernin simultaneously beg the Germans for more food supplies and oppose their annexationist wishes at the conference? As he retorted angrily, it was impossible for him to conduct foreign policy if the Monarchy could not even organize its domestic food distribution properly.[46] He was infuriated with the laxness of the Seidler administration and disgusted with Karl's failure to rectify it. Moreover, while Karl urged him to save the situation at Brest, he was seeing other political figures at Court without his knowledge. Again, it almost came to a break between them; Czernin accused the Emperor of intriguing behind his back and added sarcastically that he was ready to resign at any time but that he wanted at least to be the first one informed that his responsibilities had been terminated. A few days later, he told Karl that he was so worn out from his exertions he wondered how much longer he would even be able to stay alive, let alone hold office. Demblin anxiously reminded Czernin what would happen if he retired: "General separate peace, separation from Germany, in the best case a delayed illusory existence for a couple of years, and then a dismemberment of the Monarchy."[47] But once again, the Emperor backed down. Czernin was allowed to continue his policy of working with Berlin, even though the January events in Vienna further reduced his already constricted freedom of initiative.

IV

The stage was now set for the conclusion of the "Bread Peace" of Brest-Litovsk. The strike wave of January subsided, but the threat of a recurrence haunted Vienna. From January on, the Monarchy was racked with sporadic strikes and demonstrations against the government, all of which, though repressed, demonstrated the growing inability of the constituted authorities to deal with the situation. In early February, there was even a mutiny of the fleet at the naval base of Cattaro (Kotor). Czernin bombarded Karl with demands for severe measures against all domestic disorders and even suggested a military dictatorship to replace the ineffectual Seidler ministry in Cisleithania. Karl, however, persisted in his conciliatory domestic course, doing nothing to remove the Austrian Minister-President; Wedel reported worriedly that the gulf between Emperor and Foreign Minister was greater than ever.[48]

Peace thus had to be attained at practically any cost. Czernin needed it both to forestall a further outbreak of domestic unrest and to maintain his own position with Karl. Yet peace at Brest seemed to be fading away, for the discussions there had devolved into a meaningless and endless verbal duel between Kühlmann and Trotsky over the definition of national autonomy. It was at this point that, in desperation, Czernin turned to the separate Ukrainian delegates, hoping to play them off against the intractable Trotsky. At the height of the domestic strike wave, he informed Karl that he was negotiating separately with the Ukrainians and with the Russians, and that a peace treaty with the former would be much more important than with the latter because of Ukrainian grain. In fact, he went on, if Vienna actually tried to carry out the threat of concluding a separate peace with Petrograd, the Germans would conclude one at the Monarchy's expense with the

Ukrainian Rada.[49] Peace became linked with grain in Czernin's mind—or at least with the promise of it. Grain became the justification to a war-weary domestic population for remaining in the war on the side of Berlin. Czernin told the Austrian Delegation on January 24: "If you give our present opponents the impression that we must have *peace at once, and at any price,* we shall not get so much as a single measure of grain, and the result will be more or less platonic." [50]

But the Ukrainians drove a hard bargain. Not only did they demand the predominately Polish-inhabited district of Cholm from Congress Poland, but the transformation of East Galicia and the Bukovina into a Ruthene Crownland within the Monarchy. The precedent of constitutional reshuffles on foreign demand was dangerous enough, but the potential effect on the Poles of giving Cholm to the Ukrainians was likely to prove fatal—as Czernin well knew. For the last few months, he had urged the Austro-Polish solution as the only way of retaining the loyalty of the Galician Poles and preserving parliamentary stability in Austria. He had in fact specifically warned Karl in December against the idea of splitting Galicia into Polish and Ruthene areas for fear of throwing the entire Polish group in the Reichsrat into opposition. But by accepting the Ukrainian conditions, he completely reversed himself. Even his hope that the Polish Minister-President in Warsaw could somehow be brought to Brest to receive the odium for such a step, had it succeeded, would not have saved the situation. It only demonstrated once more that the alliance had driven Vienna into a position where there was no salvation at all, only more and more contradictory half-measures.[51]

The deliberations of the Common Ministers Council of January 22 clearly bore this out. Czernin described the annexationist demands of the German military (distinguishing sharply as always between them and the civilian authorities) as one of the greatest obstacles to peace and requested approval to conclude a separate peace with Trotsky if that step became necessary. Such a peace needed only to be a statement that hostilities had ceased; and to counter German opposition, Austria could promise support for the Western Front. Ludendorff's demands for annexations in Poland were so unacceptable that the meeting proceeded to discuss dropping the Austro-Polish solution altogether and returning to that of compensation in Rumania. But both Wekerle and Arz were against any steps that might lead to a break in the alliance, and on this Czernin was in complete agreement. He probably wanted ministerial approval to settle with Trotsky only as a bargaining counter of last resort against Berlin, and to reassure Karl, who chaired the meeting. Most of his energy was expended in arguing for the settlement with the Ukraine, which he described as "far more important" than any separate arrangement with Petrograd, and which would avoid the whole question of confronting the Germans directly. Nevertheless, Wekerle, especially, was opposed to the Ukrainian terms, and was supported by Arz and Burián. Czernin overcame their arguments with the rejoinder that the food supply situation made peace with the Ukraine a vital necessity despite its constitutional complications. He was reduced to describing himself as being "in the position of a man who finds himself on the fourth floor of a burning building and who jumps out the window as the only possibility of rescue." It was a fitting description of the state of Austrian policy by 1918, and with reluctance the other ministers agreed to take the plunge.[52] To calm the domestic population with the prospect of peace and food, an agreement had to be gotten from somebody; and if a deal with Trotsky might endanger the alliance, then it would have to come from the Ukrainians—at whatever cost. A few days later, Hohenlohe, hearing that peace was near with the Ukraine, expressed his relief that a separate peace with Trotsky was no longer necessary: "I would see in it the beginning of the collapse of our alliance with Germany, the first step with which we left a firm foundation before having assured ourselves of any other at all."[53]

With German approval, the Austro-Ukrainian negotiations were rushed through. On February 9, in a room in Brest-Litovsk decorated with floodlights and filled with reporters, the peace treaty between Vienna and Kiev was officially signed. Austria-Hungary agreed to the Ukrainian terms for Cholm and East Galicia, and was promised in return the granaries of the Ukraine. Almost immediately, the provisions for Poland, supposedly secret, leaked out. There were strikes and protest demonstrations in both Congress Poland and Galicia, the Polish government in Warsaw resigned, and the remains of the Austrian Polish Legion mutinied. The Polish reaction was so angry that Vienna soon began backing out of the whole agreement as best it could. It was a high price to pay for the Ukrainian grain even if it had existed—which it did not. Petrograd had broken with the Ukrainians, and a few days before the signature of the peace treaty, Bolshevik troops drove the Rada out of its own capital. In reality, Czernin had concluded peace with the representatives of a government that had ceased to exist. Even if grain had been available in the Ukraine, the Rada was no longer in a position to deliver it.

Why did Czernin agree to a treaty that even at its inception contained so little substantive reality? Czernin himself had more than once confessed that little grain was to be had from the Ukraine, at least in the immediate future, and a meeting of the Common Food Supply Committee on January 11 had considered substantial imports of grain "very problematic" even in the best of cases.[54] Wekerle and Arz had been equally doubtful at the January 22 Common Ministers Council. Moreover, it had been obvious to the Austrian Foreign Minister that the Rada was in dissolution; and shortly before the signing ceremony, he had considered the possibility that they would have to aid the Ukrainians against Petrograd in order to get any grain at all.[55] But convinced that the domestic situation in the Monarchy was continuing to deteriorate (which was true enough), he felt that he needed any kind of success—even a purely symbolic one—to demonstrate that his policy of maintaining the alliance was bringing an acceptable end to the war. Whether or not there really were available food supplies in the Ukraine was in a sense irrelevant. The important thing was that Czernin had a peace treaty—the first one after nearly four years of hostilities—to present to the war-weary peoples of the Monarchy. No doubt, he hoped that its propaganda value would appease their emotions long enough to enable him to find some other expedient for appeasing their stomachs.

While Vienna hopelessly undermined its standing with the Poles in order to acquire a few Ukrainian signatures on an otherwise meaningless sheet of paper, the German military was working to destroy even these ephemeral results. The Monarchy's sacrifices for peace in the East found no corresponding echo with its ally, whose plans of aggrandizement seemed rather to increase to take advantage of its plight. Ludendorff not only persisted in blocking the Austro-Polish solution but appeared intent on appropriating everything from the wreckage of Russia that he could get his hands on. Even Hohenlohe, distraught, reported from Berlin that Germany in its apparent grasp for complete control in the East was leaving Austria-Hungary no reason for fighting that could plausibly be presented to its people. But the Monarchy was helpless to do anything about it:

> Should we of necessity—I emphasize it again—eventually come into opposition to Germany through *Germany's* fault, we would—and I want to point this out today—be compelled to renounce everything granted from Germany which makes possible our daily life; for it seems to me more than problematic that the Entente, which itself suffers from every scarcity, could immediately help us in a corresponding manner. The results of a quarrel with Germany would therefore not appear simply in the future, but immediately on our body; and then, only too late, would it become clear to our public how much we are dependent on Germany today.[56]

Hohenlohe overestimated the Entente's economic difficulties, but he had no doubt about those of the Monarchy. Simply on the basis of its economic needs, he considered an Austrian break with Germany to be unthinkable.

On February 5, a conference in Berlin put the differences between Austria and Germany into full relief. Czernin argued that the Austrian sacrifices in the Ukraine entitled it to priority in receiving any Ukrainian grain: "We stand before a categorical imperative." But Kühlmann disagreed. Even stronger were German disagreements when Czernin maintained that his ally's demands made the Austro-Polish solution impossible. Without that, there could be no Mitteleuropa or compensation in Rumania, and the Monarchy would then be forced to separate from Germany after the war. But when Czernin asked for a written agreement that the alliance did not obligate Austria-Hungary to fight for German annexations, Ludendorff simply exploded. "If Germany makes peace without profit, then Germany has lost the war," he declared bluntly. Only Hertling's intercession prevented a full-dress verbal battle.[57] Meanwhile, Wedel reported the public mood in Vienna: The population refused to continue fighting simply for German aggrandizement; pressure for a separate peace was on the rise.[58]

It was against this backdrop that the events at Brest reached their climax. The Germans (or rather, General Hoffmann) decided that they had had enough of Trotsky's delaying tactics and demanded capitulation to their peace terms. Trotsky neither accepted nor refused. He announced unilaterally that the war was over; and with that, the Bolshevik delegation boarded its train and left. It was his famous "No war—no peace" declaration. Czernin and Kühlmann wanted to accept it, for both dreaded the effect on their discontented home populations if the war in the East was resumed. They were overruled by Hoffmann. The Germans denounced the armistice on February 17 and ordered their troops to advance. Vienna refused to participate in the new offensive, and Seidler announced to the Reichsrat two days later that Austria was no longer at war with Russia. On the same day, Czernin deplored to Hohenlohe the likely effect on the Entente powers of a resumption of hostilities: "I believe that Germany's unquenchable thirst for annexations permanently ruins any peace in the West." Yet despite his private misgivings, Hohenlohe was instructed to inform Berlin that he had "no objection" to its action.[59]

Austrian non-participation did not last long. Arz protested that Seidler's speech had been made without his knowledge and complained of the Monarchy's seeming lack of solidarity with Berlin in the renewed fighting. "In this," he stated, "I am again proceeding from the certain conviction that every real or apparent dissociation from Germany not only hurts us within the alliance, but is greeted with special hope by our opponents and works to prolong the war."[60] Nor was Czernin any more happy with the decision, especially as the Germans advanced virtually without opposition. He replied to Arz that he had actually been in favor of military participation until overruled by Karl and regretted the fact that the Monarchy was not sharing in the easy successes on the Eastern Front.[61] In a matter of days, Czernin had shifted from one pole to the other in his old conflict between defeatism and parity in the alliance—assuming one could still make a distinction between them, or that he was not deliberately doctoring his position with both Arz and Karl.

It was the food supply crisis that finally forced Vienna to join in the advance on the Eastern Front. All the sacrifices of the Ukrainian treaty had been made for the ostensible promise of Ukrainian grain. Even if the promise was illusory, it was the prospect of some relief, however small, which had been presented to the Austrian public with the magic word "peace". At the stormy February 5 meeting with the Germans, it had been agreed to divide any Ukrainian grain equally between the Monarchy and Germany. Yet when Berlin secured its demands in the Baltic and marched into the Ukraine, it proceeded to appropriate everything of value exclusively for itself; and it became apparent that if Vienna wanted any of the spoils, it would have to intervene actively on its own, the agreement notwithstanding. Czernin pressed Karl to change his mind, and eventually the order was given for Austrian units to advance into the Ukraine after all.

On March 3, the Bolsheviks returned to Brest-Litovsk to sign the treaty at last. They had been defenseless against the German army; Trotsky's hoped-for revolution in Berlin and Vienna had failed to materialize, and nothing remained but for them to come back and sign. Petrograd was forced to accede to all the German conditions and surrender massive areas of territory—the Baltic, Congress Poland, and the Ukraine. Though further details remained to be worked out, the war was now officially over with Russia.

Actually, Trotsky's "No war—no peace" declaration had literally come true. Whatever the propaganda value of the peace treaty of Brest-Litovsk, events in the East continued to follow their own dynamics as if it had never been signed. Once in the Ukraine, Vienna and Berlin worked out rough spheres of influence and began the task of garnering its supposed riches. It proved to be impossible; there were only endless complications. Czernin sent János Forgách, whom he had retired from office a year earlier, to Kiev to set up a supply organization, and urged him to be as energetic as possible in extracting grain from the Ukraine. For "political reasons," as he confessed, even the smallest shipment was an absolute necessity.[62] But Forgách found nothing but chaos there. The reinstated Rada was respected by nobody, the population was demoralized and hostile, and the transport system in collapse. Though the grain existed, it would be practically impossible to secure it.

"Conditions here are much worse than people in Vienna suspect," he wrote disgustedly to Berchtold. "The momentary Social Revolutionary putsch government of a few young people [is] completely useless, only supported by our bayonets—one of the many ephemeral bubbles raised up by this swamp."[63] Moreover, the new agreement with Berlin almost immediately broke down. Odessa was in the Austrian sphere, but the Germans, having gotten there first, refused to give up their control. Czernin begged Karl to send an Austrian fieldmarshal or even an archduke there to outrank the German governor. The Monarchy could not last until the new harvest without Ukrainian grain, but if the Germans got the upper hand in Odessa, the Austrians would be allowed to export practically nothing. The Germans were not impressed. Hoffmann complained in his diary that the Austrians were "behaving with their usual meanness when the knife is not at their throat."[64] The desperate domestic plight of the Monarchy thus led Vienna to embark on an enterprise demanding continuing sacrifices and offering only the dimmest prospects, made even dimmer by the Germans. By March 1918, Austria-Hungary was actually more deeply embroiled in the East than it had been in the previous December, when the Brest-Litovsk conference first began.

Czernin, in any case, had gotten another peace treaty, and he was hailed in Vienna as the maker of the "Bread Peace." Wedel had reported of him at the end of January: "He has put himself at the head of the peace efforts, and people trust that his determination will also attain the goal."[65] By March, that trust was the main thing keeping him in office, and he manipulated it almost demagogically to mute the despair of the general population, even though the practical results of the treaties so far were slim indeed. Wedel worried that he was creating expectations that could not be fulfilled, but there was no alternative. Ever more inflated expectations were all he could offer. Each new step towards "peace," presented in glowing colors to the Austrian home front, only pushed the reality of peace further away. Musulin reported from Switzerland that in the West the Eastern treaties had made a deep impression as imperialistic settlements and accentuated the belief that Germany was striving for the hegemony of the world.[66] Nobody there believed any longer that the Central Powers really wanted a peace without annexations; all of Czernin's high-sounding public declarations to the contrary had been discredited at a blow.

Neither Czernin nor Kühlmann were at Brest when the preliminary treaty with the Russians was formally signed. The breakdown of the Eastern Front and the march into the Ukraine had made the continued resistance of Rumania impossible, and early March found them both in Bucharest negotiating a treaty of peace with the Rumanians. "I hope we will never forget what baseness, betrayal, and meanness these Rumanians have committed against us," Czernin had written at the end of 1914 while Austrian Minister there, "and the hour of retribution will come."[67] Now, it had arrived—but not in the manner he had anticipated. Austro-Hungarian policy was completely divided over Rumania. The Magyars demanded massive border rectifications—it was they who had been directly invaded by the Rumanians in 1916—proposing to compensate it with Russian Bessarabia, which Bucharest had already annexed after the Bolshevik seizure of power. "If Rumania refuses to conclude peace on the basis laid down by us, our answer can only be a resumption of hostilities," Tisza wrote.[68] But Karl wanted no annexations at all, and despite Czernin's protests refused to sanction a renewal of the fighting to impose such conditions. The Emperor fumed that he would dismiss Wekerle if the Hungarian government failed to moderate its position.[69] Czernin was caught squarely in the middle and found himself paring down the Hungarian demands as best he could, while simultaneously telling Karl that he had to get as much as possible to maintain the Monarchy's prestige.

The Monarchy was much more interested in the fate of Rumania than it had been in that of northern Russia minus the Ukraine, and consequently played a more direct role in the Bucharest negotiations. Since the Austro-Polish solution still remained in limbo, thanks to German objections, there was no agreement preventing Vienna from expressing such interest. But as Wedel predicted in the middle of February, it could not afford to persist in extensive demands if they threatened to block the conclusion of peace.[70] Caught in this position of weakness, Vienna could do little more than protest ineffectually while Germany amassed for itself most of the riches of the once sought-after Milliardenobjekt. Karl telephoned to Wilhelm that inflated German economic demands could endanger the success of the negotiations, leading the Kaiser to retort angrily: "Who does this young man think he is? Who conquered Rumania?"[71] As long as the Ballplatz had to seek border rectifications for Budapest, it lost any bargaining position against Germany's pretensions to Rumania's economic riches. Those pretensions left little out of account. They extended from its oil fields to its transportation network to its harbor facilities. Vienna eventually managed to secure several border rectifications, notably the Iron Gates of the Danube, and a one-third share of the German-dominated oil monopoly which was to be established. But most of the booty fell to Berlin. One of the thorniest questions of the whole conference was the fate of the northern Dobrudja, which Bulgaria demanded stubbornly, eliciting a major clash with not only the Rumanians but the

Turks. It was finally put off by setting the area under the control of all four Central Powers together—which safeguarded Germany's interest in the rail link to the Black Sea port of Constanța as well as resolving the controversy.

German predominance in Rumania had been one of the conditions for the desired return to the Austro-Polish solution advocated by both Czernin and Kühlmann in the fall of 1917. Vienna had expected to surrender its claims on Bucharest in return for Warsaw. But by March 1918, the Austro-Polish solution seemed further away than ever, and Vienna found itself being pressed out of Rumania without getting anything elsewhere at all. Hence its almost pathetic attempts to secure at least a few crumbs at Bucharest. Kühlmann noted of the Austrians: "They are now afraid of falling between two stools: of being fobbed off economically in Rumania with a very thin dish of lentils, and also in Poland receiving little or nothing." [72]

Czernin's final hope of moderating the standpoint of the High Command through Kühlmann and preserving at least the semblance of Vienna's equality in the alliance was ended for good at Bucharest. The negotiations there drove the Austrian and German Foreign Ministers closer together than ever against the demands of the German military. "State Secretary von Kühlmann has granted me his loyal and active support in every way during the whole duration of the difficult and complicated negotiations here," Czernin tele-graphed Vienna once the main points in Bucharest had been settled.[73] Yet it was to little purpose, for Kühlmann himself had become practically isolated in Berlin. The German Foreign Minister had never really been able to get the military to agree to his Polish-Mitteleuropa concept anyway, but by March he found himself virtually alone in still advocating it. Not only the military, but also Kaiser Wilhelm and the civilian authorities, now rejected that solution, and Kühlmann realized that the Monarchy was being driven into a hopeless position. It was not going to achieve any sort of hegemony in Rumania; through the Cholm cession it had incurred the frantic animosity of the Poles and gotten little from the Ukraine; and now, with a wave of self-confidence sweeping the German government in the wake of the Eastern settlements, it was likely to be completely shut out of Congress Poland as well. Kühlmann did what he could to get something for his ally. "If we also let it fall through in the Polish question," he argued to Hertling, "a strong anti-German reaction in Austrian policy is inevitable," and he hinted at resigning if his ideas were abandoned.[74] Moderation seemed to have disappeared in Germany.

Ludendorff and Hindenburg were now the sole arbiters of the alliance. While the negotiations proceeded in the East, they steadily amassed the troops and supplies for the final offensive that would allow them to realize

their plans in the West as well. Even though nearly a million men remained
tied down from the Baltic to the Caspian, the High Command hoped to
concentrate the necessary military preponderance in France for an offensive
that would smash the Entente lines before the economic blockade and the
American army shifted the balance permanently against it. It was the last
supreme effort that was supposed to win the war, and it was launched on
March 21.

V

Czernin had now reached the pinnacle of his career. Peace had been won
in the East, and the German army considered itself on the verge of final
victory in the West. Supplies of grain and other raw materials could be hoped
for as soon as conditions in Russia were stabilized. A successful outcome of
the war seemed at last at hand, with only a few more days of patience and
sacrifice necessary to achieve it. Such, in any case, was the belief that Czernin,
through his various actions, had succeeded in nourishing among the ruling
groups of the Monarchy. If reality was less rosy, it was probably still more
than his predecessors could have accomplished in his position. A pacifist
speech by Lammasch in the Herrenhaus at the end of February created an
uproar, and it was disavowed by most of the other members. Czernin seemed
to offer both peace and the fruits of victory, and their sentiment was to
support him to the end. Even Wedel reported that his apparent success in
the East had momentarily revived the Monarchy's desire to achieve a "good"
peace. Tucher noted on March 1: "If Czernin's luck holds out and he signs
the peace with Russia and even that with Rumania, his position in the whole
country will be so strong that the courage to dismiss the successful, if often
downright uncomfortable, minister must certainly fail."[75] Czernin had, in
fact, reached a position similar to that of Hindenburg and Ludendorff in
Germany. His immediate successes gave him such standing in the leading
circles of the Monarchy that the Emperor, whatever his reservations, found
it politically impossible to act openly against him.

But however much Czernin's position seemed to have improved superficially, its underpinnings were crumbling away. On the same day that Wedel
reported a wave of confidence in victory, the Statthalter in Vienna described
sentiment among its industial workers as so bad that the possibility of a new
strike had to be reckoned with.[76] As Wedel himself pointed out, in the
unstable public mood, any confidence in victory would last only as long as
it was nourished by success. If a final settlement was not soon achieved,

renewed defeatism was bound to replace it.[77] The general situation among
the lower classes was desperate by the spring of 1918; only stopgap measures
held off complete disaster. Viktor Naumann visited Vienna in mid-February
to confer with various political and industrial leaders, and he confessed he
went with few positive expectations. "But my worst fears were surpassed by
far by what I learned during my stay in the Austrian capital." All his contacts
agreed that relations with Germany had never been so bad, and that
Ludendorff was the most hated man in the Monarchy. "From my talks with
members of parliament," he reported, "I am convinced that everything is in
flux, and that if it does not come to peace in the East soon—to a real peace—
either a collapse will result *or Austria-Hungary will conclude a separate
peace.*"[78]

The treaties with Petrograd and Bucharest brought no lasting amelioration.
The Vienna police reported that among the general population, the "downright hopeless supply conditions" pushed all other questions into the
background. There were instances of women too weak from hunger even to
spend the necessary hours of waiting in the lines outside stores without losing
consciousness and collapsing. One informant noted:

> The people give little credit to the reports in the daily papers about imports from
> the East. References are made to the difficulties of transport; and, above all, the
> fear is expressed that the supplies which can readily be gotten are already seized
> by Germany. Remarkable is the great and rather widespread resentment against
> Germany . . . [79]

For the masses of the population, Czernin's "Bread Peace" meant little.

At the beginning of March, Landwehr calculated that the Monarchy's food
administration controlled only enough grain to last until mid-April, so that
new negotiations had to be opened with Berlin for more, "difficult as this
was." Czernin was reduced to the point of awarding honorary Austrian
decorations to German economic officials in Rumania to make them more
generous with their grain supplies.[80] The peace treaties in the East remained
little more than empty promises, and even the first reports from the German
offensive in the West evoked mixed feelings. Redlich evaluated the mood of
the general populace in Vienna as the great German attack got underway:

> Despite the tremendous victory of Hindenburg-Ludendorff over the English, in
> Vienna dull dissatisfaction reigns; and the people, who are now going hungry more
> than ever, no longer expect anything good from the bloodshed and believe no
> more in a peace arising from German victories.[81]

The movement for a separate peace probably reached its height in March 1918. Each new "success" Czernin reported from the East only put it off a little longer, allowing the pressure to build up, but without releasing it. If such an end to the war was anathema to him or Hohenlohe or Arz, others besides the Meinl Group saw the need for a real peace at any price—including that of the alliance—even if they shied away from saying so outright. Baron Stjepan Sarkotić, the military governor of Bosnia, urged Karl in the summer of 1917 to conclude peace with or without Germany; and Baron Gyula Szilássy, attached to the Constantinople embassy after having headed the legation in Greece, pointed out in November that Germany ran the risk of defeat if the war miscarried, while the Monarchy faced national dissolution. The Austrian Minister to the Vatican, Prince Johann Schönburg-Hartenstein, repeatedly protested against German attempts to dictate peace.[82]

Most important of all, however, was the gulf that had developed between Czernin and Karl. The Eastern peace treaties failed to quiet the Emperor's longing for a general settlement, and Czernin's admonitions that Karl needed concrete gains to buttress the dynasty had no more than a temporary effect on him. "If I have to give up something to get a peace of understanding, that is preferable to a victorious battle for me," Mérey characterized Karl's viewpoint. Besides, the Emperor refused to accept the enormous aggrandizement the Germans secured from Brest and Bucharest.[83] Czernin made no secret of his impatience with Karl's constant proddings and often addressed him with a sharpness and lack of deference that astonished those around them. At other times, he deliberately left the Emperor in the dark about what he was doing.[84] The two had clearly lost the mutual respect and trust necessary to work smoothly together. Yet despite Karl's resistance, or rather, precisely because of it, Czernin held tightly to his course with Berlin—all the more so in that Austria-Hungary was involved in no less than five separate peace contracts with the West in the winter of 1917-1918. Czernin ended by blocking them all.

The peace feelers of this period involved all the main powers of the Entente—Britain, France, and the United States. One of the most promising occurred in mid-December 1917. Count Albert Mensdorff, the former Austrian Ambassador to London, was sent by Czernin to Switzerland to meet no less a personage than General Jan Smuts, a member of the British War Cabinet. Smuts came with the assurance that Britain had no wish to destroy the Monarchy. While it would support Italy's claim to the Trentino, that was the only Italian claim on which it would insist if the Monarchy broke with Germany and contracted out of the war. But Mensdorff had been explicitly instructed to reject any thought of a separate peace, and so the contact came to nothing.[85]

Then, in February 1918, Revertera reported a new connection with Paris, which proposed a meeting between Czernin and Georges Clemenceau, the French Premier. Czernin insisted, however, that France renounce all wishes for annexations (meaning Alsace-Lorraine) as a precondition for a meeting; Clemenceau refused; and the contact was broken off.[86] All summer in Berlin Czernin had pushed German cession of Alsace-Lorraine as a step toward peace, yet now he refused to consider it.

The renewed Revertera soundings were followed in March by a postscript to the Mensdorff-Smuts meeting. In the middle of the month, Lloyd George's private secretary, Philip Kerr, came to Switzerland to confer with Wladyslaw Skrzyński, the Councillor of the Austrian Papal delegation (which had been stationed in Switzerland since the Italian declaration of war). Kerr welcomed the similarity of views between Czernin and Lloyd George and considered a meeting between them to offer "the first step towards a general peace." [87] Yet Czernin's view of the whole affair was distrustful in the extreme. A few days before the talk with Kerr, he instructed Skrzyński to be merely receptive "and with *no word* attempt even the least drawing together." Once the meeting had taken place, he telegraphed back that peace was impossible as long as France and Italy insisted on annexations, effectively destroying any continuation of the conversations.[88]

Simultaneous with these feelers, two separate channels opened with President Wilson. Wilson made his famous 14-Point speech in early January 1918, calling for a generally moderate program of war aims and advocating "autonomous development" for the nationalities of Austria-Hungary. "Autonomous development" did not necessarily mean "independence"; Wilson in January 1918 advocated a constitutional federalization of the Monarchy— not its dissolution. He seemed to offer a clear way around the annexationist commitments of the rest of the Entente, though the 14 Points did call for a return of Alsace-Lorraine to France and Polish access to the sea, both of which could be realized only at German expense. Czernin not only answered Wilson with a positive public statement of his own, but let it be known through the King of Spain that he thought there was enough common ground in their two positions for a direct talk between their representatives. He offered to work to moderate the demands of his German allies if Wilson would do the same with the powers of the Entente. What he hoped for was a peace on the basis of the status quo ante; although there could be border adjustments, the relative positions of all the states before the war should remain unaltered.[89] Czernin hoped to avoid any commitment to domestic change in the Monarchy, but that was precisely what Wilson demanded in his answering communication: How, exactly, did Vienna propose to solve the South Slav problem? The Austrian reply, again, was the blunt assertion that the only obstruction to peace was French and Italian thirst for annexations, but the contact through Spain was lost even before that answer could be formally delivered to Washington.

The official contact with Washington was paralleled by a second, unofficial, one, through the Meinl Group. Julius Meinl was in Switzerland at the end of 1917 to pursue various soundings, but when he returned to Austria he was told by Czernin not to follow them any further.[90] Czernin wanted no such interference with his own conduct of foreign affairs. Nevertheless, a month later, Lammasch himself made the trip to Switzerland to meet with George D. Herron, a self-appointed agent of Wilson. Lammasch was ready to fulfill all Wilson's demands for a domestic transformation of the Monarchy; it was, after all, his own program. He even astonished Herron by welcoming American interference in Austria's domestic affairs. It was the only way, as he put it, to break the hegemony there of Prussia and Hungary. Domestic reconstruction had to be made a specific condition of peace. Lammasch's plan was for Karl to address a proclamation to the Pope announcing national autonomy within the Monarchy and renouncing all annexations, and then to use that proclamation as a fait accompli to force Berlin to moderate its own position. If the Germans refused, he was ready to conclude peace without them. But however much Lammasch thought he was speaking for Karl, nothing more resulted from the Herron-Lammasch talks than from any of the other contacts of 1917-1918. Czernin effectively frustrated the issuance of any proclamation.[91]

These peace contacts destroyed the last common ground between Czernin and Karl. The Emperor's reaction to the peace feelers was to pursue them all as fast and uncritically as possible, with an alacrity which the Foreign Minister found positively alarming. Wedel reported in mid-February that "His Majesty telephones and telegraphs his minister continually, as if to wear him down to compel him to bring about peace. Count Czernin's already bad nerves are thus in a hopeless condition."[92] Czernin made no secret to Kühlmann that Karl's desires for a speedy peace were causing him great difficulties.[93] The contacts with Wilson excited Karl with the idea of coming to a separate understanding with Washington, and of somehow ending the war with a series of piecemeal agreements with each of the chief belligerents until no hostile powers remained.[94] He was equally excited by the prospects of the Kerr talks.

Czernin was driven to increasingly ruthless measures in his struggle to blunt the Emperor's wishes. He did everything he could to dampen Karl's enthusiasm for Wilson, handling the matter in as dilatory a fashion as he could, despite all the Emperor's urgings for speed. The Monarchy could make no commitment without prior approval of the other Central Powers, he argued, and Vienna really had little common ground with Washington anyway. He noted that Wilson wanted to take Galicia for the new Polish state, which was simply unacceptable after all the sacrifices of the war.[95] Finally, he attempted to transfer Karl's hopes from Washington to the feeler with Kerr. "I consider these threads again taken up in Switzerland much more serious and promising than the conversation with Wilson," he instructed Demblin, his representative at the Court, on March 10 to tell the Emperor.[96] Yet he quickly ended the talks with the British, though without informing Karl of his actions. Just how much Karl was left in the dark about the end of those "more serious and promising" talks was indicated by a telegram from Demblin a week later asking how much he should divulge about the affair. "His Majesty asked me repeatedly about the result of Mr. Kerr's mission," he wrote. "I acted uninformed."[97]

The German offensive in France was undoubtedly a major reason why Czernin broke off all the peace contacts. Five years later, in a letter to Mensdorff, Lloyd George expressed the view from the British side:

> Nothing came of the conversations, because, as Mr. Kerr says, it was clear when he went out to Switzerland again at the end of February 1918 that the Austro-Hungarian Government had decided to await the result of the German offensive which began on March 21st.[98]

Hohenlohe's own opinion was that "a frightful catastrophe awaits the Entente gentlemen," as he wrote the day before the opening of the offensive. A few days later, as the attack rolled forward, he suggested doing more to demonstrate the Monarchy's loyalty to the alliance, so that it would have greater claim to German concessions at the conclusion of peace.[99] Czernin did what he could to justify the German attack to Karl, arguing that only French demands for annexations blocked the road to a general settlement. "It is thus completely clear that the Western offensive, deplorable as it is, will be in all circumstances unavoidable," he wrote a week before it began.[100] At the end of March, he urged an Austrian offensive against Italy as soon as possible to support Hindenburg in France:

> The fabulous successes of the Germans in the West downright compel this, after, it seems, troops are pulled uninterruptedly out of Italy to the West. From this, a facilitation of the offensive can be expected on the one hand; on the other we can support the action in the West by tackling the Italians. . . . Since we unfortunately

are so weakly represented in the West, we should attempt this time to be untrue to our military principle of always and at every opportunity coming too late, and seize the opportunity while there is still time.[101]

Burián in his diary characterized the mood among official circles in Vienna on the eve of the offensive: "No one will now listen to the word 'peace'. Everything is based on the forthcoming offensive, as if everyone were entrusting himself without a tremor to that decision of fate."[102]

From this, it would appear that Czernin by March 1918 had come to believe that Germany was about to compel a favorable conclusion to the war, despite all his earlier pessimism over its longterm prospects. For if Germany really were on the verge of victory, then Vienna needed to secure its own position with it in order to share in the fruits of that victory; it had to make an unequivocal decision to support the final German offensive if the Monarchy were to benefit from its expected results. Yet this, like so much with Czernin, can still not be said with complete certainty. Other members of the upper classes in Vienna might have been blinded by the prospects of the impending attack, but the desperate situation of the Central Powers was obvious enough to him. He knew that Austria-Hungary could collapse internally at any moment; and he knew, also, that conditions in Germany were not much better. Moreover, his experiences with the German military could hardly have led him to expect moderation from them if they broke through the Entente lines and reached Paris, whatever he told Karl about the necessity for the campaign. "The German military party 'fear' that the Entente may, perhaps, be inclined to agree to a general peace, and could not think of ending the war in this 'unprofitable' fashion," he had written in his diary on Christmas Eve of 1917.[103] Nothing had occurred since then to change that prognosis. Unless the German victory were absolute and total, new German demands would only steel the enemy to continue fighting— which could be done indefinitely with American troops and supplies now streaming into Europe—while the condition of the Central Powers continued to worsen. Perhaps Czernin really did believe Germany was about to win the war when he threw all his cards behind the impending attack. But more likely, he saw the offensive as a final gamble which he had to support no matter how many doubts he may actually have had.

One thing is clear, whatever Czernin's inner thoughts in March 1918: The whole logic of his "German Course" compelled him to back the German Western offensive unconditionally. His policy since the end of 1917 had involved one complication after another in its attempts to stave off final disaster, each one making him more dependent on Berlin and also undermining whatever other options might still have remained open to him. He may have had reservations about the prospects of the offensive or the tractability of the German leadership, but by March there was no alternative to wholehearted support of the offensive—except to openly break with the alliance, attempt a separate peace, and accept a radical domestic transformation of the Monarchy. If repeated contacts with the Entente encouraged the belief that only the alliance and its domestic supporters in the Monarchy stood in the way of a real peace, how long could the old elite have been expected to preserve its position there? What was to prevent both peace and domestic reform from being concluded over its head? Under these circumstances, all the peace feelers ran the risk of splitting Austria-Hungary from the alliance and initiating a domestic upheaval. In 1916, Czernin had urged "significant sacrifices" to achieve peace; in 1917, he had done all he could to establish contacts with the enemy powers to "mediate" peace; but by 1918, any further contact at all, given the chaotic domestic situation within the Monarchy, threatened to drive the situation beyond his control. Therefore, he scuttled all the peace feelers of 1918—feelers he would have seized with alacrity a year earlier—and refused concessions that he himself had urged only a few months previously when the domestic situation had not seemed so likely to get out of hand. Every prospect of peace now had to be blocked—except that which lay in a victory of the German army.

In the opening months of 1918, Czernin repeatedly linked the questions of achieving peace (through the alliance with Germany, the only form of peace he was ready to accept) with a firm domestic course. Karl, fed up with the refusal of the Wekerle government in Hungary to liberalize the regime there, found his first line of opposition not in Budapest, but at the Ballplatz. Czernin warned him against any idea of dissolving the Hungarian parliament and conducting new elections; the chief beneficiaries would be the radical elements around Károlyi. Such a result, he added, would encourage the Entente to resist all Austrian peace efforts. "No advantages which the dissolution can bring for the domestic political configuration in Hungary would be capable of balancing out these dangers," he concluded. He repeated the same message a month later, attacking Seidler's inability to control the domestic ferment in Austria.[104] Czernin blamed the failure of the March peace contacts not on his own reluctance to follow them through, but on the activities of the enemies of the alliance within the Monarchy. As he instructed Demblin to tell Karl:

I learn from an absolutely certain source that until recently the Entente had the firm intention of preparing the way for a general peace through Vienna. It seems to have fallen in time with the démarche of Herr Kerr with Herr von Skrzyński, and the inquiry known to His Majesty of Clemenceau with us. At the last moment, the current in Paris and London reversed, because the opinion that the Monarchy, thanks to the domestic political conditions in Austria, must soon be defenseless, won the upper hand. It therefore no longer made sense to negotiate with us. It seems that this thought is especially nourished in Paris and London from the side of the Czechs.[105]

Czernin was reduced to such arguments because the forces for a separate peace, despite all the apparent successes at Brest and Bucharest, refused to be stilled. Karl remained so amenable to them that his Foreign Minister had to renew his threat of resignation to keep him from pursuing them on his own. On March 18, he telegraphed Demblin to inform the Emperor "that he knows me exactly, and certainly knows that I would immediately and definitively demand my dismissal, if any sort of fait accompli were created without my knowledge." The Emperor's proclivity to conduct policy behind his back, if not promptly curtailed, was going to lead to an open break between them.[106]

Czernin felt threatened above all by Karl's continued association with the Meinl Group. Of the five recent peace feelers, that of Meinl and Lammasch, while the least official, was also the least under his own control. Unlike himself, the Meinl Group welcomed peace with the West—even a separate peace—despite its domestic implications. They in fact welcomed it precisely because of those implications. If Germany won the war, their plans to federalize the Empire would disappear forever. Having frustrated the peace contacts under his own jurisdiction, Czernin at the end of March launched a calculated campaign to discredit Lammasch and thus prevent him from pursuing any further contacts on his own. He had already disavowed Lammasch after his speech in the Austrian Herrenhaus, and now he instructed his press secretary Friedrich Wiesner to step up the press campaign against him. "It means a great deal to me," he wrote, "that the Lammasch affair not die out and everything possible be done in order to compromise this dangerous person completely."[107] Nor was he loath to mobilize the Germans against him. Kühlmann reported from Bucharest:

Count Czernin tells me that Professor Lammasch, who is highly disagreeable to him because of his pacifist intrigues with Emperor Karl, has greatly injured himself through various indiscretions in Austrian public opinion. He has instructed his press to attack Lammasch, and believes it in our common interest if also from the side of the German papers things could be written against these intriguing pacifists, without any semi-official influence being recognized.[108]

The need for such efforts was a clear indication of the essential frailty of Czernin's position. Despite its outward solidity, bolstered by the successes of Brest-Litovsk and Bucharest, his alliance policy was strained to the limit.

Czernin was certainly laboring under immense emotional and psychological pressure at this point. He had exhausted himself in vain efforts to moderate the inflexibility of the German military; at the same time, he had to struggle constantly to maintain his authority with the Emperor and to counter the pacifist ideas of Lammasch and Meinl. As he wrote to the former German Ambassador to Washington after the war, "Ludendorff's attitude on the one hand, foolish as it was violent, and the outrageous indiscretions of irresponsible elements in Vienna, were an admirable complement to each other, and destroyed the prospect of any kind of peace."[109] Someone with nerves of steel would have been hard put under those circumstances not to overreact or panic as the pressure mounted. Czernin, however, was by all accounts a man of highly sensitive and nervous temperament. By April 1918, as he moved against Lammasch and those other "irresponsible elements," he must have been close to his breaking point.

Such was the background to the famous verbal duel with Clemenceau which drove Czernin from office and sealed the fate of Austria-Hungary as an independent entity. It was Czernin's last battle as Foreign Minister for the conservative order in the Monarchy. While much about it and the resulting "Sixtus Affair" will probably never adequately be explained, it seems clear that its immediate origin was Czernin's drive to destroy once and for all the possibility of Austria-Hungary leaving the war through a separate peace, and to cement it firmly to the alliance with Germany. Only thus could the domestic order be preserved. On April 2, temporarily returned from the negotiations in Bucharest, Czernin gave an address to the city fathers of Vienna. It was a major public utterance—and his last as head at the Ballplatz. In it, he reaffirmed the loyalty of the Monarchy to the alliance and, alluding to the failure of the last round of the Armand-Revertera talks, attempted to put all the blame for the unrolling German offensive in France on Clemenceau's desire to annex Alsace-Lorraine. Significantly, he also attacked the loyalty of the Czechs: "The poor, pitiable Masaryk is not alone of his kind! There are also Masaryks within the boundary posts of the Monarchy."[110]

The interpretation of the speech by Czernin's supporters is that it was intended to undermine Clemenceau's position in France and perhaps even force his replacement by a more conciliatory statesman before the final success of the German Western offensive. That must have figured in Czernin's thinking, but it was not the only consideration. As has been pointed out by subsequent writers, exploiting a confidential peace feeler in such a polemical manner put the confidentiality of all future feelers into question, and thus made renewed contacts with the Entente highly questionable.[111] Moreover, the attack on Clemenceau was combined with an attack on the most dissatisfied nationality in the Monarchy; the speech was as much an all-or-nothing gamble as the Ludendorff offensive itself, to strike down all Czernin's domestic enemies at a single blow. It would undermine both the chances of domestic compromise between Czech and German and the ability of the Meinl Group to reach an understanding with the Entente. Baernreither noted a conversation with the Austrian Foreign Minister a week later:

> Czernin further declared to me why he brought forth the affair with Clemenceau in his speech. This was done deliberately to cut off all those poisonous connections and make them impossible for the future. Whether that is an explanation ex post, I don't know. He asserted, he knew how many originators created these connections, named Lammasch, Foerster, Meinl, and tutti quanti as dangerous informants.[112]

Whatever he originally may have intended, the impact of the speech quickly led in an unforeseen direction. Clemenceau, when he was informed of it, announced brusquely that the Austrian Foreign Minister was lying. Czernin immediately launched an answering communiqué, detailing the Armand-Revertera talks and thus again attempting to lay the blame for the continuation of the war on French annexationism. Clemenceau's answer was to hint that he had information from the Sixtus talks of a year earlier which would undermine the whole Austrian position. By now, Czernin had returned to Bucharest. He telegraphed anxiously to Karl asking if he had sent anything to Sixtus without his knowledge—which the Emperor denied. But Karl insisted that he make no further communication until he returned again to Vienna, which should have forestalled any further actions on Czernin's part. He was only too familiar with Karl's impulsiveness and past attempts to make policy without his knowledge and must have suspected some unpleasant new revelation even if he was unaware of the extent of Karl's independent dealings with Sixtus. By now, Vienna was threatened with becoming discredited not only in the West, but also in Berlin, if a false step were made. Nevertheless, Czernin issued a further communiqué denying everything that had been said in France. The result was French publication, on April 12, of the entire text of Karl's letter to Sixtus recognizing the "just claims" of France to Alsace-Lorraine

Actually, the duel with Clemenceau need not have had such catastrophic consequences. The Germans were well aware that the Monarchy had conducted peace feelers with the Entente and had wanted to use Alsace-Lorraine to end the war. Berlin had also conducted feelers with them; and it could hardly complain about strict observance of allied territorial integrity after its own efforts to influence Italy and Rumania with Habsburg real estate in 1914 and 1915. If Czernin had not persisted in his attack on Clemenceau, the Sixtus letter might well never have been published. Even its publication did not have to be an unmitigated disaster. Much of the war-weary population of Vienna rather seems to have approved of it as evidence of a serious desire for peace. It was the way the crisis was conducted that ruined the standing of the Monarchy. For Czernin insisted on pushing the affair to a conclusion at whatever cost; the intemperate statements and denials which no one believed destroyed the moral authority of both the Foreign Minister and the Emperor.

The final denouement came on Czernin's return to Vienna. Czernin demanded from Karl a signed statement that on his honor he had never sent the letter to Sixtus, to which Karl agreed—a declaration which both of them by then knew was patently false. According to some reports, Czernin, who must have been close to a nervous breakdown by this time, threatened to commit suicide if his wishes were not fulfilled.[113] Furthermore, he demanded that the Emperor temporarily retire from the conduct of the government, to be replaced by some sort of regent—a proposal tantamount to outright abdication. Clearly, Czernin had had enough of Karl's attempts to tamper with his alliance policy and intended to remove him from power altogether. But Karl finally refused to back down before the will of his Foreign Minister, his resolve perhaps stiffened by the Empress Zita. On April 14, Czernin resigned from the Ballplatz. His final communiqué asserted that the Paris publication of the Sixtus letter was a fabrication, a statement clearly contradicted by his own departure from office, and he declared the affair closed. Indeed it was, and much else with it.

How much of this Czernin intended when he made his April 2 speech remains a matter of dispute. The strain he was under by then certainly played a role in what he initially said on April 2, as well as in his subsequent conduct. But the unfolding of the whole affair was due to more than just miscalculation on his part, even if he had no knowledge of the content of Karl's letter to Sixtus at the beginning of it. Whether he expected it to lead to his own resignation has been equally disputed. It has even been argued that he deliberately engineered the entire scandal from the outset.[114] Demblin, who probably understood Czernin's thoughts better than anyone else at that time, later wrote that if the Monarchy could not attain a compromise peace together with Germany, Czernin saw only two other courses open to it: It would either be forced with Berlin under the Entente yoke, or, if Germany won the war, under the yoke of the Germans.[115] By 1918, he had opted for the second choice as the lesser of the two evils.

Whether that dichotomy had been objectively true before April 1918, Czernin's own actions now made it so. The third course of a separate peace, advocated by Meinl and Lammasch, might have been utopian in any case; it was clearly out of the question after the Sixtus scandal. Vienna lost its independent standing with both the Entente and its own peoples. The latter now turned either to Germany or to London and Washington; from April 1918, Vienna became merely a façade devoid of real power to influence its own fate any longer. Berlin moved in to fill the vacuum, welcomed by the Austrian Germans and the Magyars, while the other nationalities awaited the opportunity to abandon the Habsburg state entirely. The Entente, convinced that the Monarchy had become a powerless German satellite, finally gave up the idea of treating with it and turned to the plans of dissolution advocated by the exiles.

This was the legacy of the Sixtus Affair of April 1918. Two months later, Revertera wrote to Berchtold describing newspaper reports that France was becoming more receptive to peace talks, which he was inclined to doubt so long as Clemenceau remained in power. But he added significantly: "I nevertheless have the feeling that there would now soon be a connection, if Kari Czernin had not given his April speech. Since this speech, I have undoubtedly become unusable, and we have to give over the initiative in politicis as in militaribus to the Germans."[116] The letter is all the more revealing in that Revertera had never advocated a separate peace but had often praised Czernin's policies in his correspondence. Those policies had now destroyed all prospect of peace with the West. It was, of course, because the prospect of such a peace—without Germany—had become so enticing, that Czernin had delivered his speech in the first place. In so doing, willingly or not, he had also shattered the illusion of Austrian parity in the alliance which he had labored so hard to create. His entire diplomatic construct, which had sought to shore up the image of Austria-Hungary as some sort of independent entity despite its ties with Berlin, had crashed to pieces overnight. After April 1918, the only alternative to complete German domination appeared to be complete dissolution—such was the ultimate logic of the German Course. Now only a miracle could save the Dual Monarchy.

Chapter 8

THE MOST TERRIBLE DEATH
April-November 1918

I

As the Sixtus crisis reached its height, Wedel cabled anxiously to Berlin that Czernin's position was endangered from all sides and that the German press should avoid any expressions of mistrust in him. Czernin was the exponent of a pro-German policy based on an Austrian German and Magyar minority, and his removal from office could only have adverse consequences.[1] Three days later, he was no longer Austrian Foreign Minister.

The consequences of his fall were adverse, but not in the direction Wedel had feared. Czernin's apparent successes had given him considerable popularity in upper class circles, and it was all the Austrian censorship could do to muffle the outcry against his going. But more important, the result of the crisis was to discredit the dynasty among the Austrian Germans and the Magyars, previously its strongest supporters, while Karl's efforts to ingratiate himself with the Germans after it broke had the same effect on the other nationalities. The Emperor was rumored to be completely under the influence of the Empress Zita and her shady if not treasonable Parma family connections. The throne lost its moral authority among its subjects, perhaps the last means of countering the political and economic disintegration all around it. Their trust in the dynasty gone, the upholders of the old order had nowhere left to turn but to Berlin. A week after Czernin's resignation, Wedel reported a complete change of mood in Austrian German and Hungarian circles, which now agitated heatedly for maintaining the alliance:

> It has never been as clearly felt as now that the Monarchy, if it can continue to live at all, can do so only under the protection of the German Reich; that a departure from the ally means certain collapse. The sunken trust in the rule of the Crown has contributed strongly to this recognition.[2]

The Sixtus affair deepened the German Course and pushed it to its final conclusion. Cramon reported that the dismay in the officer corps was "indescribable," and that Arz had poured out his heart to him about Karl's actions.[3] Conrad repeated his assertions that he had been dismissed in order to give free rein to such things as the Sixtus letter. "The Amnesty, the suppression of disciplinary punishment, a hundred other things rushed in then," he asserted, reaffirming his unbroken loyalty to the alliance.[4] Perhaps no one was more upset than Hohenlohe, who made no secret in Berlin that he considered Karl's letter to Sixtus "absolutely inexcusable" and that the Emperor "had acted like a schoolboy" in the whole affair. Hohenlohe saw everything he had worked for shattered by the revelations. Berchtold noted after seeing him in Vienna:

> All his efforts since 1914 had been directed towards demonstrating to the Germans the great services of the Austro-Hungarian armies in the defense of the East, and to emphasize that in this world struggle it was Austria-Hungary which, through waves of outpoured blood, had made it possible for Germany to hold and to win. Austria-Hungary had persevered steadfastly in every phase of the war at Germany's side as a true, self-sacrificing ally, and must also at the conclusion of peace claim the corresponding reward for this. Now, this was all broken to *pieces* overnight![5]

For those who had already set so much of their faith on salvation through Germany, the scandal seemed to demand surrender of their last reservations in order to prove the loyalty of the Monarchy to the alliance and thus be able to claim some small reward for four years of brutal conflict. The Monarchy now appeared inescapably tied to the Germans, and the only question was how many crumbs it might still be able to wheedle out of them.

Czernin's successor as head at the Ballhausplatz was István Burián. Burián's appointment (or rather, re-appointment) came as a surprise to everyone; Karl probably picked him because he was an experienced and wholly predictable figure who would engage in no Czerninesque policy initiatives. The choice has never been entirely explained. Whatever his policies during his earlier tenure as Foreign Minister, even Burián realized the extent of the dependence on Germany to which the Monarchy had fallen by 1918. "Now we are really tied to the fate of Germany, whether we want it or not," he had written in the midst of the Sixtus revelations.[6] In any case, the mood both in Germany and in the Monarchy was such that, whatever his own misgivings, there was little he could do to counter the general current.

For the Germans themselves now acted to cement the connection once and for all. Wedel, earlier so sympathetic with Austrian conditions, cabled the Wilhelmstraße: "We should not let this moment go by unused, in order to reach lasting and firm agreements with Austria-Hungary first politically and militarily, and later also economically."[7] Cramon was even more explicit: "One can no longer have trust now; therefore, we must demand guarantees." He spoke of putting all political and military measures under German control.[8] Soon after Burián's return to office, Wedel had a blunt talk with the Austrian Foreign Minister. The tone was one of scarcely-veiled threats, a clear indication of how much the center of power in the alliance had shifted to Berlin. "I had to tell him openly," Wedel wrote afterwards, "that a simple yes was not enough; we had to see an actual, a practical change in policy which raised all our uncertainty, since I could not hide from him that our trust was shaken." Burián had little choice but to reply that deepening the alliance was his foremost task, and that the supposed Parma influence on Karl was merely an "episode." Wedel reflected after the interview that some of his words must have made a painful impression, but that pressure from the German side actually made it easier for the vacillating Austrians to overcome their own hesitations.[9]

The initiative to tie the Monarchy firmly to Germany did not come simply from the German side. Cramon reported that Hohenlohe had told him to be sure that Karl was made fully aware of the seriousness of his actions, since a repetition of the Sixtus affair would completely alienate the Austrian Germans and the Magyars from the Crown and bring about the collapse of the Monarchy. Arz talked in the same vein.[10] At the end of April, Hohenlohe advised German Chancellor Hertling how to handle the new head at the Ballplatz: He should be told that Vienna had so shaken its trustworthiness in Germany that none of the questions outstanding between the two countries could be discussed until the Austrian government proved through its behavior that it was once again worthy of confidence. "I believe we will do well to follow the advice of the Ambassador," Hertling noted.[11] If he was surprised to find the chief representative of another state telling him how that representative's own Foreign Minister should be manipulated, he made no mention of it.

The final humiliation of the Monarchy was proclaimed to all the world in Karl's famous trip to Spa, where German headquarters had been transferred from Kreuznach, on May 12. It quickly became known as Karl's journey to Canossa. Kühlmann, a week before the meeting, noted the opportunity the Sixtus scandal presented to tie Austria-Hungary tightly to Germany; Berlin should play deliberately on Karl's sense of guilt by giving

him the impression that he always had something to atone for.[12] At Spa, the
Austrians agreed to all the old Mitteleuropa proposals: an expanded longterm
alliance, a military union, and an economic agreement leading to complete
free trade between the two empires. There was in addition a military
protocol, providing for standardization of military organization and planning.
Actually, the Austrians agreed to much less than was first apparent. Except
for the military protocol, all they did was concede the Mitteleuropa
provisions in principle; they still had plenty of leeway for opposition and foot-
dragging since the specific details remained to be worked out. Moreover, their
acceptance of even that was made dependent on a solution of the Polish
problem—a considerable qualification. But none of this was apparent to the
public, which was told only the general lines of the agreement and assured
that the two countries were now tied more closely together than ever. The
impact of the Spa meeting came not from what the Monarchy really agreed,
but rather from what it appeared to agree. The communiqué from the
meeting, and the bombastic speeches which followed it, created the impression that without hesitation it had sold off its last shreds of independence to
the German Reich.

Whatever credit Austria-Hungary still had with either the Slav nationalities
within its borders or with the Entente was destroyed by the Sixtus scandal
and the Spa meeting a month later. Already units of Czech soldiers were
fighting alongside the Western armies in France; the Rome Congress in early
April seemed finally to bridge the worst differences between the Italians and
the Yugoslavs. From April, Western support for the aims of the exiles and
thus the complete dissolution of the Monarchy reached higher and higher
levels, from declarations of sympathy to open propaganda against the
Habsburg armies to eventual recognition of the exile committees as de facto
allied governments. Any sort of national compromise within the Monarchy
became impossible, for the Austrian Germans and the Magyars now
identified their position almost completely with a German victory, while the
other nationalities, hoping equally for a German defeat, espoused aims that
could be achieved only through the destruction of the state. There was no
longer any middle ground between them at all.

II

With all the problems facing the Monarchy by the spring of 1918, it is
perhaps amazing that it managed to remain together through the summer at
all. It had in fact become little more than a hollow shell, with the central

authority everywhere in various stages of collapse. The economy had reached a state of near paralysis, with shortages of supply and breakdowns in transportation resulting in general exhaustion. The grain crisis remained so serious that at the end of April, Landwehr, on his own authority, confiscated a fleet of Danube supply transports steaming to Germany and had their contents diverted to Vienna. The German High Command was infuriated and demanded restitution as well as guarantees against a future recurrence; Burián had to promise the German economic organizations far-reaching control rights in the Monarchy. But little else was done. As Wedel pointed out, the Austrian situation was such a mess that anything more than protests would have no effect anyway.[13] The German monetary subsidy, which had run at 100 million Marks a month for most of the war, was cut several times in 1918, despite Austrian objections. The Krone had lost so much of its value by then that only massive transfusions of currency could have saved it.

Food requisitions were at last inaugurated in Hungary by Lajos Windisch-graetz, but it was too late for them to make much difference. As inflation destroyed the value of the currency, some areas of the Monarchy were reduced to barter. The black market thrived, while instances of plundering of shops and farms occurred with dismal regularity. Strikes and work slowdowns multiplied. Still more alarming was the decay of the military, the final bulwark of the old order. The soldiers at the front were underclothed and undernourished. Shoes and changes of underwear were in short supply, and horseflesh had become a delicacy even for officers. The peace with Russia opened the prisoner camps of the East; but many returned prisoners had been radicalized by their contact with the Russian Revolution, and the attempts made to counteract this subversive influence when they were reintegrated into the army had little effect. Instances of desertion and mutiny by whole regiments became ever more common.

Despite this, it was decided to launch a new attack against Italy in June, in order to support the German Western offensive. To an extent, the decision was an independent one, to guarantee the Monarchy some share in the expected German victory; to an extent, it was compelled by the Germans themselves, in return for further shipments of food supplies. Appropriately, it was dubbed the "hunger offensive" by the starving troops, for one of its objectives was to seize the abundant supply stocks of the Italian army. It was launched on June 15, and it failed. Thereafter, though the Italians attempted no immediate counteroffensive of their own, the morale of the army steadily crumbled. It lost the last vestiges of its faith in itself. Count Karl Trauttmans-dorff, the Foreign Ministry representative at Austrian army headquarters, noted two results of the defeat within the officer corps. One was the feeling that the troops no longer had any faith in their leadership; the other, that militarily the alliance with Germany had to be "deepened" as far as possible to recover and maintain fighting efficiency.[14]

Under these circumstances, the government sank into a state of resignation, passively awaiting the outcome of the German offensive in France as if it no longer controlled its own fate—which it did not. "People have only one more hope," Wedel wrote, describing the apathy and despair in Vienna after the failure of the Italian offensive: "the German front. Even a hope in a separate peace does not exist anymore."[15] As the various nationality demands became more strident, the only solution seemed to be to put off any solution of them at all, since they all overlapped in such hopeless fashion; or rather, to subordinate them all to those of the predominant groups. In May, Seidler announced the division of Bohemia into national districts or Kreise—the old goal of the Austrian German nationalists and the Oktroi that had been discussed a year earlier—and in July he proclaimed his adherence to the "German Course" before the Reichsrat. He was applauded by Czernin in the Herrenhaus, who agreed that the Monarchy's foreign policy orientation toward Germany had to be complemented by a similar domestic orientation. Soon after, Seidler was replaced as Austrian Minister-President by Max Hussarek, but nothing was attempted to appease the Slav nationalities.

To all the other irredentas the Monarchy had to contend with, two more had now been added: those of the Germans and the Magyars. Their loyalty had always determined the domestic course of the Empire; but by the summer of 1918, they, like the other nationalities, were openly wondering whether they had more to gain outside of it than within. At the end of May, Wedel sent a report to Hertling in which he described the danger from the Slav demands to the position of the Germans in Cisleithania and how far the latter would go in order to block them:

> The Germans of Austria are fully conscious of the danger and therefore resolved to support the government in the struggle against Slavicization. If the government fails and does not find the necessary strength against the danger, they have a second iron in the fire: the irredenta. Signs of its presence are not lacking, and if the prospect of building and deepening the alliance has undercut an irredentist movement for the moment, it would nevertheless set in all the more strongly when it became certain that Slavic predominance was only a question of time.[16]

Any real concessions to the Slavs to keep them within the Empire threatened immediately to drive the Austrian Germans out of it, and only the closest tie to the German Reich still kept them loyal at all. But that very connection

completed the alienation of the Slavs and thus accentuated the process of
inner dissolution. In June, Wedel, anticipating the inevitable, advised a press
campaign to prepare for open German intervention to restore order when the
process of collapse finally became irreversible.[17]

The promise of the peace treaties in the East remained unfulfilled. In May,
it was decided to send the Austrian General Alfred Krauß to the Ukraine to
set up a military dictatorship in the Austrian area to requisition as much as
possible for the starving home population. But the Germans were so opposed
to the idea that Gusztáv Gratz, one of the Austrian Foreign Ministry
economic officials, pleaded that it be dropped for fear that Berlin would
unleash what would amount to an economic war against the Monarchy.[18]
A new agreement was worked out. In return for more supplies of grain,
Vienna consented to overall German command throughout the occupied
Ukraine, as well as making various other concessions. "The way this affair
was handled from the German side excited among all representatives of the
Monarchy . . . the deepest resentment, and only the compulsion of necessity
occasioned the Austro-Hungarian representatives not to break off the
negotiations," Arz later wrote. When Krauß actually got to the Ukraine, he
found the Germans ruthlessly exploiting everything in their own interest, and
his own hands completely bound.[19] Forgách wrote from Kiev at the end of
May: "At the moment, the acquisition of grain progresses as badly as can be
imagined."[20] A month later, Windischgraetz, in charge of Hungarian food
allocations, was in Berlin to beg for more help, but he got only half of what
he and Landwehr considered necessary. Even that, according to Windischgraetz, was given only on condition that the six Austrian divisions promised
for the Western Front be rushed there without delay.[21]

Vienna's remaining initiative was expended on trying to achieve advantages in the same drawn-out controversies that had occupied Burián for most
of his previous tenure as Foreign Minister. At the end of June, he suddenly
resurrected the old question of an agreement defining the obligations of each
partner in the alliance to the other. The Germans reacted sharply, and there
followed a series of heated exchanges that accomplished nothing.

The question of reinterpreting the alliance was easily eclipsed by the old
disputes over Poland and Mitteleuropa. Even while the domestic organism
of the Monarchy was dying, Burián still hoped to achieve German assent to
the Austro-Polish solution. In June, he attended a two-day meeting in Berlin
to begin working out the details of the general promises made at Spa. While
the question of drafting a new treaty of alliance and a customs agreement
seemed to go relatively smoothly, the issue of Poland produced a complete
stalemate. "I did not neglect to remind emphatically that the offered measure

of our receptiveness in all alliance questions has as its essential presupposition a solution of the Polish question free of complaint for us, as already expressed in the Spa agreement," Burián reported afterward to Karl in his usual verbose manner.[22] The Germans were outraged, but Burián persisted in defending the Austro-Polish solution with all his logical arguments for the rest of the summer. The only difference from his position in 1915 and 1916 was that he now envisioned a personal union rather than a sub-dualistic constitutional amalgamation. In the final weeks of the war, all Burián's efforts actually did achieve German agreement to an Austro-Polish solution of sorts. But by then it had ceased to matter. It had long since become obvious to all but a few Polish conservatives (and to Burián) that the whole controversy had become a dead issue, since the Poles could get more from the Entente than from either Austria or Germany.

A similar amount of attention was directed to the Mitteleuropa question. A new treaty between the two capitals was drafted. In July, Austrian and German economic experts began talks in Salzburg on the customs agreement. An economic settlement was finally concluded in October on the basis of a customs union (rather than the old Austrian formula of preference), but with temporary internal duties to protect Austrian manufactured products from German competition. Like the agreement over Poland, though, it remained completely meaningless.

Why did Vienna pursue these old issues so doggedly while the existence of the state itself was becoming ever more dubious? Despite all the signs of impending diaster, many upper class Austrian Germans and Magyars still believed that Germany was about to win the war. The war of position in France seemed to have ended at last, with the German army slogging slowly, but steadily, forward; it was only a matter of time until the Entente lines broke under the pressure. Victory would offer the final solution to all their problems. On July 21, Arz even expressed his relief that talk of "no annexations" had vanished, at least for the Balkans. "The victor has the right to draw up the results of the victory according to *his* judgment and *his* discretion. And we are the victors on the Balkan Peninsula, no one will argue with us about that."[23]

Neither Karl nor Burián, however, numbered among the true believers in German might. The Sixtus scandal had destroyed Karl's freedom to make any more policy initiatives away from the alliance; and he was also compelled to follow the prevailing German Course in Austrian domestic politics, reportedly telling the Czechs that their persistent refusal to engage in negotiations for any sort of compromise settlement of their demands left him no other alternative.[24] But he had lost none of his longing for peace or his skepticism that the Germans could achieve it. In June, he even predicted that the great German offensive would soon be grinding to a halt.[25] Nor was Burián any more confident in German military success. He spoke of a new peace effort in four to six weeks when the situation had become "clearer," [26] and in July began considering getting neutral mediation for a settlement. Wedel in fact called the Austrian Foreign Minister practically the only optimist in the Monarchy who believed that it still had enough strength to solve its problems on its own,[27] not a surprising judgment considering Burián's consistent overestimation of the Monarchy's resources during his first tenure as Foreign Minister.

Whatever their conception of the general situation, though, it seems to have been inconceivable to both Karl and Burián that Germany might be decisively defeated—even if it failed to achieve decisive victory. Whatever happened in the West, German armies still occupied Poland, the Baltic, the Ukraine, Rumania, Belgium, and northern France; and for that matter, the Monarchy itself occupied the western Balkans and part of Italy. The failure of the German offensive would pave the way for a peace conference where the Central Powers, even if defeated, would still hold a powerful bargaining position because of their conquests. As they liked to say in Vienna, the situation was desperate but not serious; there was still time to find solutions. At the end of July, Friedrich Wieser, the Austrian Finance Minister, had an audience with Karl, who even at that late date reckoned on peace negotiations beginning only in the fall and not leading to a conclusion until the following spring.[28] This misplaced confidence explains some of Vienna's myopic preoccupation with war aims negotiations with Berlin in the summer of 1918. It was intent to secure as much from the Germans as possible, certain that Germany's position at the peace conference, even if it was defeated, would still be strong enough to pull the Monarchy out of the war intact. There might be a defeat in France, but not a disaster. It was a fatal miscalculation.

III

In July 1914, the Austro-Hungarian Monarchy went to war in the confidence that its ally was the strongest power in the world. It was the myth of German military invincibility that sustained the alliance; four years later, after all the events of the war, the myth had still not been broken. By then that myth was practically the only thing sustaining the alliance at all—or, for that matter, the Monarchy itself. Wedel wrote in April:

The Monarchy is true to the alliance as long as we win, and it will also remain so after the conclusion of peace when Germany remains strong. Then, but only then, can Austria also continue to live. If we did not win, and did not remain strong and invincible after the struggle, then the first result would be: "Finis Austriae."[29]

By the summer of 1918, everything hinged on the outcome of the German offensive in France. But despite repeated tactical successes, Hindenburg and Ludendorff failed to break the Entente lines. Western superiority in both men and materiel had grown too overwhelming, even with the momentary German advantage of new forces diverted from the East. The great gamble, that Britain and France could be knocked out of the war before the arrival of the fresh American army, had failed. German troops by the summer had nearly reached their old Marne position of 1914, but there the offensive spent itself. The High Command may now have expected a return to the war of position, but the Entente counterattacks turned into a general advance all along the line, and, in increasing disorder, the German army was forced into retreat. Its last reserves had been expended in the offensive, and one retreat followed another without the hoped-for stabilization being achieved. August 8, which Ludendorff later called the Black Day of the German army, indicated clearly that the Entente advance could no longer be stemmed, and that the German military now faced not merely a retreat, but the prospect of a collapse of its whole position. Finally, even Ludendorff realized that the war had been lost.

The effects of the failure on the Monarchy were immediate. "The belief in the invincibility of Germany, which until then had been the main support for holding out, had lost its magic power," Landwehr later wrote.[30] The mood at the Ballplatz changed practically overnight; jarred from its earlier lack of urgency, Vienna now frantically pleaded for immediate action to end the war before the situation became completely hopeless. Arz even expressed his willingness to resign if his remaining in office might hinder a change of policy towards Berlin.[31]

On August 14, Burián, Karl, and Arz met with their German counterparts at Spa to plead for the necessity of peace as soon as possible. Backed by the Emperor, Burián proposed that the Central Powers issue a public call to all the belligerents to meet in some neutral place for a non-binding discussion of their peace conditions. His earlier idea of soliciting neutral mediation was now dropped as too cumbersome and slow; peace talks had to be started immediately. But the Germans, headed by Admiral Paul von Hintze, who had replaced Kühlmann at the Wilhelmstraße—Kühlmann, completely isolated, had finally been forced out of office in early July—objected that such a step would be seen only as a sign of weakness and despair. It was a measure of Burián's own assessment of the situation that he now doggedly persevered in pressing the need for peace on Berlin, as in his first tenure as Foreign Minister he had just as obstinately rejected it. Hintze argued in vain that neutral mediation would be better, since it would not be so obvious that it was the Central Powers that had initiated it. Nothing in any case should be done until the front in France was stabilized. For the rest of August, Burián, with Karl's support, bombarded Berlin with admonitions and urgings for his proposal—the more so as the German retreat in France continued unabated. Wedel reported that every counter-argument he made to the dogmatic Austrian Foreign Minister only elicited ten others in its stead.

Vienna was so convinced that peace talks had to begin before the situation worsened further that it was prepared to issue a peace note even without German approval. That prospect was received with alarm in Berlin, and Hintze came to Vienna at the beginning of September to try personally in a two-day conference to talk Burián out of his resolve. The whole range of Austro-German war aims was discussed. Hintze said that Germany was ready to renounce annexations, and Burián described Vienna's war aim as maintaining the integrity of the Monarchy. Despite such pious declarations, the question of Poland provoked all the usual controversies. But no agreement over the proposed peace initiative could be reached.[32]

Berlin, still hoping to head off a unilateral Austrian move, began contacts for mediation through the Netherlands while Kaiser Wilhelm sent a last-minute telegram to Karl. Nonetheless, Burián's call "To everyone" was issued on September 14. In suspense, Vienna awaited the answer. The first response was further expression of anger from Germany. Then the Entente reactions began to appear. They were all negative—those of the states that even bothered to react at all.

In the following month, the collapse that had been predicted and feared so long came to pass with bewildering swiftness. The day after the publication of Burián's peace note, the Entente army in Saloniki, which had been there since the Serbian campaign of 1915, launched an offensive against the Bulgarian lines. They broke. By the end of September, the Bulgarians had concluded an armistice and were out of the war. The Ottoman Turks, cut off from Germany and the Monarchy, soon followed suit. The way was now open to the Entente up the Vardar valley into Hungary, for there were practically no Austrian or German forces available with which to patch up a new front. The Entente army streamed northward.

The collapse of Bulgaria toppled the façade that had still hidden the dissolution of real authority within Austria-Hungary. Everywhere, the national groups began to proclaim their independence and to take over the reins of administration, finding that there was no longer any internal force capable of opposing them. The government frantically tried to repair the dissolving edifice, refusing to realize that it was already too late. Even now, in the hour of final disintegration, it was still bound by the constraints that had blocked every proposal for reform since the outbreak of the war. On September 27, a Common Ministers Council was called to discuss the situation created by the Bulgarian defection. Karl, chairing the meeting, urged the necessity of both peace and internal reconstruction, especially resolution of the South Slav question. "There is not a day to be lost," Burián agreed. "Decisions must be made if one wants to keep the people from taking their fate into their hands and deciding their future over the heads of the rulers." But the Foreign Minister insisted that any internal changes take place within the framework of the Ausgleich, and he was seconded by Wekerle, the Hungarian Minister-President. That meant in practical terms no solution at all. The problem was discussed again on October 2, and again no agreement could be reached. Austrian Minister-President Hussarek spoke of the danger of creating an Austrian German irredenta if their measures were not carefully chosen.[33]

Two weeks later, Karl issued his Autonomy Manifesto. Like so many of his measures, its idealism was matched by its practical imprecision. It sanctioned the incipient national committees without clearly defining their authority, and it was stillborn as soon as it was made public. Moreover, Wekerle had limited its application to Cisleithania, and Budapest now used its issuance to denounce the Ausgleich itself and declared only a personal union to bind Hungary any longer with Vienna. Tisza had publicly proclaimed the war lost a few days earlier, and the Magyars hoped to save themselves from the general ruin by severing all connection with the rest of the Monarchy. Their efforts were in vain. The Budapest government was overthrown in revolution at the end of the month, and Tisza himself murdered in his home on October 31.

While the domestic authority of the Monarchy was everywhere crumbling, Burián still hoped to salvage something through his diplomacy. On October 4, the Central Powers issued a joint note requesting peace on the basis of Wilson's 14 Points. Those points had posited the reconstruction of Austria-Hungary, not its dissolution; such a peace might yet save the Empire. Or so Burián hoped. But while Washington answered Berlin, it ignored Vienna; and this, coupled with its recognition of the Czechs as an allied government, showed that it was already too late. Vienna had seemed to slide away from the Germans with Burián's independent peace note of September. Now, it reiterated its solidarity with them, hoping Berlin could somehow get Wilson at least to recognize its existence. "We must strive for the Germans concluding an armistice only under the condition that we also receive one," Burián wrote on October 10.[34] The following day, he told Hohenlohe that the alliance obligated Germany to defend the Monarchy against possible demands for its dissolution.[35] His fears were well founded. When a reply to Vienna finally appeared from Washington, it noted that Point 10 of the 14 Points, which had called for the autonomous development (but not dissolution) of the Monarchy, had been invalidated by subsequent events.

Vienna's last proclamations of solidarity with Germany were of short duration. Within a week, as it grasped at any expedient that seemed to hold some prospect of salvation, the Ballplatz completely reversed itself. Wedel had reported at the end of September that morale in the Monarchy had undergone a "downright frightful change" with the collapse of Bulgaria, and that the Meinl Group had again become active. Only extensive German support could avert a catastrophe. With the reverses in France, however, that support no longer existed. Two weeks later, as Wilson's answer to the Austro-German peace note was awaited, he added that further military resistance by Vienna was impossible. "Conclusion among the people is that the Monarchy, despite every assurance to the contrary, in case of a refusal nevertheless must and will conclude a separate peace".[36] Gyula Szilássy, the former Austrian Minister to Greece, had in fact sent a memorandum to Karl in August with the unambiguous title "The Necessity of an Immediate Peace, Even a Separate Peace," arguing that continuing in the war at Germany's side meant suicide for the Monarchy. It had made enough of an impression on the Emperor that he had considered appointing Szilássy to take Burián's place; its author had been ordered to Vienna at the end of August for an audience. But then Karl had succumbed to his usual vacillations and, after letting him wait aimlessly for two weeks, changed his mind so that nothing further happened.[37]

Now, as Burián's peace efforts within the alliance got nowhere, other voices began to argue that it was not solidarity with Germany, but openly breaking with it, that offered the last chance to save the Monarchy. Their arguments were based on the hope that Britain and France, if not the United States, still favored Austria-Hungary's continued existence as a single entity, and that a quick conclusion of peace with them would preserve it intact and halt the process of domestic collapse. Nothing Germany could do would any longer have any effect; therefore, Vienna had to throw itself on the West.

János Pallavicini argued from Constantinople on October 21 that the
Monarchy had to get out of the war immediately, and that self-preservation
must take precedence over loyalty to the alliance.[38] More influential at this
point than either Szilássy or Pallavicini was Wladyslaw Skrzyński. Skrzyński,
in neutral Switzerland, the setting of so many earlier soundings between the
belligerents, had become Vienna's chief liaison with the Entente through his
contacts with its semi-official agents there, which he then reported to
Musulin, the Austrian Ambassador in Berne. The link through Switzerland
seemed to offer the last chance of staving off the growing catastrophe. He
cabled on October 24:

> It is beyond argument:
> 1. That France does not want to permit an expansion of Germany through
> German-Austria (Herr Clemenceau would be ready to take a position against
> Wilson on this), and that England wishes a loose connection of the arising states
> under the House of Habsburg.
> 2. That we *ourselves* can *not* save the unity of the Monarchy, but only with the
> help of England and France.
> 3. That neither England nor France will step in for us *as long as we remain
> Germany's ally.*[39]

By then, Burián, who had cautioned him a week earlier against any action
disloyal to Berlin, had ceased to be Foreign Minister. His successor—the last
Foreign Minister of the Habsburg Monarchy—was Count Gyula Andrássy the
younger. Andrássy had been one of the most pro-German statesmen of the
whole Monarchy, but he was appointed to office with the purpose of
dissolving the alliance. Even more ironic, it was his father, Gyula Andrássy
the elder, who, as Austrian Foreign Minister forty years earlier, had
concluded the original alliance treaty with Bismarck. Andrássy the elder had
always considered it one of his chief successes. Yet there was a certain
appropriateness to the irony. Both Andrássys were Hungarian; and the
Hungarians, however tightly they had held to the alliance and the German war
effort, had always done so out of a reasoned calculation of their own state
interests—not from the confused national loyalty that had characterized so
many Austrian Germans. As German defeat became certain and Cisleithania
broke to pieces, that same calculation spurred them to dissociate themselves
from both, as if they could somehow maintain the Crown of St. Stephen on
their own and halt at the Leitha the effects of the defeat. One of Andrássy's
motives in assuming office was to prevent the outbreak of revolution in
Budapest by attempting a separate peace with the Entente.

He lost no time in making the effort. He replaced Burián on October 24, and two days later instructed Hohenlohe to transmit a personal message from the Emperor Karl to Kaiser Wilhelm. It read:

> It is my duty, as difficult for me as this is, to tell you that my people are neither capable nor willing to continue the war. . . . Therefore, I am notifying you that I have made the unalterable decision to ask for a separate peace and an immediate armistice within the next 24 hours.[40]

Hohenlohe, when he received the telegram from Vienna, immediately tendered his resignation.

The Germans did what they could to avert the note, but without success. It became public on October 28. Wedel, who asked to see it before it was issued, was shown a draft in which the decisive passages were missing; he felt he had been deliberately deceived, even though he had warned Berlin of its coming as soon as Andrássy accepted office. The Ballplatz, fearing the effect of such opposition, in fact phrased the final draft in such a way that Skrzyński had to be instructed to make perfectly clear to his Entente contacts that it really did involve a separate peace. As he was informed from Vienna, it had been unable to say so openly because of the possible reaction of the Austrian Germans.[41] The central phrase was the declaration of the Monarchy's willingness to enter into peace talks "without waiting for the result of other negotiations." That could have only one meaning.

Andrássy's note ended the alliance that had bound Austria-Hungary to Germany for nearly forty years. But the step was a forlorn hope from the beginning, antagonizing Berlin (which, after all, had by now already asked for armistice conditions jointly with Vienna) without having any real effect on either the Entente or the domestic situation. Events continued to play themselves out as if it had never been issued, proving only that the Ballplatz had long since lost all real power. Andrássy had scarcely accepted office before the long-expected Italian offensive began. After several days of stubborn resistance, the Austrian army, its homeland already in dissolution, broke into its constituent national parts. Vittorio Veneto, the decisive victory Rome had sought since 1915, was achieved largely by default. Lammasch finally became Minister-President in Vienna, but there was nothing left for him to do but to try to make the transfer of power as bloodless as possible. The revolution Andrássy had hoped to avert in Hungary came at last with the collapse of the Italian front, putting the radical Károlyi at the head of a new regime in Budapest. It was a final irony that Károlyi was Andrássy's own son-in-law. The First World War officially ended on all the fronts on November 11, 1918. By then, Austria-Hungary had ceased to exist.

IV

With hindsight, the dissolution of Austria-Hungary seemed to many who lived through it to have been inevitable. "We were bound to die," Czernin wrote in his memoirs. "We were at liberty to choose the manner of our death, and we chose the most terrible." [42] If that was indeed the case, the alliance with Germany, which had been the Monarchy's greatest ally, certainly contributed to making it so. The alliance had caused Austria-Hungary serious problems even before 1914, but they were multiplied immeasurably after the outbreak of the war. Nevertheless, for the first three years of hostilities, the connection with Germany still served its primary purpose of safeguarding the Monarchy from its foreign enemies. Without German aid, the Habsburg armies would probably have collapsed under Russian pressure in either the spring of 1915 or the summer of the following year. In 1917, though, the threat from Russia—at least in terms of military invasion—ceased to exist. From that point on, the alliance lost its chief foreign policy raison d'être. Its maintenance after 1917 involved complications which far outweighed its benefits. It locked Austria-Hungary in insoluble conflicts over war aims with Germany and it held the Monarchy in the war until its economic and social infrastructure was reduced to ruin. One historian has even argued that without the alliance, the Austrian Germans and the Magyars would have been forced to come to terms with the demands of the Slavs, and a constitutional transformation might have been effected which would have saved the state. [43] When the attempt was finally made at the end of October to sunder the tie with Berlin, it came far too late to have even a momentary effect on the final course of events.

Why, then, did the Monarchy remain allied with Germany to the bitter end, seemingly against its own best interests? For most of its leaders, it really had no choice. By 1917, transfusions of German aid had become essential for maintaining a functioning economy. More important, the alliance seemed to them the final prop maintaining the integrity of the state itself. A separate peace would probably have cost the Crown the support of the Austrian Germans and the Magyars without increasing the loyalties of the other ethnic groups, leaving it with no positive support from any of the major peoples of the realm. The Habsburgs had faced a similar situation in 1848, when nearly all of the nationalities had attempted to go their separate ways. They had overcome the crisis then because the imperial bureaucracy and, what was decisive, the army, had remained intact. The Austrian poet Grillparzer had justly apotheosized the Habsburg army: "In your camp is Austria." That camp was a pale shadow of its former self by the last years of World War I. Even many of its chief officials were wholeheartedly loyal to it only as long as the domestic order remained unchanged. Whether 1848-49 could have been repeated in the circumstances of 1917-18 if the Crown had cut itself off from Germany is thus highly unlikely.

If the alliance created an impossible situation for Austria-Hungary, it had a similar impact on Germany. The Germans wanted a strong ally in Central Europe; they possessed in the Monarchy what many of them considered a corpse. They never developed a successful policy of dealing with it, and in a certain respect their plans to dominate Central Europe were simply the result of the Austrians' inability to provide political stability there by themselves. The alliance certainly brought Berlin as many problems as it did Vienna. The only difference was that it had greater reserves of strength with which to deal with them. As several Austrian statesmen had pointed out during the war, defeat for Germany meant some losses of territory and a new government; defeat for Austria-Hungary meant the end of its very existence.

In the narrowest sense, it might be said that the Monarchy was the hapless victim of German militarism on the one hand and Entente determination to fight for total victory over Germany on the other. But the Austrians caused much of their plight themselves, by overestimating their strength and continually postponing solution of their pressing institutional problems. The Monarchy's fate might have been different had there been no Ludendorff. But it also would have been different had there been no Stürgkhs or Buriáns. Similarly, a determined peace policy early in the war, rather than in 1917 when the Monarchy's reserves of strength had become so exhausted, might have staved off the disaster that came a year later. Karl and Czernin, whatever their faults, found themselves in a position by then which would have strained the talents of a Metternich. If the nationality conflicts had not reached such a pitch by the twentieth century, perhaps the decision to go to war in 1914 could have been avoided altogether. The list of might-have-been's and if-only's is endless. The worst that is generally said about the Dual Monarchy is that it was, in the Socialist Viktor Adler's often-quoted words, a despotism tempered by slovenliness. It certainly deserved better of its leadership than the fate it suffered in the First World War. Perhaps the moral in all this, if morals are to be sought, is simply that any political system, if it is allowed to run down far enough, reaches a point at which no amount of good will or last-minute reform attempts can save it.

"A world is perishing here, and a new one is arising," Wedel wrote in late October from Vienna.[44] Whether the new world that was replacing the Monarchy would be as much of an improvement as its protagonists alleged remained to be seen. Habsburg rule in Central Europe had, after all, endured for four hundred years—an impressive track record. In many cases, the old world had perished leaving nothing in its stead but chaos. Watching the emergence of the new German-Austrian state, Wedel observed:

> The Tyroler feels himself a Tyroler, but hardly an Austrian; it is the same for the Carinthian and the Styrian; the Salzburger and the Upper Austrian are less nationally settled because of the active communication with Bavaria. Only the Lower Austrian and the inhabitants of the Sudentenland, who gravitate to Vienna, really feel themselves to be Austrians.[45]

It was going to be no easier to convince Serbs and Croats that they shared a common identity as Yugoslavs, or Czechs and Slovaks that they were now Czechoslovakians. The confusion of loyalties that had so complicated the Monarchy's history was a legacy that had only begun to be faced when the Habsburg state ceased to exist.

The dissolution of Austria-Hungary in fact marked no end to the problems that had plagued the alliance. It simply changed their outward aspect or shifted their emphasis. The Germans had always seen shoring up the old order in the Monarchy as furthering their own interests; it was only when it was in complete collapse that they began to realize that its passing did not necessarily mean the end of those interests as well—quite the contrary. Wedel wrote at the end of October that a restoration of the Habsburgs in a restructured Monarchy would represent a danger to Germany. He added prophetically: "But it will be easier to live with the little states which will probably be formed here, since they will all have to reckon with the great German Reich."[46] His words would be more than borne out by the events of the following decades, though in tragic dimensions which no one would have dared to foretell in 1918.

NOTES

Abbreviations used:

AA   Bonn: Auswärtiges Amt.

AR   Vienna: Haus-, Hof-, und Staatsarchiv, Administrative Registratur.

DZA   Potsdam: Deutsches Zentralarchiv.

GP   Johannes Lepsius, A. Mendelssohn-Bartholdy, Friedrich Thimme, eds.,
            Die Große Politik der Europäischen Kabinette, 40 vols., Berlin, 1922-
            1927.

HHSA   Vienna: Haus-, Hof-, und Staatsarchiv (for material not in the Poli-
            tisches Archiv or Administrative Registratur).

KA   Vienna: Kriegsarchiv.

MA   Munich: Geheimes Staatsarchiv.

ÖUA   Ludwig Bittner, Alfred Pribram, Heinrich Srbik, Hans Uebersberger,
            eds., *Österreich-Ungarns Aussenpolitik,* 8 vols., Vienna, 1930.

PA   Vienna: Haus-, Hof-, und Staatsarchiv, Politisches Archiv.

SA   Brno: Státní Archiv.

SG   André Scherer and Jacques Grunewald, eds., *L'Allemagne et les Prob-
            lèmes de la Paix Pendant la Première Guerre Mondiale,* 4 vols., Paris,
            1962-1978.

Limitations of space prevent complete citations of printed sources in the endnotes;
these can be found in the bibliography.

Dates are given in common American (rather than European) usage, that is, month-day-year.

Preface: The Problem

1. Josef Stürgkh, *Im Deutschen Großen Hauptquartier,* 116.

Chapter 1: The Brilliant Second

1. James Wegs, *Austrian Economic Mobilization During World War I,* 200.

2. Alois Brusatti, "Die Wirtschaftliche Situation Österreich-Ungarns am Vorabend des Ersten Weltkrieges," in Institut für Österreichkunde, ed., *Österreich am Vorabend des Ersten Weltkrieges,* 64-65; Miklós Komjáthy, ed., *Protokolle des Gemeinsamen Ministerrates der Österreichisch-Ungarischen Monarchie,* 64.

3. Viktor Naumann, *Dokumente und Argumente,* 3-4.

4. Ottokar Czernin, *In the World War,* 359.

5. Bismarck to Schweinitz, 10-18-1888, Stephan Verosta, *Theorie und Realität von Bündnissen,* 157.

6. Fritz Klein, "Innere Widersprüche im Bündnis Zwischen Deutschland und Österreich-Ungarn zu Beginn der Imperialistischen Epoche (1897 bis 1902)," in F. Klein, ed., *Studien zum Deutschen Imperialismus vor 1914,* 225-262.

7. Treutler to AA, 3-24-14, GP, XXXIX, 337; Treutler to AA, 3-27-14, GP, XXXIX, 342.

8. Samassa to Claß, 6-16-14, DZA, Alldeutscher Verband, 704.

9. Tisza to Hugo Ganz, 4-3-15, István Tisza, *Összes Munkái,* III, 211.

10. A. Basch, *The Danube Basin and the German Economic Sphere,* 10; Henry Cord Meyer, *Mitteleuropa in German Thought and Action,* 68; Fritz Fischer, *War of Illusions,* 296-298.

11. Dörte Löding, *Deutschlands und Österreich-Ungarns Balkanpolitik,* 253-254.

12. Tschirschky to Jagow, 5-22-14, GP, XXXIX, 634.

13. Lothar Höbelt, "Österreich-Ungarn und das Deutsche Reich als Zweibundpartner," in H. Lutz and H. Rumpler, eds., *Österreich und die Deutsche Frage,* 277.

14. Löding, 247-248.

15. Fritz Fischer, *War of Illusions,* 291-298; ———, "World Policy, World Power, and German War Aims," in H. W. Koch, ed., *The Origins of the First World War,* 103.

16. Joseph Maria Baernreither, *Fragments of a Political Diary,* 4-1914, 291, 294.

17. Peter Katzenstein, *Disjointed Partners,* 98.

18. Zdeněk Jindra, "Über die Ökonomischen Grundlagen der 'Mitteleuropa'-Ideologie des Deutschen Imperialismus," in K. Obermann, ed., *Probleme der Ökonomie und Politik in den Beziehungen Zwischen Ost-und Westeuropa,* 161.

19. Baernreither, *Fragments,* 4-1914, 291-293. The situation in Berlin was if anything even more confusing: *Ibid.,* 3-10-14, 263.

20. Günter Schödl, "Paul Samassa," *Süddeutsches Archiv,* XXI, 75-104.

21. Conrad to Gina Conrad von Hötzendorf, 6-28-14, Gina Conrad von Hötzendorf, *Mein Leben mit Conrad von Hötzendorf,* 114.

22. Berchtold Memoirs, VIII, 9-28-13, 69, PA I, 524b.

23. Gyula Szilássy, *Der Untergang der Donaumonarchie,* 254-255.

24. Karl von Macchio, *Momentbilder aus dem Diplomaten-Leben des Botschafters a. D. Dr. Freiherrn von Macchio,* VIII, 10, HHSA, Nachlaß Macchio, 2; Cf. Czernin, *In the World War,* 150-151.

25. Talk with Biliński, 11-3-16, Kanner Papers, Ib, 161.

26. Baernreither, Fragments, 8-25-13, 235.

27. Franz Ferdinand to Berchtold, 7-4-13, SA, Berchtold Archive, 457.

28. Baernreither, *Fragments,* 7-5-13, 210.

29. Josef Redlich, *Schicksalsjahre Österreichs,* I, 8-11-13, 206.

30. Berchtold to Franz Ferdinand, 7-28-13, HHSA, Nachlaß Franz Ferdinand, 9.

31. Franz Ferdinand to Berchtold, 7-24-13, SA, Berchtold Archive, 457.

32. Baernreither, *Fragments,* 3-14-14, 282-283.

33. Franz Conrad von Hötzendorf, *Aus Meiner Dienstzeit,* III, 470.

34. Berchtold Tagesbericht, 10-28-13, ÖUA, VII, 512-515.

35. Burián diary, 10-26-13, István Diószegi, "Außenminister Stephan Graf Burián," *Annales,* VIII, 192.

36. Baernreither, *Fragments,* 3-1914, 270-271, 277.

37. Redlich, I, 3-25-14, 223.

38. Czernin to Berchtold, 3-11-14, ÖUA, VII, 957; Cf. Czernin to Berchtold, 12-8-13, ÖUA, VII, 628.

39. Forgách to Mérey, 4-1-14, HHSA, Nachlaß Mérey.

40. Minute by Wilhelm on Griesinger to Bethmann, 3-11-14, GP, XXXVIII, 335.

41. Mérey to Berchtold, 7-27-14, ÖUA, VIII, 800.

42. See the short articles by Fritz Klein and F. R. Bridge, both listed in the bibliography.

43. Conrad to Berchtold, 6-22-14, Conrad, *Dienstzeit,* III, 696.

44. Czernin to Berchtold, 6-22-14, ÖUA, VIII, 174-175.

45. Tisza memo, 3-15-14, ÖUA, VII, 976.

Chapter 2: Va Banque

1. Berchtold to Czernin, 11-26-13, ÖUA, VII, 592.

2. Berchtold to Macchio, 2-13-15, HHSA, Nachlaß Macchio, 1.

3. Berchtold diary, 7-8-14, Hantsch, *Leopold Graf Berchtold,* II, 570; Hantsch, II, 557.

4. Exactly how bellicose Franz Joseph was during the crisis remains a subject

of controversy. Biliński, in several later interviews with Heinrich Kanner, affirmed that the Emperor had been in favor of war ever since the Skutari crisis of 1913 (Kanner Papers, Ib, 165-166, 191, 211-212). The interviews are discussed in Robert A. Kann, *Kaiser Franz Joseph und der Ausbruch des Weltkrieges.*

5. Talk with Biliński, 11-3-16, Kanner Papers, Ib, 211.

6. Hantsch, II, 646, 761.

7. Berchtold Tagesbericht, 7-3-14, ÖUA, VIII, 277.

8. Conrad, *Dienstzeit,* IV, 36-37.

9. Kurt Riezler, *Tagebücher,* 7-7-14, 183.

10. Forgách to Mérey, 7-8-14, HHSA, Nachlaß Mérey.

11. Komjáthy, 7-7-14, 145.

12. *Ibid.,* 142. On Tisza's position, see József Galántai, *Österreich-Ungarn und der Weltkrieg,* 266-278; and the article by Norman Stone, "Hungary and the Crisis of July 1914" in W. Laqueur and G. Mosse, eds., *1914: The Coming of the First World War,* 147-164.

13. Tisza to Franz Joseph, 7-1-14, István Tisza, *Briefe,* 37-38.

14. Szögyény to Vienna, 7-6-14, ÖUA, VIII, 319-320.

15. Tisza to Franz Joseph, 7-8-14, ÖUA, VIII, 371.

16. Berchtold to Tisza, 7-8-14, ÖUA, VIII, 371.

17. Burián diary, 7-10-14, 7-12-14, Diószegi, 206.

18. Forgách to Berchtold, 11-27-25, Hantsch, II, 585-586; Cf. Diószegi, 172.

19. Berchtold diary, 7-9-14, Hantsch, II, 570.

20. Tschirschky to Bethmann, 7-14-14, Geiß, *Julikrise,* I, 164.

21. Forgách to Mérey, 7-16-14, HHSA, Nachlaß Mérey.

22. Tschirschky to Bethmann, 7-14-14, Geiß, I, 166.

23. Jagow to Tschirschky, 7-15-14, Geiß, I, 179.

24. Komjáthy, 7-19-14, 150-154.

25. Berchtold to son Alois, 7-27-14, SA, Berchtold Archive, 556.

26. Bethmann to Tschirschky, 7-29-14, Geiß, II, 280-281.

27. Szögyény to Vienna, 7-27-14, ÖUA, VIII, 778.

28. Tschirschky to Jagow, 7-30-14, Geiß, II, 387-388.

29. Conrad, *Dienstzeit,* IV, 153.

30. *Ibid.*

31. Conrad, *Dienstzeit,* IV, 72.

32. Stürgkh to Thun, 6-28-14, Paul Molisch, ed., *Briefe zur Deutschen Politik in Österreich,* 389.

33. Alexander Spitzmüller, *". . . Und Hat Auch Ursach' Es zu Lieben",* 114.

Chapter 3: The Short War

1. Istvan Deak, "The Decline and Fall of Habsburg Hungary," in Iván Völgyes, *Hungary in Revolution,* 15.

2. Berchtold to Albertini, 11-23-33, Luigi Albertini, *The Origins of the War of 1914*, II, 221.

3. Mihály Károlyi, *Fighting the World*, 61, 117.

4. Stefan Zweig, *The World of Yesterday*, 223.

5. Glaise, *Zwielicht*, 360.

6. *Ibid.*, 326-327.

7. Berchtold to Giesl, 8-20-14, PA I, 498, xlvii/2a.

8. Glaise, *Zwielicht*, 325, 328, 357, 365.

9. József Galántai, "Die Kriegszielpolitik der Österreichisch-Ungarischen Monarchie im Ersten Weltkrieg und die Ungarische Regierung," in Institut für Österreichkunde, *Österreich-Ungarn 1867-1967*, 140.

10. Redlich, I, 8-6-14, 245.

11. Berchtold to Szögyény, 8-12-14, PA I, 522, xlvii/11.

12. Tisza to Burián, 8-11-14, Tisza, *Briefe*, 50-54; Memo of meeting, 8-20-14, PA I, 522, xlvii/11; Redlich, II, 1-8-15, 7.

13. Wolfdieter Bihl, "Zu den Österreichisch-Ungarischen Kriegszielen 1914," *Jahrbücher für Geschichte Osteuropas*, XVI, 506.

14. Berchtold to Szögyény, 8-18-14, PA I, 522, xlvii/11.

15. Berchtold to Hohenlohe, 8-21-14, *Ibid.*; Hohenlohe to Vienna, 8-22-14, *Ibid.*

16. Stürgkh to Berchtold, 8-25-14, *Ibid.*

17. Tisza to Berchtold, 8-24-14, Tisza, *Briefe*, 59.

18. Hohenlohe to Vienna, 8-22-14, PA I, 522, xlvii/11.

19. On the Austrian mobilization, see the excellent article by Stone and Ronald Ernharth, *The Tragic Alliance*, 138-142.

20. Gerard Silberstein, *The Troubled Alliance*, 253. Norman Stone, *The Eastern Front*, 91, puts the total losses even higher, at 400,000. Rudolf Kiszling, *Österreich-Ungarns Anteil am Ersten Weltkrieg*, 15-16; Hugo von Freytag-Loringhoven, *Menschen und Dinge*, 216.

21. Heinrich von Lützow, *Im Diplomatischen Dienst der K. u. K. Monarchie*, 220.

22. Glaise, *Zwielicht*, 424.

23. Alfred Krauß, *Die Ursachen Unserer Niederlage*, 58.

24. Theodor von Zeynek, *Das Leben eines Österreichisch-Ungarischen Generalstabsoffiziers*, 130, KA, Nachlaß Zeynek, B151.

25. Stone, *The Eastern Front*, 127, 262, 272-273; Zeynek, *Leben*, 170, KA, Nachlaß Zeynek, B151.

26. Zeynek, *Leben*, 117, 119, KA, Nachlaß Zeynek, B151; Glaise, *Zwielicht*, 348.

27. Conrad to Bolfras, 8-27-14, Conrad, *Dienstzeit*, IV, 551-552; Conrad to Bolfras, 9-5-14, *Ibid.*, 647.

28. Conrad to Bolfras, 11-19-14, Conrad, *Dienstzeit*, V, 543.

29. Forgách to Macchio, 9-5-14, HHSA, Nachlaß Macchio, 1.

30. Forgách to Macchio, 9-12-14, *Ibid.*

31. Lützow, 229; Berchtold to Hohenlohe, 9-8-14, PA I, 500, xlvii/3; Hohenlohe to Berchtold, 9-14-14, *Ibid.*

32. Hohenlohe to Berchtold, 9-4-14, 9-13-14, SA, Berchtold Archive, 464/16.

33. Tisza to Berchtold, 9-3-14, Tisza, *Briefe,* 71; Tisza to Berchtold, 9-10-14, *Ibid.,* 77.

34. Stürgkh, 60.

35. Redlich, I, 9-19-14, 274.

36. Salomonssohn to Zimmermann, 10-7-14, AA, Öst. 72 Geh., Bd. 1.

37. Tisza to Stürgkh, 10-30-14, Tisza, *Briefe,* 100.

38. Eduard März, *Österreichische Bankpolitik,* 190.

39. Baron von Margutti, *The Emperor Francis Joseph and His Times,* quoted in Silberstein, 270.

40. Hohenlohe to Vienna, 9-19-14, PA I, 500, xlvii/3.

41. Tisza to Czernin, 9-7-14, Tisza, *Briefe,* 75; Tisza to Conrad and Berchtold, 9-10-14, *Ibid.,* 76; Tisza to Berchtold, 11-1-14, PA I, 517, xlvii/7c.

42. Komjáthy, 9-20-14, 177-184.

43. Bethmann to AA, 11-3-14, AA, Deut. 128 Nr. 2 Geh., Bd. 17.

44. Tisza to Tschirschky, 11-5-14, Tisza, *Briefe,* 104.

45. Komjáthy, 8-8-14, 159-166. German actions in Belgium were to be a recurrent concern in Vienna. A good overview of the problem is the article by Hartmut Lehmann cited in the bibliography.

46. Tisza to Berchtold, 8-26-14, Tisza, *Briefe,* 61-62.

47. Berchtold to Hohenlohe, 11-21-14, PA I, 506, xlvii/5a; Berchtold Tagesbericht, 12-13-14, *Ibid.*

48. Macchio to Berchtold, 1-6-15, Macchio, *Wahrheit! Fürst Bülow und Ich in Rom,* 73.

49. Berchtold diary, 1-9-15, Hantsch, II, 716.

50. Forgách to Macchio, 4-25-31, HHSA, Nachlaß Macchio, 1.

51. Tisza to Berchtold, 1-6-15, Tisza, *Briefe,* 146.

52. Tisza to Burián, 1-5-15, Tisza, *Briefe,* 141.

53. Macchio, 68.

54. Berchtold to Bethmann, 11-10-14, SG, I, 7-9; Bethmann to Berchtold, 11-23-14, *Ibid.,* 23-24.

55. Erlaß to Velics (Munich), 12-3-14, PA I, 842, Krieg 4a; Conrad to Berchtold, 12-14-14, Conrad, *Dienstzeit,* V, 754-756.

56. Conrad, *Dienstzeit,* V, 911.

57. Tisza to Burián, 8-30-14, Tisza, *Briefe,* 66.

58. Pallavicini to Berchtold, 11-19-14, PA I, 521, xlvii/8b; Pallavicini to Berchtold, 11-26-14, PA I, 949, Krieg 25a; Pallavicini to Forgách, 1-6-15, *Ibid.*

59. Forgách memo, 1-10-15, PA I, 496, xlvii/1c. An accompanying note, added by Forgách 5-4-15, explains that the memo was written by him to be given to Berchtold. But since Berchtold was dismissed in the middle of the month, and since Forgách knew that neither Burián, Berchtold's successor, nor Tisza, agreed with the

views expressed there, he saw no reason to give it over but deposited it in the Foreign Ministry archive some months later as a document on the then-prevailing frame of mind. Whether Berchtold actually asked him to write it is not stated. Ten years later, Forgách reflected in a letter to Berchtold that their incipient desires for peace would have foundered on German opposition in any case, but that Tisza's opposition effectively nipped them in the bud. Forgách to Berchtold, 9-3-27, SA, Berchtold Archive, 464/9.

Chapter 4: The Hard Line

1. Tisza memo, 1-18-15, Tisza, *Briefe,* 151.
2. Forgách to Macchio, 4-25-31, HHSA, Nachlaß Macchio, 1.
3. Pogatscher to Macchio, 3-31-15, *Ibid.*
4. Talk with Zimmermann, 1-19-16, Kanner Papers, IIIa, 14-15.
5. Redlich, I, 10-8-14, 280.
6. Tschirschky to Bethmann, 7-20-16, AA. Wk. 20c Geh., Bd. 3.
7. August von Cramon, *Unser Österreich-Ungarische Bundesgenosse im Welt-kriege,* 150.
8. Tschirschky to AA, 6-21-15, AA, Deut. 128 Nr. 2 Geh., Bd. 32.
9. Komjáthy, 10-6-15, 308.
10. Tisza to József Vészi, 3-2-15, Tisza, *Briefe,* 170.
11. Burián memo, 11-14-15, PA I, 501, xlvii/3.
12. Berchtold diary, 1-4-16, Hantsch, II, 761.
13. Mérey to Macchio, 1-16-15, Macchio, 97.
14. Tisza to Conrad, 1-16-15, Tisza, *Briefe,* 154.
15. Hohenlohe to Berchtold, 1-29-15, SA, Berchtold Archive, 464/16.
16. Bethmann to Tschirschky, 2-6-15, AA, Deut. 128 Nr. 1 Geh., Bd. 41.
17. Tschirschky to AA, 3-5-15, 3-6-15, AA, Deut. 128 Nr. 1 Geh., Bd. 44; Jagow to Mühlberg, 3-6-15, *Ibid.;* Tagesbericht, 3-10-15, PA I, 510, xlvii/5a.
18. Conrad to Burián, 2-26-15, KA, Conrad-Archiv, B7.
19. Egmont Zechlin, "Das 'Schlesische Angebot' und die Italienische Kriegsge-fahr 1915," in W. Schieder, ed., *Erster Weltkrieg, Ursachen, Entstehung und Kriegsziele,* 353-354.
20. Burián to Conrad, 2-12-15, KA, Conrad-Archiv, B7.
21. Forgách to Macchio, 1-21-15, Macchio, 82; Forgách to Macchio, 2-24-15, HHSA, Nachlaß Macchio, 1.
22. Hohenlohe to Berchtold, 1-12-15, PA I, 507, xlvii/5a; Macchio to Burián, 2-9-15, *Ibid.*
23. Komjáthy, 3-8-15, 215-232.
24. Riezler, 2-20-15, 250.
25. Tschirschky to AA, 11-13-14, AA, Wk. Nr. 2 Geh., Bd. 1.

26. Jagow to Bülow, 2-20-15, AA, Wk. 2 Geh., Bd. 3; Cf. Redlich, II, 3-4-15, 22.

27. Conrad to Burián, 4-2-15, PA I, 499, xlvii/2b. Conrad communicated the same ideas to the Germans: Treutler to AA, 4-2-15, AA, Wk. 2 Geh., Bd. 5; Bethmann note, "Mitteilung des Generals von Falkenhayn über sein heutiges Gespräch mit General Conrad von Hötzendorf," 4-5-15, AA, Deut. 128 Nr. 1 Geh., Bd. 49.

28. Pallavicini to Burián, 4-17-15, PA I, 842, Krieg 4a; Pallavicini to Burián, 6-3-15, PA I, 518, xlvii/7d; Wangenheim to AA, 6-10-15, AA, Wk. 2 Geh., Bd. 8.

29. Tisza to Conrad, 4-16-15, Tisza, *Briefe*, 184; Tisza to Burián, 4-27-15, *Ibid.*, 189-190; Tisza memo, 5-1-15, *Ibid.*, 199-200.

30. Szécsen memos, 4-1915, 5-23-15, PA I, 497, xlvii/lc.

31. Redlich, II, 4-27-15, 33.

32. Bethmann memo, 4-25-15, AA, Deut. 128 Nr. 1 Geh., Bd. 52.

33. Berchtold diary, 5-1-15, Hantsch, II, 738; Karl Schneller diary, 5-1-15, 349, KA, Nachlaß Schneller, B509.

34. Conrad to Burián, 5-15-15, PA I, 499, xlvii/2b.

35. Bethmann memo, 6-17-15, AA, Deut. 128 Nr. 2 Geh., Bd. 32; Tisza note, 6-17-15, PA I, 518, xlvii/7d; Burián memo, 6-25-15, *Ibid.*

36. Viktor Naumann, *Profile*, 218.

37. Conrad to Bolfras, 4-10-15, KA, Conrad-Archiv, B7.

38. Burián to Conrad, 10-23-15, *Ibid.*

39. István Burián, *Austria in Dissolution,* 79.

40. Komjáthy, 10-6-15, 285-314.

41. Baernreither to Fürstenberg, 11-20-15, HHSA, Nachlaß Baernreither, 6.

42. Bethmann note, 8-13-15, SG, I, 161; Burián memo, 8-14-15, PA I, 503, xlvii/ 3.

43. Burián memo, 11-14-15, PA I, 501, xlvii/3; Jagow memo, 11-14-15, SG, I, 218-221.

44. Fürstenberg to AA, 8-10-15, DZA, AA-Handelspolitische Abteilung, 3988.

45. Szterényi to Beck, 7-1-15, Vienna: Allgemeines Verwaltungsarchiv, Nachlaß Beck, 38.

46. Richard Kapp, *The Failure of the Diplomatic Negotiations Between Germany and Austria-Hungary for a Customs Union,* 131-132.

47. Joannovics memo, "Die Wirtschaftliche Annäherung der Mittelmächte, Richtlinien für die Wirtschaftlichen Verhandlungen mit Deutschland," 3-2-17, PA XL, 317.

48. Tucher to Ludwig, 7-8-15, MA III, 2481/3.

49. Groß to colleagues, 8-23-14, HHSA, Nachlaß Groß, 4; Dobernig to Groß, 8-24-14, *Ibid.*

50. Pogatscher to Macchio, 10-28-14, HHSA, Nachlaß Macchio, 1.

51. Gebsattel to AA, 12-6-15, DZA, AA-Handelspolitische Abteilung, 3989.

52. Tucher to Ludwig, 11-25-15, MA III, 2481/3; Albert Berzeviczy to Groß, 12-14-16, HHSA, Nachlaß Groß, 5.

53. Hohenlohe to Berchtold, 10-12-14, SA, Berchtold Archive, 464/16.

54. Hohenlohe to Berchtold, 11-27-14, SA, Berchtold Archive, 464/16.

55. Redlich, I, 12-19-14, 294; II, 12-24-15, 92.

56. Conrad, *Private Aufzeichnungen,* 207; Conrad memo for Franz Joseph, 10-10-15, KA, Militärkanzlei Seiner Majestät, 25-1/5, 1915.

57. Talk with Baernreither, 4-10-15, Kanner Papers, Ib, 80.

58. Tisza to Burián, 4-10-15, PA I, 842, Krieg 4a.

59. Bethmann note, 10-15-15, AA, Deut. 180 Geh., Bd. 1; Tschirschky to Jagow, 10-10-15, AA, Wk. 20c Geh., Bd. 1.

60. Burián memo, 11-14-15, PA I, 501, xlvii/3.

61. Jagow memo, 11-13-15, SG, I, 211-215.

62. Cramon memo, "Gedanken über eine Militärkonvention zwischen Deutschland und Österreich-Ungarn nach dem Kriege," 11-10-15, AA, Botschaft Wien, Akten des Militärattachés, Secreta: v. Cramon.

63. Note for the Germans, 11-24-15, SG, I, 221-223.

64. Klepsch-Kloth to Bolfras, 4-9-16, KA, Militärkanzlei Seiner Majestät, Sonderfaszikel 79-42.

65. Hohenlohe to Burián, 2-22-16, AR, F37, 90.

66. Stürgkh to Burián, 3-14-16, AR, F37, 89.

67. Note for the Germans, 4-1916, PA I, 501, xlvii/3.

68. Jagow to Tschirschky, 2-16-16, SG, I, 270-272.

69. Tschirschky to Jagow, 4-6-16, AA, Wk. 20c Geh., Bd. 1a.

70. Burián memo, 4-15/16-16, PA I, 500, xlvii/3.

71. Jagow to Treutler, 4-16-16, SG, I, 306.

72. Tschirschky to AA, 4-23-15, AA, Öst. 70 Geh., Bd. 1.

73. März, 174.

74. Stürgkh to Tisza, 11-16-15, Gusztáv Gratz and Richard Schüller, *Der Wirtschaftliche Zusammenbruch Österreich-Ungarns,* 234-5.

75. Stürgkh to Tisza, 1-3-16, *Ibid.,* 256; Tisza to Stürgkh, 1-6-16, *Ibid.,* 260-261.

76. Komjáthy, 6-18-15, 233-265.

77. Komjáthy, 1-7-16, 362.

78. Conrad to Burián, 7-21-15, SG, I, 143-144; Conrad to Burián, 8-6-15, PA I, 519, xlvii/7d; Bethmann note, 6-18-15, SG, I, 126; Forgách to Berchtold, 9-24-15, SA, Berchtold Archive, 464/9.

79. Burián to Hohenlohe, 11-26-15, PA I, 949, Krieg 25a.

80. Burián to Hohenlohe, 9-28-15, PA I, 952, Krieg 25g; Tisza to Burián, 10-2-15, *Ibid.*

81. Forgách to Berchtold, 10-31-15, SA, Berchtold Archive, 464/9; Jagow to Tschirschky, 10-31-15, SG, I, 199.

82. Tschirschky to AA, 1-21-16, AA, Wk. 20e Geh., Bd. 1.

83. Conrad to Burián, 12-21-15, KA, Militärkanzlei Seiner Majestät, 25-1/5, 1915. On Balkan war aims at this time, see the article by Helmut Rumpler cited in the bibliography.

84. Tisza to Franz Joseph, 12-4-15, István Tisza, *Összes Munkái,* IV, 296-301; Tisza to Burián, 12-30-15, PA I, 499, xlvii/2b.

85. Hohenlohe to Berchtold, 10-18-15, SA, Berchtold Archive, 464/16; Hohenlohe to Berchtold, 1-4-16, *Ibid.* The second letter is dated 1-4-15, which would seem incorrect from its context. Hohenlohe probably dated it 1915 by accident — a not uncommon mistake at the beginning of a new year.

86. Hohenlohe to Burián, 6-4-16, PA I, 838, Krieg 4a.

87. Stone, *Eastern Front,* 266.

88. Conrad to Burián, 6-16-16, PA I, 499, xlvii/2b; Berchtold diary, 7-12-16, Hantsch, II, 774; Musulin to Wiesner, 8-8-16, PA I, 499.

89. Hohenlohe to Berchtold, 6-27-16, SA, Berchtold Archive, 464/16.

90. Hohenlohe to Burián, 9-13-16, PA III, 172.

91. Bethmann to Wilhelm, 8-16-16, AA, Wk. 2 Geh., Bd. 20.

92. Conrad to Bolfras, 10-14-16, KA, Conrad-Archiv, B8.

93. Baernreither, *Der Verfall des Habsburgerreiches und die Deutschen,* 11-8-16, 271.

94. Jagow to Tshirschky, 7-17-16, SG, I, 400.

95. Tisza memo, 7-25-16, PA I, 501, xlvii/3; Stürgkh memo, 7-25-16, *Ibid.*

96. Burián memo, 7-27-16 (given to Jagow 7-28-16), PA I, 501, xlvii/3; Memo (without either date or signature), SG, I, 427-428; Hindenburg to Conrad, 9-7-16, PA I, 502, xlvii/3; Burián to Thurn for Conrad, 9-13-16, *Ibid.;* Note for the Germans, 9-29-16, *Ibid.;* Burián Tagesbericht, 10-8-16, *Ibid.*

97. Burián memo, 10-18-16, PA I, 501, xlvii/3.

98. Andrian to Burián, 10-25-16, 10-27-16, *Ibid.*

99. Forgách to Berchtold, 9-26-16, SA, Berchtold Archive, 464/9; Bethmann to Jagow, 7-31-16, SG, I, 422; Berchtold diary, 9-13-16, Hantsch, II, 786.

100. Tschirschky to Bethmann, 9-28-16, SG, I, 478-481; Bethmann to Wilhelm, 9-30-16, SG, I, 486; Berchtold memo, 10-9-16, SA, Berchtold Archive, 476; Burián to Hohenlohe, 9-10-16, PA III, 172.

101. Hoyos to Berchtold, 8-23-16, SA, Berchtold Archive, 464/17.

102. Burián memo, 11-15/16-16, PA I, 503, xlvii/3.

103. Burián to Conrad, 11-5-16, PA I, 524, xlvii/12.

104. Burián memo, 7-27-16 (given to Jagow 7-28-16), PA I, 501, xlvii/3.

105. Burián to Hohenlohe, 11-28-16, PA I, 503, xlvii/3.

106. German note, 12-21-16, SG, I, 623. The background and practical difficulties of the drafting of the Central Powers' peace proposal are analyzed in great detail in Wolfgang Steglich's monograph, *Bündnissicherung oder Verständigungsfrieden.*

107. Naumann to Hertling, 11-2-16, Naumann, *Dokumente,* 146.

108. Bethmann to Grünau, 11-10-16, AA, Öst. 95 Geh., Bd. 4.

Chapter 5: The New Men

1. Tschirschky to Bethmann, 9-28-16, SG, I, 478-481; Bethmann to Wilhelm, 9-30-16, SG, I, 486.

2. Deak, 16; Gratz-Schüller, *Zusammenbruch,* 118-204, 96.

3. *Ibid.,* 46.

4. Komjáthy, 7-8-15, 267.

5. *Ibid.,* 9-9-16, 392-409.

6. Joannovics memo for Burián, 10-4-16, AR, F36, 198.

7. Komjáthy, 10-16-16, 410-428.

8. *Ibid.,* 1-10-17, 428-440.

9. Hohenlohe to Czernin, 1-12-17, AR, F36, 198.

10. Tisza to Czernin, 3-14-17, Tisza, *Összes Munkái,* VI, 187.

11. Ottokar Landwehr, *Hunger: Die Erschöpfungsjahre der Mittelmächte,* 36.

12. Memo "Aufzeichnung über die in Berlin stattgefundenen Besprechungen in der Ernährungsfrage," 3-28-17, PA I, 504, xlvii/3.

13. Victor S. Mamatey, *The United States and East Central Europe,* 47.

14. Landwehr, 306.

15. Gordon Brook-Shepherd, *The Last Habsburg,* 63.

16. Wedel to AA, 1-6-17, AA, Wk. 2 Geh., Bd. 28.

17. Cramon, *Bundesgenosse,* 86.

18. Karl to Burián, 12-5-16, PA I, 955, Krieg 25p.

19. Karl draft letter to Czernin, 5-14-17, Karl Freiherr von Werkmann, *Deutschland als Verbündeter,* 170-172.

20. Conrad to Burián, 12-13-16, PA I, 524, xlvii/12.

21. Glaise, *Zwielicht,* 399; Gunther Rothenberg, *The Army of Francis Joseph,* 203.

22. Arthur Arz von Straussenburg, *Zur Geschichte des Großen Krieges,* 137.

23. Ottokar Czernin, *Politische Betrachtungen,* 18, 85-86.

24. Czernin to Hoyos, 11-20-13, Redlich, I, 215, note 1.

25. Czernin to Franz Ferdinand, 8-31-13, HHSA, Nachlaß Franz Ferdinand, 13.

26. Ottokar Czernin, *Mein Afrikanisches Tagebuch,* 177.

27. Redlich, II, 6-28-17, 212.

28. Glaise, *Zwielicht,* 447, 449, 451.

29. Czernin to Berchtold, 12-30-13, ÖUA, VII, 694.

30. Czernin to Franz Ferdinand, 2-4-14, HHSA, Nachlaß Franz Ferdinand, 13.

31. Czernin to Burián, 9-4-15, PA I, 519, xlvii/7d.

32. Czernin memo, "Gedankan über die Beendigung des Krieges," 7-6-16, PA I, 497, xlvii/1c.

33. Forgách to Mérey, 7-16-14, Hantsch, II, 594; Cf. Berchtold diary, 12-22-16, Hantsch, II, 794.

34. Tagesbericht, 12-23-16, PA XL, 57; Arthur Polzer-Hoditz, *The Emperor Karl,* 140.

35. Redlich, II, 1-24-17, 186.

36. Joseph Baernreither, 10-1916, *Verfall,* 262-269.

37. Schoen to Hertling, 12-27-16, Ernst Deuerlein, ed., *Briefwechsel Hertling-Lerchenfeld,* II, 785.

38. Report of Otto Helmut-Hopfen, 10-8-17, DZA, Alldeutscher Verband, 705; Zeynek, *Leben,* 193, KA, Nachlaß Zeynek, B151. Erich Feigl, *Kaiserin Zita, Legende und Wahrheit,* prints information from interviews with Zita but uncritically nurtures as much legend as it lays to rest. A revised version has just been published, but I have not been able to read it.

39. Komjáthy, 1-12-17, 440-452.

40. Talk with Czernin, 4-27-17, Kanner Papers, Ib, 229-230.

41. Hohenlohe to Macchio, 1-10-17, HHSA, Nachlaß Macchio, 1.

42. Czernin to Hohenlohe, 1-1-17, PA I, 954, Krieg 25p.

43. Burián to Hohenlohe, 5-17-15, PA I, 843, Krieg 4c; Hohenlohe to Burián, 2-27-16, PA I, 844, Krieg 4c.

44. Hohenlohe to Burián, 10-6-15, PA I, 842, Krieg 4a.

45. Burián to Bethmann, 10-9-16, PA I, 503, xlvii/3.

46. Czernin to Hohenlohe, 1-2-17, *Ibid.*

47. Memo of the meeting, 1-20-17, Czernin, *In the World War,* 137-140.

48. Naumann, *Dokumente,* 244-245.

49. Komjáthy, 1-22-17, 452-458.

50. Zimmermann to Wedel, 2-6-17, AA, Wk. 23 Geh., Bd. 12.

51. Czernin to Berlin, Constantinople, Sofia, the Hague, Copenhagen, Stockholm, Madrid, 12-24-16, PA I, 954, Krieg 25p.

52. Czernin to Fürstenberg, 2-7-17, PA I, 952, Krieg 25e.

53. Ingeborg Meckling, *Die Aussenpolitik des Grafen Czernin,* 32-51.

54. Czernin to Hohenlohe, 3-5-17, PA III, 173.

55. Hohenlohe to Berchtold, 3-11-17, SA, Berchtold Archive, 464/16.

56. Czernin Tagesbericht, 1-1-17, PA I, 503, xlvii/3.

57. Memo of meeting, 1-6-17, SG, II, 663-667.

58. Memo "Ergebnisse der Besprechung seiner Excellenz des Herrn Ministers mit dem Referenten III/P und den Vertretern in Warschau und Lublin," 1-29-17, PA I, 1017, Krieg 56b/3; Komjáthy, 1-12-17, 443-444; Hohenlohe to Czernin, 1-26-17, PA I, 1012, Krieg 56a/2; Czernin to Ugron, 2-25-17, PA I, 1017, Krieg 56b/3; Tisza to Czernin, 1-3-17, Tisza, *Összes Munkái,* VI, 117.

Chapter 6: Peace at Hand?

1. Wedel to Bethmann, 7-9-17, AA, Öst. 95, Bd. 22.

2. Wedel to Bethmann, 4-15-17, AA, Wk. 2 Geh., Bd. 33.

3. Baernreither, 6-24-17, *Verfall,* 229.

4. Alexander Freiherr von Musulin, *Das Haus am Ballplatz,* 291.

5. Baernreither, 5-24-17, *Verfall,* 215; Cf. Redlich, II, 6-3-17, 208.

6. Musulin to Vienna, 5-4-17, PA I, 524, xlvii/13; Czernin to Musulin, 5-5-17, *Ibid.* Nor was Czernin alone in this idea; Pallavicini was thinking along the same lines. Baernreither, 4-24-17, *Verfall,* 220.

7. Talk with Kanner, 4-27-17, Kanner Papers, Ib, 231-233.

8. Czernin, *In the World War,* 173-174; Cf. Werkmann, *Deutschland,* 179. Erzberger, however, denied Czernin's contention. Matthias Erzberger, *Erlebnisse im Weltkrieg,* 115-116.

9. Mihály Károlyi, *Fighting the World,* 160-165; Tivadar Batthyány, *Für Ungarn Gegen Hohenzollern,* 111; Cf. Berchtold diary, 1-16-17, Hantsch, II, 796.

10. Czernin to Musulin, 5-28-17, PA I, 1013, Krieg 56a/3.

11. Tucher to Ludwig, 3-31-17, MA III, 2481/5.

12. Baernreither, 4-16-17, *Verfall,* 196.

13. Czernin to Tisza, n.d., Czernin, *In the World War,* 187-188.

14. Czernin to Pallavicini, 5-10-17, PA I, 958, Krieg 25z.

15. Czernin to Hadik for Fürstenberg, 5-13-17, PA I, 959, Krieg 25z.

16. Czernin to Otto Czernin, 5-12-17, PA I, 957, Krieg 25x; Cf. Czernin to Pallavicini, 7-6-17, PA I, 524, xlvii/13.

17. Czernin memo, "Kriegsziele und die Polnische Frage," n.d., Werkmann, *Deutschland,* 152-158. Fischer erroneously credits Czernin's sentiments for peace and Rumania to Burián in 1916 (*Germany's Aims in the First World War,* 311, 323), confusing Czernin's memorandum with a letter Burián wrote to Conrad on November 5, 1916. Z. A. B. Zeman, *Diplomatic History of the First World War,* 123, repeats the error.

18. Komjáthy, 3-22-17, 482-491.

19. Czernin's note with Karl's gloss, 2-20-17, G. de Manteyer, *Austria's Peace Offer,* 51-54.

20. Otto of Habsburg, "Danubian Reconstruction," *Foreign Affairs,* XX, 1942, 246.

21. Karl to Sixtus, 3-24-17, Brook-Shepherd, 72-73.

22. Meckling, 346-347; Berta Szeps-Zuckerkandl, *My Life and History,* 238-239. On Czernin's knowledge of the Sixtus letter, Brook-Shepherd, 72-73.

23. Brook-Shepherd, 148.

24. Czernin note, 5-9-17, Manteyer, 146-147.

25. Wedel to AA, 5-30-17, AA, Wk. 2 Geh., Bd. 38; Wedel to AA, 6-6-17, AA, Wk. 2 Geh., Bd. 39.

26. Memo of meeting, 3-16-17, SG, II, 32-39.

27. Memo of meeting, 3-26-17, SG, II, 50-60; Agreement, 3-27-17, PA I, 524, xlvii/13. On these exchanges, see Rudolf Neck, "Das 'Wiener Dokument' vom 27. März 1917," *Mitteilungen des Österreichischen Staatsarchivs,* VII, 294-309.

28. Stumm to Grünau, 4-2-17, AA, Wk. Nr. 15 Geh., Bd. 2.

29. Memo of meeting, 3-26-17, SG, II, 56.

30. Czernin to Hohenlohe, 3-31-17, PA I, 511, xlvii/5g; Wedel to AA, 4-2-17, SG, II, 75-76; Czernin to Storck, 4-2-17, PA I, 511, xlvii/5g.

31. Bethmann to Wilhelm, 5-14-17, SG, II, 199-200.

32. Zimmermann to Grünau, 5-10-17, SG, II, 188.

33. Müller diary, 4-3-17, Georg Alexander von Müller, *The Kaiser and His Court,* 252.

34. Czernin memo of meeting, 4-3-17, PA I, 504, xlvii/3; Theobald von Bethmann Hollweg, *Betrachtungen zum Weltkriege,* II, 202; Erich von Ludendorff, *Ludendorff's Own Story,* II, 46.

35. Cramon, *Bundesgenosse,* 112.

36. *Ibid.,* 111; Arthur Arz, *Zur Geschichte des Großen Krieges,* 281.

37. Czernin to Hohenlohe, 4-10-17, PA I, 956, Krieg 25t; Hohenlohe to Czernin, 4-11-17, *Ibid.*

38. Czernin memo, 4-12-17, Czernin, *In the World War,* 164-168; Karl to Wilhelm, n.d., AA, Wk. 2 Geh., Bd. 32. The memo has aroused considerable controversy. The German politician Erzberger obtained a copy of it, which he used in his efforts to counter the war aims of the German conservatives. How he got it was a source of considerable dispute at the time; it seems that Karl personally gave him a copy. See Klaus Epstein, *Matthias Erzberger and the Dilemma of German Democracy,* 172-174, 206-208. More recently, the Empress Zita asserted that the memorandum was not written by Czernin at all but by Karl, and simply put under his Foreign Minister's name to make it more convincing to the Germans (Brook-Shepherd, 78). Czernin, however, claimed its authorship both at the time and later in his memoirs, and so it has been accepted by all the principals involved (except Zita).

39. Zimmermann to Wedel, 4-17-17, AA, Wk. 2 Geh., Bd. 33.

40. Czernin to Hohenlohe, 4-23-17, PA I, 956, Krieg 25t.

41. Hertling to Dandl, 4-30-17, MA, Gesandtschaft Wien, 1759; Czernin to Hohenlohe, 4-30-17, PA I, 957, Krieg 25x.

42. Hohenlohe to Czernin, 5-4-17, PA I, 536. These actions are discussed more fully in Robert Hopwood, *Interalliance Diplomacy,* 139-153.

43. Tisza to Czernin, n.d., Czernin, *In the World War,* 172.

44. Hohenlohe to Berchtold, 4-12-17, SA, Berchtold Archive, 464/16.

45. Arz to Czernin, 5-16-17, PA I, 956, Krieg 25t; Wedel to Bethmann, 4-18-17, SG, II, 127.

46. Zimmermann to Wedel, 5-3-17, AA, Wk. 2 Geh., Bd. 35.

47. Grünau to AA, 4-19-17, AA, Wk. 2 Geh., Bd. 33; Lersner to AA, 4-29-17, SG, II, 164.

48. Memo of meeting, 4-23-17, AA, Wk. 15 Geh., Bd. 3.

49. Note by Wilhelm, n.d., SG, II, 202.

50. Memo of meeting, 5-18-17, SG, II, 204-206.

51. Czernin to Karl, 5-18-17, PA I, 504, xlvii/3; Wedel to Bethmann, 5-23-17, SG, II, 212-213.

52. Czernin to Bethmann, 6-18-17, AA, Wk. 15 Geh., Bd. 3.

53. Wedel to Bethmann, 5-15-17, SG, II, 203.

54. Wedel to Bethmann, 4-25-17, AA, Öst. 86 Nr. 1, Bd. 21.

55. Wedel to Bethmann, 6-12-17, AA, Öst. 70 Geh., Bd. 51.

56. Lajos Windischgraetz, *My Memoirs*, 135; Cf. Czernin to Demblin, 12-20-17, Pa I, 1078.

57. The reports are printed in Rudolf Neck, *Arbeiterschaft und Staat im Ersten Weltkrieg*, I/2, 27-46.

58. Arz memo, "Darstellung der Materiellen Lage der Armee im Felde," 7-18-17, PA I, 500, xlvii/2b.

59. Landwehr, 37-45, 105; "Aufzeichnung über die am 3. August 1917 im k.u.k. Ministerium des Äußern in Wien abgehaltene interministerielle Besprechung betr. die Verhandlungen mit Deutschland über die Ausfuhr von Nährungs- und Futtermitteln aus Rumänien," AR, F36, 198.

60. Redlich, II, 8-20-17, 226.

61. Czernin to Hohenlohe, 4-23-17, PA I, 956, Krieg 25t.

62. Czernin memo for Karl, 7-13-17, Werkmann, *Deutschland*, 107-108.

63. Erzberger, "Bericht über meine Reise nach Wien am Sonntag 22. und Montag 23. April," AA, Wk. 2 Geh., Bd. 34.

64. Berchtold diary, 7-10-17, Hantsch, II, 799-800.

65. Czernin to Larisch, 7-6-17, PA III, 175; Redlich, II, 6-28-17, 212.

66. Wedel to Bethmann, 7-1-17, AA, Öst. 70 Geh., Bd. 51.

67. Redlich, II, 7-5-17, 214.

68. William de Hevesy, "Postscript to the Sixtus Affair," *Foreign Affairs*, XXI, 1943, 568.

69. Wedel to Michaelis, 7-22-17, SG, II, 276-283.

70. Tucher to Hertling, 8-4-17, MA III, 2481/5.

71. Seeckt to Hindenburg, 7-22-17, Hans Meier-Welcker, "Die Beurteilung der Politischen Lage in Österreich-Ungarn durch Generalmajor von Seeckt im Sommer 1917," *Militärgeschichtliche Mitteilungen*, X, 99.

72. Meinl to de Jong van Beek en Donk, 1-10-18, Benedikt, 228-229; Meinl memo for Polzer, 6-19-17, *Ibid.*, 101-110.

73. Redlich, II, 8-20-17, 228.

74. Wedel to Michaelis, 7-20-17, SG, II, 272-274.

75. Wedel to Michaelis, 7-18-17, MA I, 952.

76. Redlich, II, 8-20-17, 228; Cf. Robert A. Kann, *Die Sixtusaffäre*, 38.

77. Wedel to AA, 7-24-17, AA, Öst. 91, Bd. 17; Wedel to Zimmermann, 6-25-17, Meckling, 95.

78. Wedel to AA, 7-24-17, AA, Öst. 91, Bd. 17; Wedel to AA, 7-26-17, *Ibid.*; Redlich, II, 8-1-17, 225; Polzer, 345.

79. Hohenlohe to Berchtold, 7-26-17, SA, Berchtold Archive, 464/16.

80. Wedel to AA, 7-16-17, SG, II, 268.

81. Grünau to AA, 7-25-17, AA, Öst. 95 Geh., Bd. 4.

82. Revertera to Berchtold, 7-24-17, SA, Berchtold Archive, 464/30.

83. Revertera memo, 8-27-17, Friedrich Engel-Janosi, "Die Friedensgespräche Graf Nikolaus Reverteras," *Anzeiger der Österreichischen Akademie der Wissen-*

schaften, vol. CII, Nr. 1-25, 377; Gerhard Ritter, *The Sword and the Scepter,* IV, 37-38; Wolfgang Steglich, *Die Friedenspolitik der Mittelmächte,* 148-149.

84. Memo of meeting, 8-1-17, PA I, 504, xlvii/3.

85. Krafft to Lößl, 8-14-17, Deuerlein, II, 901-906.

86. Memo of meeting, 8-14-17, DZA, Reichskanzlei, Großes Hauptquartier, 2477, Beiheft 21.

87. Kühlmann to Wedel, 8-27-17, SG, II, 371.

88. Musulin to Flotow, 6-12-17, HHSA, Nachlaß Flotow, 1; Musulin to Czernin, 10-11-17, PA I, 841, Krieg 4i.

89. Kühlmann to Michaelis, 8-30-17, SG, II, 378-380; Kühlmann notes, 9-2-17, SG, II, 381-385; and 9-3-17, SG, II, 388.

90. Kühlmann note, 9-2-17, SG, II, 381-385.

91. Revertera memo, 10-6-17, Engel-Janosi, "Revertera," 377-378.

92. Czernin to a friend, 11-17-17, Czernin, *In the World War,* 241-242.

Chapter 7: The German Course

1. Czernin to neutral missions, 9-9-17, Meckling, 139.

2. Wedel to AA, 12-6-17, AA, Öst. 86 Nr. 2, Bd. 23.

3. Czernin, *In the World War,* 206.

4. *Ibid.,* 361.

5. Hardinge minute, 4-18-18, V. H. Rothwell, *British War Aims and Peace Diplomacy,* 221.

6. Otto von Bismarck, *Bismarck, The Man and the Statesman,* II, 273-274; Cf. Fred Iklé, *All Wars Must End,* 62-64.

7. Windischgraetz, *My Memoirs,* 140-141; Felix Höglinger, *Ministerpräsident Heinrich Clam-Martinic,* 213; Czernin to a friend, 11-17-17, Czernin, *In the World War,* 242.

8. Cramon draft report, 7-31-17, Freiburg: Bundesarchiv-Militärarchiv, Nachlaß Cramon, N266/55. Only month and day are given on the draft, but its context dates it from 1917.

9. Talk with Conrad, summer 1917, *Ibid.,* N266/63.

10. Conrad, *Private Aufzeichnungen,* 101-102, 181, 198-199.

11. Revertera to Berchtold, 10-17-17, SA, Berchtold Archive, 464/30.

12. Komjáthy, 5-6-17, 499-510.

13. Redlich, II, 6-3-17, 208.

14. Komjáthy, 9-6-17, 558-585; 7-5-17, 524.

15. Karl draft letter to Czernin, 5-14-17, Werkmann, *Deutschland,* 170.

16. Memos of meetings between 7-23-17 and 8-14-17, AR, F37, 90; Gusztáv Gratz and Richard Schüller, *The Economic Policy of Austria-Hungary during the War,* 45-46.

17. Naumann to Reichskanzlei, 9-22-17, Naumann, *Dokumente,* 278-279; Wedel to Kühlmann, 9-29-17, SG, II, 461-464.

18. Cramon, *Bundesgenosse,* 124-125.

19. Memo of meeting, 10-7-17, SG, II, 488.

20. Unsigned agreement, 10-22-17, SG, II, 521-522.

21. Memo of meeting, 10-7-17, SG, II, 488-489; Lersner to AA, 10-9-17, SG, II, 495.

22. Memo of meeting, 11-6-17, SG, II, 533-537; Austrian resumé, 11-5/6-17, PA I, 504, xlvii/3.

23. Czernin to Demblin, 10-15-17, PA XL, 262.

24. Hohenlohe to Czernin, 11-23-17, AR, F37, 90; Demblin to Vienna, 12-9-17, PA I, 1052, Krieg 70/1.

25. Czernin to Hohenlohe, 11-11-17, PA I, 956, Krieg 25t; Notiz, 11-12-17, PA I, 536.

26. Kühlmann to Wedel, 11-17-17, SG, III, 17.

27. Memo, 12-7-17, PA I, 504, xlvii/3.

28. Demblin to Czernin, 12-9-17, PA I, 504, xlvii/3; Czernin to Demblin, 12-10-17, PA I, 1052, Krieg 70/1.

29. Czernin to Wekerle, 12-12-17, AR, F36, 199.

30. Max von Hoffmann, *War Diaries and Other Papers,* II, 198; Albrecht von Thaer, *Generalstabsdienst an der Front und in der O. H. L.,* 159.

31. Czernin to Mérey, 12-14-17, PA I, 1052, Krieg 70/1.

32. Czernin to a friend, 11-17-17, Czernin, *In the World War,* 239-242.

33. Bussche note, 12-30-17, SG, III, 184.

34. Demblin to Czernin, 12-21-17, PA I, 962, Krieg 25/26; Müller to Czernin, 12-20-17, PA I, 1078; Demblin to Czernin, 12-24-17, PA I, 1080; Mérey to Czernin, 12-27-17, *Ibid.*

35. Czernin to Demblin, 12-21-17, PA I, 1078.

36. Czernin to Müller, 12-24-17, *Ibid.*

37. Czernin to Flotow, 1-9-18, PA I, 1077.

38. Memo of discussion, 1-9-18, HHSA, Kabinettsarchiv: Geheimakten, 24 (alt 22).

39. Czernin to Flotow, 1-15-18, PA I, 1077.

40. Wedel to Hertling, 1-17-18, SG, III, 278-279.

41. Flotow, Müller to Czernin, 1-18-18, PA I, 818, Krieg 1/o.

42. Czernin to Hohenlohe, 1-16-18, PA I, 1079.

43. Landwehr, 152.

44. Lersner to AA, 1-23-18, AA, Öst. 95 Geh., Bd. 4.

45. Demblin to Czernin, 1-17-18, PA I, 1079.

46. Czernin to Vienna for Landwehr, 1-16-18, PA I, 818, Krieg 1/o.

47. Müller to Demblin, 1-18-18, PA XL, 262; Czernin to Müller, 1-20-18, PA I, 1077; Demblin to Czernin, 1-18-18, PA I, 1079.

48. Wedel to Hertling, 2-10-18, AA, Öst. 70, Bd. 53.

49. Müller to Demblin, 1-18-18, PA XL, 262.

50. Czernin speech, 1-24-18, Czernin, *In the World War,* 342.

51. Czernin to Demblin, 12-10-17, PA I, 504, xlvii/3; Kühlmann to Hertling, 1-17-18, SG, III, 275-276.

52. Komjáthy, 1-22-18, 627-633.

53. Hohenlohe to Czernin, 1-27-18, PA I, 1081.

54. Memo of committee meeting, 1-11-18, AR, F36, 198.

55. Czernin to Vienna for Karl, 2-8-18, PA I, 1077; Czernin to Vienna, 1-30-18, *Ibid.*

56. Hohenlohe to Czernin, 1-31-18, PA I, 1079.

57. Memo of meeting, 2-5-18, PA I, 504, xlvii/3; Czernin diary, 2-5-18, Czernin, *In the World War,* 275; Landwehr, 162-163.

58. Wedel to AA, 1-31-18, SG, III, 318-319.

59. Czernin to Hohenlohe, 2-19-18, PA I, 1053, Krieg 70/1.

60. Arz to Foreign Ministry, 2-20-18, PA I, 1053, Krieg 70/1.

61. Czernin to Demblin, 2-21-18, PA XL, 262.

62. Czernin to Vienna, 3-3-18, PA I, 1084.

63. Forgách to Berchtold, 3-29-18, SA, Berchtold Archive, 464/9; Cf. Forgách to Czernin, 3-23-18, 3-24-18, Gratz-Schüller, *Economic Policy,* 132-134.

64. Hoffmann diary, 3-13-18, Hoffmann, I, 210.

65. Wedel to Hertling, 1-28-18, AA, Öst. 86 Nr. 2, Bd. 23.

66. Musulin to Czernin, 3-9-18, PA I, 1052, Krieg 70/1.

67. Czernin to Berchtold, 11-22-14, SA, Berchtold Archive, 464/6.

68. Tisza to Czernin, 2-27-18, Czernin, *In the World War,* 288.

69. Marsovszky to Czernin, 2-7-18, PA I, 1079; Müller to Czernin, 2-23-18, PA I, 1085.

70. Wedel to AA, 2-17-18, SG, III, 386-387.

71. Müller diary, 2-17-18, Müller, 335.

72. Kühlmann to Hertling, 2-27-18, AA, Öst. 95 Geh., Bd. 4.

73. Czernin to Demblin, 3-25-18, PA I, 1090.

74. Kühlmann to Hertling, 3-16-18, SG, IV, 36-37.

75. Wedel to Bussche, 3-11-18, AA, Wk. Nr. 2 Geh., Bd. 57; Tucher to Ludwig, 3-1-18, MA III, 2481/6.

76. Statthalter in Vienna to Minister of the Interior, 3-11-18, Neck, I/2, 404-406.

77. Wedel to Hertling, 3-2-18, AA, Öst. 70, Bd. 53.

78. Naumann to Hertling, 2-22-18, Naumann, *Dokumente,* 332-334.

79. Report from Vienna Polizeidirektion to Minister of the Interior, 3-16-18, PA I, 818, Krieg 1/o.

80. Landwehr, 178, 183; Czernin to Vienna for Arz, 3-22-18, PA I, 1084.

81. Redlich, II, 3-27-18, 262.

82. Max Schwarte, ed., *Der Große Krieg,* V, 338-339; Szilássy memo for Karl, 11-9-17, Szilássy, 379-399; Schönburg to Czernin, 1-3-18, PA I, 951, Krieg 25a; Schönburg to Czernin, 2-17-18, 2-24-18, PA I, 1084.

83. Müller to Czernin, 3-8-18, PA I, 1085. A good analysis of the widening gap between Czernin and Karl can be found in the article by Robert Hopwood, "The Conflict Between Count Czernin and the Emperor Charles in 1918," cited in full in the bibliography.

84. Glaise, *Zwielicht,* 452-453; Cf. Lützow, 254.

85. Müller to Czernin, 12-20-17 (inclosing Musulin to Vienna, 12-19-17), PA I, 1080; Smuts report, 12-18/19-17, David Lloyd George, *War Memoirs,* V, 21-35.

86. Revertera to Berchtold, 3-3-18, SA, Berchtold Archive, 464/30.

87. Musulin to Czernin, 3-15-18, PA I, 1087.

88. Czernin to Musulin for Skrzyński, 3-10-18, PA I, 1088; Czernin to Vienna, 3-19-18, HHSA, Nachlaß Mensdorff, 2.

89. Czernin to Fürstenberg, 2-17-18, PA I, 964, Krieg 25/29.

90. Czernin to Meinl, 1-2-18, Benedikt, 202-203.

91. Herron memo, 2-3-18, Benedikt, 232-238; Heinrich Lammasch, "Aus Meinem Leben: Friedensversuche mit Präsident Wilson," in Marga Lammasch, ed., *Heinrich Lammasch,* 96-102.

92. Wedel to Hertling, 2-18-18, SG, III, 288-289.

93. Kühlmann to AA, 3-4-18, SG, IV, 1-2.

94. Demblin to Czernin, 3-11-18, PA I, 1087.

95. Czernin to Demblin, 3-10-18, PA I, 1089; Demblin to Czernin, 3-9-18, PA I, 1087.

96. Czernin to Musulin (inclosing Czernin to Demblin), 3-10-18, PA I, 1088.

97. Demblin to Czernin, 3-19-18, PA I, 1087.

98. Lloyd George to Mensdorff, 6-30-23, HHSA, Nachlaß Mensdorff, 3.

99. Hohenlohe to Czernin, 3-20-18, PA I, 841, Krieg 4a; Hohenlohe to Czernin, 3-25-18, PA I, 1087.

100. Czernin to Demblin, 3-10-18, PA I, 1089.

101. Czernin to Demblin, 3-29-18, PA XL, 262.

102. Burián diary, 3-19-18, Valiani, 416-417, note 91.

103. Czernin diary, 12-24-17, Czernin, *In the World War,* 249.

104. Czernin to Demblin, 2-6-18, PA XL, 262; Czernin to Demblin, 3-8-18, PA I, 1089.

105. Czernin to Demblin, 3-28-18, PA I, 1090.

106. Czernin to Demblin, 3-18-18, PA XL, 262.

107. Czernin to Vienna for Wiesner, 3-18-18, PA I, 1084.

108. Kühlmann to AA, 3-18-18, AA, Kommissionsakten: Bukarester Akten 6, Öst. Politik.

109. Czernin to Bernsdorff, 6-1-20, Johann von Bernsdorff, *Memoirs of Count Bernsdorff,* 172.

110. Copy of speech, 4-2-18, HHSA, Nachlaß Flotow, 2.

111. Cf. Edmund Glaise von Horstenau, *The Collapse of the Austro-Hungarian Empire,* 126.

112. Baernreither diary, 4-12-18, Kann, *Sixtusaffäre,* 22.

113. Both Tamás von Erdödy, who figured as an intermediary in the original Sixtus talks, and Friedrich Funder, editor of the Christian Social newspaper the *Reichspost,* claim that Czernin told him of his suicide threat. Tamás von Erdödy, *Habsburgs Weg von Wilhelm zu Briand,* 116; Friedrich Funder, *Vom Gestern ins Heute,* 563; Cf. Brook-Shepherd, 150.

114. Peter Feldl, *Das Verspielte Reich,* 160-184.

115. August Demblin, *Czernin und die Sixtus-Affaire,* 27; Meckling, 347, note 19.

116. Revertera to Berchtold, 6-13-18, SA, Berchtold Archive, 464/30.

Chapter 8: The Most Terrible Death

1. Wedel to AA, 4-11-18, AA, Wk. 2 Geh., Bd. 59.

2. Wedel to Hertling, 4-22-18, SG, IV, 120.

3. Grünau to AA, 4-14-18, AA, Wk. 2 Geh., Bd. 59.

4. Talk with Conrad, 4-13-18, Freiburg: Bundesarchiv-Militararchiv, Nachlaß Cramon, N266/3.

5. Bussche note, 4-22-18, SG, IV, 118-119; Berchtold diary, 4-20-18, Hantsch, II, 821.

6. Burián diary, 4-8-18, Valiani, 417, note 91.

7. Wedel to AA, 4-18-18, AA, Öst. 95 Geh., Bd. 5.

8. Grünau to AA, 4-14-18, AA, Wk. 2 Geh., Bd. 59.

9. Wedel to Hertling, 4-24-18, SG, IV, 122-124.

10. Cramon to Wilhelm, 4-24-18, SG, IV, 124-126.

11. Hertling to Wedel, 4-30-18, AA, Öst. 95 Geh., Bd. 5.

12. Kühlmann to AA, 5-3-18, SG, IV, 136-138.

13. Kühlmann to Hertling, 5-4-18, AA, Kommissionsakten: Bukarester Akten 6, Öst. Politik; Bussche to Kühlmann, 5-3-18, *Ibid.*

14. Trauttmansdorff to Flotow, 6-25-18, HHSA, Nachlaß Flotow, 1.

15. Wedel to Hertling, 7-11-18, AA, Öst. 70, Bd. 53.

16. Wedel to Hertling, 5-22-18, AA, Öst. 101, Bd. 41.

17. Wedel to Bergen, 6-29-18, SG, IV, 225-228.

18. Hohenlohe to Burián, 5-16-18, PA X, 152, xi/d-1.

19. Arz, *Geschichte des Großen Krieges,* 252-253; Krauß, 257-259; Zeynek, *Leben,* 202-203, KA, Nachlaß Zeynek, B151.

20. Forgách to Flotow, 5-26-18, HHSA, Nachlaß Flotow, 1.

21. Windischgraetz, *My Memoirs,* 191; Landwehr, 237.

22. Burián to Karl, 6-13-18, PA I, 505, xlvii/3.

23. Arz to Burián, 7-21-18, PA I, 500, xlvii/2b.

24. Wieser diary, 5-11-18, HHSA, Nachlaß Wieser.

25. Marsovszky to Vienna, 6-18-18, PA I, 841, Krieg 4a.

26. Berchtold diary, 6-17-18, Hantsch, II, 824.

27. Wedel to Hertling, 6-19-18, AA, Öst. 70, Bd. 53.

28. Wieser diary, 7-29-18, HHSA, Nachlaß Wieser.
29. Wedel to Hertling, 4-22-18, SG, IV, 121-122.
30. Landwehr, 248.
31. Trauttmansdorff to Flotow, 8-10-18, HHSA, Nachlaß Flotow, 1.
32. Memos of meeting, 9-5-18, PA I, 505, xlvii/3; 9-6-18, PA I, 524, xlvii/13.
33. Komjáthy, 9-27-18, 680-687; 10-2-18, 687-695.
34. Burián to Trauttmansdorff, 10-10-18, PA I, 966, Krieg 25/31.
35. Burián to Hohenlohe, 10-11-18, PA I, 966, Krieg 25/33.
36. Wedel to Stumm, 9-21-18, SG, IV, 353-355; Wedel to AA, 10-7-18, AA, Wk. 23 Geh., Bd. 20.
37. Szilássy memo, 8-13-18, Szilássy, 400-408; Szilássy, 304-306; Windisch-graetz, *My Memoirs,* 207-209.
38. Pallavicini to Burián, 10-21-18, HHSA, Nachlaß Flotow, 3.
39. De Vaux to Vienna, 10-24-18, PA I, 966, Krieg 25/33.
40. Andrássy to Hohenlohe, 10-26-18, PA I, 966, Krieg 25/33.
41. Andrássy to de Vaux, 10-27-18, *Ibid.*
42. Czernin, *In the World War,* 38.
43. Meckling, 358.
44. Wedel to Max von Baden, 10-23-18, AA, Öst. 103, Bd. 9.
45. Wedel to Max von Baden, 10-30-18, Wk. 23 Geh., Bd. 28.
46. *Ibid.*

SOURCES

The last years of the Austro-Hungarian Monarchy have been amply documented, even if one counts only material in the major Western European languages. I would like to briefly indicate which sources I found most useful for the major sections of the text. Again, complete citations will be found in the bibliography.

The Monarchy's condition as a whole is dealt with in English in the standard studies by C. A. Macartney, A. J. P. Taylor, Robert A. Kann, Arthur J. May, and Oscar Jászi. For an excellent brief analysis of the role of the alliance in Austrian and German policy, see the article by Lothar Höbelt. The alliance's impact on the various nationalities is briefly surveyed in three articles which appeared recently in *East Central Europe:* Solomon Wank on the Austrian Germans, Gabor Vermes on the Hungarians, and Stanley Winters on the Slavs. Stephan Verosta, *Theorie und Realität von Bündnissen,* is a more theoretical study. Verosta argues that Austria-Hungary had the option of quitting the Great Power game and becoming neutral in the conflicts of the time. I must agree with Höbelt that such a notion can hardly be taken seriously in light of the Monarchy's geographic position in the heart of Europe and the appetites of its neighbors. Two different approaches to understanding the historical interactions of Germans and Austrians in various walks of life are found respectively in Peter Katzenstein, *Disjointed Partners,* and Robert A. Kann and Friedrich Prinz, eds., *Deutschland und Österreich.*

Prewar diplomacy is covered in the famous multi-volume document collections, *Österreich-Ungarns Aussenpolitik, 1908-1914,* from the Austrian side; and *Die Große Politik der Europäischen Kabinette, 1871-1914,* from the German. Luigi Albertini, *The Origins of the War of 1914,* 3 vols., remains basic. See also Hans Uebersberger, *Österreich Zwischen Rußland und Serbien.* For recent interpretations of Austrian policy, Fritz Fellner, *Der Dreibund,* and F. R. Bridge, *From Sadowa to Sarajevo, The Foreign Policy of Austria-Hungary, 1866-1914,* are essential. No less so are the articles by Fritz Klein on Austro-German alliance relations. The series of essays published by the Institut für Österreichkunde, *Österreich am Vorabend des Ersten Weltkrieges,* is informative on the immediate prewar situation. Ernst Helmreich's *The Diplomacy of the Balkan Wars* remains the standard treatment of this subject.

Equally informative, and something of classics in the historiography of the period, are the respective diaries of Josef Redlich and Joseph Maria Baernreither. Both men enjoyed extensive contacts in official circles; their entries are often far more revealing of what people actually thought and said than more official accounts. Baernreither's prewar notes have been translated into English as *Fragments of a Political Diary.* Additional selections to 1917 are found in *Der Verfall des Habsburgerreiches.* His diaries and numerous other papers are preserved in his Nachlaß in the HHSA. On the memoir literature in general, G. P. Gooch, *Recent Revelations in European Diplomacy,* 4th ed., 1940, is still a useful evaluation and summary.

There are numerous biographies of Franz Joseph, the most extensive being the multi-volume work by Egon Caesar Conte Corti. In English, see Josef Redlich, *Emperor Francis Joseph of Austria.* On Berchtold, Hugo Hantsch, *Leopold Graf Berchtold, Grandseigneur und Staatsmann,* 2 vols., contains extensive quotations from Berchtold's unpublished diaries and is excellent. There is no really good biography of Tisza. His letters and speeches were assembled in the multi-volume *Összes Munkái;* many are in German, and German translations of others appeared in his *Briefe* (which was supposed to cover the whole war period but never got beyond 1915). Burián is the subject of the short sketch by István Diószegi cited in the bibliography; it includes a German translation of his diary for 1913-1914. Burián's memoirs read like one of his official dispatches: dry and not very revealing. Tisza's and Burián's papers can be found in the Archive of the Hungarian Reformed Church in Budapest.

The standard biography of the Archduke is Rudolf Kiszling, *Erzherzog Franz Ferdinand von Österreich-Este.* More recently: Robert A. Kann, *Erzherzog Franz Ferdinand, Studien,* which contains extensive quotations from his Nachlaß; and the article by Samuel Williamson (again, the complete citation is in the bibliography). The best source on Conrad is himself: his memoirs, *Aus Meiner Dienstzeit,* 5 vols. (which extend only to the end of 1914; he died before the remaining war years could be covered); and the *Private Aufzeichnungen,* a collection of notes and observations jotted down after the war. The standard biography is that of Oskar Regele. Conrad's papers are preserved in the Conrad-Archiv of the Kriegsarchiv in Vienna.

Especially rich are the private papers of Berchtold and Franz Ferdinand, not so much for what they say of their respective subjects as for the light they cast on the opinions of the other statesmen of the Monarchy. Berchtold, even after he left office, remained in contact with many of the chief figures of the realm, and their letters to him are often invaluable. Their great virtue (as with any private correspondence) is that their writers are generally much more open about their opinions than in their official writings. Berchtold apparently made no copies of his replies, but the other half of the correspondence can often be inferred from context. The Berchtold Family Archive is accessible through the Státní Archiv in Brno, Czechoslovakia. The same can be said about the Franz Ferdinand collection in the HHSA, except that it covers only the prewar period. Mention should also be made of the Macchio Nachlaß, likewise in the HHSA. Though small, it contains some interesting private letters from Forgách, Mérey, Berchtold, and Hohenlohe.

Such collections gain in importance from the fact that the Austrians generally did not record extensive minutes on foreign ministry memoranda or dispatches like their counterparts elsewhere. A student of British diplomacy of the period can find the notations of any number of secondary officials or of the foreign secretary himself penciled in at the end of a critical document; from them, he can get a pretty good idea of who influenced whom and with what arguments. Even German documents at least have the marginalia of the Kaiser to enliven them. The best one can expect from the Austrian side are a few words underlined in blue pencil or an exclamation mark or two in the margin—a lot less to go on.

Another nonofficial source of information is the work of the Austrian journalist Heinrich Kanner. Kanner interviewed various Austrian and German statesmen during the war, including Baernreither, Czernin, Biliński, and Zimmermann. His unpublished accounts of the interviews are preserved as the Kanner Papers in the Hoover Institution at Stanford University.

The July Crisis continues to attract interest. The most detailed treatment is still that of Albertini. The old (pre-World War II) revisionist account is Sidney B. Fay, *The Origins of the World War;* the new (post-World War II) revisionist version, which in many respects returns to the pre-Fay position, the two controversial books by Fritz Fischer, *Germany's Aims in the First World War,,* and *War of Illusions, German Policies From 1911 to 1914.* Imanuel Geiß supplements Fischer with his documents and commentary in *Julikrise und Kriegsausbruch,* 2 vols. (*July 1914* in its abbreviated English version). More recently, Fritz Fellner has published an account by Hoyos of his mission to Berlin; and the Hungarian historian József Galántai, in *Die Österreichisch-Ungarische Monarchie und der Weltkrieg,* has analyzed the course of the diplomatic events with the inclusion of material from the private papers of Tisza and Burián.

A brief general survey of wartime diplomacy among all the belligerents can be found in Z.A.B. Zeman, *A Diplomatic History of the First World War.* Politics in the war—both within the Monarchy and between it and Germany—are covered by a number of volumes. On the most general level: Z. A. B. Zeman, *The Break-Up of the Habsburg Empire;* Leo Valiani, *The End of Austria-Hungary;* and Arthur J. May, *The Passing of the Hapsburg Monarchy, 1914-1918.* The essays in Richard Plaschka and Karlheinz Mack, eds., *Die Auflösung des Habsburgerreiches,* cover a wide range of political, economic, and social topics. Fritz Fischer, *Germany's Aims in the First World War;* and vols. 3 and 4 of Gerhard Ritter, *The Sword and the Scepter,* are basic for Germany, though both have much to say about Austria-Hungary as well. The Redlich diaries are essential. Also useful are the memoirs of the German publicist Viktor Naumann, *Dokumente und Argumente;* Naumann had good connections in Vienna, and excerpts from many of his wartime reports are included here.

Domestic administration in Austria is discussed in Josef Redlich, *Austrian War Government.* More recently, the political activities of the military administration have been treated in Christoph Führ, *Das K. u. K. Armeeoberkommando und die Innenpolitik in Österreich.* The economy is the subject of Gusztáv Gratz and Richard Schüller, *Der Wirtschaftliche Zusammenbruch Österreich-Ungarns,* like the Redlich book on administration part of the Carnegie Foundation-sponsored series on the social history of the war.

There are no published document collections on the scale of the government publications for the prewar years, but two compilations fill some of the gap. André Scherer and Jacques Grunewald, *L'Allemagne et les Problèmes de la Paix Pendant la Première Guerre Mondiale* gathers German Foreign Ministry material relating to war aims and peace policy in four volumes from 1914 to October 1918. The documents appear in their original German and include many communications from the German embassy in Vienna. From the Austrian side, Miklós Komjáthy has edited the minutes of the wartime meetings of the Austro-Hungarian Common Ministers Council.

The basic documents themselves are stored in the political archives of the Haus-, Hof-, und Staatsarchiv in Vienna and of the Auswärtiges Amt in Bonn. The latter were captured and filmed after World War II, but in often haphazard fashion with unrelated files (and parts of files) being combined on the same reels of film. For reasons of organization alone, it is far easier to go to Bonn to study the original documents than to try to make sense out of the microfilms. The documents of the economic section of the Austrian

Foreign Ministry are in the Administrative Registratur of the HHSA. Those of the German Foreign Ministry's economic section ended up after World War II in the Deutsches Zentralarchiv in Potsdam, East Germany.

On military affairs there is an extensive literature. The official Austrian military history, published in the 1930's by the Bundesministerium für Landesverteidigung, is the multi-volume *Österreich-Ungarns Letzter Krieg.* More accessible is the slender summary by Rudolf Kiszling, *Österreich-Ungarns Anteil am Ersten Weltkrieg.* The Austrian military establishment is viewed in more critical light in Gunther Rothenberg's *The Army of Francis Joseph,* an excellent analysis which utilizes the files of the Austrian Kriegsarchiv. Prewar relations between Conrad and Moltke are covered by Conrad himself, Ritter, and the "Moltke-Conrad" article by Norman Stone. Conrad's relations with Falkenhayn are analyzed in detail in the second part of Gerard Silberstein's *The Troubled Alliance* and in a University of Vienna dissertation by Volker Höttl. They are also touched in the work of Ritter and in Karl Heinz Janßen, *Der Kanzler und der General,* which covers more than just Bethmann and Falkenhayn as its subtitle would seem to indicate. A brilliant analysis of the Russian theater of war in general is Norman Stone's recent *The Eastern Front.* Gordon Craig has written a brief essay on the military cohesion of the alliance which is an excellent overview of the problem.

Memoir literature: Conrad left his *Aus Meiner Dienstzeit,* which, as noted earlier, only extends to the end of 1914. Arthur Arz von Straussenburg, his successor, wrote *Zur Geschichte des Großen Krieges,* which is much more circumspect; a later volume of memoirs largely repeats what is said here. Arz's Nachlaß in the KA in Vienna is rather meager. August von Cramon, *Unser Österreich-Ungarische Bundesgenosse im Weltkriege,* is basic. Also important is *Deutschland als Verbündeter* by Karl Freiherr von Werkmann, the Emperor Karl's press chief. Especially useful is the recently-published first volume of the memoirs of Edmund Glaise von Horstenau, *Ein General im Zwielicht,* which covers the years of the war. Glaise's position as an information officer with the Austrian High Command gave him occasion to observe many of the chief statesmen and soldiers of the Monarchy at close quarters. Whatever his politics, he was a perceptive observer; his memoirs offer some often fascinating portraits of their personalities and behavior.

This study is not directly concerned with military affairs except to the extent that they impinged on foreign policy. It has therefore made only selective use of the holdings of the Kriegsarchiv in Vienna. For anyone researching the military history of either Germany or Austria-Hungary during World War I, however, this collection is essential—the more so in that the

238   SOURCES

German army records for 1914-1918 were destroyed in the bombing raids
of World War II.

All the military liaison officers left material. Cramon's memoirs, *Unser
Österreich-Ungarischer Bundesgenosse im Weltkriege,* are the most important. (Glaise, *Zwielicht,* 328, asserts that most of the book was ghosted by
him or Paul Fleck, Cramon's assistant). A later volume adds little. Josef
Stürgkh wrote *Im Deutschen Großen Hauptquartier* on his experiences.
Cramon's predecessor, Hugo Freiherr von Freytag-Loringhoven, composed
Menschen und Dinge, Wie Ich Sie in Meinem Leben Sah. On Klepsch-Kloth,
see the two articles by Peter Broucek cited in the bibliography, which present
excerpts from his unpublished reminiscences. These, and his wartime reports,
are in the KA. Cramon's original reports to his superiors were apparently
destroyed with the rest of the German army records during the Second World
War. However, copies of some of these were made during the interwar period
and deposited in the KA. The Cramon Nachlaß in the Bundesarchiv-
Militärarchiv in Freiburg contains some wartime notes and postwar letters
from Conrad von Hötzendorf.

The effort by the Central Powers to win over the adjacent neutral states
is covered in detail in Gerard Silberstein, *The Troubled Alliance.* On
Rumania, see in addition the articles by Glenn E. Torrey. The Monarchy's
relations with the Ottoman Empire are the subject of brief articles by F. R.
Bridge and Wolfdieter Bihl respectively; see also the books of Trumpener and
of Weber which cover both Germany and Austria-Hungary. Italy was the
most important of the wavering neutrals, so it is not surprising that it has
received more specific attention than Bulgaria, Rumania, Greece, or Turkey.
The section in W. W. Gottlieb, *Studies in Secret Diplomacy During the First
World War,* is an anti-Austrian account. The chapter in Valiani has Italian
domestic politics as much as Austria-Hungary as its focus. Bülow left an
account of his mission to Rome in Vol. 3 of his memoirs. Karl von Macchio,
the Austrian Ambassador there, wrote a rebuttal in *Wahrheit! Fürst Bülow
und Ich in Rom 1914/1915.* From the Italian side, in English, there are the
recollections of Antonio Salandra, the Italian Premier. There are also sections
in Ritter, Janßen, and Zeman.

A great deal has been written on the Polish problem during the war.
Besides the sections in Fischer and Ritter, there is Werner Conze, *Polnische
Nation und Deutsche Politik im Ersten Weltkrieg;* and, from an East German
historian, Heinz Lemke, *Allianz und Rivalität, Die Mittelmächte und Polen
im Ersten Weltkrieg (Bis zur Febuarrevolution).* John Leslie's Cambridge
dissertation, *Austria-Hungary's Eastern Policy in the First World War,
August 1914 to August 1915,* is definitive for that 12-month period.

On Mitteleuropa, the most general treatment is Henry Cord Meyer, *Mitteleuropa in German Thought and Action, 1815-1945.* More detailed studies of the agitation in the war years are the University of Toronto dissertation of Richard Kapp, *The Failure of the Diplomatic Negotiations Between Germany and Austria-Hungary for a Customs Union, 1915-1916;* Gusztáv Gratz and Richard Schüller, *The Economic Policy of Austria-Hungary During the War in its External Relations;* and the article by Paul R. Sweet. From the strictly German side are Fischer and, of course, the original best-seller by Friedrich Naumann (*Central Europe* in its English translation). Efforts to achieve closer military ties are discussed in Peter Broucek's article, "Die Deutschen Bemühungen um eine Militärkonvention mit Österreich-Ungarn."

The period 1917-1918, with its momentous events, has received more attention than the earlier years of the war. A fascinating reinterpretation is Peter Feldl, *Das Verspielte Reich,* which argues that the final dissolution was anything but inevitable, even after the Sixtus scandal. On politics between the two Central Powers, the Hungarian historian Imre Gonda, *Verfall der Kaiserreiche im Mitteleuropa,* provides a Marxist view. Peace diplomacy is the subject of Wolfgang Steglch, *Die Friedenspolitik der Mittelmächte, 1917-1918* (which actually covers only 1917; the concluding volume on 1918 has never appeared). The secret peace feelers are briefly summarized in the surveys of Launay and Pedroncini, as well as in Fischer, Ritter, Zeman, May, Valiani, and the documents in Scherer and Grunewald. They of course receive detailed treatment in the studies of the Emperor Karl and of Czernin, discussed below. Ottokar Landwehr, *Hunger: Die Erschöpfungsjahre der Mittelmächte,* is a compelling description of the Monarchy's food problems and Landwehr's activities. Police reports on conditions in general and signs of unrest in particular are collected in Rudolf Neck, ed., *Arbeiterschaft und Staat im Ersten Weltkrieg.*

Entente policy towards the Monarchy is treated in several works. British views are discussed in Kenneth J. Calder, *Britain and the Origins of the New Europe;* Wilfried Fest, *Peace or Partition, The Habsburg Monarchy and British Policy, 1914-1918;* and V. H. Rothwell, *British War Aims and Peace Diplomacy.* An equivalent volume on the French side is lacking, but D. Stevenson, *French War Aims Against Germany, 1914-1919,* also provides light on French policy towards Austria-Hungary. See as well the memoirs of Raymond Poincaré and Alexandre Ribot; and the two articles by Pierre Renouvin cited in the bibliography. The United States is covered in the pro-exile treatment of Victor S. Mamatey, *The United States and East Central*

Europe, as well as the dispatches collected in the *Foreign Relations of the United States.*

The exile movements are one of the most extensively-covered aspects of Austrian history during the war. There are lengthy sections in Zeman, Valiani, and May. The Czech leaders Masaryk and Beneš both left memoirs which have been translated into English and give a good idea of the exiles' tactics and difficulties.

Several biographies of the Emperor Karl have recently appeared, all very sympathetic. Gordon Brook-Shepherd, *The Last Habsburg,* draws on extensive material from interviews with the Empress Zita. See also the studies of Lorenz and Rieder. Several of Karl's aides left accounts of their association with him: Arthur Polzer-Hoditz, *The Emperor Karl;* and Karl Freiherr von Werkmann, *Deutschland als Verbündeter.* Both publish extensive excerpts from primary documents. The view these works present should, however, be compared with the more critical assessments in Singer, Meckling, Hopwood, and Demblin (see below) for a balanced picture. Conrad's dismissal, and Karl's relations with both the Austrian and German military while he served on the various war fronts before ascending the throne, is the subject of Helmut Hoyer, *Kaiser Karl I. und Feldmarschall Conrad von Hötzendorf.* On Arz, besides his memoirs mentioned above, there is the study of Oskar Regele.

A satisfactory interpretation of Czernin's entire career remains to be written. A good summary is Hans Friedl, "Ottokar Graf Czernin," in the *Neue Österreichische Biographie ab 1815,* XVII, 106-118. Czernin's own view is presented in *In the World War;* Ladislaus Singer, *Ottokar Graf Czernin,* largely follows this. Ingebord Meckling, *Die Aussenpolitik des Grafen Czernin,* is authoritative on Czernin's policies as Foreign Minister. Meckling's depth of understanding and command of the material make this an essential study for anyone interested in the politics of the period. Czernin's attempts to create a moderate German war aims program are covered in the Stanford University dissertation of Robert Hopwood, *Interalliance Diplomacy, Count Czernin and Germany, 1916-1918.* Hartmut Lehmann's article, "Czernins Friedenspolitik," is a brief introduction. On Czernin's prewar activities, especially his relations with Franz Ferdinand, see Robert A. Kann, *Archduke Franz Ferdinand, Studien,* 157-205 (a revised version of his earlier article "Count Ottokar Czernin and Archduke Francis Ferdinand" in the *Journal of Central European Affairs*). See also Gary W. Shanafelt, "Activism and Inertia: Ottokar Czernin's Mission to Rumania, 1913-1916," forthcoming in the *Austrian History Yearbook.*

On the Meinl Group, the main source is Heinrich Benedikt, ed., *Die Friedensaktion der Meinlgruppe 1917-1918.* Also useful are the essays in

Marga Lammasch and Hans Sperl, eds., *Heinrich Lammasch;* and the brief discussion in Valiani, 267-285.

The basic documents of the Sixtus exchanges are printed in G. de Manteyer, ed., *Austria's Peace Offer, 1916-1917.* Czernin's view (he makes no mention of the affair in his memoirs) was given to Baernreither and is printed in Robert A. Kann, *Die Sixtusaffäre.* Kann includes a lengthy bibliography on the subject. Gordon Brook-Shepherd's biography of Karl prints testimony from Zita on Karl's actions. One of the intermediaries, Tamás von Erdödy, has left memoirs of his involvement. For a sharply negative post-Versailles German view of Karl's actions and the motives of Sixtus and Zita, see Richard Fester, *Die Politik Kaiser Karls und der Wendepunkt des Weltkrieges.* Meckling, Steglich, and Ritter all discuss the exchanges.

The best introduction to the Brest-Litovsk negotiations, though composed without benefit of access to the archives, is probably still John W. Wheeler-Bennett, *Brest-Litovsk, the Forgotten Peace.* On Austria, see Wolfdieter Bihl, *Österreich-Ungarn und die Friedensschlüsse von Brest-Litowsk.* Czernin, Kühlmann, and Hoffmann have all left accounts. There are sections in the more general works already cited, and a few vignettes of the surface atmosphere in Glaise, *Zwielicht;* Glaise was posted there as part of the Austrian military delegation.

The literature on the Sixtus scandal is immense. A pro-Czernin account is the small volume of August Demblin, *Czernin und die Sixtus-Affaire,* which prints Czernin's exchange of telegrams with Karl from Bucharest in the final days of the crisis. See also Singer, *Ottokar Graf Czernin,* 287-305. The other side: Brook-Shepherd, *The Last Habsburg,* 142-153, which has the Empress Zita's testimony. The pro-Karl camp argues that Czernin had full knowledge of the Sixtus letters and in general attempts to put his behavior in as treacherous a light as possible in order to establish the innocence of the Emperor. As should be obvious from the events of the previous months, neither man was completely free of blame for the final denouement; but Czernin's conduct as the duel with Clemenceau unfolded practically assured that its outcome would have catastrophic consequences. Czernin's own depiction is in Kann, *Die Sixtusaffäre.* Meckling's account, 340-358, is an excellent synthesis of the available information.

There is a large literature on the last months of the Monarchy, but the focus is generally on the national and social movements coming into their own rather than foreign or military policy per se. An exception is Feldl, who tries to emphasize the Monarchy's strengths even in its final months of existence. An old account of the final debacle which is still useful is Edmund Glaise von Horstenau's *The Collapse of the Austro-Hungarian Empire.* The standard histories of the dissolution—Zeman, Valiani, and May—all have extensive sections. Helmut Rumpler has written studies of Max Hussarek, the last-but-one Austrian Minister-President, and of Karl's Autonomy Manifesto.

The Austro-German alliance received its official coup de grâce with Andrássy's peace note of October 1918. The Monarchy's last Foreign Minister and the note are covered in Andrássy's memoirs, *Diplomacy and the War,* which are rather general; and his article in the *Neue Freie Presse* cited in the bibliography. Wedel gives his version in an earlier article in the same paper. Windischgraetz, *My Memoirs,* adds useful details; Windischgraetz was a close associate of Andrássy and himself traveled to Switzerland in the last days of the war to try to make contact with the Entente (see, however, Wedel's review of Windischgraetz's book). There are also the articles by Opočenský and Krizman.

BIBLIOGRAPHY

1. UNPUBLISHED SOURCES

VIENNA: HAUS-, HOF-, UND STAATSARCHIV

Politisches Archiv

I. Allgemeines

496-524	Korrespondenzen aus dem Komplexe der Verhandlungen während des Krieges
524a, 524b	Memoiren des Grafen Berchtold
536	Botschaftsarchiv Berlin, Geheime Korrespondenzen 1914-1918
582-583	Delegationen 1914-1918
615-620, 629	Kabinett des Ministers: Akten 1914-1918
818	Interne Maßnahmen: Lebensmittelnot von Mitte Jänner 1918
837-844	Haltung Deutschlands
880-884	Rumänien 1914-1916
949-966	Friedensverhandlungen 1914-1918
1011-1017	Polen seit der Proklamation vom 5.XI.16
1047-1049	Der verschärfte Unterseeboot-Krieg 1917-1918
1052-1055	Friedensverhandlungen
1077-1082	Brester Kanzlei: Akten 1917-1918
1083	Aus dem Nachlaß des Gesandten von Wiesner
1084-1091	Friedensdelegation Bukarest: Akten

III. Preußen (Berlin)

171-175	Berichte, Weisungen, Varia 1914-1918

IV. Bayern (München)

58-59	Berichte, Weisungen, Varia 1914-1918

X. Rußland (Petersburg)

152-153	Die Ukraine 1918

XVIII. Rumänien (Bukarest)
45-48   Berichte, Weisungen, Varia, 1914-1916

XL. Interna
57-61   Tagesberichte des Ministeriums des Äußern 1916-1918
261   Korrespondenz zwischen dem Minister und dem Ministerium 1914-
                   1918
262-263   Verschiedene Telegramme von und an Graf Demblin 1917-1918
318   Kopien von Denkschriften 1914-1918

Administrative Registratur

F34 Handel und Gewerbe (Schiffahrt)
66-68   Generalia I, Agenturen: Handelsverkehr, Österreich-Ungarn

F36 Krieg 1914-1918
189-199   Dept. 9, Abt. 50, Deutsches Reich: Getreide Verhandlungen mit
                   Deutschland
374-377   Dept. 7: Friedensverhandlungen und Friedensverträge mit Rumä-
                   nien, Ukraine, Finnland, Rußland

F37 Flußverhandlungen (Binnenseen)
89-96   Deutsches Reich 21: Wirtschaftsverhandlungen im 1. Weltkrieg

Kabinettsarchiv: Geheimakten

Nachlässe

Joseph Baernreither, Erzherzog Franz Ferdinand, Ludwig von Flotow, Gustav Groß,
Erasmus Handel, Hans Löwenfeld-Ruß, Karl von Macchio, Gustav Marchet, Albert
Mensdorff, Kajetan Mérey, Ernst von Plener, Franz von Schießl, Friedrich Wieser

VIENNA: ALLGEMEINES VERWALTUNGSARCHIV

Nachlaß Wladimir von Beck

VIENNA: KRIEGSARCHIV

Conrad-Archiv, B7, B8
Nachlaß Arthur Arz von Straussenburg, B63
Nachlaß Karl Schneller, B509
Nachlaß Theodor von Zeynek, B151
Militärkanzlei Seiner Majestät, Faszikeln 25, 28; Sonderfaszikel 79

BONN: AUSWÄRTIGES AMT, POLITISCHES ARCHIV

Abteilung IA

Deutschland

128 Nr. 1 Geheim	Bündnis zwischen Deutschland, Österreich-Ungarn und Italien 1914-1915
128 Nr. 2 Geheim	Beitritt Rumäniens zum Bündnisverträge 1914-1916
128 Nr. 5 Geheim	Beitritt Türkei 1914-1919
128 Nr. 8	Frage des Anschlusses Bulgariens an den Dreibund 1913-1919
135 Nr. 6, Nr. 6 Geh.	Die Botschaft in Wien
180 Geheim	Europäischer Staatenbund 1915-1920

Preußen

1, Nr. 1 Nr. 3d	Korrespondenz des deutschen Kaisers mit dem Kaiser von Österreich
1, Nr. 1 Nr. 4c	Begegnung Seiner Majestät mit dem Kaiser von Österreich

Österreich

70, 70 Geheim	Allgemeine Angelegenheiten
72, 72 Geheim	Finanzen Österreich-Ungarns
85	Kroatien
86 Nr. 1, Nr. 1 Geh.	Österreichisches Kaiserhaus
86 Nr. 2	Österreichische Staatsmänner
86 Nr. 4	Österreichische Generäle
88	Die Österreichischen Ministerien
91	Parlamentarische Angelegenheiten Österreichs
91 Nr. 2	Österreichisch-Ungarische Delegationen
92 Nr. 1	Innere Zustände Ungarns
92 Nr. 2	Ungarische Ministerien
92 Nr. 3	Parlamentarische Angelegenheiten Ungarns
92 Nr. 5	Militärische Angelegenheiten Ungarns
92 Nr. 6a	Ungarische Staatsmänner
92 Nr. 10	Beziehungen Ungarns zu Deutschland
95, 95 Geheim	Beziehungen Österreichs zu Deutschland
97	Österreichisch-Ungarischer Ausgleich
98	Beziehungen Österreichs zu Kurie
101	Böhmen
103	Allgemeine Österreichische Politik, auch im Hinblick auf die zukünftige Gestaltung Österreich-Ungarns

104	Siebenbürgen und die Stellung der Deutschen und Rumänen in Ungarn

Weltkrieg

2 Geheim	Vermittlungsaktionen; Friedensstimmung und Aktionen zur Vermittlung des Friedens
2 ganz Geheim	Geheime Friedensanregungen
2 adh. 1	Ganz geheime Friedensanregungen
2f Nr. 1	Waffenstillstandsverhandlungen mit Rußland
2f Nr. 2	Waffenstillstandsverhandlungen mit Rumänien
5e Geheim Öst.	Funksprüche: Österreich 1918
11b adh.	Polnische Legion
15 Geheim	Material zu den Friedensverhandlungen
20a, 20a Geheim	Zukunft der besetzten Gebiete: Belgien
20c, 20c Geheim	Zukunft der besetzten Gebiete: Polen
20d, 20d Geheim	Zukunft der besetzten Gebiete: Rußland
20e Geheim	Zukunft der besetzten Gebiete: Serbien
20f Geheim	Zukunft der besetzten Gebiete: Montenegro
20h Geheim	Zukunft der besetzten Gebiete: Rumänien
23 Geheim	Friedensaktion der Zentralmächte 1916-1918
25	Friedensappel des Papstes 1917

Weltkriegsfriedensverhandlungen
Rußland
Politisches Nr. 1 Friedensverhandlungen in Brest-Litowsk
Politisches Nr. 4 Österreichisch-Russische Sonderverhandlungen

Rumänien
Politisches Nr. 1 Friedensverhandlungen in Bukarest

Großes Hauptquartier
23   Österreich-Ungarn

Kommissionsakten Brest-Litowsk/Bukarest
Friedenspräliminarien zu Brest-Litowsk 2: Allgemeine Politik
Bukarester Akten 6: Österreich Politik

Botschaft Wien
Geheim III (V) Ganz geheime Sachen; Korrespondenz Jagow-Tschirschky
Geheim III   Privatbriefe des Botschafters; Akten des Militärattachés, Secreta: v. Cramon

POTSDAM: DEUTSCHES ZENTRALARCHIV

Reichskanzlei

Stammakten
6-6/1   Österreich-Ungarn
7   Akten betr. Brief Kaiser Karls an den Prinzen Sixtus von Bourbon-
           Parma
8   Salzburger Verhandlungen
403-407   Mitteleuropäische Wirtschaftsbund
2254   Mitteleuropäische Wirtschaftsverein

Vertreter des Reichskanzlers bei der OHL
23   Wirtschaftsfragen Österreich-Ungarns: Wochenberichte der Bevoll-
           mächtigten des Kriegsernäherungsamtes in Budapest und Wien

Großes Hauptquartier
2477   Vorbereitungen des Friedensschlusses, Beiheft 21: Besprechungen
           über Kriegsziele

Stellvertreter des Reichskanzlers
15-16   Österreich-Ungarn

Auswärtiges Amt, Handelspolitische Abteilung
3986-4003 Österreich: Gestaltung der deutschen auswärtigen Handels- und
           Wirtschaftsbeziehungen nach dem Kriege, 1914-1918

Alldeutscher Verband
691-697, 699-   Correspondence and documents concerning Austria-Hungary
700,
703-705

MUNICH: GEHEIMES STAATSARCHIV

MA. Deutsches Reich
95070   Beziehungen mit Österreich-Ungarn und Deutsch-Österreich
97575   Versammlung in der österreichischen Politischen Gesellschaft über
           die Kriegsziele 17.VII.17
97675-97680 Friedensverhandlungen in Brest-Litowsk und Bukarest

MA I. Politisches Archiv
952   Prof. Foerster
964   Hertling, Reise nach Wien 1.V.17

MA III. Diplomatische Berichte
2481/2-6   Berichte Tuchers aus Wien 1914-1918

Gesandtschaft Wien
1756-1760 Berichte, Konzepte, Varia 1914-1918

FREIBURG-IM-BREISGAU: BUNDESARCHIV-MILITÄRARCHIV

Nachlaß August von Cramon, Bestand N266

BRNO: STÁTNÍ ARCHIV

Berchtold Family Archive

457	Correspondence from Franz Ferdinand, 1912-1914
460	Correspondence from Bolfras, Montenuovo, and Schießl, 1912-1916
462	Correspondence from Apponyi, Burián, Krobatin, Stürgkh, and Tisza, 1902-1917
464	Correspondence from Czernin, Forgách, Hohenlohe, Hoyos, Musulin, Revertera, and Szápáry, 1903-1930
465	Correspondence from Tschirschky, 1912-1916
466	Correspondence from Conrad von Hötzendorf, 1912-1914
476-481	Miscellaneous papers
526	Berchtold letters to his wife
543	Berchtold letters to his son Zsiga
556	Berchtold letters to his son Alois

STANFORD UNIVERSITY: THE HOOVER LIBRARY

Heinrich Kanner Papers

2. OFFICIAL DOCUMENTS, GOVERNMENT PUBLICATIONS

Austria, Bundesministerium für Landesverteidigung, *Österreich-Ungarns Letzter Krieg, 1914, 1918,* 7 vols., Vienna, 1930-1938.

Austria, Ministerium des Äußern, *Jahrbuch des K. u. K. Auswärtigen Dienstes,* Vienna, 1914-17.

Austria, Reichsrat, *Stenographische Protokolle der Delegation des Reichsrates,* Vienna, 1914-1918.

——, *Stenographische Protokolle über die Sitzungen des Hauses der Abgeordneten des Österreichischen Reichsrates,* Vienna, 1914-1918.

——, *Stenographische Protokolle über die Sitzungen des Herrenhauses des Österreichischen Reichsrates,* Vienna, 1914-1918.

Ludwig Bittner, Alfred Pribram, Heinrich Srbik, Hans Uebersberger, eds., *Österreich-Ungarns Aussenpolitik, von der Bosnischen Krise 1908 bis zum Kriegsausbruch 1914, Diplomatische Aktenstücke des Österreichisch-Ungarischen Ministeriums des Äussern,* 8 vols., Vienna, 1930.

Ernst Deuerlein, ed., *Briefwechsel Hertling-Lerchenfeld, Dienstliche Privatkorrespondenz Zwischen dem Bayerischen Minister-Präsidenten Georg Graf von Hertling und dem Bayerischen Gesandten in Berlin Hugo Graf von und zu Lerchenfeld,* 2 vols., Boppard, 1973.

Imanuel Geiß, ed., *Julikrise und Kriegsausbruch 1914,* 2 vols., Hannover, 1963-1964.

Miklós Komjáthy, ed., *Protokolle des Gemeinsamen Ministerrates der Österreichisch-Ungarischen Monarchie, 1914-1918,* Budapest, 1966.

Johannes Lepsius, Albrecht Mendelssohn-Bartholdy, Friedrich Thimme, eds., *Die Große Politik der Europäischen Kabinette, 1870-1914, Sammlung der Diplomatischen Akten des Auswärtigen Amtes,* 40 vols., Berlin, 1922-1927.

Erich Ludendorff, ed., *Urkunden der Obersten Heeresleitung über Ihre Tätigkeit 1916-1918,* Berlin, 1920.

Rudolf Neck, ed., *Arbeiterschaft und Staat im Ersten Weltkrieg, A. Quellen, I. Der Staat,* 2 vols., Vienna, 1964, 1968.

André Scherer and Jacques Grunewald, eds., *L'Allemagne et les Problèmes de la Paix Pendant la Première Guerre Mondiale,* 4 vols., Paris, 1962-1978.

James B. Scott, ed., *Official Statements of War Aims and Peace Proposals, December 1916 to November 1918,* Washington, 1921.

Wolfgang Steglich, ed., *Der Friedensappell Papst Benedikts XV vom 1. August 1917 und die Mittelmächte, Diplomatische Aktenstücke,* Wiesbaden, 1970.

United States, State Department, *Papers Relating to the Foreign Relations of the United States,* Supplement: *The World War, 1914-1918,* 9 vols., Washington, 1928-1933.

3. MEMOIRS, DIARIES, PRIVATE LETTER COLLECTIONS

Gyula Andrássy, *Diplomacy and the War,* trans. J. H. Reece, London, 1921.

————, "Die Sonderfriedensaktion von Oktober 1918, der Brief des Kaisers Karl an Kaiser Wilhelm," *Neue Freie Presse,* May 23, May 29, 1920.

Arthur Arz von Straussenburg, *Kampf und Sturz der Mittelmächte,* Vienna, 1935.

————, *Zur Geschichte des Großen Krieges, 1914-1918,* Vienna, 1924.

Moritz Auffenberg-Kamarów, *Aus Österreichs Höhe und Niedergang,* Munich, 1921.

Joseph Maria Baernreither, *Fragments of a Political Diary,* ed. Josef Redlich, London, 1930.

————, *Der Verfall des Habsburgerreiches und die Deutschen, Fragmente eines Politischen Tagebuches 1897-1917,* ed. Oskar Mitis, Vienna, 1938.

Carl Freiherr von Bardolff, *Soldat im Alten Österreich, Erinnerungen aus Meinem Leben,* Jena, 1938.

Tivadar Batthyány, *Für Ungarn Gegen Hohenzollern,* Zürich, 1930.

Edvard Beneš, *My War Memoirs,* trans. Paul Selver, Boston, 1928.

Leopold Berchtold, "Russia, Austria, and the World War," *Contemporary Review,* 133, 1928, 422-432.

Johann von Bernstorff, *Memoirs of Count Bernstorff,* New York, 1936.

Theobald von Bethmann Hollweg, *Betrachtungen zum Weltkriege,* 2 vols., Berlin, 1919, 1921.

Otto von Bismarck, *Bismarck, The Man and the Statesman,* trans. A. J. Butler, 2 vols., New York, 1899.

Bernhard von Bülow, *Memoirs of Prince von Bülow,* vol. 3, *The World War and Germany's Collapse,* trans. Geoffrey Dunlop, Boston, 1932.

István Burián, *Austria in Dissolution,* trans. Brian Lunn, New York, 1925.

Heinrich Claß, *Wider den Strom,* Leipzig, 1932.

250 BIBLIOGRAPHY

Franz Conrad von Hötzendorf, *Aus Meiner Dienstzeit, 1906-1918,* 5 vols., Vienna, 1922-1925.

————, *Private Aufzeichnungen, Erste Veröffentichungen aus den Papieren des K. u. K. Generalstabs-Chefs,* ed. Kurt Peball, Vienna-Munich, 1977.

Gina Conrad von Hötzendorff, *Mein Leben mit Conrad von Hötzendorf,* Leipzig, 1935.

Ernest U. Cormons (E. Urbas), *Schicksale und Schatten, Eine Österreichische Autobiographie,* Salzburg, 1951.

August von Cramon, *Unser Österreich-Ungarischer Bundesgenosse im Weltkriege, Erinnerungen aus Meiner Vierjährigen Tätigkeit als Bevollmächtigter Deutscher General beim K. u. K. Armeeoberkommando,* Berlin, 1920.

————, and Paul Fleck, *Deutschlands Schicksalsbund mit Österreich-Ungarn: von Conrad von Hötzendorf zu Kaiser Karl,* Berlin, 1932.

Alois Czedik, *Zur Geschichte des K. K. Österreichischen Ministerien, 1861-1916, Nach den Erinnerungen von Alois Czedik,* 4 vols., Teschen-Vienna-Leipzig, 1917-1920.

Ottokar Czernin, *In the World War,* New York, 1920.

————, *Mein Afrikanisches Tagebuch,* Zürich, 1928.

————, *Politische Betrachtungen,* Prague, 1908.

August Demblin, *Czernin und die Sixtus-Affaire,* Munich, 1920.

Constantin Dumba, *Memoirs of a Diplomat,* trans. Ian F. Morrow, Boston, 1932.

Tamás von Erdödy, *Habsburgs Weg von Wilhelm zu Briand, vom Kurier der Sixtus-Briefe zum Königs Putschisten, die Memoiren des Grafen Tamás von Erdödy,* ed. Paul Szemere and Erich Czech, Zürich, 1931.

Robert Ehrhart, *Im Dienste des Alten Österreich,* Vienna, 1958.

Matthias Erzberger, *Erlebnisse im Weltkrieg,* Stuttgart-Berlin, 1920.

Erich von Falkenhayn, *The German General Staff and its Decisions, 1914-1916,* New York, 1920.

Friedrich Wilhelm Foerster, *Erlebte Weltgeschichte,* Nürnberg, 1953.

Hugo von Freytag-Loringhoven, *Menschen und Dinge, Wie Ich Sie in Meinem Leben Sah,* Berlin, 1923.

Friedrich Funder, *Vom Gestern ins Heute, Aus dem Kaiserreich in die Republik,* Vienna-Munich, 1953.

Wladimir Giesl, *Zwei Jahrzehnte im Nahen Orient,* ed. Ritter von Steinitz, Berlin, 1927.

Edmund Glaise von Horstenau, *Ein General im Zwielicht, die Erinnerungen Edmund Glaises von Horstenau,* ed. Peter Broucek, vol. 1, *K. u. K. Generalstabsoffizier und Historiker,* Vienna-Graz-Cologne, 1980.

Karl Helfferich, *Der Weltkrieg,* 3 vols., Berlin, 1919.

William de Hevesy, "Postscript to the Sixtus Affair," *Foreign Affairs,* 21, 1943, 566-570.

Max von Hoffmann, *War Diaries and Other Papers,* trans. Eric Sutton, 2 vols., London, 1929.

Alexander Hoyos, *Der Deutsch-Englische Gegensatz und Sein Einfluß auf die*

Balkanpolitik Österreich-Ungarns, Berlin-Leipzig, 1922.

Bogdan von Hutten-Czapski, *Sechzig Jahre Politik und Gesellschaft,* 2 vols., Berlin, 1936.

Gottlieb von Jagow, *Ursache und Ausbruch des Weltkrieges,* Berlin, 1919.

Joseph of Habsburg, "Un Entretien de l'Archiduc Joseph avec l'Empereur Charles I/IV (d'Après les Memoires de l'Archiduc Joseph)," *Revue d'Histoire de la Guerre Mondiale,* 11, 1933, 240-249.

Mihály Károlyi, *Fighting the World: The Struggle for Peace,* New York, 1925.

Alfred Krauß, *Die Ursachen Unserer Niederlage, Erinnerungen und Urteile aus dem Weltkrieg,* 2nd ed., Munich, 1921.

Stefan von Kray, *Im Dienste der Kabinettskanzlei Während des Weltkrieges, Episoden und Charakterbilder aus dem Leben der Kaiser Franz Joseph und Karl,* Budapest, 1937.

Richard von Kühlmann, *Erinnerungen,* Heidelberg, 1948.

Ottokar Landwehr von Pragenau, *Hunger: Die Erschöpfungsjahre der Mittelmächte 1917/1918,* Zürich, 1931.

David Lloyd George, *War Memoirs of David Lloyd George, 1914-1918,* 6 vols., Boston, 1933-1936.

Erich von Ludendorff, *Ludendorff's Own Story, August 1914-November 1918,* 2 vols., New York, 1920.

Heinrich von Lützow, *Im Diplomatischen Dienst der K. u. K. Monarchie,* ed. Peter Hohenbalken, Vienna, 1971.

Karl Freiherr von Macchio, *Wahrheit! Fürst Bülow und Ich in Rom 1914/1915,* Vienna, 1931.

Baron von Margutti, *The Emperor Francis Joseph and His Times,* London, n. d.

Tomáš Masaryk, *The Making of a State, Memories and Observations, 1914-1918,* New York, 1927.

Albert Mensdorff and Nikolaus Revertera, "Die Friedensgespräche der Grafen Mensdorff und Revertera im Dezember 1917 und Februar 1918 nach Ihren Berichten an den Grafen Czernin," *Berliner Monatshefte,* 15, 1937, 401-419.

Georg Michaelis, *Für Staat und Volk, Eine Lebensgeschichte,* Berlin, 1922.

Anton Monts, *Erinnerungen und Gedanken,* ed. F. K. Nowak and F. Thimme, Berlin, 1932.

Georg Alexander von Müller, *The Kaiser and His Court, The Diaries, Notebooks and Letters of Admiral Georg Alexander von Müller, Chief of the Naval Cabinet, 1914-1918,* ed. Walter Görlitz, trans. Mervyn Savill, London, 1961.

Alexander Freiherr von Musulin, *Das Haus am Ballplatz, Erinnerungen eines Österreich-Ungarischen Diplomaten,* Munich, 1924.

Friedrich Naumann, *Central Europe,* trans. Christabel Meredith, New York, 1917.

Viktor Naumann, *Dokumente und Argumente,* Berlin, 1928.

———, *Profile,* Munich, 1925.

Otto of Habsburg, "Danubian Reconstruction," *Foreign Affairs,* 20, 1942, 243-252.

Friedrich Payer, *Erinnerungen von Bethmann Hollweg bis Ebert,* Frankfurt am Main, 1934.

252 BIBLIOGRAPHY

Ernst von Plener, *Erinnerungen,* 3 vols., Stuttgart-Leipzig, 1911-1924.

Raymond Poincaré, *Au Service de La France, Neuf Années de Souvenirs,* 10 vols., Paris, 1926-1933.

Arthur Polzer-Hoditz, *The Emperor Karl,* trans. D. F. Tait, Boston, 1931.

Josef Redlich, *Schicksalsjahre Österreichs, 1908-1919, Das Politische Tagebuch Josef Redlichs,* ed. Fritz Fellner, 2 vols., Graz-Cologne, 1953-1954.

Alexandre Ribot, *Journal et Correspondances Inédites 1914-1922,* Paris, 1936.

Kurt Riezler, *Tagebücher, Aufsätze, Dokumente,* ed. Karl Dietrich Erdmann, Göttingen, 1972.

Max Ronge, *Kriegs- und Industrie- Spionage, Zwölf Jarhe Kundschaftsdienst,* Zürich-Leipzig-Vienna, 1930.

Rupprecht of Wittelsbach, *Mein Kriegstagebuch,* ed. Eugen von Frauenholz, 3 vols., Munich, 1929.

Antonio Salandra, *Italy and the Great War: From Neutrality to Intervention,* London, 1932.

Hans von Seeckt, *Aus Meinem Leben, 1866-1917,* ed. Friedrich von Rabenau, Leipzig, 1938.

Ernst von Seidler, "Aus Schwerer Zeit," *Neue Freie Presse,* July 20, 25; August 2, 9, 14; September 2; 1924.

Rudolf Sieghart, *Die Letzten Jahrzehnte einer Großmacht: Menschen, Völker, Probleme des Habsburger-Reiches,* Berlin, 1932.

Alexander Spitzmüller von Harmersbach, *Der Letzte Österreichisch-Ungarische Ausgleich und der Zusammenbruch der Monarchie, Sächliches und Persönliches,* Berlin, 1929.

———, *". . . Und Hat Auch Ursach' Es zu Lieben",* Vienna, 1955.

Edmund Steinacker, *Lebenserinnerungen,* Munich, 1937.

Josef Stürgkh, *Im Deutschen Großen Hauptquartier,* Leipzig, 1921.

Berta Szeps-Zuckerkandl, *My Life and History,* trans. John Sommerfield, New York, 1939.

Gyula Szilássy, *Der Untergang der Donaumonarchie,* Berlin, 1921.

Albrecht von Thaer, *Generalstabsdienst an der Front und in der O.H.L., Aus Briefen und Tagebuchaufzeichnungen 1915-1919,* ed. Siegfried A. Kaehler, Göttingen, 1958.

István Tisza, *Briefe (1914-1918) Nach der von der Ungarischen Akademie der Wissenschaften Veröffentlichten Originalausgabe,* ed. Oskar von Wertheimer, Berlin, 1928.

———, *Összes Munkái,* 6 vols., Budapest, 1923-1937.

Botho von Wedel, "Österreich-Ungarns Sonderfriedensversuch von Oktober 1918," *Neue Freie Presse,* July 11, 1920.

———, "Windischgraetz und Seine Erinnerungen," *Preußische Jahrbücher,* 182, 1920, 289-297.

Karl Freiherr von Werkmann, *Der Tote Auf Madeira,* Munich, 1923.

———, *Deutschland als Verbündeter, Kaiser Karls Kampf um den Frieden,* Berlin, 1931.

Wilhelm II of Hohenzollern, *The Kaiser's Memoirs,* trans. Thomas R. Ybarra, New York, 1922.

Crown Prince Wilhelm of Hohenzollern, *Erinnerungen des Kronprinzen Wilhelm, Aus den Aufzeichnungen, Dokumenten, Tagebüchern und Gesprächen,* ed. Karl Rosner, Stuttgart-Berlin, 1922.

Lajos Windischgraetz, *Ein Kaiser Kämpft für die Freiheit, So Begann Ungarns Leidensweg,* Vienna-Munich, 1957.

————, *My Memoirs,* trans. Constance Vessey, London, 1921.

Stefen Zweig, *The World of Yesterday, An Autobiography,* New York, 1943.

4. SECONDARY SOURCES

Luigi Albertini, *The Origins of the War of 1914,* trans. Isabella Massey, 3 vols., Oxford, 1967.

Johann Allmeyer-Beck, *Ministerpräsident Baron Beck, Ein Staatsmann des Alten Österreich,* Munich, 1956.

Charles Appuhn, "Les Negociations Austro-Allemandes du Printemps de 1917 et la Mission du Prince Sixte," *Revue d'Histoire de La Guerre Mondiale,* 13, 1935, 209-223.

Bertrand Auerbach, *L'Autriche et la Hongrie Pendant la Guerre, Depuis le Début des Hostilités Jusqu'à la Chute de la Monarchie (Août 1914-Novembre 1918),* Paris, 1925.

Harald Bachmann, *Joseph Maria Baernreither,* Neustadt, 1977.

A. Basch, *The Danube Basin and the German Economic Sphere,* New York, 1937.

Werner Basler, *Deutschlands Annexionspolitik in Polen und Baltikum 1914-1918,* Berlin 1962.

Henryk Batowski, "Pläne zur Teilung der Habsburger-Monarchie im Ersten Weltkieg," *Österreichische Osthefte,* 10, 1968, 129-140.

Heinrich Benedikt, ed., *Die Friedensaktion der Meinlgruppe 1917-1918, Die Bemühungen um einen Verständigungsfrieden nach Dokumenten, Aktenstücken und Briefen,* Graz-Cologne, 1962.

Hans Beyer, *Die Mittelmächte und die Ukraine 1918, Jahrbücher für Geschichte Osteuropas,* Beiheft 2, 1956.

Wolfdieter Bihl, "Die Beziehungen Zwischen Österreich-Ungarn und dem Osmanischen Reich im Ersten Welkrieg," *Österreichische Osthefte,* 24, 1981, 33-52.

————, *Die Kaukasus-Politik der Mittelmächte, Teil I, Ihre Basis In der Orient-Politik und Ihre Aktionen 1914-1917,* Vienna-Cologne-Graz, 1975.

————, *Österreich-Ungarn und die Friedensschlüsse von Brest-Litowsk,* Vienna, 1970.

————,"Zu den Österreichisch-Ungarischen Kriegszielen 1914," *Jahrbücher für Geschichte Osteuropas,* 16, 1968, 505-530.

Ernst Birke, "Die Französische Osteuropa-Politik 1914-1918," *Zeitschrift für Ostfor-*

schung, 3, 1954, 321-359.

Ludwig Bittner, "Das Österreichisch-Ungarische Ministerium des Äußern, Seine Geschichte und Seine Organisation," *Berliner Monatshefte,* 15, 1937, 819-843.

———, "Graf Johann Forgách," *Berliner Monatshefte,* 13, 1935, 950-959.

Joachim Böhm, "Czernin, Adler und Stockholm, über die Zusammenarbeit Österreichischer Rechtssozialisten mit der Regierung im Jahr 1917," *Zeitschrift für Geschichtswissenschaft,* 16, 1968, 615-623.

Francis Roy Bridge, "Austria-Hungary and the Ottoman Empire in the Twentieth Century," *Mitteilungen des Österreichischen Staatsarchivs,* 34, 1981, 234-271.

———, *From Sadowa to Sarajevo, The Foreign Policy of Austria-Hungary, 1866-1914,* London, 1972.

———, "Tarde Venientibus Ossa: Austro-Hungarian Colonial Aspirations in Asia Minor, 1913-1914," *Middle Eastern Studies,* 6, 1970, 319-330.

Mitchell Pirie Briggs, *George D. Herron and the European Settlement,* Stanford, 1932.

Gordon Brook-Shepherd, *The Last Habsburg,* New York, 1968.

Peter Broucek, "Chef des Generalstabes und Oberster Kriegsherr, Aus den Erinnerungen des Feldmarschalleutnants Alois Klepsch-Kloth von Roden, K. u. K. Delegierten im Deutschen Großen Hauptquartier, 1915/1918," *Mitteilungen des Österreichischen Staatsarchivs,* 27, 1974, 385-401.

———, "Der K. u. K. Delegierte im Deutschen Großen Hauptquartier General-Major Alois Klepsch-Kloth von Roden und Seine Berichterstattung 1915/1916," *Militärgeschichtliche Mitteilungen,* 15, 1974/1, 109-126.

———, "Die Deutschen Bemühungen um eine Militärkonvention mit Österreich-Ungarn (1915-1918)," *Mitteilungen des Instituts für Österreichische Geschichtsforschung,* 87, 1979, 440-470.

E. C. Brunauer, *The Peace Proposals of Germany and Austria-Hungary, 1914-1918,* Stanford, 1929.

Eldon Ray Burke, *The Polish Policy of the Central Powers During the World War,* Chicago, 1936.

Kenneth J. Calder, *Britain and the Origins of the New Europe, 1914-1918,* Cambridge, 1976.

François Charles-Roux, *La Paix des Empires Centraux,* Paris, 1947.

Werner Conze, *Polnische Nation und Deutsche Politik im Ersten Weltkrieg,* Cologne-Graz, 1958.

Egon Caesar Conte Corti and Hans Sokol, *Der Alte Kaiser, Franz Joseph I. vom Berliner Kongreß bis zu Seinem Tode,* Graz-Vienna, 1956.

Gordon Craig, "The Military Cohesion of the Austro-German Alliance, 1914-1918," in *War, Politics and Diplomacy, Selected Essays,* New York, 1966, 46-57.

R. J. Crampton, "The Balkans as a Factor in German Foreign Policy, 1912-1914," *Slavonic and East European Review,* 55, 1977, 370-390.

Istvan Deak, "The Decline and Fall of Habsburg Hungary, 1914-1918," in Iván Völgyes, ed., *Hungary in Revolution, 1918-19, Nine Essays,* Lincoln, 1971, 10-30.

István Diószegi, "Außenminister Stephan Graf Burián, Biographie und Tagebuch-stelle," *Annales,* Universitatis Scientiarum Budapestinensis de Rolando Eötvös Nominatae, Sectio Historica, 8, 1966, 161-208.

Günter Dolezal, *Baron (Graf) Burián als Außenminister: Die Verhandlungen mit Deutschland über Polen 1915 und 1916,* Doctor Thesis, University of Vienna, 1965.

Jacques Droz, *L'Europe Central, Evolution Historique de l'Idée de "Mitteleuropa",* Paris, 1960.

Friedrich Engel-Janosi, "Die Friedensgespräche Graf Nicholaus Reverteras mit Comte Abel Armand 1917-1918," *Anzeiger der Österreichischen Akademie der Wissenschaften,* Philosophisch-Historische Klasse, 102, Nr. 1-25, 1965, 369-381.

————, *Geschichte Auf dem Ballhausplatz,* Vienna, 1963.

————, *Österreich und der Vatikan,* 2 vols., Graz, 1958-60.

———— "Über den Friedenswillen Kaiser Karls," in Emil Franzel, ed., *Virtute Fideque, Festschrift für Otto von Habsburg zum Fünfzigsten Geburtstag,* Vienna-Munich, 1965, 37-48.

Klaus Epstein, "The Development of German-Austrian War Aims in the Spring of 1917," *Journal of Central European Affairs,* 17, 1957, 24-47.

————, *Matthias Erzberger and the Dilemma of German Democracy,* Princeton, 1959.

Gusztáv Erényi, *Graf Stefan Tisza, Ein Staatsmann und Märtyrer,* Vienna, 1935.

Ronald Ernharth, *The Tragic Alliance: Austro-German Military Cooperation, 1871-1918,* Doctor Thesis, Columbia University, 1970.

L. L. Farrar, Jr., *Divide and Conquer, German Efforts to Conclude a Separate Peace, 1914-1918,* Boulder, 1978.

Sidney B. Fay, *The Origins of the World War,* 2 vols., New York, 1966.

Oleh Fedyshyn, *Germany's Drive to the East and the Ukrainian Revolution, 1917-1918,* New Brunswick, 1971.

Erich Feigl, *Kaiserin Zita, Legende und Wahrheit, Nach Gesprächen und Doku-menten,* Vienna-Munich, 1977.

Herbert Feis, *Europe, The World's Banker, 1870-1914,* New Haven, 1930.

Peter Feldl, *Das Verspielte Reich, Die Letzten Tage Österreich-Ungarns,* Vienna-Hamburg, 1968.

Fritz Fellner, *Der Dreibund, Europäische Diplomatie vor dem Ersten Weltkrieg,* 2nd ed., Munich, 1960.

————, "Die 'Mission Hoyos'," in *Les Grandes Puissances et la Serbie à la Veille de la Première Guerre Mondiale,* Recueil des Travaux aux Assises Scientifiques Internationales, Assises Scientifiques de l'Academie Serbe des Sciences et des Arts 4, Classe des Sciences Historiques No. 1, Belgrade, 1976, 387-418.

Wilfried Fest, *Peace or Partition, The Habsburg Monarchy and British Policy 1914-1918,* New York, 1978.

Richard Fester, *Die Politik Kaiser Karls und der Wendepunkt des Weltkrieges,* Munich, 1925.

Fritz Fischer, *Germany's Aims in the First World War,* New York, 1967.
———, *War of Illusions, German Policies from 1911 to 1914,* trans. Marion Jackson, New York, 1975.
———, "World Policy, World Power and German War Aims," in H. W. Koch, ed., *The Origins of the First World War, Great Power Rivalry and German War Aims,* London, 1972, 74-144.
K. Forster, *The Failures of Peace: The Search for a Negotiated Peace During the First World War,* Washington, 1941.
Paul K. Freiwirth, *Germany and Austria-Hungary as Allies, 1914-1916,* Doctor Thesis, University of Maryland, 1961.
Hans Friedl, "Ottokar Graf Czernin, (1872-1932)," *Neue Österreichische Biographie ab 1815, Große Österreicher,* Vienna-Munich-Zürich, 1968, vol. 17, 106-118.
Christoph Führ, *Das K. u. K. Armeeoberkommando und die Innenpolitik in Österreich 1914-1917,* Graz, 1968.
Alexander Fussek, *Minister Präsident Karl Graf Stürgkh,* Doctor Thesis, University of Vienna, 1959.
József Galántai, "Die Kriegszielpolitik der Österreichisch-Ungarischen Monarchie im Ersten Weltkrieg und die Ungarische Regierung," in Institut für Österreichkunde, ed., *Österreich-Ungarn 1867-1967,* Vienna, 1970, 137-147.
———, *Die Österreichisch-Ungarische Monarchie und der Weltkrieg,* Budapest, 1979.
———, "István Tisza und der Erste Weltkrieg," *Annales,* Universitatis Scientiarum Budapestinensis de Rolando Eötvös Nominatae, Sectio Historica, 5, 1963, 185-205.
Harald Gardos, "Die 'Balkanstraße' im Kriegsjahr 1915," *Mitteilungen des Österreichischen Staatsarchivs,* 22, 1969, 279-310.
Edmund Glaise von Horstenau, *The Collapse of the Austro-Hungarian Empire,* trans. Ian F. D. Morrow, London, 1930.
Imre Gonda, *Verfall der Kaiserreiche in Mitteleuropa, Der Zweibund in den Letzten Kriegsjahren (1916-1918),* Budapest, 1977.
G. P. Gooch, *Before the War, Studies in Diplomacy,* 2 vols., London, 1936, 1938.
———, *Recent Revelations in European Diplomacy,* 4th ed., London, 1940.
Roderich Gooß, *Das Wiener Kabinett und die Entstehung des Weltkrieges,* Vienna, 1919.
W. W. Gottlieb, *Studies in Secret Diplomacy During the First World War,* London, 1957.
Gusztáv Gratz, "Etienne Tisza," *Nouvelle Revue de Hongrie,* 51, 1934, 121-128.
———, "Vor dem Zusammenbruch der Monarchie, Die Letzten Briefe des Grafen Stefan Tisza," *Berliner Monatshefte,* 16, 1938, 1098-1110.
———, and Richard Schüller, *The Economic Policy of Austria-Hungary during the War in its External Relations,* trans. W. Alison Phillips, New Haven, 1928.
———, and Richard Schüller, *Der Wirtschaftliche Zuzammenbruch Österreich-Ungarns, Die Tragödie der Erschöpfung,* Vienna-Yale, 1930.

Helga Grebing, "Österreich-Ungarn und die Ukrainische Aktion 1914-1918," *Jahrbücher für Geschichte Osteuropas*, 7, 1959, 270-296.

Harry Hanak, "The Government, the Foreign Office, and Austria-Hungary, 1914-1918," *Slavonic and East European Review*, 47, 1969, 161-197.

———, *Great Britain and Austria-Hungary During the First World War, A Study in the Formation of Public Opinion*, Oxford, 1962.

Péter Hanák, "Die Ungarischen Staatsmänner und der Kriegseintritt Italiens, Beiträge zur Außenpolitik Österreich-Ungarns in der Zeit von Juli 1914 bis Mai 1915," *Österreichische Osthefte*, 11, 1969, 197-215.

Hugo Hantsch, *Leopold Graf Berchtold, Grandseigneur und Staatsmann*, Graz, 1963.

———, *Österreichs Friedensbemühungen*, Brixlegg, 1935.

Bascom Berry Hayes, *The German Reich and the "Austrian Question", 1871-1914*, Doctor Thesis, Yale University, 1963.

Roger Lee Heacock, *Diplomatic Relations Between the Austro-Hungarian Empire and the German Reich in World War I, 1916-1918: A Study Based on Documents from the Austrian State Archives*, Doctor Thesis, University of Denver, 1967.

H. Hielbronner, "The Merger Attempts of Serbia and Montenegro, 1913-1914," *Journal of Central European Affairs*, 18, 1958, 281-291.

Ernst C. Helmreich, "The Conflict Between Germany and Austria over Balkan Policy, 1913-1914," in Donald McKay, ed., *Essays in the History of Modern Europe*, New York, 1936, 130-148.

———, *The Diplomacy of the Balkan Wars*, Cambridge, 1938.

F. Hertz, *The Economic Problem of the Danubian States*, London, 1947.

Lothar Höbelt, "Österreich-Ungarn und das Deutsche Reich als Zweibundpartner," in Heinrich Lutz and Helmut Rumpler, eds., *Österreich und die Deutsche Frage im 19. und 20. Jahrhundert, Probleme der Politisch-Staatlichen und Sozialkulturellen Differenzierung im Deutschen Mitteleuropa*, Munich, 1982, 256-281.

Felix Höglinger, *Ministerpräsident Heinrich Graf Clam-Martinic*, Graz, 1964.

Hajo Holborn, "The Cohesion of the Austro-German Alliance in World War I," in *Germany and Europe, Historical Essays*, Garden City, 1970, 151-162.

———, "The Final Disintegration of the Habsburg Monarchy," *Austrian History Yearbook*, 3, part 3, 1967, 189-205.

Erwin Hölzle, "Das Experiment des Friedens im Ersten Weltkrieg 1914-1917," *Geschichte in Wissenschaft und Unterricht*, 13, 1962, 465-522.

Robert F. Hopwood, "The Conflict Between Count Czernin and Emperor Charles in 1918," *Austrian History Yearbook*, 4-5, 1968-1969, 28-43.

———, *Interalliance Diplomacy: Count Czernin and Germany, 1916-1918*, Doctor Thesis, Stanford University, 1965.

Volker Höttl, *Die Beziehungen Conrads von Hötzendorf zu den Deutschen Generalstabschefs 1914-1917 auf Politischem Gebiet*, Doctor Thesis, University of Vienna, 1967.

Kalervo Hovi, *Cordon Sanitaire or Barrière de l'Est? The Emergence of the New French Eastern European Alliance Policy 1917-1919*, Turku, 1975.

Helmut Hoyer, *Kaiser Karl I. und Feldmarschall Conrad von Hötzendorf, Ein Beitrag zur Militärpolitik Kaiser Karls,* Doctor Thesis, University of Vienna, 1972.

Institut fur Österreichkunde, ed., *Österreich am Vorabend des Ersten Weltkrieges,* Graz-Vienna, 1964.

Fred Charles Iklé, *Every War Must End,* New York, 1971.

William Jannen, Jr., "The Austro-Hungarian Decision for War, July 1914," in S.R. Williamson and P. Pastor, eds., *Essays on World War I: Origins and Prisoners of War,* Social Science Monographs of Brooklyn College, New York, 1983, 55-81.

Karl Heinz Janßen, *Der Kanzler und der General, Die Führungskrise um Bethmann Hollweg und Falkenhayn, 1914-1916,* Göttingen, 1967.

Konrad Jarausch, *The Enigmatic Chancellor, Bethmann Hollweg and the Hubris of Imperial Germany,* New Haven-London, 1973.

Oscar Jászi, *The Dissolution of the Habsburg Monarchy,* Chicago, 1964.

Zdeněk Jindra, "Über die Ökonomischen Grundlagen der 'Mitteleuropa'-Ideologie des Deutschen Imperialismus," in Karl Obermann, ed., *Probleme der Ökonomie und Politik in den Beziehungen Zwischen Ost- und Westeuropa vom 17. Jahrhundert bis zur Gegenwart,* Berlin, 1960, 139-162.

Volkwart John, *Brest-Litowsk, Verhandlungen und Friedensverträge im Osten 1917 bis 1918, Beiträge zur Geschichte der Nachbismarckischen Zeit und des Weltkrieges,* Stuttgart, 1937.

Robert A. Kann, "Count Ottokar Czernin and Archduke Francis Ferdinand," *Journal of Central European Affairs,* 16, 1956, 117-145.

————, *Die Sixtusaffäre und die Geheimen Friedensverhandlungen Österreich-Ungarns im Ersten Weltkrieg,* Vienna, 1966.

————, *Erzherzog Franz Ferdinand, Studien,* Vienna, 1976.

————, *A History of the Habsburg Empire, 1526-1918,* Berkeley, 1974.

————, *Kaiser Franz Joseph und der Ausbruch des Weltkrieges, Eine Betrachtung über den Quellenwert der Aufzeichnungen von Dr. Heinrich Kanner,* Österreichische Akademie der Wisssenschaften, Philosophisch-Historische Klasse, Sitzungsberichte, 274. Band, 3. Abhandlung, Vienna, 1971.

————, *The Multinational Empire, Nationalism and Reform in the Habsburg Monarchy, 1848-1918,* 2 vols., New York, 1950.

————, and Bela K. Király, Paula S. Fichtner, eds., *The Habsburg Empire in World War I, Essays on the Intellectual, Military, Political and Economic Aspects of the Habsburg War Effort,* Boulder, 1977.

————, and Friedrich E. Prinz, eds., *Deutschland und Österreich-Ungarn, Ein Bilaterales Geschichtsbuch,* Munich, 1980.

Richard Kapp, *The Failure of the Diplomatic Negotiations Between Germany and Austria-Hungary for a Customs Union, 1915-1916,* Doctor Thesis, University of Toronto, 1977.

Peter J. Katzenstein, *Disjointed Partners: Austria and Germany Since 1815,* Berkeley, 1976.

Hugo Kerchnawe, *Der Zusammenbruch der Österreichisch-Ungarischen Wehrmacht im Herbst 1918,* Munich, 1921.

Fritz Kern, *Skizzen zum Kriegsausbruch im Jahre 1914,* ed. Hans Hallmann, Darmstadt, 1966.

Rudolf Kiszling, "Die Militärischen Beziehungen und Bindungen Zwischen Österreich-Ungarn und dem Deutschen Reiche vor dem Weltkrieg," *Berliner Monatshefte,* 4, 1926, 820-835.

————, *Erzherzog Franz Ferdinand von Österreich-Este, Leben, Pläne, und Wirken am Schicksalsweg der Donaumonarchie,* Graz-Cologne, 1953.

————, *Österreich-Ungarns Anteil am Ersten Weltkrieg,* Graz, 1958.

Fritz Klein, "Die Rivalität zwischen Deutschland und Österreich-Ungarn in der Türkei am Vorabend des Ersten Weltkrieges," in F. Klein, ed., *Politik im Krieg, 1914-1918, Studien zur Politik der Deutschen Herrschenden Klassen im Ersten Weltkrieg,* Berlin, 1964, 1-21.

————, "Innere Widersprüche im Bündnis Zwischen Deutschland und Österreich-Ungarn zu Beginn der Imperialistischen Epoche (1897 bis 1902)," in F. Klein, ed., *Studien zum Deutschen Imperialismus vor 1914,* Berlin, 1976, 225-262.

————, "Probleme des Bündnisses Zwischen Österreich-Ungarn und Deutschland am Vorabend des Ersten Weltkrieges," in Wolfgang Schieder, ed., *Erster Weltkrieg, Ursachen, Entstehung und Kriegsziele,* Cologne-Berlin, 1969, 309-316.

————, ed., *Österreich-Ungarn in der Weltpolitik, 1900 bis 1918,* Berlin 1965.

Arthur G. Kogan, "Germany and the Germans of the Habsburg Monarchy on the Eve of the Armistice 1918: The Genesis of the Anschluss Problem," *Journal of Central European Affairs,* 20, 1960, 24-50.

Titus Komarnicki, *Rebirth of the Polish Republic: A Study in the Diplomatic History of Europe, 1914-1920,* London, 1957.

Jiři Korálka, "Germany's Attitude Towards the National Disintegration of Cisleithania, (April-October 1918)," *Journal of Contemporary History,* 6, 1969, 85-95.

————, "la Montée du Pan-Germanisme et L'Autriche-Hongrie," *Historica,* 10, 1965, 213-253.

Christine Kosnetter, *Ministerpräsident Dr. Ernst Ritter von Seidler,* Doctor Thesis, University of Vienna, 1963.

Bogdan Krizman, "Austro-Hungarian Diplomatic Activity on the Eve of the Collapse of the Monarchy, Autumn 1918," *East European Quarterly,* 5, 1971, 27-46.

Alfred Kruck, *Geschichte des Alldeutschen Verbandes 1890-1939,* Wiesbaden, 1954.

Marga Lammasch and Hans Sperl, eds., *Heinrich Lammasch, Seine Aufzeichnungen, Seine Wirkung, und Seine Politik,* Vienna-Leipzig, 1922.

Lászlo Lanyi, *Le Comte Etienne Tisza et la Guerre de 1914-1918,* Doctor Thesis, University of Paris, 1946.

Jacques de Launay, *Secrets Diplomatiques 1914-1918,* Brussels-Paris, 1963.

Hartmut Lehmann, "Czernins Friedenspolitik 1916-1918," *Die Welt als Geschichte,* 23, 1963, 47-59.

————, "Österreich-Ungarns Belgienpolitik im Ersten Weltkrieg," *Historische*

Zeitschrift, 192, 1961, 60-93.

Heinz Lemke, *Allianz und Rivalität, Die Mittelmächte und Polen im Ersten Weltkrieg (Bis zur Februarrevolution),* Berlin, 1977.

————, "Die Deutsche Polenpolitik 1914 bis 1916 in der Sicht Eines Österreichisch-Ungarischen Diplomaten, Der Bericht Baron Andrians vom 30. Dezember 1916," *Jahrbuch für Geschichte der UdSSR und der Volksdemokratischen Länder Europas,* 7, 1963, 495-504.

————, "Die Politik der Mittelmächte in Polen von der Novemberproklamation 1916 bis zum Zusammentritt des Provisorischen Staatsrates," *Jahrbuch für Geschichte der UdSSR und der Volksdemokratischen Länder Europas,* 6, 1962, 69-138.

John Leslie, *Austria-Hungary's Eastern Policy in the First World War, August 1914 to August 1915,* Doctor Thesis, Cambridge University, 1975.

Joachim Lilla, "Innen- und Außenpolitische Aspekte der Austropolnische Lösung, 1914-1916," *Mitteilungen des Österreichischen Staatsarchivs,* 30, 1977, 221-250.

Dörte Löding, *Deutschlands und Österreich-Ungarns Balkanpolitik von 1912-1914 unter Besonderer Berücksichtigung Ihrer Wirtschaftsinteressen,* Doctor Thesis, University of Hamburg, 1969.

Hans Loewenfeld-Ruß, *Die Regelung der Volksernährung im Kriege,* Vienna-Yale, 1926.

Reinhold Lorenz, "Aus dem Kriegstagebuch des Generaladjutanten Freiherrn von Marterer," in Institut für Österreichische Geschichtsforschung, *Österreich und Europa, Festgabe für Hugo Hantsch zum 70. Geburtstag,* Graz-Vienna-Cologne, 1965, 483-504.

————, *Kaiser Karl und der Untergang der Donaumonarchie,* Graz, 1959.

Imre Lukinich, *Die Ungarische Regierung und die Polnische Frage in den Ersten Jahren des Weltkrieges,* Budapest, 1938.

C. A. Macartney, *The Habsburg Empire, 1790-1918,* New York, 1969.

Victor S. Mamatey, *The United States and East Central Europe 1914 to 1918, A Study in Wilsonian Diplomacy and Propaganda,* Princeton, 1957.

G. de Manteyer, ed., *Austria's Peace Offer 1916-1917,* London, 1921.

Eduard März, *Österreiche Bankpolitik in der Zeit der Großen Wende, 1913-1923, Am Beispiel der Creditanstalt für Handel und Gewerbe,* Munich, 1981.

Arthur J. May, *The Hapsburg Monarchy, 1867-1914,* Cambridge, 1965.

————, *The Passing of the Hapsburg Monarchy, 1914-1918,* 2 vols., Philadelphia, 1968.

Arno J. Mayer, *Political Origins of the New Diplomacy, 1917-1918,* New Haven, 1959.

Ingeborg Meckling, *Die Aussenpolitik des Grafen Czernin,* Vienna, 1969.

Hans Meier-Welcker, "Die Beurteilung der Politischen Lage in Österreich-Ungarn durch Generalmajor von Seeckt im Sommer 1917," *Militärgeschichtliche Mitteilungen,* 10, 1968/2, 87-104.

Henry Cord Meyer, *Mitteleuropa in German Thought and Action, 1815-1945,* The

Hague, 1955.

Masaki Miyake, "J. M. Baernreither und 'Mittleuropa', Eine Studie Über den Nachlaß Baernreither," *Mitteilungen des Österreichischen Staatsarchivs,* 17-18, 1964-1965, 359-398.

Paul Molisch, ed., *Briefe zur Deutschen Politik in Österreich von 1848 bis 1918,* Vienna-Leipzig, 1934.

―――, *Geschichte der Deutsch-Nationalen Bewegung in Österreich,* Jena, 1926.

―――, "Zur Politik Kaiser Karls von Österreich," *Preußische Jahrbücher,* 231, 1933, 4-23.

Rudolf Neck, "Das 'Wiener Dokument' vom 27. März 1917," *Mitteilungen des Österreichischen Staatsarchivs,* 7, 1954, 294-309.

Karl Friedrich Nowak, *The Collapse of Central Europe,* trans. P. Lochner and E. W. Dickes, London, 1924.

Jan Opočenský, "The Discussion of Responsibility for War," *Journal of Modern History,* 4, 1932, 415-429.

―――, "La Genèse de la Note Austro-Hongroise du 28 Octobre 1918," *Le Monde Slave,* October 1925, 62-97.

―――, *Umsturz in Mitteleuropa, Der Zusammenbruch Österreich-Ungarns und die Geburt der Kleinen Entente,* trans. K. L. Reiner, Hellerau, 1931.

Leo Pasvolsky, *Economic Nationalism of the Danubian States,* New York, 1928.

Guy Pedroncini, *Les Negociations Secrètes Pendant La Grande Guerre,* Paris, 1969.

M. B. A. Peterson, "Das Österreichisch-Ungarische Memorandum an Deutschland vom 5. Juli 1914," *Scandia,* 30, 1964, 138-190.

Anton Pitreich, *Der Österreichisch-Ungarische Bundesgenosse im Sperrfeuer,* Klagenfurt, 1930.

Richard Plaschka, *Cattaro-Prag, Revolte und Revolution, Kriegsmarine und Heer Österreich-Ungarns im Fever der Aufstandsbewegung vom 1. Februar und 28. Oktober 1918,* Graz-Cologne, 1963.

―――, and Horst Haselsteiner and Arnold Suppan, *Innere Front, Militärassistenz, Widerstand und Umsturz an der Inneren Front der Donaumonarchie, 1918,* 2 vols., Vienna, 1974.

―――, and Karlheinz Mack, eds., *Die Auflösung des Habsburgerreiches, Zusammenbruch und Neuorientierung im Donauraum,* Vienna, 1970.

Sándor Popovics, *Das Geldwesen im Kriege,* Vienna-Yale, 1925.

Alfred Pribram, *Austrian Foreign Policy, 1908-18,* London, 1923.

―――, *The Secret Treaties of Austria-Hungary, 1879-1914,* ed. A. C. Coolidge, 2 vols., Cambridge, 1920-1921.

Günther Ramhardter, *Geschichtswissenschaft und Patriotismus, Österreichs Historiker im Weltkrieg, 1914-1918,* Vienna, 1973.

Joseph Redlich, *Austrian War Government,* New Haven, 1929.

―――, *Emperor Francis Joseph of Austria,* New York, 1929.

Oskar Regele, *Feldmarschall Conrad, Auftrag und Erfüllung, 1906-1918,* Vienna, 1955.

——, *Gericht über Habsburgs Wehrmacht, Letze Siege und Untergang unter dem Armee-Oberkommando Kaiser Karls I — Generaloberst Arz von Straussenburg,* Vienna, 1968.

Joachim Remak, "1914 — The Third Balkan War: Origins Reconsidered," *Journal of Modern History,* 43, 1971, 353-366.

Pierre Renouvin, *The Immediate Origins of the War (28th June-4th August 1914),* trans. Theodore Hume, New Haven, 1928.

——, "Le Gouvernement Français et les Tentatives de Paix en 1917," *Revue des Deux Mondes,* October 15, 1964, 492-513.

——, "Les Buts de Guerre du Gouvernement Français 1914-1918," *Revue Historique,* 235, 1966, 1-38.

Heinz Rieder, *Kaiser Karl, Der Letzte Monarch Österreich-Ungarns, 1887-1922,* Munich, 1981.

Richard Riedl, *Die Industrie Österreichs Während des Krieges,* Vienna-Yale, 1932.

Gerhard Ritter, "Die Zusammenarbeit der Generalstäbe Deutschlands und Österreich-Ungarns vor dem Ersten Weltkrieg," in *Zur Geschichte und Problematik der Demokratie, Festgabe für Heinz Herzfeld,* Berlin, 1958, 523-549.

——, *The Sword and the Scepter: The Problem of Militarism in Germany,* trans. Heinz Norden, 4 vols., Coral Gables, 1969-1973.

Gunther Rothenberg, *The Army of Francis Joseph,* West Lafayette, 1976.

V. H. Rothwell, *British War Aims and Peace Diplomacy, 1914-1918,* Oxford, 1971.

Helmut Rumpler, *Das Völkermanifest Kaiser Karls vom 16. Oktober 1918, Letzter Versuch zur Rettung des Habsburgerreiches,* Munich, 1966.

——, "Die Kriegsziele Österreich-Ungarns auf dem Balkan 1915/1916," in Institut für Österreichische Geschichtsforschung, *Österreich und Europa, Festgabe für Hugo Hantsch zum 70. Geburtstag,* Graz-Vienna-Cologne, 1965, 465-482.

——, *Max Hussarek, Nationalitäten und Nationalitätenpolitik in Österreich im Sommer des Jahres 1918,* Graz, 1965.

Bernadotte Schmitt, *The Coming of the War, 1914,* 2 vols., New York, 1930.

Günter Schödl, "Paul Samassa, Eine Biographischer Beitrag zur Vorgeschichte des 'Extremen Nationalismus' in Deutschland und Österreich," *Südostdeutsches Archiv,* 21, 1978, 75-104.

Paul Schroeder, "World War I as Galloping Gertie: A Reply to Joachim Remak," *Journal of Modern History,* 44, 1972, 319-345.

Max Schwarte, ed., *Der Große Krieg,* vol. 5, *Der Österreich-Ungarische Krieg,* Leipzig, 1922.

Robert Seton-Watson, "Austro-German Peace Plans for the Future of Serbia, 1915," *Slavonic and East European Review,* 7, 1929, 705-724.

Gerard E. Silberstein, *The Troubled Alliance, German-Austrian Relations, 1914 to 1917,* Lexington, 1970.

Ladislaus Singer, *Ottokar Graf Czernin, Staatsmann einer Zeitenwende,* Graz, 1965.

Wolfgang Steglich, *Bündnissicherung oder Verständigungsfrieden, Untersuchung zu dem Friedensangebot der Mittelmächte vom 12. Dezember 1916,* Göttingen, 1958.

————, *Die Friedenspolitik der Mittelmächte, 1917-1918,* Wiesbaden, 1964.

Eduard Ritter von Steinitz, ed., *Erinnerungen an Franz Joseph I, Kaiser von Österreich, Apostolischer König von Ungarn,* Berlin, 1931.

————, *Rings um Sasonow,* Berlin, 1928.

D. Stevenson, *French War Aims Against Germany, 1914-1919,* Oxford, 1982.

Wilhelm Stieger, *Das Zweite Reich und die Innenpolitik Österreich-Ungarns 1871-1914,* Doctor Thesis, University of Vienna, 1938.

Friedrich Stieve, *Die Tragödie der Bundesgenossen, Deutschland und Österreich-Ungarn, 1908-1914,* Munich, 1930.

Norman Stone, "Die Mobilmachung der Öst.-Ung. Armee 1914," *Militärgeschichtliche Mitteilungen,* 16, 1974/2, 67-95.

————, *The Eastern Front, 1914-1917,* New York, 1975.

————, "Hungary and the Crisis of July 1914," in W. Laqueur and George Mosse, eds., *1914: The Coming of the First World War,* New York, 1966, 147-164.

————, "Moltke-Conrad: Relations Between the Austro-Hungarian and German General Staffs, 1909-14," *Historical Journal,* 9, 1966, 201-228.

Georges Suarez, *Briand, Sa Vie — Son Oeuvre, Avec Son Journal et de Nombreux Documents Inédits,* 6 vols., Paris, 1938-1952.

Paul R. Sweet, "Germany, Austria-Hungary, and Mitteleuropa, August 1915-April 1916," in H. Hantsch and A. Novotny, eds., *Festschrift für Heinrich Benedikt,* Vienna, 1957, 180-212.

Zoltán Szende, *Die Ungarn im Zusammenbruch, Feldherr/Hinterland, Ein Beitrag zu Österreich-Ungarns Letzter Geschichtsepoche auf Grund Unveröffentlichter Archivakten und Personalquellen,* Oldenburg, 1931.

A. J. P. Taylor, *The Habsburg Monarchy, 1809-1918, A History of the Austrian Empire and Austria-Hungary,* London, 1966.

Gyula Todoky, "Die Pläne des Alldeutschen Verbandes zur Umgestaltung Österreich-Ungarns," *Acta Historica,* 9, 1963, 39-66.

Glenn E. Torrey, "Irredentism and Diplomacy, The Central Powers and Rumania, August-November 1914," *Südostforschungen,* 25, 1966, 285-332.

————, "Rumania and the Belligerents, 1914-1916," in Walter Laqueur and George Mosse, eds., *1914: The Coming of the First World War,* New York, 1966, 165-185.

John Treadway, *The Falcon and the Eagle: Montenegro and Austria-Hungary, 1908-1914,* West Lafayette, 1983.

Karl Tschuppik, *Francis Joseph I., The Downfall of an Empire,* trans. C. J. S. Sprigge, New York, 1930.

Julius von Twardowski, "Bilińskis Memoiren," *Jahrbuch der Österreichischen Leo-Gesellschaft,* 1926, 161-192.

Hans Uebersberger, *Österreich Zwischen Rußland und Serbien, zur Südslawischen Frage und der Entstehung des Ersten Weltkrieges,* Graz-Cologne, 1958.

August Urbanski von Ostrymiecz, *Conrad von Hötzendorf, Soldat und Mensch,* Graz-Leipzig-Vienna, 1939.

Leo Valiani, *The End of Austria-Hungary*, London, 1973.

Gabor Vermes, *Count István Tisza, A Political Biography*, Doctor Thesis, Stanford University, 1966.

————, "The Impact of the Dual Alliance on the Magyars of the Austro-Hungarian Monarchy," *East Central Europe*, 7, 1980, 310-325.

Stephan Verosta, *Theorie und Realität von Bündnissen, Heinrich Lammasch, Karl Renner, und der Zweibund (1897-1914)*, Vienna, 1971.

Bruno Wagner, *Der Waffenstillstand von Villa Giusti, 3. November 1918*, Doctor Thesis, University of Vienna, 1970.

Solomon Wank, "The Impact of the Dual Alliance on the Germans in Austria and Vice-Versa, *East Central Europe*, 7, 1980, 288-309.

————, "Some Reflections on Conrad von Hötzendorf and His Memoirs Based on Old and New Sources," *Austrian History Yearbook*, 1965, 1, 74-88.

Frank G. Weber, *Eagles on the Crescent: Germany, Austria-Hungary, and the Turkish Alliance, 1914-1918*, Ithaca, 1970.

Oswald Wedel, *Austro-German Diplomatic Relations, 1908-1914*, Stanford, 1932.

Alfred von Wegerer, ed., "Graf Berchtolds Interview über den Kriegsausbruch," *Berliner Monatshefte*, 13, 1935, 518-528.

James Wegs, *Austrian Economic Mobilization During World War I: With Particular Emphasis on Heavy Industry*, Doctor Thesis, University of Illinois, 1970.

John W. Wheeler-Bennett, *Brest-Litovsk, The Forgotten Peace, March 1918*, London, 1938.

Andrew Whiteside, *The Socialism of Fools, Georg Ritter von Schönerer and Austrian Pan-Germanism*, Berkeley, 1975.

Samuel R. Williamson, "Influence, Power and the Policy Process: The Case of Franz Ferdinand, 1906-1914," *Historical Journal*, 17, 1974, 417-434.

————, "Vienna and July 1914: The Origins of the Great War Once More," in S.R. Williamson and P. Pastor, eds., *Essays on World War I: Origins and Prisoners of War*, Social Science Monographs of Brooklyn College, New York, 1983, 9-36.

Stanley B. Winters, "The Impact of the Dual Alliance upon the Slavs of the Austro-Hungarian Monarchy: A Centennial Reappraisal," *East Central Europe*, 7, 1980, 326-344.

K. Wortmann, "Ottokar Czernin und die Westmächte im Weltkriege," *Historische Vierteljahresschrift*, 24, 1927, 199-252.

Friedrich Würthle, *Die Spur Führt Nach Belgrad, Die Hintergründe des Dramas von Sarajevo 1914*, Vienna-Munich-Zürich, 1975.

Egmont Zechlin, "Das 'Schlesische Angebot' und die Italienische Kriegsgefahr 1915," in Wolfgang Schieder, ed., *Erster Weltkrieg, Ursachen, Entstehung und Kriegsziele*, Cologne-Berlin, 1969, 346-372.

————, "Österreich-Ungarn und die Bemühungen um einen Russischen Sonderfrieden 1915," in *Krieg und Kriegsrisiko, zur Deutschen Politik im Ersten Weltkrieg, Aufsätze*, Düsseldorf, 1979, 290-315.

Z. A. B. Zeman, *The Break-up of the Habsburg Empire, 1914-1918, A Study in*

National and Social Revolution, Oxford, 1961.
————, *A Diplomatic History of the First World War,* London, 1971.
Hans Karl Zeßner-Spitzenberg, *Kaiser Karl, Aus dem Nachlaß,* ed. Erich Thanner, Salzburg, 1953.

5. GUIDES AND BIBLIOGRAPHIES

American Historical Association, *A Catalogue of Files and Microfilms of the German Foreign Ministry Archives, 1867-1920,* Oxford, 1959.
Ludwig Bittner, ed., *Gesamtinventar des Wiener Haus-, Hof-, und Staatsarchivs,* 5 vols., Vienna, 1936-1940.
Peter Broucek, "Der Nachlaß Feldmarschall Conrads und das Kriegsarchiv," *Mitteilungen des Österreichischen Staatsarchivs,* 28, 1975, 164-182.
Walter Schinner, *Bibliographie zur Geschichte Österreich-Ungarns im Weltkrieg,* Stuttgart, 1934.
Robert Stropp, "Die Akten des K. u. K. Ministeriums des Äußern 1848-1918," *Mitteilungen des Österreichischen Staatsarchivs,* 20, 1967, 389-506.
————, "Die Akten des K. u. K. Ministeriums des Äußern 1848-1918: Administrative Registratur," *Mitteilungen des Österreichischen Staatsarchivs:* Pt. 1, 30, 1977, 398-453; Pt. 2, 32, 1979, 306-349; Pt. 3, 33, 1980, 356-415; Pt. 4, 34, 1981, 411-456.

INDEX